1 Lad

The Holtzman
Inkblot
Technique

*A Handbook
for Clinical Application*

Evelyn F. Hill

Foreword by Wayne H. Holtzman

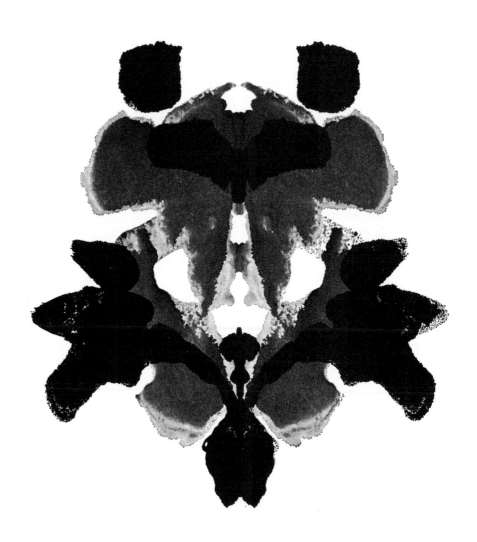

THE HOLTZMAN
INKBLOT
TECHNIQUE

Jossey-Bass Inc., Publishers
San Francisco • Washington • London • 1972

THE HOLTZMAN INKBLOT TECHNIQUE
A Handbook for Clinical Application
and The Hill Clinical Summary Form
      by Evelyn F. Hill

Copyright © 1972 by Jossey-Bass, Inc., Publishers

Published in Great Britain by
Jossey-Bass, Inc., Publishers
St. George's House
44 Hatton Garden, London E.C.1

Library of Congress Catalogue Card Number LC 74-184959

International Standard Book Number ISBN 0-87589-121-7

Manufactured in the United States of America

JACKET DESIGN BY WILLI BAUM

FIRST EDITION

Code 7205

The Jossey-Bass
Behavioral Science Series

General Editors

WILLIAM E. HENRY
University of Chicago

NEVITT SANFORD
Wright Institute, Berkeley

Foreword

When Joseph Thorpe, Jon Swartz, Wayne Herron, and I developed the Holtzman Inkblot Technique, our primary aim was to produce a psychometrically sound instrument that retained the clinical versatility and qualitative richness of its predecessor, the Rorschach. Along with Marguerite Hertz, Joseph Zubin, and others in the early fifties, I was convinced that the Rorschach was an ingenious, significant approach to the study of subtle but important aspects of personality, an approach that was severely hampered by lack of adequate reliability, objectivity, and standardization as well as by unsubstantiated clinical folklore surrounding interpretation. Spurred on by rising criticisms of the Rorschach, we experimented with various ways of extending the range of stimulus variables and lengthening the test while simplifying the procedures for administration and scoring. We soon realized that most of the psychometric difficulties inherent in the Rorschach could be overcome by encouraging only one response per inkblot, by increasing the number of blots from ten to forty-five, and by standardizing a simple inquiry immediately following the response. As we were undertaking a major test development program, it was a simple matter to develop two parallel forms, making it possible for the first time to study personality change over time with some precision in the same individuals.

The major developmental work for the Holtzman Inkblot Technique took five years and involved the testing of several thousand individuals drawn from a wide range of clinical and normal populations. Since publication of the test materials and accompanying research monograph eleven years ago, the Holtzman Inkblot Technique has been employed in a wide variety of research studies and clinical settings. Several hundred articles and scores of book chapters and reviews have been published, most of them indicating significant findings and promising applications in psychiatric screening of mental patients and assessment of creativity and healthy personality attributes as well as in studies of psychopathology, experimental studies of altered states, and cross-cultural studies of personality development. Availability of computer-scored, group-administered versions of the test has accelerated its use in large-scale studies and personality screening. The materials and monograph accompanying them have been translated into other languages, resulting in rapid spread to many countries.

Until the present book, however, little had been written about the clinical applications of the Holtzman Inkblot Technique. Sufficient experience has been gained in the past ten years to justify a major effort by a competent clinician to organize and present interpretative material. Evelyn Hill has had extensive clinical practice at The Johns Hopkins Hospital and in private practice—experience that gives her a unique vantage point from which to blend together the early work with the Rorschach, clinical applications of the Holtzman Inkblot Technique, and contemporary research in the field of inkblot perception and personality.

Parts II, III, and IV are completely original with Evelyn Hill. She has spent countless hours tracking down studies with the Rorschach as well as with the Holtzman Inkblot Technique and has woven these into her clinical interpretations in a skillful manner. She has been careful to distinguish between those interpretations that are based on solid empirical evidence from research studies and those that have been gleaned from the writings of experienced clinicians working with the Rorschach or the Holtzman Inkblot Technique. The clear presentation of detailed responses, scoring, and interpretation makes the case analyses in Part IV especially useful for student and experienced clinician alike.

Normative tables for seven new samples are presented in the Appendix, augmenting substantially the original norms published in 1961. Norms for average adults, college students, seventh graders, elementary school children, five-year-olds, chronic schizophrenics, mentally retarded individuals, and depressed patients are reprinted from our original standardization work. New normative tables based on data from a variety of sources are given for large samples of first graders, fourth graders, emotionally disturbed children, emotionally disturbed adolescents, juvenile delinquents, neurotic adults, and alcoholics. Altogether 1987 individuals are represented in the fifteen different reference groups for which normative tables are provided.

The Hill Clinical Summary Sheet is a convenient interpretive aid employed by Hill in her clinical work. It should prove especially useful for diagnosticians who are thoroughly familiar with the Rorschach since many of the subcategories often employed in Rorschach analysis are singled out for special attention.

The integration of the Rorschach literature and clinical experience with the Holtzman Inkblot Technique is long overdue. In addition, Hill's original contributions not only make the method useful in clinical settings but also are sufficiently significant to merit the serious attention of anyone concerned with the assessment of personality through inkblot perception.

Austin   WAYNE H. HOLTZMAN
January 1972

Preface

The Holtzman Inkblot Technique (HIT) was introduced by Holtzman, Thorpe, Swartz and Herron in 1961. It is a derivative of the Rorschach technique. The HIT has such obvious advantages over other projective inkblot tests, such as the Rorschach, that it is rapidly displacing the older techniques, particularly in the field of research. The ever expanding HIT literature also attests to its impact on clinical psychology. Those using the HIT have long felt the need for a guide to the interpretation of the scoring variables. Holtzman's guide (1961) provides only administration, scoring and normative data. In 1961 the clinical nuances of the HIT scores in assessing personality had not been fully explored. However, after using the HIT for ten years, both in clinical settings and in research and after gathering the main research of a decade with the HIT, it is now possible to present material which gives the clinical psychologist a highly sensitive projective tool.

For the beginning student, the comparative ease with which one can learn to administer and score the HIT and the different levels of interpretation are a great advantage. For the practiced clinician who is versed in the Rorschach, the transition is natural, there is much transfer of training to the HIT. I have written *The Holtzman Inkblot Technique* for the mature clinician who wishes to acquire a standardized new projective tool for clinical and research use, for the beginning clinician as a proper tool on which to cut his projective teeth, and for the research psychologist in clinical and personality theory who needs an inkblot technique which lends itself to statistical manipulation.

The Holtzman Inkblot Technique has four parts, each dealing with a more advanced level of clinical application. Part One is concerned with the mechanics of administration and scoring. This part contains refinements in scoring which have been developed since the publication of the original manual, and everyone using the book will want to use this section to assure complete understanding of the subsequent sections. Part Two deals with the first level of interpretation based on the scoring variables. It considers in depth the various interpretive aspects of these variables and is basic to the deeper level of interpretation found in Part Three. Part Three studies the relationship of scoring variables to personality variables, such as intelligence and ego strength. Personality dynamics as they might appear in a particular protocol are discussed and exemplified. The interpretations in this part are supported by research published on this and other projective techniques, but the interpretations do not adhere to any one personality theory. Part Four summarizes the material in the preceding sections and gives samples of the scoring and interpretation of test responses. One of these samples is a test-retest of a patient undergoing psychotherapy and demonstrates his progress. Another is of a normal college student and gives a useful reference point.

I make the hopeful prediction that the next decade will prove the value of the Holtzman Inkblot Technique and that we will see much research in this area, not only by clinical psychologists, personality theorists, and others in psychology but also by those in allied fields such as sociology and anthropology.

Acknowledgments

I acknowledge with thanks the assistance of the NIMH in awarding me grant 1R03MH13489-01 on January 1, 1967, which made possible the research of the literature. I am particularly grateful to Wayne H. Holtzman for his encouragement, review of successive drafts of the manuscript, suggestions, criticisms, and assistance. I am especially indebted to Helen E. Peixotto for her support, advice, and careful scrutiny of the evolving manuscript. I also thank the following persons who have been helpful in a variety of ways in making possible the presentation of *The Holtzman Inkblot Technique:* Seymour Fisher, Donald R. Gorham, Edwin I. Megargee, Soloman Shapiro, and Jon D. Swartz. I am thankful to Edith Scheppler for her assistance and advice in the preparation of special materials. I thank my secretary, Teresa H. Clark, for her patience and skill in following the many drafts through the final typing.

Dedication

Finally, for their continuous support, assistance, and sharing in the travail of writing this book, I am deeply grateful to my husband, Kenneth, to whom I dedicate this book, and my daughters, Jane and Susan.

Baltimore   EVELYN F. HILL
February 1972

Contents

Abbreviations for HIT Variables

Variables	Subvariables	
A		Animal
	a	Active movement
	b	Body or part of animal
	h	Head or face of animal
	o	All other A 1 responses
	p	Passive movement
AA		Affect arousal
Ab		Abstract
At		Anatomy
Ax		Anxiety
B		Balance
Br		Barrier
C		Color
	Ac	Achromatic color
	C+	Positive color content
	C−	Negative color content
FA		Form appropriateness
FD		Form definiteness

Variables	_Subvariables_	
H		Human
	a	Active movement
	b	Body or body part
	F	Female
	h	Head or face of human
	M	Male
	O	Sex not identified
	o	Other percepts scored H 1
	p	Passive movement
Hs		Hostility
I		Integration
L		Location
M		Movement
	AM	Animal movement
	HM	Human movement
	m	Inanimate movement
	ma	Inanimate movement affecting animate objects
P		Popular
Pn		Penetration
R		Rejection
RT		Reaction time
S		Space
	s	Secondary space
Sh		Shading
	df	Dark film shading
	f	Light film shading
	t	Texture
	v	Vista

Variables	*Subvariables*	
Sx		Sex
V		Pathognomic verbalization
	AB	Absurd response
	AL	Autistic logic
	CT	Contamination
	DC	Deterioration color
	FB	Fabulation
	FC	Fabulized combination
	IC	Incoherence
	QR	Queer response
	SR	Self-reference

The Holtzman
Inkblot
Technique

*A Handbook
for Clinical Application*

BACKGROUND AND TECHNIQUE

PART ONE

The need to understand how individuals function in order to predict future behavior led psychologists to develop many assessment tools. Personality evaluation is now an important part of the work of clinical settings, schools, research laboratories and institutions.

The selection of a test (or tests) which the examiner can use with confidence (because he understands the intent of the test and what it is able to measure) is of great importance. The Holtzman Inkblot Technique (HIT) is a well standardized tool for personality assessment.

But the tool is no better than the workman. Maximum effectiveness of a test is obtained when the examiner is trained in its use. Proper administration is critical. Only if the examiner follows the standard administration and scoring of the HIT can the obtained scores be compared with normative data and interpreted according to the individual scoring variables, clusters of variables and personality variables discussed in Parts II and III.

Part I of this book discusses the theoretical foundations of inkblot testing and the development of the HIT. Part I also includes instructions for administration and scoring.

1

Theoretical Foundations

I

Projection was first defined by Freud as an unconscious defense mechanism by means of which an individual proscribes to another a trait or desire of his own which would be painful for his ego to admit. Freud also stated (1938): "But projection is not specially created for the purpose of defense, it also comes into being where there are no conflicts." What we project to outer reality, he believed, results from the coexistence of a current perception, which is conscious, and the memory of past perceptions. Thus, present perceptions are influenced by past perceptions. Part of the rationale behind the projective technique is to explore the process of free association and to deal with unconscious defensive reasoning in the perceiver as the stimulus evokes in him a chain of associations. Projection, however, is not only defensive. Other influences are recognized within this process. Frank (1939) takes a holistic approach based on Gestalt theory. He states that the dynamic conception of personality is a process of organizing experiences within the context in which one finds himself, namely, a field. We can determine how an individual organizes his experiences by means of his perceptions. These perceptions disclose (or provide insight into) the individual's private world of meanings, significances, patterns, and feelings. Schachtel (1966) views projection as the attributing of one's own qualities, feelings, attitudes, experiences, and strivings to objects (people, animals, things). The process of projection, he states, "usually takes place outside of awareness," but the content of the projection "may or may not be known to the person as part of himself." He believes that the processes of perceiving an inkblot, associating ideas and images with it, and trying to integrate the ideas and images into the stimulus play a decisive role in the typical response. The result of this process is the communication of the response.

3

Projective tests as we know them today were introduced into psychology by Hermann Rorschach. In 1924, David Levy introduced Rorschach's test in the United States. However, several years elapsed before projective tests became part of the typical test battery.

Today, psychological test batteries to assess personality usually include an inkblot technique as the projective test of choice. Projective techniques are based on assumptions regarding how an individual responds to an ambiguous situation. The examiner assumes that the responses are based on past experience and contain information on how inner feelings and relationships with objects and persons are organized into one's life experiences.

The inkblot technique is one part of a group of projective tests which vary in the degree of structure. Most projective techniques which are popularly used (such as figure drawings, sentence completion, word association, or Thematic Apperception Test—TAT), provide a stimulus which directs the individual toward a generalized goal. In response to these kinds of tests, he is able to formulate associations based on the test demands. The inkblot technique, however, offers the least structure of any projective test. The stimulus is a design which has form and may be symmetrical or asymmetrical. The stimulus also has color; black, gray and white are the achromatic colors and there are chromas of many hues. Shading is present which provides a grainy quality, or it provides various delineations and alterations of hue, or a dotted, hazy appearance. The shading on some blots gives the appearance of dimension. Finally, there is the figure-ground component wherein the whiteness of the card itself represents the field upon which the blot is placed. From these cues the perceiver must organize a response based on his experience and personality and communicate this response.

Current theories of perception provide explanations for many of the interactions between the projective stimulus and the response. For example, Werner and Wapner (1949), in their sensory tonic field theory, describe perception as a total dynamic process. They maintain that perception is not only an interaction of sensory and tonic factors but acts as a field in which the body and the perceived object interact. The sensory experience either is conscious or results from the functioning of a physiological system which produces the sensation by means of receptors, afferent neurons, and sensory cortical processes. Tonic factors are visceral and somatic muscle activity; for example the change of muscle tension as in posture and the spastic contractions which are components of movement. Helson (1964) states that an individual establishes an adaptation level with a true zero of functioning. This zero of functioning represents an average of all his experiences pooled and is a frame of reference, or standard, against which external stimuli can be judged. In 1949, Bruner and Postman developed a "hypothesis theory." Their "hypothesis" is defined as a set or tendency of the individual to perceive in a certain way, based on his past experiences. The set precedes the perception and determines the percept. Upon inspection of a stimulus, the perceiver forms a hypothesis concerning the object and then proceeds to confirm it. To do so, he must have sufficient information so that the strength of the hypothesis verifies its appropriateness. The frequency of past confirmations helps to determine how strong the hypothesis is. In addition, having fewer conflicting percepts increases the likelihood that the hypothesis will be confirmed.

An inkblot as a stimulus has little evidence upon which to confirm the hypothesis of a percept, especially in terms of past experience. Bruner's theory of perception (1957) makes a distinction between that which is perceived and the perceptual report. He states that the perceptual process is less docile than the cognitive process, and he reduces perception to four steps. First Bruner distinguishes an initial or primitive categorization of the percept. Categorization is followed by a cue search, in which the perceiver seeks cues in the stimulus to assist him in formulating the hypothesis. Once the cues have all been considered, the perceiver makes a decision concerning the perception, which he does not change. Finally, he seeks confirmation of the percept fitting the stimulus. When the confirmation is completed and a certainty exists in the perceiver's mind, the percept is ready to be expressed. The fewer the cues in the stimulus, as is the case with the inkblot, the more difficult the task of drawing on specific object associations from past experience. The task of eliciting a response becomes dependent upon inner resources. The inkblot technique provides an opportunity to observe the organization of an individual's perceptions and how he patterns and responds to his life situations. His responses are based on physiological and sociological growth and maturation. The inkblot technique also reveals how a person copes with the problem-solving nature of a novel task. It identifies, as well, the degree of the relationship between reality and imagination.

Knowledge of the functional aspects of personality aids in understanding the relationship between reality and imagination as expressed in the percepts. Personality theories which shed most light on this relationship are those of Freud (1953), Dollard and Miller (1950), Adler (1927), Murphy (1947), and Sullivan (1958), who place strong emphasis on continuity of development. These theorists imply that events taking place in the present are systematically linked to events which took place in the past. They state that development is an orderly and consistent process definable in a single set of principles. The theorists consistently emphasize holism, namely, the importance of the individual as a total functioning unit (both in his biological and psychological makeup and in his interactions with the environment).

Most personality theorists today show an increasing interest in the self-concept. The self is seen either as a group of psychological processes which determine behavior or as a cluster of attitudes and feelings which the individual has about himself. Also, the significance of the psychological environment (or private world of experience) is accepted by most personality theorists, and several make it a matter of emphasis. Hall and Lindzey (1957) state: "It is probably fair to say that personality theorists are more impressed with the importance of the psychological environment than the importance of the physical environment." Finally, motivation is assigned importance in most theories of personality.

Historically, psychologists have constructed tests based on the concepts of reliability and validity. Projective techniques, however (and inkblot techniques in particular), do not generally meet these criteria. Scoring techniques, for example, have been developed for the Rorschach Inkblot Test but are not statistically verifiable. No reliability has been established for the Rorschach scoring methods, and Holtzman (1959) concludes that actuarial predictions from the Rorschach test are no better than those that can be expected from a chance relationship. Zubin, Eron, and Schumer (1965) point out, for example, the troublesome question of the number of responses. The total number of responses can vary from fewer than ten to over one hundred. But the relationship of the scoring determinants to the number of responses affects the interpretation of results. Thus, the scoring is unreliable. Holtzman and his colleagues, in developing the Holtzman Inkblot Technique (HIT), set out to construct an inkblot technique which would avoid some of the pitfalls of the parent instrument.

The most important difference between the HIT and the Rorschach is the psychometric advantage of the HIT. The reliability of the HIT has been established, and split-half reliability coefficients in the high eighties and low nineties exist for most variables for immediate and delayed intrasubject stability. In addition, interscorer consistency has been established with a median value of all correlations at .86. The number of responses per protocol is held relatively constant—an important psychometric advantage. Only one response per blot is asked for. Theorists believe that the loss of number of responses as a variable is minor compared with the increase in stability of the test and the stability of the important variables such as location, form definiteness, form appropriateness, movement, color, and shading. Furthermore, each response stems from an independent stimulus, providing a medium for interplay between the subject and the test blots. This procedure avoids lumping responses together. The test, which consists of two sets of forty-five blots, provides a rich variety of stimuli which enable the administrator to understand the elements which evoke responses in the subject. The large number of blots increases the reliability of the scores and the confidence with which an interpretation can be made. Two parallel sets of cards—called *Form A* and *Form B,* each with forty-five highly equivalent blots, make the administration of alternate forms possible (Holtzman, Thorpe, Swartz, and Herron, 1961).

Because only one response per blot is requested, special effort was made in constructing the test to develop and select inkblots with high "pulling power"—for responses involving small details, space, color, and shading attributes to compensate for the tendency to give form-determined wholes as the first response.

The study of the response characteristics of many inkblots in constructing the HIT was based on the principles of traditional variables. For location scoring, the blots should have reasonably good form in some segment (including space) so that fragmentation can occur. Inkblots having a popular response to the whole blot or little internal form delineation or outer form irregularity evoke little variation in the location of the response. Shading responses evoked by the texture of the blot occur most frequently when the blot has indefinite form, little variation in hue, and fairly light shading. Responses to color are most likely to occur when considerable color is present which can be integrated easily with the form, which is usually indefinite. Color responses are rare in popular form-definite concepts in which color plays no part. Figure-ground reversals leading to a space response are difficult to obtain when the subject is limited to one response per blot. These responses occur most frequently when there is a fairly well-formed, definite concept using space for figure and blot for ground.

Such traditional variables as movement and form level are sufficiently independent of the stimulus attributes of the blot so that special consideration was not necessary in constructing and selecting the inkblots for experimental testing (Holzman, Thorpe, Swartz and Herron, 1961).

The standardized scoring provided in the HIT consists of twenty-two scoring variables, which are usually represented by six factors. The twenty-two variables are designed to capture most aspects of inkblot perception currently scored in the Rorschach test, but in such a way as to permit reliable unidimensional quantification. The individual variables can be examined for interpretation. The interpretation of those variables which constitute a specific factor gives an added degree of confidence in assessing personality. Normative data are available against which responses can be examined.

The standardized inquiry given following the response to each blot captures the association and affect of the subject as he experiences the blot stimulus. This procedure eliminates the variable of memory or later blocking, which occurs when the inquiry is given after all responses have been made. The standardized inquiry identifies the subject's customary mode of defining an ambiguous stimulus and the extent to which he is able to structure it. In the interview type of inquiry, the degree of freedom with which the subject is able to interact with the blot is limited. Therefore the eliciting of responses becomes a matter of skill between the examiner and subject and the examiner influence is at its highest. More meaningful data is obtained when the subject can respond spontaneously to a standard inquiry. Examiner influence is minimal. Furthermore, normative data are based on the administration and inquiry as defined and are part of the standardization of the HIT.

We must consider three aspects of personality in order to understand the meaning of the subject's response to the inkblot stimulus: the pervading emotional state of the individual, his impulse upsurges, and the amount of control of these internal reactions which he demonstrates. Emotions correspond to certain states of the body, and emotional responses are discerned by means of the behavior. Experiences of pleasure and displeasure are reflected both in overt reactions and mannerisms and internally. Happiness may be reflected in good posture, a springy step, the brightness of one's eyes, and a smile on one's face. But it will also be felt in all the systems under autonomic control—deep breathing, strong pulse, good appetite, food is enjoyed, and digestion and elimination are effortless. When a person is under stress it is apparent behaviorally in his inability to function well, in his nervousness, his shortness of breath, his frequent sighing, and anger in his physical movement. His internal organs reflect this stress in a rapid heart beat, dry mouth, and cold hands, and so on.

A general emotional state exists in the testing situation even before the individual interacts with the stimulus material. Some individuals approach tasks in the test situation with indifference and a desire to get them over with as quickly as possible and with as little involvement as possible. Others approach the task with intellectual curiosity and a desire to know what is going on. They see it as a challenge to their ability to develop percepts. Still others find the situation stressful. The strange and ambiguous nature of the stimuli generate tension.

The responses of an individual to a projective inkblot technique reflects his ability to control and direct his cognitive and affective reactions in accordance with the demands of the situation. When an individual is functioning comfortably with little disturbance in his emotional state, he is able to control his reactions rationally and to elicit percepts that reflect this state. In a stressful state, the individual may not be able to control his reactions, and his percepts are a function more of his inner needs and fantasies (revealing emotional disturbance) than of intellectual conceptualization.

Administration

II

The inkblots have no counterpart in reality. They can be responded to by subjects of any age or socioeconomic or cultural group. Language is no barrier in administering the test as long as the subject and examiner can communicate. However, the responses to these stimuli must be *interpreted* not only in the light of meanings derived from the percept but according to the age, socioeconomic level, educational level, and experience of the perceiver.

The role of the examiner in test administration is important (Schachtel, 1945; Gibby, Miller, and Walker, 1953; Simkins, 1960; Hamilton and Robertson, 1966; Megargee, Lockwood, Cato, and Jones, 1966). Repeated evidence shows that the interaction between the examiner and the subject affects the test performance, although the differential impact is less for the HIT than for the Rorschach because of the standardized administration. For the least possible influence of transient environmental events on the subject's response, the examiner should be as inobtrusive as possible. In administration of a battery of psychological tests, the inkblot test is frequently one of the last tests given. This practice is sound because the subject has had an opportunity to interact with the examiner in the structured tests which are not as threatening as the less structured inkblot test. When the inkblot test is given alone, a neutral task should first be introduced to develop rapport with the subject. Before administering any test, the examiner should assess the subject's level of anxiety as overtly manifested, his general physical condition, and his attitude toward being tested.

In order to administer the test, the examiner needs a set of HIT cards, the appropriate Holtzman record form, and a stopwatch. Two sets of cards are available, Forms A and B. Although Forms A and B are equivalent, clinical psychologists have acquired more experience with Form A. Form A may be preferable to Form B if the subject has not been previously tested with the HIT. Form B can then be reserved for retesting. Normative samples, however, include records using both Forms. Each set contains forty-seven inkblots. An X and a Y trial blot in each set are the same. The balance are numbered one to forty-five on the reverse side of the card with a letter A or B to identify the set. The record forms for A and B are different. A schematic diagram of each blot is at the left of the space provided for recording the responses. Samples of record forms A and B are part of the case analyses in Part IV.

The cards should be inversely stacked and placed face down with card X on top. Seating is a matter of choice. Evidence does not indicate that the response of the subject is influenced by the examiner's sitting on his left, right, or opposite him. Whatever is most convenient is suitable. However, the examiner should be able to see the blot.

The top of the record form should be filled in with the subject's name, age, sex, and so on. If the information is not already available, it should be secured from the subject. The age and educational level are especially needed for proper reference to normative data in interpretation.

The examiner gives a standardized set of instructions so that the subject knows what to expect and what is expected of him. The instructions should be given slowly and clearly in a conversational tone, emphasizing the points enumerated below, so that the subject interacts with the blots in a way that is meaningful for later interpretation. The examiner informs the subject that the inkblots are not made to look like anything: that different people are reminded of different things, and therefore there is no right or wrong answer. He is told that he will be asked to look at each inkblot and to tell what it reminds him of, what it might resemble. Although he may perceive several things in each inkblot, he may relate only one thing about each blot. The examiner must point out that he will ask some questions concerning the responses because he wants to see the percept in the same way that the subject does. The subject must also be informed that the examiner will write down what the subject says and note the time taken to respond, but that he is to take as long as he wishes. The exact wording of the instructions may vary from one subject to another in order to avoid stiffness and maintain rapport. I would suggest the following as a typical verbatim instruction: "I have a set of inkblots which were made by dropping ink on paper and folding it. I would like you to look at each inkblot and tell me what it reminds you of. Since these are only inkblots, there are no right or wrong answers. Different people see them in different ways. While it is possible for you to be reminded of several things, I want you to tell me only one thing about each blot. After you tell me what the inkblot reminds you of, I will ask you some questions because I want to see it the same way you do. I will be writing down what you say and making a note of the time but you may take as long as you wish on each card. Do you have any questions?" The card should be presented to the subject right side up. The form and number of the blot is printed on the bottom of the reverse side of the card. Should he inquire whether he can turn the card, he should be informed that it is entirely up to him. Any turning should be recorded on the schematic diagram by a caret ($\wedge$), indicating the direction of up when the response is made (Holtzman, Thorpe, Swartz, and Herron, 1961).

The examiner records the reaction time (in seconds)—the time from the presentation of the card to the time the subject responds or rejects the card when no response can be given. If the subject fails to respond after one minute and has not returned the card, he is probably inhibiting his response or trying to put it into words. Examiner encouragement may then evoke the response. He may ask again: What does the inkblot remind you of? Encouragement may help the subject over the hurdle and avoid a rejection. However, if he still cannot respond and rejects the card, no further attempt should be made on that card. The rejection should be marked with an R on the record form. The subject rarely rejects a sufficient number of cards to interfere with the evaluation. If the number of rejections is high (more than twenty) and the subject has not given any of the well-defined percepts commonly seen in some cards (the populars), the examiner may wish to resubmit some of these cards (for example, cards 4A, 12A, 19A, 25B, 34B, 36B) to the subject to determine whether he is able to see the popular percept. Testing of the limits, such as is done with the Rorschach, is unnecessary with the HIT because even with a large number of rejections the examiner has sufficient responses to allow him to determine the subject's approach to unstructured stimuli.

Sometimes the subject makes comments which are not part of the percept before he responds to the blot. These comments should be recorded and put in brackets in order to separate them from the response. However, the reaction time should not be recorded until the response is made. The percept and the responses to the inquiry should be recorded verbatim or essentially so. Descriptions of the details of the percept may be written directly on the schematic of the blot. Unusual behaviors, side remarks, and exclamations during the testing should be recorded for clinical use. These behaviors provide information in assessing the affect which a blot may have aroused and which blots were the most affect-arousing.

The part of the blot which the subject responds to (location) should be identified on the blot schematic by circling the area (unless the response is to the whole blot). Form appropriateness (FA)—how well the percept resembles the form of the blot—should be noted on the record when the response is recorded in order to assist scoring. FA is determined by the examiner from the information supplied by the subject. Until the examiner is sufficiently familiar with FA scoring to discriminate rapidly between a fair and a good response, he should place a check mark on the schematic drawing if the response is judged appropriate to the blot. The check facilitates later scoring, when a comparison of the subject's response with the samples in the scoring guide (Holtzman, 1961) determines the weight of the FA score.

An inquiry is made for each blot immediately after the subject has given the percept for that blot. The purpose of the inquiry is to determine the location of the percept and also to identify exactly which stimulus in the blot was the cue for the response. The inquiry is also designed to encourage an elaboration of the percept.

Three kinds of questions are permissible in the standard inquiry. The exact wording may vary and should be natural for the examiner. The following are typical questions. For location (QL): "Where in the blot do you see the ——————?" For characteristics (QC): "What is there about the blot that reminded you of the ——————?" To elicit elaboration (QE): "Is there anything else you care to tell me about the ——————?" Conducting the inquiry in this manner provides sufficient information for scoring and interpretation. To minimize examiner influence there should be no further questioning because the subject will be influenced in subsequent responses by previous questioning. The examiner should try to encourage the subject to discuss the response without providing cues. If the inquiry is kept standard the typical subject develops a set as to what is expected in his response. Frequently, by the time the test is half through, the subject is providing all (or most) of the information without a full inquiry. He delineates the location, often identifies the stimulus correlates, and provides elaboration. Sometimes the subject's response does not clarify the question asked. In that case the examiner should either repeat the question or say: "I am not sure I understood what you said." This question does not bias the reply and often brings the desired results. With experience, the examiner is able to clarify responses without influencing the spontaneity of the subject's association.

Occasionally a subject may disregard the instruction to give only one response per card. This situation can usually be controlled by repeating the instructions concerning the single response. If the subject still feels compelled to give more than one response, he should be asked which of the two responses the blot reminds him of more. This is the primary response. The second response should be scored only for V (pathognomic verbalization), a variable which will be discussed later. Sometimes the subject gives a premature response to the blot. This response may be mistaken for the primary response. Therefore the subject should be questioned as to which response he means to give. The additional response, although not scored, is useful in interpreting the subject's typical mode of relating to unstructured situations.

The time required to administer the test varies from forty to eighty minutes, depending upon the examiner's experience and the speed with which the subject responds. The examiner can keep the tempo moving and still provide a warm and unhurried atmosphere if he is comfortable with the test, if he is able to conduct a simple inquiry, and if he is able to interact minimally with the subject. If the examiner is uncomfortable with the number of cards in the test and views consideration of forty-five cards as a time-consuming effort, his discomfort is communicated to the subject. In comparison with the Rorschach in which an effort is made to secure as many responses for each card as possible (five responses per card is considered average) the HIT, with forty-five single responses, is not excessively long. Furthermore, giving the inquiry after the response to each card, means that the examiner does not need to return to the card later. At times the subject may comment on the number of cards, for example: "Do I have to go through all of the cards?" The examiner's response should be short, specific, and as casual as possible. An appropriate answer would be "yes," communicating that the examiner does not consider the task excessive for either of them.

In some circumstances it is clinically useful to administer a projective test to more than one person at a time. Group administration of the HIT has been standardized (Swartz and Holtzman, 1963). Group administration is useful in institutions, hospitals, schools, seminaries, and so on. Data thus obtained may be used as part of a basic test battery for screening new admissions. The HIT, using colored slides projected on a screen, lends itself to group administration because of the requirement of only one response per card. The simple, standard inquiry allows the subject to record his responses. A number of subjects can thus be tested at the same time and in one place, providing each subject has a good view of the screen. The test can still be adequately handled by one examiner and is more economical than individual administration.

This method has limitations. For example, the printed inkblots and the projected images on the slides are not identical. Differences in projection equipment and setting may also have effects. Swartz and Holtzman (1963) found (using one response per card) that the group method and the individual method yield identical results for most major variables. There is a loss of relationship between the examiner and the subject. The subject is also restricted to viewing the inkblots in the upright position, and the examiner may have difficulty in scoring some variables, particularly form appropriateness and pathognomic verbalization. Because the inkblots are presented on slides which automatically change every fifty to seventy-five seconds, the independent reaction time and its relationship to rejections are lost. In large-scale use, especially in research projects, the advantages of group administration outweigh the disadvantages. However, the examiner must be cautious in interpreting results for an individual.

Individual record forms and instruction sheets are distributed to each subject. Instructions for group administration are read aloud, while the subjects are silently reading for themselves from a booklet.

> You will be shown a series of inkblots, each of which will be projected on the screen before you for one minute or so. Using your imagination, write down in the space provided a description of the first thing the blot looks like or reminds you of. Include in your description the particular characteristics or qualities of the inkblot which are important in determining your responses; i.e., what about the blot made it look that way? Give as complete an answer as you can in the time available. None of these inkblots has been deliberately drawn to look like anything in particular. No two people see exactly the same thing in a series of inkblots like these. There are no right or wrong answers.

Trial inkblot X is then projected on the screen. The examiner states that a common response is a bat or winged creature. He outlines on the screen the area where the bat is seen and points to the various parts, briefly mentioning the role of form in determining the response. The examiner then explains that such a response might be written as "bat because of the form" in the space provided. Next, the examiner points out that another response to this card could be pool of oil. This response is based on the color and shading rather than form. Next, the examiner states that still another response to the inkblot might be a steer's head. He outlines the head and discusses the role of form, color, and shading. Card Y is then projected on the screen and the examiner points out the common response, human figure. He mentions the role of form in determining the response. Using the same area, he then cites another common response, skeleton, and points out the role of form and shading as determinants. Finally, the examiner states that still another response to this inkblot, blood, is determined by color alone. The initial instructions are then repeated and the subjects are asked whether they have any questions.

In accordance with a prearranged schedule, subjects are occasionally reminded of important aspects of the instructions. Eight inkblots scattered through the series are verbally reenforced. For instance, after cards 2 and 24: "Write out as complete a description as you can in the time and space available." After card 3: "Just let your imagination run and put down what the inkblot suggests to you, what you see in it." After card 6: "This is another one of those blots where you'll have to be careful in outlining that part of the area which you use." After card 8: "Write out as best you can what characteristics of the inkblot were deciding factors in your response." After cards 9 and 19: "Be sure to draw a line around that part of the blot that suggested your response." And after card 14: "We're particularly interested in knowing what aspects of the inkblot influenced your response." Inkblots 1, 2, and 3 are exposed for one hundred twenty seconds each; 4, 5, and 6 for one hundred seconds; 7, 8, and 9 for ninety seconds, and the remaining thirty-six blots are exposed for seventy-five seconds each (Swartz and Holtzman, 1963).

Group administration provides protocols which can be hand-scored accurately for eighteen of the twenty-two variables. Reaction time cannot be scored. In addition to the loss of reaction time, scorable material for the abstract, sex, and balance variables is sufficiently rare that they are generally not used in the group method. Although group administration saves time, scoring and interpretation time remain unchanged because of the necessity to decipher handwriting and inadequate or unclear responses. Subjects need reading and writing ability at about the fourth grade level.

The usefulness of an abbreviated form was investigated by Herron (1963). For specialized research purposes he found it possible to use only thirty cards and prorate the scores.

Scoring

III

The Holtzman Inkblot Technique: Administration and Scoring Guide (hereafter referred to as the guide), the Holtzman Inkblot Technique Summary Sheet (hereafter referred to as the HIT summary), and the Hill Clinical Summary Sheet (hereafter referred to as the clinical summary) are needed for scoring and clinical analysis. The guide contains samples for assigning scoring weights for the twenty-two variables. The appendix to the guide contains a replica of each blot for Forms A and B with samples for scoring form appropriateness (FA) and popular (P) in relation to various locations of the percept on the blot.

On the HIT summary a circle is placed around the letter A or B (appearing in the upper right-hand corner) to identify which form was used. The variables appear in rows, and the blot numbers are in the left-hand column. Raw scores are recorded for each card under the appropriate variable letters along the line for the particular blot. For efficiency in scoring, the space may be left blank for 0. The beginner may prefer to record the zeros to make sure he has not overlooked any scorable variable. However, this practice soon becomes unnecessary.

The clinical summary is a new form developed to facilitate interpretation. Data from the record and HIT summary forms are recorded here. Tables for recording scoring refinements in color, shading, movement, human and animal, and types of pathognomic verbalization make the interpretation easier. In addition, content themes are listed for use in sequence analysis of the blots.

Twenty-two scoring variables were selected in the standardization and factor analysis of the HIT (Holtzman, Thorpe, Swartz, and Herron, 1961). These variables include nearly all the important scoring dimensions of the Rorschach. A glossary of the abbreviations of the variables appears in the front

15

of the book for ready reference. The factor analyses resulted in a clustering of the twenty-two variables into six factors. Factor 1 includes integration (I), movement (M), human (H), popular (P), and form definiteness (FD). Barrier (Br) also loads highly on factor 1 for all groups except five-year olds. Factor 2 includes color (C) and shading (Sh). Form definiteness which is inversely loaded on factor 2, is a positive marker variable for factor 1. When form definiteness loads high on factor 1, it will load low on factor 2 and vice versa. Factor 3 includes pathognomic verbalization (V), anxiety (Ax), and hostility (Hs). Movement loads on factor 3 as well as on factor 1. Among children, factors 1 and 3 are correlated. Factor 4 usually includes location (L) and form appropriateness (FA). Factor 5 usually includes reaction time (RT) and rejection (R) and animal (A) reversed; that is, the longer the RT and the larger the number of R, the lower the A. Factor 6 is a residual factor that varies from one sample to the next. It often includes space (S), anatomy (At), sex (Sx), abstract (Ab), penetration (Pn), and balance (B). In addition, it may include affect arousal (AA), which is not listed as one of the twenty-two scoring variables but is discussed below.

For maximum ease in interpretation I have grouped the twenty-two scoring variables into six categories, each relating to a separate aspect of inkblot perception. Response set reveals the subject's definition of the test situation and includes RT and R. Perceptual differentiation deals with the subject's ability to discriminate and includes L, FA, and S. Determinants include variables that have direct stimulus characteristics within the inkblot (C, Sh, and B). Form is identified as a determinant by the absence of C, Sh, and B, together with sufficient form definiteness to justify its use. Ideational organization includes those variables which reveal the manner in which the subject organizes and responds to his perceptions. These variables are FD, M, I, Br, and P. Content follows the traditional usage and includes H, A, At, Sx, and Ab. Disturbed thought processes reveal autistic thinking which is derived primarily from the subject's fantasy life with little regard to the demands of reality. The variables in this category are V, Ax, Hs, Pn, and AA. Affect arousal (AA) was included in the earlier studies of the HIT but for normative purposes proved too sensitive to examiner differences and was therefore eliminated. When the individual administering the test is also scoring it, AA is a useful variable because it provides data on the intensity of the individual's reaction to the blots.

The guide contains sample responses with scoring weights for use in scoring the protocol. The responses are scored by the numerical weighting of each test variable. This weighting results in a codification of the responses, blot by blot, for easier manipulation and evaluation. After the entire set is coded, the data are converted into meaningful language for interpretation. The original HIT scoring has been modified in the categories of space, color, shading, movement, human, and animal. These changes are listed at the end of the scoring section for these variables.

Variables

Reaction time (RT) in seconds is transferred from the record form to the HIT summary and placed in the first row under the heading for that variable. The final score is the mean reaction time (total divided by 45).

Rejection (R) is scored 1 when the subject returns the inkblot without giving a scorable response. When the examiner scores a 1 for R, all other variables for that blot automatically are scored 0. Rejections require corrections in the FD, FA, and V scores after all scores are summed. The subject may give marginal responses, and the examiner may be uncertain whether the verbalization constitutes a rejection. As a general rule, when nothing is verbalized that is otherwise scorable, a rejection should be scored. Any reference to the color, shading, or symmetry of the blot is scorable even though no percept is given. The final score is the sum of scores in the rejection column for the forty-five blots.

Location (L) scores indicate whether the response is to the whole or to a part of the blot. A score of 0 is given when the percept includes the whole blot or the whole blot with minor portions excluded. A score of 1 is given if the percept includes a large area of the blot, such as an entire side, the center, or the top or bottom half. A score of 2 is given if the percept is seen in only a small area of the bolt. The major criteria in scoring L is the size of the area in relation to the total area of the blot. Appendix A of the guide contains illustrations of each blot for Forms A and B with location symbols. The letter W is scored 0, the capital D is scored 1, and the lower-case d is scored 2. Sometimes responses do not lend themselves to a clear-cut score. When two or more small areas are combined or when two large areas are used in a single response, scoring is determined by the size of the combined area, even if the integration is minimal. If the subject recognizes the mirror image of a percept on the other side of the card, the L score should be determined by the size of the area on the one side. In some instances the subject may give formless borderline responses which are almost rejections, such as paint smears. In this situation an L score of 0 is appropriate, as if the subject had rejected the blot. The final L score is the sum of the scores in the L column for the forty-five blots.

Space (S) scoring requires a true figure-ground reversal, namely, the inkblot serves as background to delineate the form of a white area. A score of 0 is given if the inkblot is the dominant aspect of the response, even though the white area may be included in a secondary manner. A score of 1 is given if the percept is seen primarily as a white area surrounded by the inkblot. For example, the following response to card 7B is scored 0 for space: "A bat with dark wings and a white body." However, the response "a man (D_2S) lying in the mud" is scored 1 for space.

Another response to the white areas (although not scorable as a true space response) occurs when the subject includes holes, gaps, and cut-outs in his percepts. These are often referred to as lakes, rivers, or roads as seen on maps or landscapes. They are also often seen as eyes. When such secondary use of space occurs, an s should be placed in the appropriate S block *but not scored*. This information is used in the interpretation. The final score for space is the sum of the scored S responses to the forty-five blots.

   Form definiteness (FD) scores the definiteness of the form of the percept based on the content of the response and the stylized level of the verbalization regardless of the goodness of fit to the inkblot. For instance, a vast difference in the definiteness level exists between the response "fire," which has no specific form in reality (when comparing one fire with another), and violin, which is a stylized instrument with a specific form including many parts. Form definiteness is scored from 0 to 4 ranging from an amorphous entity such as fire to highly specific, definitely formed objects such as the violin. Reference lists of concepts for scoring FD are found in the guide. An elaboration of a response, however, may alter the FD score from the rating given in the guide. When the form is made either more specific or more vague because of the position, action, or clothing described, the FD score increases or decreases accordingly. For example, a person is scored FD 2. However, a person wearing an Indian costume is scored FD 3. Conversely, a score of FD 3 for a man's face would be reduced to FD 2 by the elaboration "seen through a dirty window." The final FD score is the sum of the FD scores for the forty-five blots. When a rejection is scored, a correction is made to estimate the probable FD score which the subject would have obtained if there had been no rejected cards. (See guide, pp. 18, 19.) The corrected score may be derived by the formula: corrected score $= 45/(45-R)S$. This correction is consistent with standard formulas used in objective pencil and paper tests when items are omitted. The corrected score becomes the final score. Only FD, FA, and V make use of corrected scores.

   Form appropriateness (FA) is concerned with the goodness of fit of the percept to the form of the blot. This variable is subjective and requires the examiner to make a judgment based on the information obtained from the subject during the inquiry. In order to do this, the examiner must clearly understand where and in what way the concept is seen. FA is scorable if the examiner can recognize the percept in the area described or if a vague concept (such as an abstract response) which does not challenge the form of the blot is given. FA is scored from 0 to 2. A score of 2 is reserved for good FA, 1 is given when FA is fair or does not apply (for instance, "sorrow"), and 0 is given when FA is poor. The guide should be used in scoring FA. When discrepancies occur between the examiner's rating and the guide rating, the guide rating should be the final criterion.

   The form appropriate and form definite scorings are related. Responses scored FD 0 are scored FA 1, except in rare instances when the goodness of fit is so bad that even for a concept with indefinite form the inkblot is inappropriate. A response scored FD 0 is never scored FA 2, even though the form may seem appropriate at first glance. Scoring such a response FA superior distorts the meaning of the variable. At the other extreme, a response scored FD 4 implies a concept with invariant form and makes severe demands upon the form of the inkblot if one is to produce a score of 2 for goodness of fit. Such a combination is rare, especially if the whole inkblot is used. The only combination of the two scores which cannot occur at all is FD 0 and FA 2.

The examiner should continue to use the scoring samples in determining FA until he becomes proficient in the use of the test. Even when he has gained this proficiency he should refer from time to time to the guide in order to avoid any systematic shifting in his scoring values. Beginners often give too many ratings of 1 and shy away from the extremes of the scale.

The examiner must also be aware of the position of the card. When the card is positioned one way, the concept (in a particular area of a blot) may deserve a score of 2, while when the card is held in a different position the same concept might rate a score of 1 or even 0. The beginner may be cautious in scoring FA but should be careful not to distort the effect of this variable for later comparison with the normative samples. He should make every effort to determine where the subject sees the percept, and if the percept is acceptable, the response should be scored at least FA 1.

The total FA score is the sum for the forty-five blots unless the subject has rejected some cards. Correction scores appear in the guide or may be derived by the formula: corrected score $= 45/(45\text{-}R)S$. The corrected score becomes the final score.

Color (C) scoring is based on the importance of color (both chromatic and achromatic) in determining the response. C scores are generally reserved for responses in which the subject explicitly mentions color as a determinant for the response or when the subject points to the color obviously involved in the percept. On some occasions, however, color is not explicitly mentioned, and the examiner cannot easily determine whether color played an important role. The examiner should then ascertain whether the response would have been made without the presence of color. If not, he should score C (even though color was not mentioned). The examiner should not extend the inquiry beyond the standard questions, however, in order to facilitate his color scoring. He should avoid direct reference to color in the inquiry unless the subject has already mentioned it. The subject may identify fire or blood and point to a colored area without verbalizing that color elicited the response. Such responses nonetheless receive a C score. C is rated on a four-point scale from zero to 3. C 1 is equivalent to the Rorschach score FC; C 2 is equivalent to CF; and C 3 is equivalent to C in the Klopfer system (Klopfer, Ainsworth, Klopfer, and Holt, 1954). When color is not used as a determinant, score 0. When color is used in a secondary manner as an elaboration of the percept, score 1. Score 2 if color is used as the primary determinant but form (though indefinite) is implied in the response. Score 3 when color is used as a primary determinant with no form present in the percept. Scoring for achromatic color requires that the individual mention black, gray, or white as having elicited the response. Sometimes the blackness, grayness, or whiteness of the card is perceived not as color but as shading. The examiner should be alert to this difference.

The C and the FD scores are related. Sometimes only a small part of the percept involves color. However, the response as a whole is scored for color. If the definiteness of the form of the total concept is sufficient to merit a score of 3 or 4, C should be no higher than 1, even though the part of the percept involving color, if seen alone, would probably rate a score of C 2. For example, on card 12A a response "girls dancing by a campfire" is scored FD 3. C is rated no higher than 1 for campfire even though, if seen alone, campfire would be csored C 2. As a general rule, when a concept has a definite form in reality, the primary determinant is form and not color, particularly if the score on FA is 1 or 2. However, there are some exceptions. For example, on card 16A the response "an orange" would receive a high FD score (4) because of the invariant shape of the orange. Color would be scored 3 because of the integral relationship between color and the percept in this response. The FA score would be 0.

If the examiner is unsure whether color played a determining role in the percept and the individual has not clarified this question in the standard inquiry, the examiner should not pursue the questioning. The examiner is better off relying on the person's verbalization and scoring C 0 than incorrectly assuming the use of color. Sometimes the subject talks of the coloring or the coloration of the inkblot meaning the shading or texture rather than color or chroma. At other times a subject uses color in order to delineate the percept without using it as a determinant. For example: "This blue part could be ——————." "The red parts look like ——————." In these instances C is not scored.

For later interpretation the examiner should indicate while scoring whether a color percept is positive or negative. Color responses reflect the degree and direction of emotional responsivity to the external environment. They may disclose a positive reaching out toward the world of people or a negative withdrawal. Positive color responses include references to flowers, landscapes, and beautiful objects. Negative color responses are associated with violence, injury, disgust, decay, disorganization, and deterioration. They include responses such as blood and destructive fire. A plus or minus sign placed beside the color score indicates whether the response is positive or negative. When the scoring is completed, the color values (plus, minus, or neutral) are transferred to the clinical summary for interpretation. The total C score is the sum of all C scores for the forty-five blots.

Shading (Sh) is scored according to its primacy as a percept determinant. Shading is scored 1 when it is used in a secondary manner as an elaboration of a percept. Shading is scored 2 when it is explicitly used as the primary determinant with little or no form determinant. When the subject fails to verbalize a shading response, the examiner must interpret its role himself. If the subject rubs an area of the blot indicating sensitivity to texture, Sh should be scored. Any reference to fuzziness, hairiness, or coloring by which the subject clearly means shading is scored for Sh. Rain is a borderline response. For example, a rain response to card 35A (because of the streaky lines) approaches a texture response and should be scored Sh 1 or 2, depending on the form characteristics of the primary concept.

In some instances the examiner may have to distinguish between a fuzzy outline (a form response) and a fuzzy surface (a Sh response).

In standardizing the HIT, all the traditional Rorschach shading distinctions were pooled into one variable. The normative data are based on the accumulation of the shading values. However, for specialized clinical uses, this scoring is too gross. A letter should be added to the shading score to pinpoint the shading specified. If the percept is based on an actual textural quality of the blot a t should be placed beside the Sh score. Often the subject rubs or touches the blot. Such behavior should be noted at the time of administration for later scoring. Any reference to furriness or fuzziness is also a textural response (for example, animal skin, wool, vegetation, or topographical map).

Film is another shading variant and is of two types, light or dark. Light film Sh responses include diffusion such as fog, smoke, steam, cloud, water, or transparencies (photographic negatives or a reflection which is not based on form). When film is a shading determinant, an f should be added to the Sh score. Dark film responses (scored df) include darkness or dysphoric shading. Examples are dark storm clouds, gloomy night, despair, coal, black fog, nightmare, looks slimy and dirty.

The third shading variable is vista, represented in the scoring by v. Vista responses are scored when the subject perceives the shading in a three-dimensional manner. The examiner must be careful not to confuse vista with representations of depth by other cues such as linear perspective or size. More than one letter may be used to qualify shading if the response warrants it. The total shading score is the sum of that column for the forty-five blots.

Movement (M) scoring is based on the energy level or dynamic quality of the movement invested in the percept. M is scored on a five-point scale. Zero indicates neither movement nor static potential for movement. A score of 1 indicates static potential for movement, such as sitting, looking, resting, or lying. A score of 2 is given for passive and casual movement, such as walking, talking, climbing, reaching. A score of 3 is given for dynamic movement, such as lifting, dancing, running, weeping. A score of 4 is given for violent movement, such as whirling, exploding, fighting, or killing. M is scored only when the subject voluntarily ascribes movement or potential for movement to the percept. The examiner should make no attempt to elicit a movement response beyond the standard inquiry. Since the M score is designed to record the degree of movement, tension, or dynamic energy projected onto the percept by the subject, concepts clearly involving tension and dynamic energy should be scored even though motion is not verbalized. Potential for movement is exemplified by responses of stance: "a lion ready to spring" or the "looking-alive" quality described by the subject. Sometimes the tension level may be high even though visible motion is minimal—for example, "two men struggling in a tug of war." Score this response 3 even though the men appear relatively motionless. The examiner should always score the level of energy invested in the percept. The elaboration and description of the percept should be evaluated for a properly rated score.

The M score combines both animate and inanimate movement. This all-inclusive M score limits a full clinical interpretation. There are different dynamic interpretations offered for animate and inanimate movement. Although the special variations traditionally used in the Rorschach test can be derived later by configural scoring of M, H, and A for each response, the clinician may find it simpler to mark the differences while scoring. When the movement relates to abstract forces acting on a situation and the movement is not instigated by a human or animal, an m should be added to the M score. The subject sometimes sees inanimate movement affecting animate objects. When this combination occurs, an ma should be placed beside the M score. Examples of the m scoring are "raining" (2 m) and "volcano erupting" or "nuclear explosion" (both 4 m). Examples of ma scoring are "a person battered by a storm" (4 ma) and "an animal eaten by disease" (3 ma). Some responses contain both animate and in-animate movement. The examiner should note each. The highest score of the two should be recorded for the M score of that blot. For example, for "a volcano erupting and a man is walking away from it," "volcano erupting" is scored 4 m and "man walking away" is scored M 2. The whole blot is scored M 4. The refinements in the M scoring are needed for transfer to the clinical summary. The total M score is the sum of the scores in M column for the forty-five blots.

Pathognomic verbalization (V) reflects the degree of autistic, bizarre thinking in a response (compared with rational, logical reasoning). This thinking is usually manifested in the subject's description of the percept or his explanation of why he saw the percept, rather than in side remarks or personal references incidental to the response. V is difficult to classify and quantify especially if the examiner has had little experience with psychotic processes. Nevertheless, from the viewpoint of personality assessment or differential diagnosis, V represents some of the most important material in inkblot responses. Experienced clinicians usually rely more heavily on such qualitative signs of mental disturbance than on many of the standard variables. Because of the difficulty in scoring this variable, especially for the student and inexperienced clinician, numerous specific examples are included in the guide for each of the nine scoring categories which fall within the V grouping. The scoring for V is weighted on a five-point scale, but some of the nine categories use only part of the scale, depending on the severity of the pathology evident in the response. The scale values and categories for pathognomic verbalization appear in Table 1. Because of the difficulty in assessing pathological thought processes, this scale should be scored last. The other variables are comparatively simply derived and do not require the degree of reference that the V scale requires. If an examiner suspects that a response has pathognomic content, he should place a check in the V block of the HIT summary. After he completes all other scoring, he can compare these responses with the examples in the guide to determine their proper V value. In scoring, the category of the V score should be included so that later, during interpretation, the total scores in a category can be accumulated and evaluated according to the meaning of the category. When a response belongs to more than one V category, both are noted, but the

Table 1

SCALE VALUES AND CATEGORIES OF PATHOGNOMIC VERBALIZATION

Category	Abbreviated Symbol	Possible Scale Values
Fabulation	FB	1
Fabulized Combination	FC	2, 3, 4
Queer Response	QR	1, 2, 3
Incoherence	IC	4
Autistic Logic	AL	1, 2, 3, 4
Contamination	CT	2, 3, 4
Self-Reference	SR	2, 3, 4
Deterioration Color	DC	2, 3, 4
Absurd Response	AB	3

Source: Holtzman and others, 1961.

highest score is recorded for the blot. When a subject provides a secondary percept or makes a side remark with additional evidence of disordered thinking, the examiner may include this response as an additional V score for the blot (to a maximum of two V scores). However, a scale value greater than 8 may not be scored for any one blot. The nine V scoring categories and their meanings are described below.

(1) Fabulation (FB) is a response in which the associative elaboration has notable affective components. Feelings, motives, and similar qualities are ascribed to the concept in an unusual manner. The percept reveals nothing which would account for this elaboration. The only scoring for this category is 1 because such responses are often given by sensitive persons who enjoy a colorful play of language. For example, "two elephants looking at each other, one happy, one sad" is a response to the whole card 26B and should be scored FB 1.

(2) Fabulized combination (FC) is scored when the subject combines different elements of the inkblot into one response and the resulting combination is fantastic. The combination is based on spatial contiguity rather than on logical relationships. Such responses reflect a loss of distance as evidenced by the subject's acceptance of the combination as real "because it is there." Scoring of this category is either 2, 3, or 4, depending on the degree of disturbed thinking evident in the response. For example, "two men carrying a wishbone," a response to the whole card 34A, is scored FC 2.

(3) Queer response (QR) scoring requires subjective guidelines of the examiner. The scoring should therefore proceed with caution, particularly by the inexperienced. Considerable clinical experience is necessary to sense peculiarity in the verbalizations. The queer response has an odd flavor which implies psychotic reasoning, although illogical reasoning may not be directly revealed. Scoring for this group is 1, 2, or 3 depending on the severity of pathology evident in the response. For example, "head of an animal with the face carved out of it" (a response to the whole card 7A) is scored QR 2.

(4) Incoherence (IC) is scored when rational controls completely break down. The response contains queer elements, and the percept appears as nonsense to the examiner. Responses in this category are always given the maximum weight of four points. For example: "Two colors, or three, that would be the masculine, where have I seen that! It's a prison, presentable, that's masculine" (a response to the whole card 22B) is scored IC 4.

(5) Autistic logic (AL) implies faulty, fantastic reasoning given as justification for the response. The reasoning is given with an air of certainty, even though it bears little or no relationship to reality or conventional forms of logic. For example, the response to card 35A "two bulls, fairy bulls—because they're dressed in pink." This kind of reasoning can appear in a mild, subtle form which is difficult to detect, or it can be so severe that an untrained observer recognizes it. The confabulation response is a special form of autistic logic in which a small part of the inkblot triggers off a percept including a larger area, even though the larger area bears no resemblance to the percept. In the sample of scoring variables in the guide, confabulated responses are those which have an asterisk in front of the number of the blot. Another kind of autistic logic is evident in responses in which parts of the percept are determined solely by position. AL scoring is 1, 2, 3, or 4, depending on the degree of faulty reasoning. For example, "Alaska" (and after the characteristics query) "because it's cold and blue" and (d_3 is seen as an igloo), a response to the D1 area of card 33A, is scored AL 2.

(6) Contamination (CT) occurs when conflicting percepts are fused or when the same area simultaneously stands for two (or more) interdependent, logically separate concepts. The two superimposed concepts are reported as one percept because the subject is unable to separate the disparate associations. Normally an individual can suppress such conflicting elements, giving one or the other as his response. CT is scored 2, 3, or 4. When a subject unduly vacillates between two concepts or when the characteristics of the rival concept influence the response selected, a score of 2 is given. A score of 4 is generally given when two (or more) different concepts are fused, such as: "a man, no a bat, a batman" (in response to the d_1 area of card 26A). A score of 3 is given for responses that fall between vacillation and fusion.

(7) Self-reference (SR) is scored when an individual draws himself into the response and gives the percept a personal meaning. Self-reference demonstrates loss of distance between the subject and the inkblot. When the subject reveals such a loss of distance (in a side remark or in the main response) the examiner scores a 2, 3, or 4, depending on the degree of involvement. If a subject refers to a personal experience as a means of explaining why he gave a particular response, the loss of distance between him and the blot is slight. For example, the response to card 10A "Organisms under a microscope" explained as "I'm studying slides of organisms in biology this week and these resembled some." Such a self-reference is not considered pathological and therefore is not scored. However, the distinction should be clearly made. For example, "A face. God, I'm

seeing faces in everything but I can't help it" (a response to the whole card 31A) is scored SR 2.

(8) Deterioration color (DC) is scored when loose, fantastic color associations which have bizarre content are given with an air of reality. Such responses are often gory, arbitrary, or symbolic elaborations. They are often haphazard associations of an object colored like the area in the blot. DC may be scored 2, 3, or 4, depending on the degree of pathology. For example, "a green sky" (a response to the whole card 13A) is scored DC 2.

(9) Absurd response (AB) is scored when a subject assigns a form definite concept to an area of the blot which by no stretch of the imagination can be conceived of as appropriate and to which no other stimuli (such as color or shading) are contributing factors. These responses show complete disregard for form quality where the form of the percept can not be ignored. Perseverative responses can often be scored as absurd responses because the same response is repeated blot after blot without regard to the blot itself. Scoring in this category is always 3. For example, "King Tut's tomb, a pyramid" (a response to the whole blot 32A) is scored AB 3.

The total V score is the sum for the forty-five blots. A correction for rejections is necessary. Corrected scores appear in the guide or may be derived by the formula: corrected score $= 45/(45\text{-}R)S$.

Integration (I) is scored when the subject organizes two or more adequately perceived blot elements into a larger whole. In scoring integration, three other variables need to be considered. FD and FA must be scored at least 1 or higher, and V must be scored no higher than 1. Four classes of integration responses are recognized: *Functional integration* responses are scored on the basis of interaction between two or more conceptually independent subunits, for example, "two men talking to each other." In all cases of functional integration M must be scored at least 1 (in addition to a consideration of the three variables mentioned above). *Collective integration* responses concern overall grouping. The essential feature of collective integration is evidence of a conceptualizing, classifying process, distinct from sheer enumeration, for example, "a group of," "garden," "collection of," or "pair of." *Positional integration* is scored when a spatial relationship is perceived between the elements (except for fabulized combinations). The relationship between blot elements must have a positional character, as in the response "a candle stuck in the neck of a bottle" or "two natives dancing around a fire." A secondary elaboration, such as clothing, and the organization of two or more otherwise independent concepts are not scored as integration. *Structural integration* responses concern color boundary crossing with recognition of the boundary as part of the response. In this kind of integration, a single content is perceived by unifying two or more colored areas, including white space. Occasionally, when the blending of different colored areas is gradual rather than abrupt, scoring may be complicated. Usually, however, two or more generally independent, sizable colored areas have been integrated into a single content. For example (in card 16B) "a candle in a bottle packed in green moss" (D_2 and d_1). The crossing of color boundaries is not considered integrative when one of the colors is of no concern to the subject and occupies a minor area or nearly all of the area, for example, card 36B, "a mask with beady eyes" for the whole response. The total score for integration is the sum of that column for the forty-five blots.

Content is scored for the five independent categories (human, animal, anatomy, sex, abstract) which follow. A response may be scored under two or more content variables.

Human (H) scoring depends upon the degree of human quality in the response. When no human or part of a human is perceived, the H score is 0. Parts of human beings, featureless or distorted human bodies, and mythological or cartoon characters are scored H 1. A score of 2 is given when a whole human being (with differentiable parts) is seen. (Small parts, such as a hand or a foot, can be missing.) A score of 2 is also given for a human face if the features are elaborated, or for parts of a human being provided that the subject assumes the remainder of the person is present but hidden.

For later interpretation and transfer to the clinical summary, the examiner should note the exact H 1 response. He should add an h if the head or face only is reported, b if the body or part of the body is reported, and o for other percepts. If H is scored 2, the examiner should add an M if the person is male, F if the person is female, and 0 if the sex is not identified. If the human is seen in movement, the examiner should add p for passive movement (M 1) and a for active movement (M 2, M 3, or M 4). The total score for H is the sum of the forty-five blots.

Animal (A) scoring depends on the degree of animal qualities in the content of the response. The examiner should score 0 when the response contains no animal or animal parts. He should also score 0 for animal objects, vaguely described animal skins, and skins serving a nonanimal purpose such as "fur coat" or "bear rug." Microscopic animal life should also be scored 0. The examiner should score 1 when the response includes animal parts such as animal heads or faces (even if highly elaborated) and for elaborated descriptions of animal skins (head or legs), bugs, or insects. The examiner should score 2 when the percept includes a whole animal (small parts such as a foot, leg, or tail may be missing), or major parts of an animal, provided the subject assumes the whole animal to be present but partially hidden. Sometimes the examiner may be unable to tell whether the subject is referring to an animal or a human when he gives a response such as face or open mouth. The examiner cannot assume that the subject means a human face (and so on), although in most instances he does. The examiner should not attempt to clarify this point in the inquiry. Sometimes other details in the response clarify it. However, when the examiner has a genuine doubt whether A or H should be scored, he should give a score of 1 to both. When animals are engaged in an activity which is strictly human in nature, score H 1 as well as A 1 or A 2, depending upon the scoring criteria for A.

When A is scored 1, add h if the head or face only is included, b if only the body or part of the animal is included, and 0 for all other A 1 responses. If movement is scored and A is scored 2, add p if the movement is passive (M 1) and a if it is aggressive (M 2, M 3, or M 4). The total score for A is the sum of the forty-five blots.

Anatomy (At) is scored when penetration or implied penetration of the body wall of a human or animal is expressed. The examiner scores a 0 if this variable is not present. X rays, medical drawings, and all bone structures are scored 1. Visceral and crude anatomy responses and all soft internal organs are scored 2. Blood, which presumes penetration of the human or animal, is also scored 2. Blood without any other anatomical reference was not scored as At in the original HIT scoring but is included here because of its clinical implications. Anatomy and penetration (Pn) scores are related. A score of 1 on At may imply a score of 1 on Pn. A score of At 2 usually implies a score of Pn 1. The total At score is the sum of the forty-five blots.

Sex (Sx) scoring reflects the degree of sexuality in the response. Percepts including lips, dancing, hips, or holding hands are not scored for sex unless the subject elaborates the percept to include sexual content. A score of 1 is given to socially accepted sexual percepts such as thighs, buttocks, bust, nude figures, pregnant woman, petting, kissing, embracing. A score of 2 is given for blatant sexual content such as man and woman having intercourse, a penis, vagina, anus, breast. The total is the sum of the Sx responses for the forty-five blots.

Abstract (Ab) is scored according to the degree of abstract quality in the response. A score of 0 is given when no abstract qualities are present. A score of 1 is given for abstract elements which accompany other elements that have form such as "two people meeting in a blur of indifference." A score of 2 is given if the reference is wholly abstract, for example, "It reminds me of happiness." The total score is the sum of the Ab column for the forty-five blots.

Anxiety (Ax) is scored when signs of anxiety in the content are identifiable. The scoring of the anxiety element is patterned after the work of Elizur (1949). Ax is scored 0, 1, or 2 according to the following four categories.

(1) Emotions and attitudes expressed or implied include responses that reveal fear, unpleasantness, sorrow, and pity. A score of 1 is given for responses such as a sad child, a whimpering dog, or a gloomy cave. A score of 2 is given for responses such as a weeping child, a mad dog crazy with fear, or a dark and dangerous cave.

(2) Expressive behavior in the projection of movement into the percept can sometimes be interpreted as a sign of anxiety. M must be scored at least 1 to score Ax in this category. Ax is scored 1 when the evidence for Ax is debatable and indirect. Ax is scored 2 when the evidence is clear-cut. A score of Ax 1 is given for responses such as a mouse caught in a trap or someone caught in a rainstorm. A score of Ax 2 is given for responses such as a man crawling in the desert, dying of thirst, a pile of rocks falling on a man, or two men being hanged.

(3) Symbolic responses which reflect anxiety should be conservatively

scored. Although psychologists generally recognize that anxiety is often manifest in a symbolic or disguised form, the particular form varies considerably from person to person. Also, the "universal" meaning of symbols can be seriously questioned, even within relatively homogeneous subcultures. Score 1 when symbolism is present but is of a subtle and questionable nature. Score 2 for responses which have a clear-cut symbolic meaning. For example, Ax 1 is scored for responses such as animal carcass in the desert or bouquet of dead flowers. Ax 2 is scored for a dead person, black represents death and destruction, a bottomless pit, and a diseased lung.

(4) Cultural stereotypes of fear also require conservative scoring. Treating cultural stereotypes as universal signs of anxiety is difficult. Undoubtedly some of the concepts listed in the guide (especially those scored Ax 1) vary from one subculture to another in the degree of anxiety signified. Nevertheless, some concepts do have a general connotation of fear for most individuals in our culture, even though the percepts may be given without any elaboration. A score of 0 is given to percepts such as campfire, bugs, X ray, or bones. A score of 1 is given to cultural stereotypes of questionable universality such as bat, explosion, witch doctor, storm clouds, volcano, or animal skeleton. A score of 2 is reserved for percepts which have distinctively universal fear-producing properties such as vampire bat, snake, spider, witch, blood, tornado, and ghost. Sample Ax responses are given in the guide. If the examiner is in doubt after examining the samples, he should not score for this variable. Anxiety is better underscored than overscored. The total score is the sum of Ax for the forty-five blots.

Hostility (Hs) scores are based on symbolic, implicit, or explicit signs of hostility in the response. The hostility scale was derived from Elizur (1949) and Murstein (1956). As with anxiety, some clinical sensitivity on the part of the scorer is essential. Scores can be lowered or raised, depending upon the elaboration of the percept. Two general rules are helpful in scoring Hs. As the hostility varies from vague or symbolic to direct and violent, the score increases. The score also increases as the objects in the percept vary from inanimate to animal and then to human. Examples of scoring categories for Hs scores of 1, 2, or 3 are listed in the guide. The total score for Hs is the sum of the Hs column for the forty-five blots.

Barrier (Br) scoring is based on the degree of definiteness of the body-image boundary. It refers to perception of objects with definite and well delineated boundaries and protective coverings, membranes, shells, or skins. If the subject makes no reference to such items, Br is scored 0. Otherwise Br is scored 1. All references to enclosed openings in the earth such as valley, mineshaft, and well are scored for Br. All references to unusual animal containerlike shapes such as bloated cat, pregnant woman, kangaroo, and udder are scored. All references to overhanging or protective surfaces such as umbrella or awning are scored. All references to things that are armored or depend on their own containing walls for protection such as car, airplane, dirigible, and rocket are scored. All references to things being covered, surrounded, or concealed such as person behind a tree, man covered with a blanket, and bowl overgrown by a plant are scored. All references to objects with unusual containerlike shapes or properties such as throne, chair, and ferris wheel are scored. All references to figures which can be identified only by their uniforms such as warrior, nun, fireman, and policeman are scored. Additional general examples of barrier responses are included in the guide. Although masks or buildings are generally scored 0, some exceptions where the structure is unique merit a score of 1, for example, tent, igloo, or quonset hut.

The scoring of Br as a HIT variable is derived directly from the work of Fisher and Cleveland (1958), although it was later modified to include more items. The original HIT classification of Br categories is used, however, because normative data are based on that scoring. The total score for Br is the sum of the Br scores for the forty-five blots.

Penetration (Pn) is scored for percepts which imply that the body exterior is of little protective value and can be easily penetrated. If such a feeling is not evident in the response, penetration is not scored. Otherwise the score is 1. Three concepts are included in a penetration score: any penetration, disruption, or wearing away of an outer surface; any mode or channel for getting into the interior of an object or passing from the interior to the exterior; and surfaces which are easily permeable or fragile. The guide gives examples for all these categories. Pn scoring is related to scoring of At. When At is scored 1, Pn may be scored 1. When At is scored 2, Pn is usually scored 1.

The use of Pn as a HIT variable is derived directly from the work of Fisher and Cleveland (1958). This work was subsequently modified to include more items. The original classifications of Pn categories are used, however, because normative data are based on that scoring. The total Pn score is the sum of the Pn column for the forty-five blots.

Balance (B) is scored 0 or 1. The examiner scores a 1 when the subject expresses interest in the symmetry (or asymmetry) of the blot, for example, "just alike on either side" or "nearly perfect mirror image." References to minor discrepancies in the symmetry are also scored 1. Occasionally the subject may react to the symmetry of the blot without interpreting it in any other way. If the response is adequate (complies with the instructions), B should be scored 1. The total score is the sum of the B column for the forty-five blots.

Popular (P) responses are percepts that have been statistically defined for a specific area of an inkblot in earlier normative studies. P responses are based on a core concept which is the essential factor defining their presence or absence. The response need not be identical with the core concept; alternative concepts are admissible variations. For example, if the popular area of a blot is a "person" but the subject elaborates and adds other portions of the blot, even the total blot, the examiner nonetheless scores for P because the popular figure was seen in the appropriate location. Also, even if the popular area is labeled with a specific concept, such as a butterfly, a similar concept, such as a moth, is scored for P. If the popular response for an area is a person, a response of goblin, witch, or clown (all people) is scored for P. If the popular area is defined as a common four-

legged animal, then a response of dog, horse, or any other such animal is acceptable. Some cards have two areas, each of which has a different popular concept.
The HIT scores twenty-five populars each for Forms A and B. The total score
for popular can be no greater than twenty-five. Samples of P core concepts are
in the guide. The total score for P is the sum of the P column for the forty-five
blots.

    Affect arousal (AA) is not included in the variables usually scored. How-
ever, when the HIT is administered, scored, and interpreted by the same person,
he may use the AA score. This score is *not* based on the content. To score AA,
the subject must explicitly express an affective or emotional reaction either to his
own response or to an inkblot. Such reactions are determined by the adjectives in
the elaboration of his response or by side remarks. In order to score AA the
examiner must record all comments and side remarks concerning the inkblot.
These comments should be enclosed in parentheses so that they are not confused
with the percept itself. AA may be scored in the first blank column after popular.
AA scoring employs two three-point scales, one positive and one negative. The
examiner should score a 0 if no affect is indicated and plus or minus 1 or 2 if it
is. The plus and minus indicate the direction of the affect (pleasant plus and unpleasant minus). Only one AA score is given for each card even though the
subject may make more than one comment. The affective remark with the
highest plus or minus rating is scored. Some responses are directionless and ambivalent. Both a plus and minus symbol (±) are added to the score to indicate
the neutral affect. Scoring for the direction of affect may depend largely on the
subject's tone of voice or other nonverbal behavior such as facial expression or
body movement. The examiner should be alert for such expressions of affect and
record a plus or minus in the record together with the verbalization. AA should
be scored conservatively, and when the examiner is in doubt, he should not enter
a score. Although the following examples appear to be content-oriented, the
reader must keep in mind the nonverbal elements available to the administrator.
The significance of the nonverbal behavior makes scoring impossible by someone
other than the examiner. Typical −2 reactions are a horrible beast, a hideous insect, a terrifying witch. Unpleasant reactions to responses (scorable −1) are a
leering face, tigers growling at each other, a blouse with terrible coloring. The
following examples typify the neutral or indifferent affect and are scored 0 in
spite of the affect implicit in the content: war, an odd-looking monster, a mashed
butterfly, a decomposed body. Examples of pleasant affects (scorable +1) are a
happy clown, a cute little puppy, a gaily colored dress. Very pleasant reactions
(+2) are exemplified by a gorgeous dance scene, a feeling of happiness, a beauti-
fully colored garden. Ambivalent or directionless affect responses (scorable ±1)
are: "For goodness sakes, it looks like a lollypop" or "Gosh! Well it could be a
bat." Those scorable ±2 are "Good God Almighty! I see my mother's face" or
"Lord! It looks like a girl undressing." Side remarks scorable −2 are: "I don't
know why but these are making me ill." "Smudges . . . who the hell made these
anyway?" Side remarks scorable −1 are: "A merry-go-round; I don't like to ride

on them" or "Finger painting of a child; I don't like this one." Side remarks scorable +1 are: "A dog running; I like dogs" or "It doesn't remind me of anything, but the colors are pretty." Side remarks scorable +2 are: "I love looking at these cards, it's lots of fun" or "This is a beautiful card, it's like a painting." The total for AA should be expressed in two scores: one plus, and one minus. The guide contains no normative samples for comparison, but these data are useful in interpretation.

Developing Scoring Facility

It is suggested that the novice begin by testing several cooperative subjects and use the results to develop facility in scoring. For the first ten to twenty records some of the difficult variables should be scored vertically for all forty-five blots. This practice develops sensitivity in discriminating among the weights of a variable. The guide aids in avoiding bias in scoring. Some variables can be scored horizontally without referring to the guide. These variables include reaction time (which is transferred directly from the record sheet to the summary sheet), rejection (a score of 1 is indicated when no response is given), space, and balance. Some variables are learned more quickly than others. As the examiner becomes competent, he scores more variables horizontally than vertically. In scoring location, form appropriateness, and popular, the examiner should refer to the appendix of the guide. The areas of the schematics are marked for location. W represents areas which are scored 0, D areas scored 1, and d areas scored 2. FA judged during administration can be reexamined for scoring weight against the samples. Such reference may necessitate a change in the rating originally given. Examiners are often overcautious in scoring FA. When the response is appropriate, the subject should be given a score of at least fair (1). The inexperienced examiner will probably continue to refer to the guide in scoring FA for a long time because of the difficulty in scoring subjective variables. Scoring P requires reference to the blot schematics. Responses which are scored for P are included in the samples. A list of the core concepts is also needed for accurate P scoring because all possible variations are not contained in the samples provided. When the examiner is familiar with the use of core concepts and recognizes the amount of variation that can still be scored P, he no longer needs to use the guide and can rely solely on the list of core concepts.

Form definiteness, anxiety, hostility, barrier, penetration, pathognomic verbalization, and affect arousal are the most difficult variables to score for accuracy. Frequent reference to scoring samples in these categories is essential. Even after the examiner has acquired experience and scoring proficiency, he may need to review the scoring criteria occasionally to avoid drift in scoring—perpetuation of scoring errors which he may have developed. Minor scoring disagreements among scorers are inevitable. However, averaged over the forty-five blots, inter-scorer agreement has been found to be exceedingly high.

Initially, the scoring time may be as long as an hour because of the need to refer to the samples and because of the unfamiliarity with scoring. However, once the examiner gains experience, he can score most records in less than thirty minutes.

Relationships Between Variables

Some relationships between variables should be reviewed for accurate scoring. When form definiteness is 0, form appropriateness is at no time scored 2, although it may be scored 1. FD 4 and FA 2 seldom occur together, especially when location is 0. When FD is scored 3 or 4, color is no higher than 1. As a rule, C 3 is not scored when FD is 2 or higher, particularly if FA is 1 or 2. FD 4 and C 3 is a rare but possible combination only when FA is 0—for example, when nothing but color is appropriate to the blot even though the percept is FD high as in "an orange" for card 16A. When FD is 2 or higher, shading cannot exceed 1. A shading score of 2 can combine with FD 0 or FD 1. C 3 and FD 0 or FD 1 permits a FA score of 1 (any color reference or naming is appropriate to the blot). FD and FA must be 1 or higher and pathognomic verbalization no higher than 1 to permit an integration score of 1. When anatomy is scored, a score of 1 for penetration is frequently scored too. FA 1 and B 1 (balance) are scored when the subject responds only to the symmetry or asymmetry of the blot.

Part IV of this book includes case analyses with HIT records scoring all variables. The reader may use this scoring as a prototype.

Protocols obtained from group administration in which the prescribed method for hand scoring has been used can be scored on all the above variables except reaction time. Balance, sex, and abstract occur rarely with this method.

The Hill Clinical Summary (see p. 33) contains tables for transferring data from the HIT summary. The final raw scores for all variables, percentile norms, and the subscores for the responses to the fifteen highest- and lowest-saturated color cards are placed in the categories table. The six categories correspond to the grouping of the variables for interpretation. The card numbers of the blots having the highest degree of saturated color are listed (a) at the bottom of the categories table, and those with the lowest degree of color saturation are listed (b).

The summary includes separate tables for color, shading, movement and pathognomic verbalization. The movement table records the responses in the human and animal categories. The sequence analysis section provides space for the examiner to transfer the basic themes of the percepts.

The cumulative responses for all C 1, C 2, and C 3 weights of color are entered in the color table in the appropriate sections for positive, negative, or neutral responses. The number of achromatic responses is entered in the column headed Ac (achromatic). Shading information should also be transferred to the appropriate section of that table. Sh responses should be broken down into four categories: texture, light film, dark film, and vista.

The movement table has separate lines for M scored 1, 2, 3, and 4 and is

HILL CLINICAL SUMMARY
for the
HOLTZMAN INKBLOT TECHNIQUE

Form A or B

Name: _____   Date: _____

Norms: _____

CATEGORIES

	I		II				III		IV					V				VI				
	RT	R	L	FA	S	C	Sh	B	FD	M	I	Br	P	H	A	At	Sx	Ab	Ax	Hs	V	Pn	AA
Final Score																							
Per-centile																							
High (a) Stim. Color																							
Low (b) Stim. Color																							

Form A (a) 3, 6, 9, 15, 16, 17, 19, 20, 26, 27, 28, 35, 39, 42, 44
        (b) 1, 2, 5, 7, 18, 22, 24, 29, 30, 32, 33, 36, 37, 38, 43
Form B (a) 3, 6, 7, 11, 15, 17, 21, 24, 29, 34, 36, 39, 41, 42, 44
        (b) 2, 5, 8, 9, 10, 16, 18, 19, 23, 25, 26, 30, 32, 33, 45

COLOR

Score	+	–	N	Ac
1				
2				
3				

SHADING

Score	Texture	Light Film	Dark Film	Vista
1				
2				

MOVEMENT

	HUMAN									ANIMAL					m	
	1			2						1			2		Inanimate	Animate
Score				M		F		O								
	H	B	O	P	A	P	A	P	A	H	B	O	P	A		
1																
2																
3																
4																
NO M																

PATHOGNOMIC VERBALIZATION

FB	FC	QR	IC	AL	CT	SR	DC	AB

Notes: _____
_____
_____
_____
_____

SEQUENCE ANALYSIS

1. _____
2. _____
3. _____
4. _____
5. _____
6. _____
7. _____
8. _____
9. _____
10. _____
11. _____
12. _____
13. _____
14. _____
15. _____
16. _____
17. _____
18. _____
19. _____
20. _____
21. _____
22. _____
23. _____
24. _____
25. _____
26. _____
27. _____
28. _____
29. _____
30. _____
31. _____
32. _____
33. _____
34. _____
35. _____
36. _____
37. _____
38. _____
39. _____
40. _____
41. _____
42. _____
43. _____
44. _____
45. _____

divided into three sections. These sections include animate (human and animal) movement and inanimate movement. The human (H) and animal (A) sections are further divided to identify the movement as a score of 1 or 2. Under both H 1 and A 1 are sections for recording M responses of head or body or other types of H 1 and A 1. Under H 2 a division is provided for recording M responses reported as male, female, or other, and a subdivision under both H 2 and A 2 is provided for recording the movement as passive or active. M scores of 1 are passive; M scores 2, 3, and 4 are active. The m scores are divided according to the recipient of the m (animate and inanimate). A line is also provided at the bottom of the M table labeled No M. In this space both H and A responses which had no movement can be recorded under all the groupings on the table. These scorings provide data for independent interpretation of H and A.

Each of the scoring categories of pathognomic verbalization is listed. The number of V responses in each category should be posted. The quality of the responses may be indicated under notes if desired. Interpretation is done directly from the clinical summary.

Norms

Normative data for the standardization population are presented in the guide. These data plus norms for additional population samples are presented in the Appendix. Normative data may be used for hand-scored protocols which are obtained from either an individual or noncomputer-style group administration.

The relevant normative group is the group in which the subject belongs at the time of testing. If the subject is in school, his test is scored against the normative group of the appropriate level. Norms for eleventh graders are combined with those of average adults. For subjects in grades eleven and twelve use average adult norms. If the subject is no longer in school, norms for the average adult are appropriate. If the subject is in a pathological group, his test can be scored against the norms for several types of pathological groups. In the clinical setting the examiner may wish to refer to a second normative sample, namely, the group to which the subject is suspected to belong.

Scores at or below the twentieth percentile and at or above the eightieth percentile should be designated for interpretive evaluation because of the tendency toward the extremes. The examiner should make particular note of scores below the fifth percentile and above the ninety-ninth percentile.

INTERPRETATION
BASED ON
SCORING VARIABLES

PART TWO

Webster defines interpretation as: "(1) the act of interpreting, explanation of unintelligible words in language that is intelligible; (2) the act of expounding or unfolding what is not understood or not obvious."

When an artist's creative endeavors are interpreted, the critic considers them the product of an inner formulation, particularly when the artist is a painter or poet. Creative expression is the artist's interpretation or inner formulation of some external stimulus. The same creative process occurs in the interpretation of inkblot stimuli. In responding to an inkblot, the subject draws on his inner self to formulate a percept. Thus, the subject's response is a creative act and, like the creative expression of the artist, is available for interpretation by the expert. The examination of inkblot responses over the years indicates that most people respond in specific patterns. These patterns have been classified to identify particular personality groups in the same way artists are classified as belonging to a particular school. The interpretation of inkblot responses, however, requires more than categorizing an individual; it also requires identifying his unique characteristics and the way he consistently organizes his thoughts and feelings. The level at which he functions, his experiences, intelligence, verbal fluency, defensive maneuvers, and response set determine his perception of the test situation and his ability to

*cope with its demands. Thus, clinical judgment is made of the individual's inter-
pretation of the inkblots based both on his perception of external reality (the
stimulus) and on the role of internal factors as reflected in his ideational effort
and overt behavior. The interaction between subject and examiner affects the
subject's response. The subject may react in many ways to the behavior and
personality of the examiner and how he perceives the expectations of the situation.
The examiner needs to evaluate the subject's self-concept, the impression he hopes
to create (to enhance or negate himself), his level of cooperation, and his attitude
toward his own responses. The subject may take a concrete attitude toward interpreting the blot and try to find likenesses to specific objects. This attitude is
frequently taken when the examiner asks: "What does it look like?" rather than
"What does it remind you of?", or he may get involved in the task of association
and appear not to realize that he is interpreting. Responses flow smoothly and
appear to be without any conscious effort. Some persons are always aware of the
discrepancy between the response and the stimulus and call this discrepancy to
the attention of the examiner. This awareness makes the test a continued effort for
the subject. Schachtel (1966) states that the free flow of associations may be
deterred by a narrow definition of the test task, by rigid repressiveness, by a feeling of being under pressure, or by the fear that responses may reveal something
about himself that he does not wish to reveal.*

*An interpretation is more than the identification of the manner in which
an individual structures his responses to the environment. It should also include
a prediction about a future pattern of behavior and a diagnostic evaluation. The
psychologist is seldom asked to evaluate a subject solely to identify personality
variables. He is more interested in the formulation and prediction of future
behavior so that appropriate planning can be done. He is frequently asked to
answer questions such as: "Will this individual be a good candidate for psychotherapy?" If so, "Can therapy be assayed in an open setting?" He may also be
asked whether individual or group psychotherapy is indicated. Other questions
may concern aid in relocation planning, as in the case of a child. The agency
needs to know what kind of controls the child possesses. Test reports should include strengths as well as weaknesses.*

*Although this text is concerned with the HIT, and this section is specifi-
cally concerned with interpretation of HIT responses, psychologists generally (and
appropriately) give more than one test to a subject before they try to answer
questions and substantiate hypotheses which arise from the responses. The more
information available on the individual's functioning in response to different stimuli, the greater the confidence with which questions can be answered. Basic data
should contain quantitative information describing the intellectual functioning
and emotional inner world of the subject, evidence of behavior reflecting the
quality of the inner emotional life, available controls for coping with inner
needs and pressures, and the individual's adaptive solutions to his life problems
(types of defenses). From this information, a valid picture of the individual's
mode of operation is provided along several dimensions: how he feels, how he*

thinks, and how he attempts to maintain his psychological homeostasis (Beck, 1952).

Zubin, Eron, and Schumer (1965) state that the basic hypotheses underlying interpretation of the Rorschach technique also apply to the HIT. They note that Rorschach paved the way for interpretive assumptions based on empirical observations or hunches. Psychologists are aware that not all the rationale behind interpretation of inkblot responses is empirically tested. The interpreter must apply judgment as he rates and makes decisions about a subject.

Inkblot perception parallels perception of the everyday world. Responses to the ambiguous character of the blots permits the observer to study the perceptual process. Because the stimulus imposes little organization from without, the laws of color constancy, size constancy, and form constancy do not apply in the subject's adjustment to the stimulus (Zubin, Eron, and Schumer, 1965). The responses reflect habitual modes and patterns of subjective organization and reveal the way the subject projects his view of the world. The HIT provides enough sampling of behavior patterns to lend confidence to the examination of the subject's perceptions. The technique is designed to include enough blots with the same "stimulus pull" to identify common modes of response.

Psychology literature indicates that considerable research is being carried on with the HIT, but the results of clinical usage are limited. Although the major modifications introduced by the HIT represent fundamental improvements over the Rorschach, the qualitative richness of the projective responses remains unchanged. Thus, clinical experience and research with the Rorschach, as well as research with the HIT, are applicable in interpreting HIT responses. Interpretations based on Rorschach experience are derived from working hypotheses shown to be most useful by Rorschach authorities and found clinically applicable to the HIT. A synthesis of Rorschach and HIT research and clinical experience is presented in this text. Much material is based on clinical application, and inferences concerning individual cases should be regarded as working hypotheses to be discarded or accepted after examining all the information available.

Because of the newness of the HIT and the need for extensive normative data, clinical interpretations are cautiously applied. The cut-off points used in assessing deviant behavior cover the extremes for each variable. In the upper ranges, scores that fall at or above the ninetieth percentile (for some variables) are considered only as tendencies toward deviations. In most cases, however, those that are above the ninety-ninth percentile are defined as deviant. In the lower range of the normative scale, scores which fall at or below the tenth percentile are considered sufficiently distant from the mean to require some explanation, while those that fall below the fifth percentile are considered deviant. Later research may demonstrate that these limits are too narrow. However, to err in the direction of caution is preferable to mistakenly classifying an individual as deviant. Therefore, scoring which approaches the extremes should be interpreted with prudence. In evaluating the individual's behavior in interacting with the blots, the examiner should be aware of biological factors which affect the subject and of his cultural background (Zubin, Eron, and Schumer, 1965). This information may clarify the interpretation of such factors as verbal fluency and peculiar verbal expressions. Caution, for example, should be exercised in applying HIT norms to Negro subjects. Current norms are based solely on white samples. Megargee (1969), who compared the scores of white and Negro male juvenile delinquents using three projective tests, found that HIT norms for white subjects are applicable to Negroes of equivalent IQ in custodial settings. He suggests, however, that his results cannot be assumed to be valid for other populations, and equivalence should not be assumed in clinical practice until further comparisons can be made. Differences were found between his groups on three of the variables. White subjects scored higher on pathognomic verbalization and popular, Negroes scored higher on anatomy. Minor differences were discovered in three other variables with whites scoring higher in reaction time, form appropriateness, and color. Megargee speculated that the inkblot technique is more sensitive to interracial differences than are the apperceptive tests.

Response Set

IV

Some subjects perceive the inkblot test as a challenge and pursue it as a cognitive exercise. Some participate in response to a need for reaching a therapeutic goal. These persons are generally cooperative and place no conscious restrictions on their associations to the inkblots. Others impose limitations on their responses and impair their freedom of association. These individuals may have a response set that the inkblots are supposed to look like something or that the examiner prefers a particular type of response over another. They may lack the motivation to cooperate or may wish to resist the examiner. Such an attitude is reflected in a deliberate set to make themselves appear in an especially favorable or unfavorable light. Both reaction time and rejections reflect the subject's ability to respond.

Reaction Time (RT)

Reaction time is the elapsed period (in seconds) from the presentation of the stimulus to the verbal response. Presumably, perceptual processes begin immediately after the stimulus is perceived but remain internalized until the response is made. Reaction time is an index of the complexity of the inner process for a specific response. The more complicated the process, the longer the response takes (Woodworth and Schlosberg, 1958). Generally speaking, neither the stimulus nor the instructions exert too much control or restrict the subject. The direction and content of the response are determined primarily by the subject's own experiences, present feelings, and attitudes. This variable (reaction time) is associated with the level of intellectual functioning, impulse control, and emotional disturbance as evidenced by blocking. RT reveals the subject's ability to consciously direct his thinking, concentrate on a task, and demonstrate the availability of inner resources.

REACTION TIME BELOW THE FIFTH PERCENTILE. Based on normative samples, the shortest RT for all populations is for five-year olds. This short reaction time is normal for young children and reflects their spontaneity, impulsiveness, and limited capacity for concentration (Holtzman, Thorpe, Swartz, and Herron, 1961). The next shortest RT is for emotionally disturbed children and then for emotionally disturbed adolescents. These norms reflect the impulsiveness of these groups.

Various reasons are given as to why persons react quickly to blots. Some persons have difficulty in dealing with ambiguous stimuli. They make little attempt to provide their own structure, and they withdraw as quickly as possible because they cannot otherwise cope with the demands of the situation. These persons do not take time to interact with the blot and frequently give superficial percepts. They respond with the first thought that comes to mind, which is often unrelated to the stimulus. This uncritical free association reflects an inner need to get away from the task and precludes their effective handling of reality.

Some persons who have short reaction times feel threatened by the interaction with the examiner and the test demands. An uncooperative individual who is hostile to the test situation responds rapidly to the blots. His responses are brief and of mediocre content. Some intelligent individuals have an overriding need to give good responses quickly in order to prove their flexibility and to demonstrate normality. These persons drive themselves. Short reaction time is usually accompanied by low scores in form appropriateness, and possibly location and form definiteness. High scores are expected in barrier and anxiety.

REACTION TIME ABOVE THE NINETY-NINTH PERCENTILE. The highest mean RT is found in alcoholics, followed by chronic paranoid schizophrenics, depressives, and retardates. RT for other groups is fairly normally distributed. These findings are consistent with results of Rorschach studies. Many factors interfere with the process of association and lengthen RT. Long RT may be a function of emotional or intellectual difficulties. In subjects with intellectual difficulties, long RT indicates psychomotor retardation or slow thinking—individuals who are overly careful and precise and need to organize and perfect concepts before verbalizing them. Such individuals may also experience difficulty shifting from one association to another. Most frequently, however, long RT signals emotional problems. Two or more responses may be competing, one getting in the way of the other; or the first association may remind the individual of something which distracts him from the task and causes him to wander into other associations. The subject may experience a short period of blankness during which he makes no progress toward a response. When such blankness occurs, the response process is being interfered with, probably at an unconscious level (Woodworth and Schlosberg, 1958). For some subjects, longer RT results from efforts to inhibit the affect aroused by the stimulus so that an appropriate cognitive response can be made.

Response delays also occur when the subject cannot state aloud the first concept or association. This inhibition may result from a disturbance within the subject or from his impression that the response is socially inappropriate. The possibility that the subject's perceptual processes are disturbed should never be overlooked.

Piotrowski (1957) states that intellectual deterioration as a result of intracranial pathology is often found in subjects with a very long RT (probably at or above the ninety-ninth percentile on the HIT). Long RT is also found in repressive individuals who avoid interacting with the stimulus for fear of revealing their inner fantasies. Relaxation of repressive barriers in the interest of imaginative creativity and self-expression presents the danger of breaking down defenses. Therefore, they delay responding and repress free association (Shafer, 1954). Evidence also indicates that RT tends to increase with suspiciousness. Shafer found that paranoid individuals who are not sure of the significance of the stimuli or of their own responses and who fear being "found out" are mistrusting and slow in reacting to inkblots. These persons see the examiner as hostile, and they are not sure what he has in mind. Those with severe paranoid problems are likely to freeze, clam up, or go into hiding. They are often overcautious and reject their own responses as inadequate.

VARIANT REACTION TIME. Occasionally, RT varies considerably from card to card. Zubin, Eron, and Schumer (1965) believe that such variations in RT reflect attempts on the part of the respondent to repress responses. The variation may also reflect confusion resulting from several responses occurring simultaneously. Hill (1966) found that the reaction time to the high and low stimulus-strength color cards varies between normal and schizophrenic populations. Normal subjects have a longer RT to high stimulus-strength color cards than to low stimulus-strength color cards, but schizophrenic subjects do not show this difference. Apparently the process which intervenes between the presentation of the stimulus and verbalization of the response is fairly consistent for schizophrenics. In normal subjects, the high stimulus-strength color appears to arouse more affect, and the longer RT reflects the inhibition of this affect before making an "acceptable" response.

RELATIONSHIP TO OTHER VARIABLES. Reaction time loads on Factor 5 together with two other variables: rejection and animal (reversed). Long RT usually coincides with high rejections. Caution or interference which causes delays in response time may prevent the subject from responding altogether. Animal responses are given less frequently when RT is long and R is high.

Rejection (R)

Inability to respond may be attributed to a variety of causes, just as the entire test performance is influenced by many factors. Rejection may reflect the subject's style and characteristic manner of responding in general. It may reflect the person's set, namely, the attitudes and expectations he has brought with him to the test. Rejection may be a product of the interaction between the subject and the examiner. According to the test instructions, the choice of responding or not responding is open to the subject. If he decides to respond, he can accept the task at face value and verbalize a percept, or he may have difficulty in making appropriate associations as evidenced by long delays. He may accept the task and nevertheless respond in an evasive manner which amounts to near rejection. (These near rejections include responses such as map, rock formation, clouds, or descriptions of color or shading nuances.) He may also reject the card entirely.

Holtzman, Thorpe, Swartz and Herron (1961) found the distribution of rejections sharply skewed and truncated for all the standardization groups. Most college students failed to reject a single card, while the reverse proved true for nearly all the other groups. Significantly higher mean scores are obtained by chronic schizophrenics, mental retardates, depressed patients, and emotionally disturbed children than for normal groups. Earlier Rorschach studies indicate this difference also.

Rejection of inkblot cards indicates great disturbance in psychological functioning (Bohm, 1958). The rejection may represent a conscious refusal to associate or an unconscious temporary blocking of the associative process. Rejections may also reflect a lack of intellectual capacity. Whether willful or unwillful, rejection is a defensive tactic and Beck (1952) states that some process prevents the subject from making an association.

Rejections usually indicate that affect has been aroused. Affect arousal can block use of available ideational resources and oblige the individual to consciously inhibit the affect from "breaking through" before he is able to deal with the inkblot. If the subject is unable to consciously inhibit the affect from blocking the intellect, he will reject the card. If the subject is successful in inhibiting the affect he can at least give an evasive (near rejection) response. The evasive response indicates that, given enough time, the subject can control the arousal of affect and use intellectual faculties to cope with situations in which he finds himself. Thus, the near rejection is a more adaptive response than is the complete rejection.

Some persons consciously refuse to make an association or, if they do, they refuse to report the association because of hostility. Rejections based on hostility are found most frequently in paranoids who reject more than half of the cards. The responses they do make are usually to blots with high form level which can be responded to as a perceptual task by identifying a popular area rather than a response revealing inner associations. Such behavior is equivalent to refusing to take the test.

An outright rejection, however, is not necessarily a willful refusal to take the test; it may be an unwillful temporary blocking. The rejection may reflect the intellect unconsciously protecting the ego by blocking the affect. Beck (1952) points out that rejection in this instance maintains a distance between the subect and the painful feelings aroused by the blot. Rejection by blocking may be the subject's characteristic mode of behavior. Habitually, the intellect may unconsciously inhibit and control affect through avoidance of confrontations which are likely to create affective discomfort. Whatever the reason for rejection, it indicates a paucity of constructive inner resources. The individual has not learned to adapt to and cope with ambiguous stimuli.

DEVELOPMENTAL TRENDS. Rejections are frequent in children up to the age of six or seven and may be caused by boredom, inattention, or fatigue. Occasionally, children reject cards due to blocking. Such blocking suggests inner disturbances, which can be verified by evaluating the child's behavior and the quality of the responses he gives to the rest of the test. A cooperative child rejects only difficult or disturbing cards, whereas an indifferent child discards easier blots.

At age six and seven, the child's concern with correctness or incorrectness of his responses may account for rejections. However, a large number of rejections given by persons older than six or seven are likely to reflect emotional disturbances, revealing inner conflicts. At age ten, any emotionally charged situation is perceived as threatening, and rejections increase because of the child's uncertainty about himself and his role in relation to others.

DIAGNOSTIC IMPLICATIONS. With the exception of very young children (preschool age), who may reject as many as twenty blots, the only other normative populations in which many rejections occur are the mentally retarded and chronic schizophrenics. A rejection of half of the cards is exceedingly rare. When such rejections occur, the balance of the record is usually sparse, and the responses are either near rejections or elucidations of populars. Persons giving this many rejections are relatively inaccessible for therapeutic intervention. They have difficulty accepting interpersonal relationships on a one-to-one basis and are incapable of insightful self-evaluation. These persons usually lack a free fantasy life and are unable to discharge their feelings through imagination. They frequently evidence impulsively explosive behavior because they have no other way of coping with affect.

RESEARCH. Thorpe and Swartz (1963) found the role of intelligence and social status negatively related to rejections on the HIT. For the population studied (ninety-eight male and ninety-nine female seventh-graders), rejections are not based solely on intellectual level. They are the result of a complex combination of factors, among which are social status and the subject's perception of the test situation.

Megargee and Swartz (1968) studied the relationship between HIT scores and the extraversion and neuroticism scales of the Maudsley Personality Inventory (MPI). The study showed a negative correlation between R on the HIT and the neuroticism scale on the MPI. This relationship is expected because neurotic persons tend to conform to instructions and are therefore not likely to reject cards.

Codkind (1964) studied the relationship of personality maturity and attitudes toward the imaginary based on HIT responses. Persons who demonstrate a high degree of acceptance of the imaginary are able to control and use fantasy at will. They are able to realistically differentiate the fantasy from reality. Persons who reject the use of the imaginary organize responses around the object world, avoiding associations which are not objective or perceptually mediated. The former group has significantly fewer rejections.

Perceptual Differentiation

V

A process of perceptual organization occurs when the subject is faced with the task of responding to a stimulus. He becomes aware of the inkblot and of the test instructions through his senses. Once he has the information concerning the external demands, he interprets the task and responds on the basis of its meaning to him. His response is subjectively derived from his attitudes, motives, values, and affect. If he is functioning without undue internal pressures, he should be capable of recognizing and responding to relevant objects in the inkblot stimulus by using perceptual cues and past experience. If, however, he is beset with internal stress and anxiety, he will be more apt to rely on perceptual defenses to modify the external stimulus so that he can deal with it. Inner determinants dominate his definition of the test task and are reflected in the subsequent response. The way in which the individual deals with the task of responding to the inkblot is revealed largely by his scores on location, form appropriateness, and space.

Location (L)

Location scores provide data concerning the individual's organizing ability and intellectual functioning. Responses to the whole blot reflect conceptual and organizational ability and show how he goes about making judgments. Responses to the whole blot do not, however, indicate why the individual organizes in the way he does. Schachtel (1966), referring to location in the Rorschach, points out that the choice of structuring the blot is left entirely to the individual. The quality of the structuring may vary from vagueness to clarity, reflecting explora-

45

tory curiosity. The inkblot task, however, requires more active structuring than do tasks in everyday life because daily demands have limitations.

Responses to the whole blot are of two varieties. First, the subject may give a diffuse, amorphous response and not attempt to organize blot elements or deal with the reality of the stimulus field. These diffuse responses are typical of young children, mental defectives, and psychotics. The responses of these groups are based on the dominance of their emotional reactivity. Fantasy and imagination control their behavior. The content of whole-blot responses given by some schizophrenics reflects poor planning and a lack of persistence in their drive to realize their plans, which are often confused. Second, the subject may make adequate use of the entire blot. Such responses are a reflection of his ability to synthesize. Other scores support an interpretation of realistic organizational ability. For example, the integration score reveals the ability to appropriately relate two or more areas of the blot. To score integration, form appropriateness must be scored at least 1, and the content of the response cannot be pathognomic because a V score greater than 1 precludes an I score. Persons who use the entire blot (responding in a cognitive manner) usually score high in form appropriateness, form definiteness and integration and low in pathognomic verbalization. Individuals with this combination of scores have an integrated approach to life situations and are capable of systematic thinking. These scores are also correlated with adequate intelligence since a good response demonstrates the ability to use cognitive processes. Beck and Molish (1967), referring to the Rorschach, state that individuals scoring high in well-integrated whole responses (LO on the HIT) can be expected to have strong egos which are not severely modified by defensive strategies.

Bohm (1958) considers the whole response in the Rorschach which is accompanied by well-integrated blot elements and good form level an expression of affective drive for achievement. He theorizes that such individuals are capable of attacking a situation without having all the facts before coming to a conclusion. Use of the whole blot also reflects an aptitude for diligence and an ability to put ideas into action. The greater the use of integrated whole responses, the more intensive the awareness of the future as a result of personally planned activities. Ronald Kuhn (in Rickers-Ovsiankina, 1960) states that integrated whole responses in the Rorschach reflect a richness of association and an availability of memory engrams and activity strivings.

LOCATION BELOW THE FIFTH PERCENTILE. Extensive use of the whole inkblot is reflected in low L scores. Such scores are typical of the very young child who is immature and self-preoccupied. Other groups scoring low in L usually have low form definiteness scores and high pathognomic verbalization scores and include schizophrenics, retardates, emotionally disturbed adolescents, emotionally disturbed children, and depressives. In order to assess properly the low L score, the examiner must view it in relation to other variables. When the L score is low and the FD and FA scores are below average, the examiner can assume that the individual makes little effort to organize his experience beyond a global perception of the situation. This lack of effort results from either low intelligence or interference with the constructive use of the intellectual capacity (as found in emotional maladjustment). In the latter case, little interest is manifested in seeking relationships between different facets of experience and in achieving an organized view of the world (Klopfer, Ainsworth, Klopfer and Holt, 1954). If the V score is above average, the individual has poor reality contact and lacks the ability to use his intellect for critical evaluation of the task. A low L score may be caused by a high rejection score. This relationship should be examined before making an interpretation.

LOCATION ABOVE THE NINETY-NINTH PERCENTILE. Scores in this range indicate abnormally high use of small detail areas of the blot. Psychologists agree that it is easier to provide a good response to the blot with good form level when a smaller portion of the blot is used. Small details require little, if any, integration or synthesis. Fourth graders have the highest L scores. At that age the child becomes more reality bound and is capable of responding with high form level. For the percept to be more appropriate to the stimulus small areas are used since the child is not yet able to integrate small blot areas into a whole.

Generally, a high score in location and a high score in form definiteness go together with an average or above average form appropriate score. The combination of detail responses with good form present on the Rorschach reflects the subject's interest and ability to differentiate perceptually with relatively little interest in integrating, organizing, or seeking relationships among the different facets of experience (Klopfer, Ainsworth, Klopfer, and Holt, 1954).

Psychologists agree that excessive use of small detail seems to be a mechanism to control anxiety. Such concentration on small detail identifies an individual as having a differentiated interest in factual things (Beck, 1952; Klopfer, Ainsworth, Klopfer, and Holt, 1954; Piotrowski, 1957; Bohm, 1958; Schachtel, 1966; Beck and Molish, 1967). He clings to trivia, irrelevant detail, and flaws for the sake of the details and not as part of an observation for an overall effect. These individuals control their anxiety by keeping busy with small but exacting tasks. They are likely to talk about nonessentials and tend to steer away from that which they would rather not recognize, thereby restricting their perception to a portion of the visual field. Less tension is experienced when time is filled with work, even if the work makes no sense. If the subject responds to many small-detail areas on the edges of the blot, he may also have a need to stay on the fringe of things without becoming too deeply involved (Klopfer, Ainsworth, Klopfer, and Holt, 1954). Although excessive use of detailed areas may reflect lack of initiative, it does not necessarily reflect lack of intelligence. Persons of superior intelligence often reveal fear and anxiety in their need to stick to obvious, small details.

Extensive use of small detail on the Rorschach identifies the pedant who places great emphasis on accuracy and exactness (Klopfer, Ainsworth, Klopfer, and Holt, 1954). Beck (1952) states that excessive use of small-detail responses on the Rorschach may reflect compulsiveness.

Piotrowski (1957) found that irreversibly deteriorated patients with intracranial pathology make considerable use of detail responses because of the relative simplicity of responding to the smaller parts of the blot. He found that obsessive neurotics also use small details excessively, frequently those located along the edges and those including heads and faces.

There is relationship between L scores and other HIT variables. Low location scores are usually accompanied by high scores in color and shading because the whole blot is most often used when color and shading determine the response. A high L score is usually associated with a high score in form definiteness because of the variety of well-defined concepts possible when only small areas are used. The combination of a high integration score and a low L score indicates an ability to combine and organize well-defined percepts in two or more parts of the blot. Such integration also reflects the ability to grasp relationships among separate facets of experience in solving problems. The combination of a low score in location, average scores in form definiteness, form appropriateness, and integration, and an above average score in human movement reflects imagination in the normal person. Small-detail responses seldom accompany human-movement responses (Schachtel, 1966). L and FA constitute Factor 4 and are bipolar scores. Both scores, when in the average range (twentieth to eightieth percentile), identify the individual with perceptual-differentiation ability. Whole-blot responses in a normal population indicate reality contact and inner resources. The use of small blot areas by deteriorated schizophrenics or retardates shows limited resources and the ability to differentiate parts as opposed to their usual vague, amorphous whole responses. This correlation reenforces the general belief that the location area and level of FA in a percept are related to organizational ability and intellectual functioning of the person.

DEVELOPMENTAL TRENDS. Location scores are considerably influenced by the age of the subject. Age trend studies for L reveal that scores increase steadily until late adolescence and then drop, (Thorpe, 1960; Holtzman, Thorpe, Swartz, and Herron, 1961; Thorpe and Swartz, 1965). The L score, however, must be considered (at all age levels) in a pattern with FD, FA, and I. In the young child, responses to the entire blot predominate, resulting in a low L score. He pays little attention to FA and FD. These scores are also low. By age ten the child has become reality bound and responds in a manner more appropriate to the stimulus. At the same time he is capable of a response with high form level. To achieve goodness of fit to the blot, the child foregoes the response to the whole blot and uses smaller areas. As the child gets older he can maintain good form level and appropriateness of the responses to the inkblot and at the same time increase the area of the blot used. Thus he integrates smaller parts of the blot into the entire response. For college-age subjects, the L scores drop. The individual is capable of increased perceptual organization; he can synthesize the various parts of the blot and integrate them into a whole response. The college student is concerned with reality and obtains high FA scores. His human, movement, color, shading, and balance responses also increase. The peak developmental trend is reached in college-age students.

Holtzman, Thorpe, Swartz, and Herron (1961) found a low but significant correlation between the ability for perceptual differentiation, as defined by Factor 4 (which includes L and FA), and Factor 1 (which defines well-organized ideational activity).

RESEARCH. In studying the relationship between whole responses and problem-solving ability, Blatt and Allison (1963) found a highly significant positive correlation between well-articulated whole responses to the Rorschach which included good form level and the integration of two or more parts of the blot.

Codkind (1964) found significant differences between persons who demonstrate a high degree of fantasy acceptance (the ability to use fantasy material at a cognitive level) and persons who do not engage in the use of the imaginary but organize responses around associations reflecting objective reporting of the stimulus. The former group score lower in L and higher in integration.

Schmidt and Fonda (1953), studying the Location score of the Rorschach, found that feeble-minded persons give few whole responses and also score low in integration. Schmidt and Fonda attributed these low scores to the mental torpidity of the group. They report similar scores for brain-damaged populations. The scores reflect the loss of abstracting powers and an inability to make associations.

Barnes (1963) used the HIT along with six other tests for assessing brain damage in order to determine whether the inclusion of the HIT increased the discrimination of the battery. His results indicated that six HIT variables (location, form appropriateness, color, hostility, penetration, and anatomy) increased the discrimination between groups of brain-damaged and non-brain–damaged subjects. The brain-damaged group obtained significantly lower scores in L and FA and higher C scores than did the non-brain–damaged group. Differences in Hs, Pn, and At were not equally significant and should be cautiously applied.

Clark, Veldman, and Thorpe (1965) studied the convergent and divergent thinking abilities of talented youngsters, using the HIT as one of the test measures. (Divergent thinking is defined as "the most readily delineated aspects of creative activity." Convergent thinking is defined as "the ability to select a single correct response from a series of alternatives or to deduce it from multiple stimuli.") The HIT responses showed freer imaginative content for divergent-thinking subjects than for the convergent thinkers. The high divergent population made greater use of whole responses and thus scored lower on L than did the low divergent group. High divergent subjects also scored significantly higher on movement, anxiety, hostility, color, and penetration than did low divergent subjects (Holtzman, Thorpe, Swartz, and Herron, 1961).

Correlations have also been demonstrated between HIT scores and standard measures of intelligence, scholastic achievement, and convergent thinking for the seventh-grade sample of the HIT standardization population. Compared with scores of ten mental ability tests, significant HIT variables were rejection (reversed), location, form appropriateness, shading, anxiety, hostility, and barrier (Holtzman, Thorpe, Swartz, and Herron, 1961).

Form Appropriateness (FA)

The ability of the subject to verbalize a percept which is appropriate to the blot reflects several dimensions of personality functioning. Primarily, good FA demonstrates a conscious effort of attention to the distinctive features of the stimulus as separate from the needs of the viewer. This effort of attention depends on acquired habits of perception and reflects the degree of contact with reality. Reality contact is directly related to practical intellectual functioning. Impractical functioning is characteristic of persons who live in a fantasy world and are only partially aware of external demands. The ability to produce a response appropriate to the form of the blot also indicates ego control. Perceptual autonomy permits the individual to control and use his cognitive processes without interference from the unconscious or emotional impulsivity. Also, responding appropriately to a blot indicates an ability to discriminate and demonstrates the availability of memory images from which the subject can select fitting percepts.

FORM APPROPRIATENESS BELOW THE FIFTH PERCENTILE. If we recall that Holtzman, Thorpe, Swartz, and Herron (1961) allow even abstract and vague responses to be scored 1, a score as low as the fifth percentile is highly significant. Low FA scores are typical of five-year olds, emotionally disturbed children, neurotics, and alcoholics. In addition, low FA scores are found in populations of feeble-minded persons, some organics, and schizophrenics. Research results also indicate that low FA scores are found in persons with low intelligence because they do not observe environmental events clearly. Beck (1952) states that a large number of F minus scores on the Rorschach (low FA) reflect inadequate ego strength in individuals who distort reality and determine their responses on the basis of personal needs and drives. Beck also found F minus scores on the Rorschach for feeble-minded, brain-damaged, and schizophrenic persons, caused by a lapse in attention, which, he explained, may result from an unbridled temper. The lower the form level (FA) the more disturbed the individual. Low FA scores suggest lack of ability to concentrate. Insufficient attention is directed to the immediate physical and social environment, and the subject is unable to remain detached, indifferent, or objective. The capacity for recall may also be impaired even if the person has sharp memory traces. The disturbance may be for recent or past memories. Such impairment is found in organic as well as functional disorders (Bohm, 1958). When the pathognomic verbalization score is also very high, a distortion of reality accompanied by thinking disorders and confusion is implied.

FORM APPROPRIATENESS ABOVE THE EIGHTY-FIFTH PERCENTILE. Too much emphasis on fitting likenesses to the form of the blot reflects an excessively narrow attitude toward the test. According to Schachtel (1966), some individuals try so hard to find something closely similar to the stimulus that they are unable to satisfy their aspirations. They are likely to be critical of their achievements because they take the world at face value, accepting what is presented as immutable truth. They lack the intellectual flexibility necessary for questioning or critical evaluation.

DEVELOPMENTAL TRENDS. FA, L, FD, and I permit a refined interpretation of genetic level, using the analysis of pattern scores in the work of Thorpe and Swartz (1965). The young child tends toward low scores in L, FA, and FD. By age ten, the scores for all three variables increase as he becomes capable of attending to reality. With further increase in age, the FA and FD scores are maintained and the L score drops. At this point the I score increases, indicating ability to integrate and differentiate parts of the blot to form a total response.

Holtzman, Thorpe, Swartz, and Herron (1961), in their standardization population, identify low FA scores in five-year olds, which is consistent with the Rorschach literature. Beck (1952) found that form level is low up to about age six, after which expectations are for average scores. Ames, Learned, Metraux, and Walker (1952) place the developmental age for attaining average limits of form level (the equivalent of FA scores) at about age ten. Thorpe and Swartz (1965) found that FA rose fairly rapidly in the preadolescent years and leveled off afterward. They identify the college years as a peak period for perceptual organization and differentiated concern with reality, which would be characterized by a high FA score.

OTHER RESEARCH. Codkind (1964) found that individuals with a high degree of fantasy acceptance who also have complex cognitive organizing ability and openness to experience have significantly higher FA scores than do those who do not accept fantasy. Moseley, Duffey, and Sherman (1963) found a relationship among a guilt scale, low FA scores, and high anatomy and pathognomic verbalization scores for depressed patients. The researchers were also able to discriminate schizophrenics from depressives by using a formula that included higher FA scores for the depressive group than for the schizophrenics. Holtzman, Thorpe, Swartz, and Herron (1961) found that schizophrenics have significantly lower FA scores than do normals. Conners (1965) found differences in HIT scores between neurotic children and children with conduct disorders. The neurotics have higher scores in FA and L (both variables of Factor 4). He also found that disturbed children have lower scores on FA than do normals. In a study of brain-damaged subjects, Barnes (1963) found that FA scores (along with L and C) increase the ability to predict brain damage. Holtzman, Thorpe, Swartz, and Herron

(1961) found that FA correlates high with intelligence as measured in ten mental-ability tests.

Space (S)

The S response, as discussed earlier, is scored for a complete figure and ground reversal. A secondary S response, although not scored, is noted on the summary sheet and refers to the use of areas of space within the blot (as part of the response) without a true reversal of figure and ground.

Psychologists disagree on the interpretation of the space response. Some believe it indicates a negative attitude toward life and some see it as a positive sign. The traditional interpretation based on the work of Rorschach (1942), regards the space response as a reflection of oppositional tendencies, aggression, and tension between the individual and his environment (Rapaport, 1946; Beck, 1952; Bohm, 1958). These authors also type the individual's attitude (passive or aggressive) on the basis of the color and human-movement scores. Space responses in the aggressive personality (identified by high color scores and low human-movement scores) reveal difficulty in controlling impulses which are discharged in immature and undisciplined patterns. Such individuals defend themselves from inner fears by attacking the environment. Beck (1952) reports evidence of space responses in records of paranoids who are tenacious in sticking to their delusional ideas.

Space responses given by passive introverted individuals (identified by high scores on human movement and low scores on color) indicate shyness and depression, feelings of inferiority and self-distrust, and overall insecurity. These individuals are self-critical. When the number of human-movement responses and color responses are relatively equal, space responses are interpreted as indicating indecisiveness, pessimism, and self-distrust coupled with the perplexity that goes with compulsive thinking. Beck (1952) identifies this pattern with obsessive compulsiveness—the patient fighting both the world and his own unconscious needs. Clinical or laboratory research data verifying interpretations based on the passive or aggressive personality do not exist. Therefore this information should be considered speculative.

Those who disagree with the traditional interpretation believe that space responses are a positive trait, based on an adaptive need for self-protection (Bandura, 1954; Klopfer, Ainsworth, Klopfer, and Holt, 1954; Levy, 1955; Piotrowski, 1957; Fonda, 1960). The antitraditionalists believe that the individual is acting in response to a need for autonomy and in making the reversal is exerting inner forces to reduce the tensions associated with this need. The number of space responses indicates the extent to which the individual needs to demonstrate his autonomy. Fonda (1960), recognizing that conflicts over self-determination are at the core of personality disorders, finds it easy to understand why Rorschach defined the space response in terms of neuroses. Fonda cites laboratory investigations of the primary S response in which clear-cut findings show that the higher the individual's rate of S responses, the more likely is he to be bright, productive, flexible, ingenious, and self-sufficient. Present evidence does not confirm the hypothesis associating S responses with persistence, intellectual oppositional tendencies, antagonism, and hostile resistive tactics. Fonda did find that persons who give many space responses are more hesitant and indecisive than other persons but that they are no more likely to concede that they have feelings of inadequacy than are those who do not give space responses. Space responses are found in both passive and aggressive individuals. Fonda also found no evidence to support a positive correlation between S responses and color-dominant responses (or between lack of control and color-dominant responses). In fact, S responses appear inversely related to the impulsive color-dominated responses. Therefore, those who oppose traditional space interpretation believe that the space response indicates an effort on the part of the ego to control and assert autonomy or mastery over external situations. They believe the S response is not as negative as it was originally thought to be and it may indicate ego strength and resources to resist environmental pressures. The S response may prove to be a function of the strength of the need for autonomy or of the need to gratify autonomy. Or it may prove to reflect the degree to which satisfactions of this need involve resistance on the part of the individual.

Bandura (1954) found twice as many space responses given in the last two minutes of exposure to the inkblot (Rorschach technique) than in the first two minutes and concluded that prolonged observation and not impulsivity may be the facilitator of the space response. This phenomenon may explain the occurrence of space responses in the Rorschach in which many percepts to the same card are encouraged. In the HIT, however (where only one response per card is elicited) length of exposure to the card and the production of S responses do not appear to be related, even though some cards have been specifically chosen for their pulling power for space (which is not true for the Rorschach). Whether the S responses are interpreted as a need for autonomy or as a need for aggression, they reflect behavior contrary to instructions and provide information regarding the character of the individual.

Even though some cards are expected to have pulling power for space (for instance, card 22A), the space response is rare. Fifty per cent of all subjects fail to give even one true figure-ground reversal for all forty-five blots. The distribution of this variable for all normative sample groups is severely truncated. Among the normal populations, school children give slightly more S responses than do adults or five year olds. Alcoholics, emotionally disturbed adolescents, and children give slightly more S responses than do normal adults. For most samples, more than two space responses put the individual at or above the ninety-fifth percentile (for this variable) except for the elementary-school group, for whom three space responses is at the nintieth percentile. Therefore, one or two space responses are within the range of the normal personality.

THREE OR MORE SPACE RESPONSES. Excessive use of S responses is interpreted as overconcern with problems of autonomy. A high number of S responses on the

Rorschach are given by negativistic adolescents and negative students who are also suggestible (Fonda, 1960). HIT norms for emotionally disturbed adolescents show a large number of S responses. Both Beck (1952) and Fonda (1960) regard excessive use of the S response in the Rorschach to be prevalent in persons who have a paranoid character and rely heavily on projection. Beck labels such a person unbending, rigid, and tenacious in clinging to a paranoid delusional system. Fonda states that an individual with a high number of S responses who becomes psychotic is likely to cling to paranoid delusions. He also suggests that a high rate of S responses in the passive person reflects paranoid personality adjustment. Such a person is constantly on guard to protect his separateness and the integrity of his delusional system. High S responses in the aggressive individual may indicate acting out behavior. If the aggression is acted out, it is likely to be self-willed and destructively delinquent. If not, it may be evident in the form of a reaction formation, isolation, or projection. In reaction formation the aggressive behavior (which the individual does not wish to acknowledge) is countered with sweetly reasonable, compliant, and scrupulously trustworthy behavior. If the defense is isolation, the overt behavior may vacillate between obstinancy and compulsiveness. If the defense is projection, suspicion, truculence, grandiosity, and delusions occur.

Excessive S responses given by children may indicate feelings of insecurity about the environment. Bohm (1958) believes that in difficult children the S responses may be the differential diagnostic indicator of traumas brought about by the environment. S used by a child as young as three or four may reflect an unconventional exploration of the environment (Halpern, 1953).

SECONDARY SPACE RESPONSES. Secondary space responses do not require a complete reversal of figure and ground but are scored when the subject uses the white spaces in the blot as holes, gaps, or cut-outs. These areas may also be alluded to as lakes, rivers, or roads. Sometimes they are identified as eyes. Secondary space responses occur more frequently than the complete figure-ground reversal. Up to five secondary S responses are considered normal. Interpretation is based on clinical usage with the Rorschach and, for the most part, not on empirical evidence. Thus, the following hypotheses are speculative. Bandura (1954) believes that the use of many secondary S responses indicates excessive sensitivity because of the subject's awareness of the lack of solidity in the blot. Bandura also believes that this response reflects lack of stability in interpersonal relationships. Secondary S responses do not reflect favorable personality characteristics. The necessity to account for everything on the blot and to delineate each space in describing a scene implies a need for thoroughness or obsessive attention to detail. Frequent use of the secondary S as eyes suggests projection in the form of ideas of reference or possible paranoid trends, particularly if some of the responses are "eyes staring at me." Schachtel (1966) states that space (either primary or secondary) perceived as an entrance to a cave indicates a need for shelter or a fear of enclosure. Halpern (1953) believes that the use of secondary space by a child indicates undue awareness of open spaces, which in turn evokes tension concerning his own adequacy. The greater the use of the secondary S response for the child, the greater the degree of tension and preoccupation with inescurity. If this response is given only to the first few blots and not to subsequent ones, the tension and inadequacy may be part of the test situation itself.

In summary, the variables in this chapter reveal how the subject organizes situations on the basis of his perceptions and how he relates these situations to past experiences—in short his reasoning ability. These variables also reveal the degree of his perceptual autonomy, reality contact, and ego control.

Determinants

VI

In this chapter I discuss three stimulus attributes of the blot: (color, shading, and balance). All the blots are colored. The colors include achromatic black, gray, and white, and chromas of many hues—the total range of color stimulation. The color can have varying degrees of saturation. On some of the blots, the saturation is low (pastel); in others the color is highly saturated. The interpretation of color applies to subjects who are not color blind. Another characteristic of the blot is shading. The gradations of color may cause the shading to appear textured and grainy, or dotted, hazy, and filmlike. For the most part, the left and right sides of the designs are symmetrical, but in some instances they are asymmetrical. The role of balance is briefly discussed at the conclusion of the chapter.

Color (C)

The interpretation of color responses has caused disagreement over the influence of the affective value of color on the cognitive processes. Some theorists believe that the color response is a reflection of affect and emotionality. Others hypothesize that these responses reflect cognitive processes. Schachtel (1943) aligns himself with the theorists who favor the emotionality concept and he describes passivity to the perceiver when experiencing color. He states that color impresses itself on the observer and motivates his behavior as reflected in the content of the response or in the affect aroused by the response. Shapiro (1960) agrees with this interpretation. He cites the affective responses and affect arousals of chronic schizophrenics and organics as examples of passivity in the face of color stimulus. He explains this affect as an impairment of organization ability—

a helplessness in coping with the world. Goldstein (1942) asserts that "color swings the individual toward the outside world or away from it to concentrate on himself." Drechsler's (1960) intrusion hypothesis theorizes that colors are affect-stimulating agents. They intrude on the perceiving individual so that the on-going thought processes are interrupted until the intrusive stimulant can be removed or assimilated. Drechsler states that the intrusion is similar to the intrusion of threatening environmental or internal stimuli. It arouses and breaks through the defenses used against threat.

Those who take a cognitive view of color include the Committee on Colorimetry (1953), who state that colors are perceived as surface or volume and are commonly associated with meaningful objects or composition. The committee states that most people pay so little attention to colors which are unattached to familiar objects that they find it hard to believe that a typical affective response to color can be anything but weak and indifferent. Norman and Scott (1952) state that color is nearly always associated with some object. They believe that a response to color is a cognitive process requiring a higher level of functioning than does one based solely on reaction of affect.

Baughman (1965), in his reviews of color studies using the Rorschach technique, concludes that the blots elicit little in the way of behavior that could be taken as a basis for inferring color affects. He does caution, however, that his studies do not automatically preclude this possibility. Sufficient evidence exists that color does affect subjects, most notably in the preference for or liking of particular blots that have a color stimulus. Baughman also states that color does affect to some extent the content elicited by the blot.

Some theorists incorporate the interaction between perceiver and stimulus in their theories. Woods (1954), in discussing responses to Rorschach inkblots, states that the more conforming the individual, the more his responses to color are determined by social and acquired values. Adults who resist social pressures are influenced by the universal (unlearned) color values. Piotrowski (1957) questions the power of learned and environmentally conditioned color values to modify and overshadow unlearned and universal color values. Werner (1949) finds that the adult with pathology is stimulus bound and reacts passively to sensory stimulation—traits commonly found in the young child. Both adults with pathology and children have gross color perception, which is an immediate passive perceptual process. Witkin, Lewis, Hertzman, Machover, Meissner, and Wapner (1954) state that the structure of the field and the personality of the perceiver are the significant factors in the responses. They dichotomize individual differences based on active (field-independent) or passive (field-dependent) coping with the environment and on the nature of the person's self-concept. These personality differences were confirmed in a schizophrenic population. Hill (1966) theorizes that response to color is an interaction between the property of the stimulus and the personality of the perceiver. In studies using the HIT (1966, 1968) the affect expressed in response to color in the inkblot was found to be a function of the saturation of the color and the degree of autism (field-dependence/independence) of the observer. Schaie (1966) studied color in its relation to mood, affect, and emotion. The excitation potential of a color stimulus may be strong or weak, depending on the emotional state of the subject which is identifiable in the corresponding emotional response. Schaie also points out that the degree of excitation potential may be associated with the saturation of the color. All-or-none theories espousing either a purely affective or a purely cognitive explanation are inadequate. A workable theory must include the interaction effect between the stimulus strength of color and the personality of the perceiver.

Block and Greenfield (1965), using the HIT, studied the effects of order of presentation, context, and stimulus characteristics. They found that color is the preferred stimulus condition regardless of the order of presentation or context. The presence or absence of color affects adaptation to the blot.

COLOR SHOCK. Color shock is a phenomenon described by Rorschach as an "associative stupor" which results from the impact of chroma in the inkblot. He identified this disturbed reaction with neurotic inhibition. Van de Castle and Spicher (1964), in a study of the affective impact of color on the HIT, examined the relationship between neuroticism and color shock as it relates to the Rorschach theory. They found no difference between their extremely neurotic subjects and the so-called normal subjects. They did, however, find a difference in the reaction to the same card presented both in its chromatic form and an achromatic counterpart. The authors concluded that if color shock exists, it may be caused by the specific coloration or by the administration of the Rorschach because it is not evident in the HIT. I do not find sufficient evidence to consider color shock a HIT occurrence. Various affective reactions that relate to the subject's interaction with the inkblot are examined in Part II (affect arousal).

COLOR RESPONSES IN THE AVERAGE RANGE. When color scores fall in the average range, a predominance of C 1 responses is expected. Sometimes the color responses are all C 1. At other times other color responses are included. (See clinical summary.) When C 1 is the dominant response, C 2 and C 3 responses are not significant if the quality of the content is positive, well integrated, and not pathological. Such scores indicate that the respondent is able to use affect and "regress in the service of the ego" (Kris, 1952) without the loss of emotional control. Beck (1952) states that color is not necessarily a disruptive entity but may enrich the level of association. Therefore C 1 responses are free percepts indicating a wider range of sensitivity, greater flexibility, and greater adaptation than are found in persons whose responses are based only on form or only on color. C 1 responses reflect a combination of the social, emotional, and intellectual aspects of the individual.

The ability to integrate the form of the blot with the color in a secondary manner identifies the individual who is capable of smooth interpersonal relationships (Beck, 1952; Bohm, 1958; Klopfer, Ainsworth, Klopfer, and Holt, 1954; Piotrowski, 1957; Schachtel, 1966). He can establish rapport in a warm, empathic manner. Such an interpretation is reenforced if the subject also gives human-movement responses. Such a person is sensitive and responsive to environmental cues and achieves mastery over his feelings, exerting conscious control of the emotions. His behavior is directed toward the outer world, and he is considerate of others. Because the C 1 is a controlled response it also implies elements of conformity and dependence on others, which are important in maintaining good external relationships.

Beck (1952) found that when the subject's color score on the Rorschach is average but consists mainly of FCs (equivalent to HIT C 1) without any CFs (C 2) or Cs (C 3), the individual is inhibited and compulsive, especially when many responses depend entirely on form (C 0). Inhibition, however, should not be judged solely on this basis. Other indicators of constriction and compulsion in the test record should also be considered. Klopfer, Ainsworth, Klopfer, and Holt (1954) believe that a predominance of C 1 responses reveals an overconforming, overdependent individual who is afraid to be different. Under emotional stimulation he tends to withdraw unless the situation is free of threat.

COLOR BELOW THE FIFTH PERCENTILE. When the C score falls below the fifth percentile, the use of color is very limited or completely absent, indicating that form dominates the responses. The lowest color scores are found in the records of fourth graders, retardates, juvenile delinquents, and depressives. Absence or near absence of color responses is attributable to various personality types (Schachtel, 1966; Shapiro, 1960; Bohm, 1958; Piotrowski, 1957). One type consists of those upon whom color makes little impact, even though they may notice it. Three different groups exist within this personality type. Schachtel (1966) identifies in the first subgroup severely neurotic depressives and many psychotic depressives. He attributes their absence of the use of color to dulled and blunted senses. These persons often verbalize their perceptions of things around them as gray and colorless. Neither the colors in the environment nor the colors in the inkblots register significantly. These persons tend to be self-rejecting and self-recriminating. Schachtel designates the second subgroup as indolent. Persons in this group have a dulled capacity for warmth. They show neither the effort nor the self-rejection of the depressive. The third subgroup is normal persons who are emotionally flat and insensitive to the enriching quality of the color. Their capacity to enjoy the exhilarating values of the world around them is not developed, either because of lack of opportunity or because of lack of incentive.

Schachtel (1966) identifies a second personality type giving minimum color responses as persons who are habitually rigid and show compulsive attitudes. This behavior is usually associated with the pedantic personality. The pedant has an excessively strained and narrow definition of the test situation, which prevents him from being receptive to the blot and its colors. His efforts are consciously and consistently directed toward accurate form likeness.

A third personality type identified by Schachtel (1966) are those who are passively open to the impact of colors. They cannot freely interact with the color and either give in to it helplessly or avoid it because it disturbs them. The result is usually a sparse record with either no color responses or perhaps a single C 3 response. Schachtel reports this openly passive attitude most frequently in pre-schizophrenics and attributes it to the fear that their underlying chaos and panicky thoughts may be revealed. The avoidance of color responses and the occasional extreme use of C 3 both reflect the breakdown of the capacity for active coping, structuring, integrating, and organizing. Shapiro (1960) also found no color responses or many C 3 responses in records of chronic schizophrenics, subjects with severe schizoid character disorders, and subjects with severe narcissistic character disorders. He attributes this restraint of affect to depressive inhibition, neurotic inhibition, or psychotic affective arridity. The schizophrenic characteristically experiences a dulling of affect. Lack of use of color is not in itself a sign of affective depressive, neurotic, or psychotic inhibition. Bohm (1958) believes that the dullness of the torpid mental defective, whose affective life is as weak and superficial as is his intellectual life, also renders him unable to respond with color. The other extreme of this personality is the mental defective who is excitable and emotionally labile and who uses many color responses. Piotrowski (1957) quotes Z. Drohocki, who claims that the quality of the color response drops with a decrease in mental efficiency and temporary loss of emotional interest in others. Such tendencies are evident in records of epileptics.

In general, lack of color response shows intellectual and emotional withdrawal and narrowing of functioning. Inhibition, guardedness, and defensiveness are expected. Lack of color responses may also indicate that ordinary channels for expressing emotion are not available, that socialization of emotional impulses appears to be deficient, and it is doubtful that the individual can give of himself to establish a good reciprocal relationship.

COLOR ABOVE THE NINETY-NINTH PERCENTILE. The greatest use of color is found among neurotics, alcoholics, and some schizophrenics. College students are also among the high color users. When the C score falls above the ninety-ninth percentile, C 2 and C 3 responses are always excessive. These responses usually indicate unrest and lack of emotional stability (Beck, 1952). They also reveal immaturity, lack of restraint, and impulsivity. Sensitive interpretations consider whether C 2 or C 3 responses are predominant.

Psychologists agree that Rorschach CF (C 2) responses reflect an immature, even infantile, reaction in an individual with labile affect and poor controls (Beck, 1952; Bohm, 1958; Piotrowski, 1957). Nevertheless, some restraint is demonstrated by the presence of form which indicates that reality has not been entirely excluded. Such an individual desires and strives for contacts but is unable to establish a stable relationship with the object of the affect. The reason, Bohm (1958) explains, is that restless fluctuation (overshooting of the mark) occurs without adequate involvement in the situation. The affect is objectless. Beck (1952) believes that CF (C 2) responses indicate an easy state of irritability such as is frequently found in the adolescent type, whether the adolescent is young or old. Persons who give many C 2 responses are more egocentric than allocentric, although they may have some insight into the needs of others. Egocentricity is found in neurotics who disregard the rights and welfare of others, although they try unsuccessfully to be considerate. Bohm (1958) believes that persons who give an excessive number of CF (C 2) responses are much more accessible to the emotional impact of others and therefore are receptive to suggestion. The degree of suggestibility varies in strength and direction in direct proportion to the number of these responses given. Bohm points out that suggestibility is also determined by other variables. When high human-movement scores are combined with CF (C 2) scores, the individual is resistant to suggestions, whereas the presence of few or no human-movement responses indicates that the person is open to suggestion.

Beck (1952) states that schizophrenics give more CF (C 2) responses to the Rorschach than FC (C 1) responses. Although these scores indicate affective regression, the individual is still holding onto controls, perhaps accounting for the sporadic nature of the schizophrenic's outbursts. Beck also found CF responses predominant in feeble-minded persons who are also hypersuggestible.

Two other important groups give a preponderance of C 2 responses. Both lack the capacity to delay affective responses but adapt to reality and are not psychotic. The first group—the hysterical group—has a repressed tendency to react in a highly charged fashion but yet with some control. The second group—persons with character disorders—are more impulsive, react immediately, are often shallow in feeling, bland, cool, and disregarding of what others think. Beck (1952) finds these responses also in normal persons, especially those who are creative, sensitive, and sympathetic. These individuals have genuine feelings and a capacity for varying degrees of freedom. However, C 2 minus responses are not found in a normal population. Generally, the person with C 2 minus responses uncovers emotional pressures with too little self-discipline, has undirected flights of ideas, and pushes personal needs and desires. The total protocol is frequently erratic with a low FA score in support of these findings.

The C 3 response is a projection of impulsivity, the discharge of which serves only to release the uninhibited feelings of the individual. When C 3 responses predominate, the question of adaptation no longer exists and impulsive affectivity is the sole goal. The subject does not try to adjust to the environment but is overwhelmed by his emotions and is ready only to let off steam. Bohm (1958) states that when (in addition to the pure color responses) few or no human-movement responses are present, the impulsive outbursts may take the shape of frequent weak discharges like "the crackling of a machine gun." But, when many human-movement responses are given, the impulsiveness emerges in infrequent but more massive and powerful discharges like "the explosion of a bomb." Therefore, the combination C 3 and HM is potentially dangerous because when other inhibitors lapse accumulated explosive energy can suddenly explode. Bohm found the danger is greater if location responses of the D 1 variety are also present (equivalent to HIT L 1).

Beck (1952) states that the Rorschach C (C 3) response reflects the diffuse lability manifested as crotchetiness and irritability in the chronic neurotic. These responses are also found in aging individuals in whom the awareness of aging is attended by a morose mood. Klopfer, Ainsworth, Klopfer, and Holt (1954) state that C responses in the Rorschach are rarely found in the older adult except in deteriorated organics. A predominance of C 3 responses reflects ungovernable impulses, lack of participation of the intellect, and the potential for rage reactions often found in schizophrenics. Schizophrenics generally give many C 3 responses and frequently obtain color scores above the ninety-ninth percentile. Some schizophrenics, however, give no color responses. This lack suggests that the individual is devoid of the intellectual processes necessary to cope with emotional stimulation. Records of organics may also show either a complete lack of color responses or the presence of many florid color responses. Both reveal a limited capacity to articulate or organize the blots. C 3 responses are normal for young children.

SPECIAL COLOR RESPONSES. *Color-plus responses* are given when the affect aroused in the subject by color is positive. These responses reveal warm, cheerful, optimistic feelings. Records in which color-plus responses predominate identify a person with the personality to attract people to him and the ability to enjoy warm, close rapport with others (Piotrowski, 1957).

Color-minus responses are given when the subject is negatively affected by the color. These responses contain negative content, for example blood or disease. Color-minus responses signal depressive affective undertones. Individuals who avoid intimate relationships have a predominant number of color-minus responses. Such persons associate pain with closeness because of unpleasant past experiences. They tend to be self-centered and to disregard the feelings, needs, rights, and comforts of others. They fear others and feel aggressive toward them. Color-minus responses are found in the records of deteriorating schizophrenics. Their percepts depict mental or physical destructiveness. Blood is a common color-minus response. Persons who give this response experience fear and anxiety in emotional closeness with people. Therefore they tend to dissociate themselves from others. The person who is not in close contact with others does not need as much self-control as the one who is dependent and must suppress his fear and hatred. Negative color responses, according to Bohm (1958), are found in the records of individuals who try to adapt but are largely unsuccessful because of intellectual shortcomings. The affect influences the thought processes and the thinking influences the affect. Emotion and reason do not remain separate.

Color naming reflects superficial affect (Piotrowski, 1957). The subject has given only the afferent phase of the color response without the efferent phase. This response reflects the inability of the subject to integrate and react to the affect aroused other than by identifying the stimulus. Color naming is found most often in the records of organics or very disturbed individuals. Frequently it is found in patients with brain damage who are easily irritated. Color naming in this group reveals a helpless reaction—defective affect rather than emotional evasion. Bohm (1958) contends that color naming is a sign of genuine or traumatic epilepsy and is usually accompanied by symmetry responses (B). In the emotionally disturbed individual, color naming reveals an inability to control and direct the reaction to affect. However, Klopfer, Ainsworth, Klopfer, and Holt (1954) hypothesize that this response is an attempt to control the situation without actually coming into contact with it. In the very young child, color naming is not unusual and may represent pride in displaying the learned skill of naming a color (Schachtel, 1966).

Color denial reveals superficiality in dealing with emotions. In the adult, it represents a neurotic avoidance of reality. If other test indicators concur, color denial may be considered a strength. It indicates the ability to resist the impact of affect.

Achromatic-color responses are an extension of the individual's receptivity to color. According to Halpern (1953), black reflects depression, white elation. For the child, good is white and bad is black. Achromatic-color responses occur in the records of persons who have variegated reactions to the environment and may be artistic (Klopfer, Ainsworth, Klopfer, and Holt, 1954). Such responses are often given by highly intellectual persons. Responding to color without chroma is a toned-down way of handling emotional stimuli and is a depressive sign if there is an absence of chromatic color responses and content indicators show depression. Schachtel (1966) believes that the achromatic response reflects perceptual sensitivity. The perceiver seeks out the achromatic colors in order to respond to them, whereas chromatic colors intrude on him and he is obliged to respond to them. Bohm (1958) contends that when achromatic colors are used and the response is fairly concise, it is an indicator of epilepsy. If the responses, however, are amorphous, Bohm contends that the subject is indolent or lacking emotional fixation or a traumatic effect may be present.

Achromatic color responses are rare, and research in support of interpretations is limited. Their meaning should be considered with caution, and the balance of the record should support the interpretation.

White is an infrequent response and is associated with remoteness and detachment. White responses frequently have amorphous content such as ice or snow. These responses given by a child suggest that he perceives the environment as hard, unyielding and ungiving. According to Hans Binder (in Piotrowski, 1957), more than one white response in an adult Rorschach record warrants an interpretation of mood swings which are the euphoric aftermath of depression. White indicates the emergence of the individual from a depressive state into a state of euphoria, peace, joy, and certitude. According to Schaie (1966), white represents lightness, release, and unboundedness as well as emptiness and lack of identification. Zulliger (1954) found white-color responses in the records of oversensitive, easily hurt subjects who try to hide their sensitivity. When white responses are accompanied by high anxiety scores, the subject may demonstrate uncertitude, sadness, and inattention.

Black responses are found most frequently in children from age four and one-half to six. They are found more often in the records of disturbed children than in those of well-adjusted children, but may appear in both. Black is closely associated with conflict with authority figures. Black responses increase during the Oedipal period, when the child is trying to come to terms with objective reality and to internalize authority. Black responses indicate that the individual is still at odds with authority and views the world in terms of these frustrating contacts. He has not overcome early feelings of being denied, disappointed, or opposed. Therefore subsequent disturbances and disappointments are likely to arouse infantile reactions. A reduction in the number of black responses after age six or seven does not always mean that conflict relationships have been resolved. The conflict can still be manifested through explosive outbursts or marked withdrawal. Exaggerated repression may also indicate unresolved problems with authority figures. Klopfer, Ainsworth, Klopfer, and Holt (1954) refer to the person who uses black and gray in his responses as the burned child, meaning that he has experienced a series of traumatic events. This interpretation gains weight if achromatic responses outnumber chromatic responses by two to one. Such scores imply great affectional need. The person is inhibited in his overt reactions to others for fear of being hurt or rejected. Schaie (1966) contends that black signifies depression, constraint, and inhibition.

Color-shading responses are given by subjects who react both to the color and to the shading of an area, for example, dried blood—the color red for the blood and the shading for the dried, caked-on impression. Applebaum and Colson (1968) report a study using Rorschach records in which they found statistically significant differences (chi square $< .0005$) between C-Sh responses given by hospitalized psychiatric patients who had made suicidal attempts and responses of a group of patients who had made no such attempts. Individuals reacting to the C-Sh combination adopt an affective distance which makes it possible to think or act as if they were removed while in a situation potentially rife with feeling. They can tolerate the fear, pain, and horror entailed in suicidal actions. Some individuals are remarkably dispassionate in preparing for suicide.

RELATIONSHIP BETWEEN COLOR AND OTHER VARIABLES. Reaction time is related to the color response. Fast reaction time (RT low), according to Beck (1952), may be a clue to quickened emotional sensitivity. Hypomanic individuals characteristically react rapidly to color cards. Their feelings and pressures permit no delay or restraint. The thinking of these individuals is dominated by intense emotion, and centers on particular topics in the color-determined associations. When these themes are pathological or regressive, they may be reflected in sick anatomy and sex associations or crude fire, blood, or violence motives. Fast reaction time also reflects the need to withdraw from a threatening stimulus as quickly as possible, giving the first available response. Often the response is superficial, but it may also contain healthy content such as art and nature. A fast response may also reflect the spontaneity and impulsiveness of the child.

Slow reaction time (RT high) particularly in responses to high-stimulus strength color cards reveals blocking in dealing with affective elements because of emotional factors. The subject may be inhibiting an unacceptable response or inhibiting all affective content. Slow RT to color cards also reveals inhibition of free fantasy.

Shading responses and C scores, when approximately equal, show adequate control over emotional impulses if other variables are in the normal range. High form-definite scores reenforce a prediction of control over impulses. A predominance of dark Sh responses, however, precludes the interpretation of self-control. Individuals giving dark Sh responses are subject to intermittent depressions, but they tolerate tension because of the subjective release they experience through acting-out behavior.

Movement scores reveal fantasy living. Color scores are a function of affective pressures. When C and M scores are equal (or almost equal) and both are in the high-average range, the subject has inner resources and accessibility for treatment can be predicted.

C scores in excess of M also indicate responsiveness. The exception is persons who give C 2 and C 3 responses exclusively. These people are at the mercy of their emotions. Schizophrenics, retardates, and five-year olds follow this pattern. (For the five-year old, emotional responsivity is expected and normal.)

When M scores predominate with few or no C scores, the individual is withdrawn and retreats from emotional involvement. Klopfer, Ainsworth, Klopfer, and Holt (1954) found this pattern typical of adolescents. Similar results have been recorded using the HIT for seventh and eleventh graders and for college students. In emotionally disturbed adolescents, the excess of M over C is greater than it is for normals. High M scores in such individuals are accompanied by high V scores. The records of alcoholics are similar to those of emotionally disturbed adolescents. Depressives and juvenile delinquents respond like normal adolescents.

Inanimate movement (m) is a sign of motor restraint. When positive color responses (C plus) occur with m responses, aggressive needs are controlled. The combination, however, is rare. Generally when C and m appear together the responses are explosive (C minus). This combination reflects a grandiose and overwhelming need to increase one's power and to reject emotional ties with others, although these needs are not really desired. In the absence of other indicators, this combination does not indicate a tendency for explosive aggressiveness. Piotrowski (1957) found m-C minus responses mainly in adolescents, indicating a struggle against environmentally imposed limitations.

The combination of high location and high C scores identifies the individual who is not impelled to exert himself to accomplish outstanding personal achievements. He enjoys pleasurable emotional impulses, and although he dislikes painful emotions he does not act on them because of indolence. When the L score is low (many whole responses) and the C score is high, the individual is ambitious to achieve, especially if FD, FA, and I are average or higher. If L is low and C is high, the individual may act impulsively and have poor control, particularly if FD and Sh are low.

When *abstract* responses are derived from color, the subject's thinking is dominated by feelings. One needs a strong ego to handle such strong emotions. Beck (1952) found this combination in schizophrenics, hypomanics, and neurotics. When emotions are projected in this manner in schizophrenics and hypomanics they are dissociated from their direct control.

RESPONSES TO HIGH- AND LOW-SATURATED COLOR. Responses to color saturation identify the mode of coping with affect. Inhibition of or inability to deal with affect aroused by color occurs most frequently in response to the high stimulus-strength color cards. The low stimulus-strength cards have little affect-arousal value. A difference of more than five points in the score on any one of the variables comparing the high stimulus-strength color cards with the low stimulus strength color cards, indicates this disparate affect and requires interpretive attention. The following differences were found between ten high and ten low stimulus-strength color cards in a study comparing a high autistic (self-dependent) group with a low autistic (field-dependent) group (Hill, 1966). The study combined high- and low stimulus color cards from Forms A and B. The high stimulus-strength color cards selected were 9A, 16A, 17B, 18A, 20A, 26A, 27A, 35A, 36B, and 42A. The low-stimulus-strength color cards were 2B, 7A, 8A, 8B, 10A, 19B, 30A, 30B, 33A, and 45A. Both groups of subjects obtained higher scores in rejection, anxiety, hostility, and affect arousal and lower scores in form appropriateness when responding to the high stimulus-strength color cards compared to responses to the low stimulus-strength color cards. In response to the low stimulus color cards, no differences were found between the groups on form appropriateness, form definiteness, location, anxiety, hostility, color, and affect arousal. In responses to the high stimulus-strength color cards the following differences occurred between the groups. High autistic subjects obtained lower scores on FD, FA, and C and higher scores on R, L, and AA than did the low autistic subjects. Low autistic subjects had a longer RT to the high stimulus-strength color cards than did high autistic subjects. High autistic subjects showed no difference in RT as a function of the stimulus strength of color.

In a subsequent study carried out in 1968, Donald R. Gorham, Louise Green, and I compared the responses elicited by the fifteen highest (3, 6, 9, 15, 16, 17, 19, 20, 26, 27, 28, 35, 39, 42, 44) and fifteen lowest (1, 2, 5, 7, 18, 22, 24, 29, 30, 32, 33, 36, 37, 38, 45) stimulus-strength color cards of HIT Form A, using a population of one hundred normals (college students) and one hundred schizophrenics. In response to the high stimulus-strength color cards, both groups obtained significantly lower scores in M and higher scores in location, shading, and color as compared with responses to the low stimulus-strength color cards. The normals, in response to the high stimulus-strength color cards, scored significantly higher in anatomy and lower in human. Schizophrenics, in response to the high stimulus-strength color cards, had higher pathognomic verbalization scores than normals did in their responses to the low stimulus-strength color cards. These differences may help to identify the population to which an individual most likely belongs.

DEVELOPMENTAL TRENDS. Color responses for young children are primarily dominated by the color in the blot. They pay little attention to form (Halpern, 1953; Ames, Learned, Metraux, and Walker, 1952; Piotrowski, 1957). Color-dominant responses of the two-year old are the result of sporadic, short-lived emotional reactions. Needs are expressed in a crude, uncontrollable, and demanding fashion (Halpern, 1953). Up to age four or five, emotional reactions are essentially egocentric, demanding, and impulsive. By age six the child who is still self-centered continues to give C 3 and C 2 responses, but these responses begin to decline. Color responses with form as the primary determinant and color secondary (C 1) begin to emerge. Sanders, Holtzman, and Swartz (1968) studied developmental trends in color in the HIT using the records of more than three hundred youngsters who are part of a long-term longitudinal study (Holtzman, 1965; Holtzman, Diaz-Guerrero, Swartz, and Lara Tapia, 1968). The subjects were divided into three age groups: Group 1 ages 6.7 to 9.7; Group 2 ages 9.7 to 12.7; and Group 3, ages 12.7 to 15.7. Group 1 demonstrated a marked decline in C 3 responses and some decline in C 2 responses over earlier years. C 1 responses in this group remained fairly constant across the three years. Holtzman, Thorpe, Swartz, and Herron (1961) confirm this high use of color by the prepubertal-age child in their normative samples. Elementary-school children ages six to ten use C 3 and C 2 responses well in excess of the other normal population samples, but with the onset of puberty feeling with and for others gradually increases. In addition, the child is developing certain emotional controls along with increased maturity and these changes are reflected in the increase in the number of color-secondary responses in which form is predominant. Studies by both Halpern (1953) and Ames, Learned, Metraux, and Walker (1952) found that after age ten the FC (C 1) response in the Rorschach increases for both sexes. The latter authors found that even though the FC (C 1) color response gradually increases from age ten to sixteen, CF (C 2) responses still dominate. FC (C 1) responses do, however, dominate C (C 3) responses. Sanders, Holtzman, and Swartz (1968) found that in Group 2, C 1 responses are fairly high around age 9.7 but decrease steadily through the three years to age 12.7. They also found minor fluctuations from year to year in the mean color score when they combined Groups 2 and 3. They were unable to account for these fluctuations and for the steady drop in C 1 for Group 2. This fluctuation and the decline in C 1 can be attributed to adolescence. Both internal and external pressures cause the early adolescent to be in a fairly constant state of turmoil. During this period he is reworking his self-concept. He also needs to understand and control his emotions. Not until the beginning of the late adolescent period, (approximately age sixteen) is the adolescent able to stabilize the inner emotional turmoil and use his cognitive processes to control his emotions or develop a mature outlook toward the environment. From this point on, color responses are similar for all age groups. Holtzman, Thorpe, Swartz, and Herron (1961) found that color responses distribute normally for college students and average adults.

The affect disclosed in the color response indicates the developmental level at which the individual is functioning emotionally. For example, the more extensive the use of C 3 and C 2 responses, the more infantile and primitive the emotional state of the subject. When C 3 is predominant, the individual has not effectively achieved differentiation from his environment through exploration. When C 2 is predominant, the individual is beginning to effect an objective reconciliation with the environment. The subject may still be at the unstable stage of search for stimulation, comparable to that of the young child who has a weak drive toward the environment and is predominantly egocentric. Bohm (1958) states that a record in which FC (C 1) responses predominate with an occasional CF (C 2) is characteristic of the adult making a normal effective object relationship in the environment. To determine whether the developmental level of an individual is a fixation or a regression, the balance of the record must be considered. Simply knowing the developmental stage does not indicate whether the subject is neurotic, psychopathic, or psychotic. Psychologists agree that C 1 responses should emerge during the latency period (Sanders, Holtzman, and Swartz, 1968; Halpern, 1953). Therefore, if no C 1 responses are given during this period, we can assume that the educational process of the child is not making itself felt and the capacity for emotional maturity is not evolving appropriately. When the C 3 responses continue to predominate or are the only affective reaction in latency, affective development lags. Many C 1 responses in the child younger than nine or ten, indicates that he has developed strong control of affects comparable to those of the adult. Such control implies that the child has been subjected to repressive forms of training and that his insecurity has made him subject to exaggerated efforts of control and compliance. In this instance, the maturity normally associated with a C 1 response is not present. The response is forced and precocious. This type of control can be verified from the balance of the record. Exaggerated inhibition is seen in curtailed production, resulting in either rejections or responses which are near rejections. Repression may show itself in the denial of fantasies. Poor form definiteness usually accompanies this kind of C 1 response.

Shading (Sh)

The shading characteristics of the blots contribute a further dimension of ambiguity to the already unstructured stimulus. For many persons the shading makes a response difficult. Shading imparts lightness and darkness to the blot, which tend to obscure, dim, or darken some areas. Shading also creates a vague, diffuse quality, the unevenness of which seems to evoke a corresponding sense of vagueness and uncertainty in some observers. When a person is faced with the task of imposing structure on this ambiguous stimulus, the shading presents an additional potential threat to his equilibrium (Halpern, 1953). Rapaport (1946) believes that shading creates difficulty in articulation and makes it hard for the person to integrate his thoughts. Rorschach scholars agree virtually unanimously that shading responses reflect anxiety and reveal the manner in which the individual deals with anxiety.

Schachtel (1966) believes that to most people overall shading (exclusive of texture) is not sufficiently disturbing to become a determinant. Schachtel believes that discrete nuances of shading become important only when they are sought out, implying perceptual sensitivity. This sensitivity to shading on a test correlates with the sensitivity of the individual to emotional overtones and undercurrents in the environment, for example, physiognomic and gestural expressive nuances, intonations and mannerisms, and the manifest content of speech. These persons have an underlying perceptual attitude which makes them aware of the presence or absence of hostility, indifference or friendliness, disapproval or approval, rejection or acceptance, anxiety and tension or security. Responses to the overall shading reveal anxiety and tension, although the individual may not be aware of them. This anxiety is found in his attitudes both toward other people and toward himself. Beck and Molish (1967) believe that shading impinges on a deeply centralized core of anxiety and that the defensive strategies used in responding were established early in life. Typical defenses are the obsessive compulsive behaviors—ritual thoughts, counterphobic flight, conversion symptoms, expression of anxiety in depression, and aggression against the environment to relieve the tension—all the defenses found in children. Thus, shading seems to provide an index of the qualitative affect of mood. It indicates manifest and potential anxiety, subjectively and consciously felt, and the degree of control of the outward manifestations of this anxiety. Shading responses, particularly texture responses, also indicate an affectional anxiety with regard to primary security needs, relating to feelings of adequacy and to the self-concept.

In the HIT, shading is considered a determinant only if it is (or appears to be) a main factor in the response. No attempt was made in the original HIT work to score or record subtle qualitative shading differences. In developing standard scores and normative data this single shading measure is appropriate and sufficient. For clinical interpretation, however, qualitative distinctions are meaningful. Some persons respond predominantly to textural qualities. Others respond to depth cues, and still others to the film quality of the shading (they are drawn to either the light or the dark values of the blot). Some use a variety of shading elements. The HIT lends itself readily to the examination of these distinctions. The section on scoring (in part 1) describes how these qualitative differences can be recorded.

Interpretations are made according to the qualitative aspects of the shading response. The hypotheses offered for the interpretation of vista, texture, and light and dark film are based primarily on research and clinical use of the Rorschach. Some of the information is speculative and not empirically derived. Therefore it is offered tentatively.

SHADING BELOW THE FIFTH PERCENTILE. Few or no shading responses may reflect a helplessness in integrating shading elements with form elements. It may also reveal passivity or repression in dealing with moods which evoke anxiety or affectional components (Schachtel, 1966). The individual overwhelmed by stress makes no attempt to deal with the stressful agent or denies its presence. Such behavior suggests difficulty in establishing meaningful object relationships because the individual is unable to deal with the threatening aspects of interpersonal interactions.

A pedant who defines the test task narrowly is likely to give responses which have good form and to avoid dealing with affective elements of the blot such as shading.

SHADING ABOVE THE NINETY-NINTH PERCENTILE. Sh responses are based on affective modes of responding to anxiety and are generally automatic. Therefore (as in the color responses) some individuals are compelled to relate to the shading and to the mood thus activated. They are oversensitive to environmental pressure, which arouses anxiety, and they pay excessive attention to the mood qualities of the blot.

VISTA. Vista responses reflect a special perception of the shading elements of the blot. Individuals giving vista responses appreciate depth dimensions as well as the distance cues provided by the shading. The ability to perceive perspective suggests a comparable ability to objectify personal problems and to gain perspective or distance in regarding them. Vista responses reflect a capacity for self-evaluation in handling affectional needs (Beck, 1952; Klopfer, Ainsworth, Klopfer, and Holt, 1954). However, insight is not necessarily implied in these responses and must be gleaned from other data in the record. Beck (1952) believes that persons giving vista responses may be involved in painful ruminative concern about their own shortcomings and inadequacies and may have intrapunitive feelings of destruction. If the subject has given a greater than average number of Sh responses in addition to many vista responses, he may have compensating defensive maneuvers for these feelings of inferiority which are revealed by a need for self-autonomy and self-will. If pathognomic verbalization responses are high, location responses are very low, and integration and form definiteness are high in the average range, the defense is an extended effort toward personal achievement.

Beck (1952) feels that a subject has a consciousness of inferiority when vista responses occur together with film responses. This inferiority aggravates the individual's psychological pain. This combination indicates depression and anxiety, a deepening of the individual's passivity, and an accenting of his submissiveness. If shading elements are prominent in color cards, painful depression and free-floating anxiety are expected.

According to Ames, Learned, Metraux, and Walker (1952), vista responses are absent in young children. They begin to appear at age thirteen through fifteen, and by age fourteen through sixteen vista is the third leading shading response.

TEXTURE. Predominantly textural responses imply tactual awareness of objects. This awareness is verbalized as rough or smooth or as grainy or furry. Schachtel (1966) states that the texture response is a discrete differential response compared with the overall vagueness of other shading responses. Focus on the tactual surface elements points to a particular sensitivity to contact interaction and implies affectional needs and expectations for basic security from the environment. Beck and Molish (1967) suggest that the anxiety aroused by the texture of the blot is caused by the deprivation of basic contacts, and the defensive strategy activated is passive dependent longing. These authors contend that texture responses are concomitant with a sensed rejection and deprivation. This deprivation reveals pressure rooted in the early symbiotic mother-child relationship. Schachtel (1966) believes that in addition to this deprivation, texture responses reveal concern with wishes for pleasure and comforting physical contact or with fear and discomfort over the unpleasantness of such contact. Differentiation can be made by examining the balance of the record.

Texture responses scored 2 indicate that no form or very little form is present in the response. According to Klopfer, Ainsworth, Klopfer, and Holt (1954), texture responses with no form indicate a primitive, infantile, undifferentiated need system, which can be gratified only by physical contact. The reason for these strong drives is frequently frustration of physical contact needs in early childhood accompanied by strong feelings of deprivation. Need for contact may no longer be present, but the subject may still be aware of the former need. Texture responses scored 2 are commonly found within normal populations. Whether the need for closeness and contact is acted upon depends upon other aspects of the record.

Texture responses scored 1 indicate that form is dominant and texture secondary. These responses also reveal a sensual, tactual need for closeness, but gratification need not be immediate and may be sought from an appropriate object. However, if the record shows an excessive number of these responses and shading responses are above the ninety-ninth percentile, a disproportionate need for affection is indicated in spite of the mitigating aspects implied by the presence of form.

Absence of texture responses implies a lack of awareness of the need for affection but does not necessarily mean that the need is not present. Inability to respond to texture usually reflects denial of the need for affection or a reluctance or inability to deal with the need.

FILM. When shading is scorable as film, the perceiver has been aroused by the diffuse quality of the pervasive shaded areas which imply that the blot is no longer solid (Schachtel, 1966). Film responses are divided into light or dark categories. Bohm (1958) believes that film responses reflect the influence of mood (or central feeling tone) and generally imply undifferentiated emotional reaction. Such reaction indicates vague anxiety, which relates to the need for security in interacting both with other people and with oneself. Film responses imply a disintegration of disruption in this area. Klopfer, Ainsworth, Klopfer, and Holt (1954) refer to this reaction as a free-floating anxiety. The individual is aware of the anxiety but has not developed adequate defenses with which to counteract it. A predominance of film responses when Sh is above the ninety-ninth percentile indicates severe anxiety and acute loss of subject-object relationship. The subject may experience feelings of nothingness in the sense of having nothing to hold on to, either in the self or with respect to the environment. Therefore there is more than average frustration of affectional needs.

Predominant use of light film values of shading reflects emotional passivity with the concomitant defense of decreased involvement in areas which activate fear and anxiety. This passivity is not a withdrawal but a reduction or dampening of the general activity level. The individual is cautious, prudent, tends to be hesitant, and often submissive. He experiences depression, restlessness, and a low energy level. The level of anxiety remains because of his unwillingness to act when confronted with a situation which creates inner anxiety. The more light film responses, the more acute the manifest anxiety and the greater the need for behavioral inhibition. Beck (1952) states that when anxiety is extremely high, activity is minimal, almost to the point of catatonic stupor, with barely enough activity to survive.

In the normal individual, many light film responses may indicate a temporary reduction in activity level or, as Beck (1952) defines it, a temporary homeostatic letdown. It indicates inhibition in the timid individual who feels personally inadequate and depressed and is hypersensitive to environmental threat. The total record determines how constrictive the defenses are. Piotrowski (1957) suggests that the light film response indicates an ability to tolerate stress and anxiety.

Elstein (1965), in studying behavioral correlates of Rorschach Shading determinants, found that persons who give many light film shading responses are more passive toward the environment than are those who give few. The former are less openly critical of their surroundings and more inhibited and resigned than the latter. Persons with few light shading responses tend to be critical of the environment.

In the neurotic, the use of light film responses may be a defensive maneuver to avoid the discharge of affective impulses. The discharge of affect poses the threat of retaliation. Therefore the neurotic responds with anxiety. He takes recourse in inactivity and develops passive adjustment to contain his hostility. The concomitant indicators of such labile affect are C 2 and C 3. These scores in combination with light film shading indicate a hypersensitive emotional state. Impulsiveness and a chronic readiness for easily becoming upset are counteracted by passivity, a low threshold of irritability, and inner tension (Beck, 1952).

The predominant use of dark values in the film response indicates anxiety and depression in insecure persons (Binder, 1933). Schachtel (1966) believes that such individuals are passively impressed by the darkness of the blot and experience it as threatening. He believes that depressive patients look for elements in the environment which fit into their depressed mood. They seem disappointed when something good happens to them. He therefore suggests that dark-film responses reveal an assertive quality. The subject asserts himself by calling attention to how black, unpleasant, and depressing everything is so that others may share the feeling. Schachtel found this reaction in the milder depressives in whom reproach and anger are manifest although not always acknowledged. The anger of these persons stems from feelings of being half wanted and half unwanted.

Shading and color have an important relationship. Factor 2 is best defined by color. Shading has significant positive loading on Factor 2 throughout the standardization population samples. Because color is essentially a pure measure of Factor 2, the higher the loading on shading, the more operationally identical it is to color (Holtzman, Thorpe, Swartz, and Herron, 1961). This similarity between shading and color supports the inference that the behavior control implied by shading is primarily part of the affective mood rather than of the cognitive mode of responding because these responses (C and Sh) are more automatic and less conscious than intellectual. The extent of the use of color determines the degree of affect control. It indicates if the action tendency will be toward continuing or severing associations, pleasurable or painful, in relationships with people. Shading, particularly the light film response, indicates whether this tendency will become overt. When light film responses exceed the number of C responses, the subject is unlikely to engage in acting-out behaviors. If, however, the subject gives few or no shading responses, he may have little or no control on the action tendencies revealed in the color responses. In the absence of shading responses, FD scores in the high-average range indicate adequate controls. Dark film responses do not indicate the capacity for control, delay, or suppression of emotional impulses; the person may act despite the pressure of anxiety. Therefore, if color responses reflect a tendency toward overt action, the presence of many dark-film responses indicates the capacity to implement this tendency. The greater the number of dark-film responses when Sh is above the ninety-ninth percentile, the greater the danger of acting out when internal or external pressures become acute. Bohm (1958) states that when shading and color responses are both positive and in the average range, the person has an especially good empathic capacity.

Affect arousal evoked by shading responses reflects fear and the potential for becoming upset. Beck and Molish (1967) believe that when this combination occurs, the core of the anxiety which has been deeply encapsulated in the character structure is opened, and complex defense maneuvers are operating. The defense most frequently evoked is reaction formation. The subject denies the acute anxiety by increasing productivity and seeking recourse in fantasy. Persons using this defense show a unique interest in shading details and appear to hold on to the stimulus by paying attention to minutia. In obsessive patients who are primarily phobic, the reaction pattern is less well defined, and the defense is denial and counterphobic flight.

DEVELOPMENTAL TRENDS. Developmental trends for shading (found in the HIT standardization population) show that shading responses are lowest for young children, especially for five-year olds. This group's shading scores are comparable to the low scores of mental retardates. The highest shading scores are in the records of college students (Holtzman, Thorpe, Swartz, and Herron, 1961). In a study of developmental trends, Thorpe (1960) and Thorpe and Swartz (1965) found that the number of shading responses increases regularly with age in the five-to twenty-year-old group.

Halpern (1953) states that for two-and-one-half to three-and-one-half year olds, patterns of acceptable and unacceptable behavior are simple and not yet well defined. Disturbances in acceptance are likely to result either in violent emotional outbursts, hangdog looks, or in complete denial of the criticism. The child is unable to relate in subtle, controlled, and decisive ways. He may also experience vague uneasiness in responding to the shading. This uneasiness may be reflected in the use of light or dark film responses. The older child (ages five through ten) gives relatively few, if any, shading responses. The sensitivity necessary to respond to shading nuances is rarely developed before puberty.

Deviations from the developmental expectation require an explanation. Excessive Sh responses in the young child, for example, reflect special needs and problems. Halpern (1953) believes that such children are trying to adapt to a world they do not as yet understand and with which they are not as yet in harmony. Excessive Sh responses indicate guardedness and defensiveness and reflect a disturbed, suspicious attitude toward life. The exaggerated sensitivity implicit in this condition is often a disturbance in itself if the child does not have the maturity to control and integrate his reactions constructively. An abnormal number of film or texture responses suggests tension and agitation of a disruptive nature. Halpern (1953) finds that some children give form-dominant, film-secondary (or texture-secondary) responses. She questions, however, whether these responses are a sign of maturity or only of pseudomaturity. A combination of control and spontaneity, as well as good judgment and self-expression must accompany these responses if they are to be considered mature. An overall judgment can be made from the entire record.

Emotionally disturbed children (average age 9.6) give the lowest number of Sh responses of any norm group. This lack reflects difficulty in dealing with environmental threats and reveals a retreat into an earlier mode of response—denial or violent emotional outbursts.

The normative data show that Sh responses for alcoholics are higher than for average adults, reflecting alcoholics' oversensitivity. Klopfer, Ainsworth, Klopfer, and Holt (1954) suggest that alcoholism is symptomatic of a lowered tolerance for frustration which is based on confusion in relating to other people.

Balance (B)

Symmetry is a quality of almost all the blots. It serves as the stimulus for many of the responses. Most subjects are aware of the symmetry. Some verbalize it, others do not. In some instances, the balance response is incidental to the awareness of the symmetry. The subject refers to the symmetry to fill in time while he is temporarily unable to give a response or can perceive nothing else in the blot. Some subjects make a forced search for symmetry and actively try to find balance or lack of it. Such behavior reflects inner insecurity and a fear of one's own impulsiveness (Bohm, 1958).

Psychologists find no basis for considering a lack of B responses to be significant. Four or more B responses are considered excessive. An absorption in the symmetry indicates obsessive, compulsive defenses. An excess of balance responses may also indicate suspiciousness of the test situation. If the individual is suspicious, he examines the inkblot in an attempt to find some element which he perceives as being included deliberately to evoke an uncontrolled response. Sometimes symmetry is used as the only determinant for a response, and the elaboration of the symmetrical position is the percept. Frequent responses of this type indicate pathological thinking. The subject elaborates on the symmetry or balance and does not relate to the blot. The scores on the other variables are needed, however, before the examiner can judge the subject with any certainty.

Holtzman, Thorpe, Swartz, and Herron (1961) found balance responses rare in most groups. The distribution of B scores is skewed and truncated. Five out of six children in a group of five-year olds, elementary-school students, and seventh graders gave no B response. B responses appeared appeared most often among college students and frequently among depressives.

Ideational Organization

VII

Any behavior that uses ideas is called thinking. Thinking is of two kinds: directed and undirected. Undirected thinking is also called associative thinking and may sometimes seem purposeless and uncontrolled, although it often has unconscious direction. At other times undirected thinking may appear rational but is guided by personal drives and desires rather than external reality. Directed thinking involves critical thought. The individual makes judgments concerning a proposition or a value. But directed thinking may also be creative. The individual achieves new solutions to problems, discovers new relationships, invents methods or devices, or produces original artistic objects or forms (Hilgard, 1963).

The inkblot response reflects both associative and directed thinking. The manner of responding reveals how the individual consistently organizes and responds to life situations. Regardless of the particular stimulus, the individual approaches the world in a consistent manner based on his physical and social growth and his level of maturation. His responses also reveal how he copes with the problem-solving nature of a novel situation such as the inkblot task. The variables which reveal ideational organization are form definiteness, movement, integration, popular, and barrier.

Form Definiteness (FD)

Form definiteness is a concept-centered variable which does not depend on the goodness of fit to the blot. The ability to express well-defined percepts is found in persons with adequate intellectual functioning (Rapaport, 1946; Beck, 1952; Shafer, 1954; Bohm, 1958; Holtzman, Thorpe, Swartz, and Herron, 1961; Holtzman, 1965). The form level of the response reflects mental activities which are under the influence of the most rational and impersonal processes. Good form-level responses require an ability to attend to the task and depend upon concentration and a good attention span. Through a process of association, the individual selects a percept and makes a response, thereby revealing his ability to articulate and differentiate. He draws upon experience and memory, using his creative resources (Codkind, 1964; Richter and Winter, 1966). The higher the number of superior form elaborations, the greater the likelihood that the individual is of superior intelligence (Phillips and Smith, 1953). Affect aroused by the stimulus or the test situation is under conscious control, and emotions do not disrupt the task of eliciting a well-defined response. Such control indicates ego strength. Persons verbalizing good FD percepts are expected to show a sense of responsibility both for themselves and toward others. The higher the FD score, the more responsible the person is. Holtzman, Thorpe, Swartz, and Herron (1961) found FD to be one of the variables which identifies perceptual maturity, integration of ideational activity, and awareness of conventional percepts.

FORM DEFINITENESS BELOW THE FIFTH PERCENTILE. Low FD scores indicate lack of control over thought processes. Poor form level characterizes persons of low intellectual caliber. Such persons may have an inferior capacity for observation or a disturbance in their ability to concentrate. Organics have low FD scores because of both their inability to concentrate and the presence of depressive feelings (Bohm, 1958).

Shafer (1954) states that large numbers of poorly formed or unformed responses identify persons whose ego functioning concerned with restraint and modulation of impulse and affect appears to be feeble or overwhelmed. These individuals tend to be tense and impulsive and to have weak defensive and adaptive abilities. If movement and color scores are also low, behavior is likely to be unpredictable and uneven. These persons are afraid of contact or responsibility and tend to be excessively cautious in making up their minds.

Holtzman, Thorpe, Swartz, and Herron (1961) found that chronic schizophrenics, depressives, and retardates have lower mean FD scores than do normal subjects. Emotionally disturbed children (average 9.8 years) also have low mean FD scores.

FORM DEFINITENESS ABOVE THE NINETY-NINTH PERCENTILE. An interpretation of scores this high needs to be considered in relation to other variables. When FD responses are exceptionally high and the subject gives few or no color, shading, or movement responses, the individual is likely to be rigid and inflexible in his adaptiveness. He is limited in feelings and his fantasy is stifled (Shafer, 1954).

When FD scores are high, low form-appropriate scores are expected because of the difficulty in finding highly stylized percepts within the blot. When the FD score is high and the location score is low (and form-appropriate and integration scores are at least average), above-average persistence is expected. When the FD and I scores are low and the L score is high, the individual is likely to be petty, meticulous, and critical.

DEVELOPMENTAL TRENDS. The child under four years cannot be objective and detached in his feelings on the basis of experience. Therefore his grasp of reality tends to be weak and fluid. He also lacks a good vocabulary and is unable to structure his responses effectively. FD responses for this group are weak, but by school age the form level should begin to increase (Halpern, 1953; Ames, Learned, Metraux, and Walker, 1952). Holtzman, Thorpe, Swartz, and Herron (1961) found that by age ten the child is reality oriented and achieves satisfactory FD.

Thorpe (1960) and Thorpe and Swartz (1965) found that FD rose fairly rapidly in the preadolescent years and leveled off after that time. They also found significant correlations between FD, FA, and I. Young children give whole responses without much attention to FD or FA. By age ten (when the child is becoming reality oriented) he achieves satisfactory FD and FA by choosing smaller areas. As he grows older he can maintain this good form level and increase the area of the blot, integrating small parts into the whole. These findings are consistent with theories of the development of higher level thinking, reasoning, and abstracting abilities in the preadolescent and early adolescent years. The child also accumulates experiences which serve as the basis for more complicated thinking. Thus, experience and natural development account for the rapid preadolescent increase in FD responses. By the time the individual reaches college, his peceptual organization, ability to project dynamic qualities into the percept, and sensitivity to color, shading, and symmetry are at their peak.

RESEARCH. Richter and Winter (1966) examined the correlation between HIT scales and high- and low-scoring groups of women on the intuitive-perceptive scales of the Myers-Briggs Type Indicator (a self-inventory personality measure). They found that women with high creativity of the intuitive perceptive type have significantly higher FD scores on the HIT. Richter and Winter concluded that the HIT measures creative potential. Other HIT variables on which they scored significantly higher were C, M, H, I, V, Ax, Hs, and Ab.

Codkind (1964) used the HIT to study the personalities of individuals who accept and use fantasy and the imaginary and compared them with those who do not. FD was one of the scores used to measure articulation or differentiation in the subject's responses. No significant differences were found in FD scores for those who could and those who could not use the imaginary. The ability to articulate responses does not appear to be related to the use of fantasy in the content.

Conners (1965) studied the effect of brief psychotherapy as compared with initial consultation only and use of drugs on children with restlessness and conduct disorders. He used the HIT to measure changes. Brief psychotherapy (five sessions over eight weeks) caused a significant increase in FD and I responses over initial consultation only. Although the drug group demonstrated no changes in individual variables, a highly significant change occurred in Factor 1. This factor includes FD as well as integration, movement, human, pathognomic verbalization, barrier, and penetration reversed. FD (reversed) is also associated with Factor 2.

Megargee (1965) studied the HIT performance of seventy-five male juvenile delinquents (average age 15.5) who were awaiting hearing. He found differences between the juvenile delinquents and normal populations. The delinquents had lower mean scores on FD, FA, I, M, H, and V. These scores were similar to the scores of seventh graders and reflected the immaturity of the delinquents.

Movement (M)

Movement is experienced in two different ways: movement which takes place in the environment and can be observed, and movement that is a personal kinesthetic experience. The inkblot itself has no movement; it presents a stationary field. The exact stimulus which causes the subject to project movement to the inkblot is unknown, although many have speculated about it. When a person perceives movement in a blot he is attributing something to it which comes from within himself. Rorschach (1942) states that the subject imagines the object to be in motion and often reveals this kinesthetic influence in his actions. Movement, then, is a creative addition to the percept. Schachtel (1966) discusses the significance of the movement response in relation to three variables within the individual and to the dynamic-energy level of the movement reported. The movement response reflects both kinesthetic experience and creative experience. It reveals the basic attitudes of the individual toward himself and toward others. The individual's ability to identify with the action of the percept, whether consciously or unconsciously, stems from the constitutional and experiential life of the perceiver. The subject's own feelings and kinesthetic experiences are projected onto the person, animal, or object seen in the movement.

Creative experience is the ability to live within the self and rely on one's own experience and intelligence. Creativity requires openness and sensitivity in experiencing the world and the freedom to contribute inner attitudes to the perception of stimuli. The individual projecting movement onto a blot is putting something of himself into the response. Such projection reflects creative experience. Schachtel (1966) believes that the creativity revealed in movement responses is important in understanding the creative factors of experience rather than serving as a clue to creative production. The creative experience may enhance the percept or add a nightmarish quality. The addition of negative qualities reveals disturbed thought processes which were dominant at the time.

By means of projection, the subject attributes personal strivings and feelings to humans, animals, and objects. These feelings and attitudes may be conscious or unconscious, but they reveal the inner compulsions which direct the individual's life. Frequently they are unconscious and are represented symbolically, somewhat in the manner of dreams. When the projection is a distortion and does not relate to the object, it serves a defensive need, and the subject derives the meaning entirely from within himself. Qualities are ascribed to the percept by the subject which he denies and of which he is unaware.

Rorschach (1942) defined a response as a movement response if the percept involved humans or animals capable of humanlike movement (as found in monkeys, bears, and so on). However, he found that some subjects can perceive movement not only in human and humanlike figures but also in all kinds of animals, plants, and so on. Rorschach's criterion for a movement response was the "sensation of motion." For example, "a bird, in flight" might be considered a form response with no movement actually felt. The examiner would score M, however, for "a bird fluttering his wings" possibly accompanied by a descriptive hand motion.

Schachtel (1966) emphasizes the importance of the dynamic-energy level of the movement reported. This concept is used in HIT scoring. The HIT movement score combines all movement regardless of who or what is seen as moving, and the normative data are based on this single measure. This score is sufficient and appropriate for experimental purposes. The clinician, however, needs to scrutinize types of movement closely. I am presenting movement as two types, animate and inanimate. Animate movement is divided into two categories: human movement (HM) and animal movement (AM). Inanimate movement is movement of or caused by inanimate objects (m).

Basic attitudes toward the self and others are revealed in the attitudes projected onto the M responses such as in the physiognomic expressions of humans and animals and in the kinesthetic actions. Both HM and AM reflect the individual's current drives and feelings. Schachtel (1966) states that when overt or covert identification takes place, regardless of whether the movement is that of a human or animal, the strivings and attitudes expressed tend to be either partially or wholly in the person's awareness or are accessible to awareness without much resistance. Although there is a greater tendency to identify with HM than to identify with AM, some people find it more acceptable to project movement onto animals rather than humans, because of taboos toward certain behavior. Identification with AM reflects attitudes which are more repressed than those represented in the HM responses. Children express their feelings readily through AM because they relate more easily to animals than to humans. As they mature and become increasingly interested in people, HM responses increase. By adolescence HM responses equal and may exceed AM responses, although AM responses are present at all ages. An equal number of HM and AM responses reflect the mature, spontaneous individual who accepts his impulses. He is able to regress in the service of the ego and to use his fantasy at will.

When the subject is severely repressed, denial of self-identification with the movement projected onto the blot is revealed in the m responses. Schactel (1966) refers to this as the "not me" response. Such acute difficulty with identification is not usually reflected in HM or AM responses. Threatening HM or AM responses, however, are those which reveal a "not me" quality and are accompanied by fear and maximum repression.

Animate movement reveals basic personality attitudes toward the self and others. In order to determine these attitudes, the examiner must consider the quality of the movement, the content of the response, the relationship of the movement to the perceiver, and the quantity of movement. Several similar M responses may indicate tension surrounding an unsatisfied basic drive.

The quality of the movement (whether active, passive, indecisive, or other) reveals significant attitudes and drives that dynamically affect the subject's present personality structure (Schachtel, 1966). It reflects the energy level of the individual and indicates whether he is weak and incapable of functioning effectively, tense and rigid, or relaxed and spontaneous. Movement is not the only variable that indicates basic attitudes, nor does all movement reveal basic attitudes. Many M responses are so stereotyped that they reveal only conventional ways of seeing things. These responses are generally to obvious stimulus properties which yield popular M percepts. With this type of movement, P responses are usually high.

Passive movement may indicate the completely helpless individual who waits for someone to come to his assistance. Or it may reflect an individual's bid for help by reaching out for assistance. In either instance, the characteristic attitude is dependency. Humans and animals seen sitting, kneeling, lying down, resting, bending, and so on are passive responses and are scored M 1. Gestures of begging for help or asking for material aid are also passive as are oral responses (for example, eating). The manner in which the subject gratifies dependent needs is revealed in the activity level of all M responses. If the movement is predominantly passive, the individual sits and waits for help. If the movement is predominantly active, he actively seeks gratification of the need (Schachtel, 1966). The passive individual feels threatened by the world, and these fears prevent activity. He may express helplessness and inactivity in the belief (conscious or unconscious) that he shows pity or contempt for the attitude of others who are not meeting his needs, without realizing that it is his own feelings of pity and contempt toward himself that he is expressing.

Active movement may reflect strength, qualities of leadership, and co-operativeness, or it may reveal aggressive competitive hostility. The individual, in projecting active movement onto the percept, reveals the importance of aggressive impulses in his life even though he may not be aware of what he is revealing. Persons whose aggressive responses reveal spontaneous activity and positive interactions between people or animals are likely to be confident and capable of independent pursuit of goals. In the records of these individuals, anxiety and hostility scores are usually in the average range or lower. Active-movement scores, M 2, M 3, or M 4, cover running, walking, dancing, jumping, lifting, and fighting. When humans or animals are seen as aggressively trying to exploit one another by grabbing, pulling, or fighting for food or some other object, oral sadistic drives are present (Schachtel, 1966). An element of dependency is also involved in such taking from others instead of finding one's own. The overt behavior of persons who give aggressive, exploiting M responses is assertive and

competitively aggressive. Hostility and anxiety scores are generally high. Emotionally disturbed adolescents who have high mean M scores and the highest
mean Ax and Hs scores of all the normative groups appear to have this pattern
of behavior.

Blocked movement may indicate ambivalence when the action is indecisive.
When contradictory movement is reported in the same figure, one action neutraliz-
ing the other, the individual is unable to make decisions because he is uncertain of
his wants. He exerts much energy but nothing happens. For example, "a man
running, his feet are caught in the mud; he can't move."

Posture responses reflect potential for movement (scored M 1) but do not
actually include movement. When a figure is seen standing erect with legs pressed
closely together and arms close to the body, the response reveals basically unfree,
rigid, defensive attitudes in which spontaneous relations with others are threatened
(Schachtel, 1966).

Beck (1952) states that stance responses are an indication of a homosexual
orientation. Submissive responses are feminine, and self-assertive responses are
masculine. If the subject gives many responses in which the dominant pose is
contrary to that expected for his sex (males in clinging feminine stances or females
with self-assertive masculine postures), the examiner may consider the possibility
of homosexual strivings. Fantasy content specific to homosexuality strengthens
such findings.

INANIMATE MOVEMENT. No data on the inanimate-movement (m) response have
as yet been established for the HIT. However, Rorschach scholars have found
that the m response expresses maximum repression and lack of identification with
the content. The percepts appear to exist outside of the individual and without
his participation. In all movement responses the individual is a spectator. However, in the m response his dissociation with the activity makes him an impotent
spectator. He can do nothing about the action and therefore cannot be held
responsible for it (Schachtel, 1966). Individuals giving m responses are incapable
either of asserting themselves or of defending themselves against threats. They
can only project their feelings (at the greatest possible distance) onto inanimate
objects.

Movement in objects which are disintegrating or falling apart reveals deep
insecurity and feelings of helplessness in protecting the self against impending
danger. Explosions and eruptions reveal the desire to release impulses or the fear
of releasing impulses or both. Aggression toward animate objects from inanimate
sources suggests the greatest dissociation of hostile, aggressive impulses. For example, a bullet ripping through a body, a machine crushing someone, or a crucifixion
scene all depict helplessness and disaster.

Not all m responses are of this destructive dissociative nature. The subject
may have positive wishes and hopes which he feels incapable of realizing and
which become externalized through inanimate forces. Objects seen as soaring or
floating without human effort may indicate the desire to elevate one's position or

break away and escape from confinement. Because the movement is projected to an inanimate source, the subject has no confidence that the aspirations can be fulfilled. The response represents magical wish-fulfillment fantasies (Schachtel, 1966).

Five or more m responses are considered excessive and may indicate ego weakness. The person tends to take recourse in daydreaming and observing himself or others, thus appreciably reducing overt activity.

MOVEMENT BELOW THE FIFTH PERCENTILE. Few or no M responses indicate inability to express empathic projection and creative experience. This inability may be due to excessive repression or to the unavailability of inner resources. Excessive repression prevents the projection of inner feelings through imagination and reduces affect. In the depressed person, inner resources are temporarily repressed, and color responses may also be low or absent. Form definiteness, however, should still be in the average range. This rigidity is a safety device and does not mean that inner resources are absent (Schachtel, 1966). The balance of the record may reveal creative, empathic, and imaginative resources which counteract the lack of M.

In conversion hysteric patients, lack of insight into their own roles or those of others prevents M responses. Other clinical groups with low M include persons in anxiety states and some with psychosomatic disorders (Phillips and Smith, 1953). Persons with such limited resources are either fixated at, or have regressed to, a lower level of development. Included in this group are mental defectives and persons with organic impairment. The small number of M responses reflects their typically low level of perceptual functioning. The chronically immature (psychopaths and adults with simple maladjustments) also fit this category (Phillips and Smith, 1953).

When FD and M are both low, the individual is unable to express himself and acknowledge his impulses. This does not mean, however, that impulses may not be acted on. The norms for very young children, emotionally disturbed children, depressives, schizophrenics, and retardates all include low mean M responses. These groups are prone to act irresponsibly and without ego participation.

MOVEMENT ABOVE THE NINETY-NINTH PERCENTILE. An excessive number of M responses suggest that the individual is preoccupied with his own ideas at the expense of being responsive to external stimuli. They may also reveal reduced overt activity, particularly if color responses are low. The additional presence of excessive pathognomic-verbalization responses indicates the extent of withdrawal from reality. When animal-movement responses are excessively high in an adult record and exceed human-movement responses, the individual may be frustrated because of the partial repression of feelings in identifying with the AM. Such an individual is expected to behave at the level of the young child who acts on impulse and without inhibition. The addition of a large number of color responses supports a prediction of acting-out behavior.

RELATIONSHIP BETWEEN MOVEMENT AND COLOR. Rorschach believes both movement responses and color responses identify individuals in whom particular groups
of functions are developed to a marked degree. Persons who give M responses
predominantly compared with their C responses are considered introversive. Persons whose C responses predominate are considered extratensive. The strength of
introversiveness or extratensiveness is a function of the absolute number of M or
C responses.

The introversive person tends to live within himself (with his own thoughts
—often fantasies) rather than in the outside world. He adapts with difficulty. He
may achieve adaptation partially through consciously acquired ways of thinking.
He has difficulty changing his emotional tone, is stable and taciturn, and indulges
in less physical activity than does the extratensive type. Normals with predominant
M responses are intelligent, differentiated in their inner lives, independent thinkers
and creative. Schizophrenic paranoids also fall into this category. They have more
or less systematized delusions of persecution and grandeur.

The extratensive person lives in the world outside himself and can adapt
as long as excessive lability does not interfere and other functions are not disturbed. The extratensive person who is disturbed is motoric and has unstable
emotional reactions. Normals who are extratensive make emotional adaptations
easily. They are practical, light hearted, flighty, and intellectually more reproductive than creative. Records of retardates are C predominant. Retardates react
to every passing emotion. Organics are also extratensive as are schizophrenics with
motor excitement.

Rorschach also discusses what he calls the coartated personality type—
persons who give neither M nor C responses and whose introversive and extratensive personality features are minimal. The pedant is a coartated type who
compulsively controls his inner living and abhors fantasy. He avoids relationships
with the world outside and controls lability of emotional expression. Depressives
are also coartated types. They are constricted by the paralyzing nature of their
depressions. This constriction is seen in their inability to think, love, or enjoy
themselves, and in their complaint of inner emptiness. Some persons give approximately equal numbers of M and C responses but only a few of each. These persons
are considered coartative and show a tendency toward constriction. Few but equal
M and C responses is a relatively frequent pattern in persons with depressed
moods. Other subjects respond with equal but high numbers of M and C responses
which are relatively equal. Rorschach refers to these subjects as "ambiequal types"
with distinctly coartated features. He reports this as a suppression phenomenon
where the need is for form responses but C and M appear almost against the will
of the individual. The following groups are included in this ambiequal category:
compulsive neurotics who constantly and consciously check their introversive and
extratensive tendencies and elated manics who have multitudes of ideas and feel
that they can do anything and everything. Manics also seek emotional rapport
with anyone at any time. Normals with this pattern are highly talented. They are
markedly introversive, creative, subjective, and engage in intensive rapport. They

are also markedly extratensive, enjoy extensive rapport, have the ability to make sympathetic reproductions, and have an excellent emotional approach (Rorschach, 1942).

DEVELOPMENTAL TRENDS. Holtzman, Thorpe, Swartz, and Herron (1961) found that the number of M responses increases from age five through college age. The median score for five-year olds is 9, whereas only one college student in a hundred scored 9 or less. The variability about the mean was least for five-year olds and greatest for elementary-school children seven to eleven. The latter group includes preadolescents. The increased variability for the elementary-school group is attributed to the variable rate at which these children develop.

Thorpe (1960) found significant age trends for M using the four normal populations included in the HIT standardization. Thorpe and Swartz (1965) extended the analysis using groups from five to twenty years of age and found significant developmental trends with a regular increase with increasing age throughout the span studied. M responses not only increase in quantity with age but Rorschach research shows that the type of M response changes as well.

Movement responses are given as early as age four. Halpern (1953) states that explosion and fire responses are numerous in children four-and-one-half to six or even eight years. These responses reflect pent-up, aggressive impulses and frustration in the struggle to win approval from authority via compliance. Although inanimate-movement (m) responses are typical at this age, animal-movement responses begin to be given as the child moves toward feelings of oneness with animals rather than the world in general. Occasionally, the child gives human movement responses at this period. The number of M responses (other than the m) given as the child approaches age six indicate the extent to which he is becoming differentiated as an individual. In the years between six and ten AM responses are more numerous than is any other movement response. In the child, AM responses are expected and accurately reflect his inner feelings. He expresses his dreams and conflicts through this kind of fantasy. In the adult predominant use of AM may reveal partial repression of those impulses which he cannot ascribe to himself. Because of this repression he is also unable to project these impulses to human percepts.

Levi and Kraemer (1952) studied the Rorschach records of children ages four to ten who had been seen in a guidance center. They found that only a small number of them produced a significantly higher number of human-movement responses than would normally be expected. Those who did had common behavioral characteristics: temper tantrums, attention-getting acts, difficulty in learning, and creating classroom disturbances. The evidence indicates the presence of depression and sexual traumas. These children experienced the effects of conscious or unconscious partial or marked rejection by one or both parents as well as marked overprotection by the mother who may have been the (unconsciously) rejecting parent. These parents cannot accept childish modes of behavior and force the child to act in a mature manner before he has developed the emotional resources to do so. The authors hypothesize that forced curtailment of physical activities appropriate to the age results in a regression to temper tantrum behavior and other emotionally inappropriate behavior. They also speculate that the disproportionate number of human-movement responses (over animal-movement responses) reveals a possible defense aiding repression. Emotional outbursts are probably the mode of releasing the energy damned up by the repressive defenses. Halpern (1953) states that an excessive number of human-movement responses in the child under age six indicate that the child has an apparent need to try out many different roles. She suggests that the child may never have found emotional support and therefore may be seeking a role which pleases the people in his environment. Some schizophrenic children are overly concerned with adult reactions, and the large number of human-movement responses in their records suggests an attempt at becoming a person. The content of the human-movement responses of such children has, however, an artificial and forced quality (Halpern, 1961).

In the prepuberty period (beginning about age ten) and during the early puberty stage, a drastic and important change occurs as the child begins to perceive himself in a different way. He is suddenly interested in the opposite sex but afraid to show that interest. He is seeking to know who and what he is, and there is a tendency to withdraw from his old peer group. During this period, human-movement responses increase and at least equal animal-movement responses. During early adolescence, there should be fewer animal- than human-movement responses (Halpern, 1953).

In the preadolescent child (after age ten) failure to give HM suggests deviation in personality development. The kind of deviation can be determined by studying the entire record. If intelligence and emotional control are good (or even exaggerated), failure to internalize feelings may stem from fear of the individual's own fantasy activity. He may repulse fantasy while developing exaggerated pseudoconforming behavior patterns in response to the environment. When controls are absent and emotional responses reveal impulsivity and infantile judgment, the subject is probably suffering from a general lag in personality development due either to mental retardation or to emotional distortion.

RESEARCH. Clark, Veldman, and Thorpe (1965), in a study of the convergent and divergent thinking ability of talented adolescents, found a positive correlation between divergent thinking and the movement, anxiety, and hostility scores on the HIT. The results indicate a tendency for subjects high in divergent thinking to be freer in imaginative production (when given the opportunity to do so) than are those low in divergent thinking. Highly divergent subjects also had adequate form-definite and form-appropriate scores. Individuals characterized by divergent thinking are mature in their ideational and perceptual processes. These subjects have adequate controls but are not conventional. Their fantasy production is free and active but not pathological and they have significantly greater verbal facility than do the convergent thinkers.

Megargee (1965), using the HIT, compared the performance of seventy-five juvenile-delinquent males (mean age 15.5 years) awaiting court hearing with the HIT nondelinquent sample. The scores of the delinquents reflect immaturity and are similar to scores of the normal seventh grade HIT sample. The mean scores for movement, form appropriateness, form definiteness, integration, human, and pathognomic verbalization were low. M scores were similar to those of the younger age groups, reflecting the immaturity evident in the level of overt behavior of the delinquents. General immaturity such as is reflected in these inkblot scores seems to be a good indicator of the potential for delinquency.

Low scores in M, L, FD, I, and FA indicate that the subject is making little effort to reconcile the responses to the blot stimuli. This lack of concern for accuracy is a typical pattern of underachievement and is found in the juvenile delinquent. Megargee quotes Klopfer, Ainsworth, Klopfer, and Holt (1954), who argue that high use of the whole blot area in the Rorschach with few human-movement scores and low form level reflect either general interference in the use of intelligence or low intellectual capacity. In either case, the subject's efforts to gain an integrated view of the world are ineffectual, and a gap exists between the level of aspiration and the ability to achieve. Another explanation for under-achievement on the HIT is guardedness. The subjects of Megargee's study knew that the psychological examination would influence their cases. Therefore they guarded their responses. The result was minimal, tersely worded percepts to the threatening, unfamiliar blots.

Conners (1965) conducted a study with children considered restless who exhibit conduct disorders. Some were treated with dextroamphetamine, others with a placebo. Those treated with the drug show a significant increase in Factor 1 responses. (M is included in Factor 1.)

Swartz (1965), using the HIT, reports that children with high test anxiety produce significantly fewer movement and pathognomic verbalization responses and more rejections and affect-arousal responses than do normal children. Richter and Winter (1966) found a relationship between HIT scores and scores on the intuitive-perceptive scales of the Myers-Briggs Type Indicator. Women high in the type of creativity measured by the intuitive-perceptive scales have significantly higher movement, human, form-definiteness, color, integration, pathognomic-verbalization, anxiety, hostility, and abstract scores than do those with low scores on these scales. This finding supports the HIT as a measure of creative potential. Mueller and Abeles (1964) found a correlation of .44 between the M score on the HIT and the judged degree of empathy in the subject.

Megargee (1966), in a comparison of the HIT records of seventy-five male juvenile delinquents awaiting court order with a sample of eighty-four college students, found that the length of the response correlates significantly with the number of HIT categories used. Length of response is also positively related to the M score. Megargee speculated that the response length may be a mechanism through which personality is reflected in the inkblot score. For example, one of the most stable relationships between inkblot perception and personality is the relationship between M scores and intellectual ability. Altus and Thompson (1949) state that intelligent individuals tend to give more M responses because they are more verbal. Verbal facility is related to the length of the response. Therefore intellectual individuals should produce more M responses. Based on these assumptions, length of response could be considered an intervening variable. Megargee (1966) believes that variability in response length may be a function of the examiner. A warm, unhurried approach results in longer responses than does a cold, peremptory manner. Because of the relationship between length of response and M, the number of M responses may also be a function of the examiner.

Megargee and Swartz (1968) studied the relationship between scores on the extraversion and neuroticism scales of the Maudsley Personality Inventory (MPI) and HIT variables. The extraversion scale of the MPI and scores on the HIT did not correlate at all. High scores on the neuroticism scale, however, correlated positively with movement, pathognomic-verbalization, anxiety, and hostility scores and negatively with rejection and form-appropriateness scores on the HIT. The positive correlation with M is consistent with expectations for the individual who is turned in upon himself. The principal loading of the neuroticism scale (.49) was on HIT Factor 3, which reflects disordered thought processes and emotional disturbance (Holtzman, Thorpe, Swartz, and Herron, 1961). This finding can also be viewed as further evidence of the construct validity of the MPI neuroticism scale.

Integration (I)

The integration score assists in determining the intellectual efficiency at which the individual functions. It expresses his ability to integrate various areas of the blot in order to provide a good percept. The integration score is 0 if the percept is either inappropriate to the blot or pathognomic. Therefore an I score indicates at least a fair response. It indicates the subject's ability to analyze material into its component parts, determine relationships among them, and integrate them into a final percept. The higher the I score, the greater is the subject's ability to perform work requiring difficult and complex intellectual effort. High I scores reveal persons who are capable of relatively high mental functioning and have effective drive states. These persons are capable of realistic and logical thinking and the complex cognitive organization necessary to use fantasy. They are more open to experiences than are people who are concrete and restricted in their thinking (Codkind, 1964). Richter and Winter (1966) found a positive correlation between creativity and I scores in women. Holtzman, Gorham, and Moran (1964) found low but significant correlations between the Wechsler-Belleview Vocabulary Score and integration, movement, and form appropriateness in ninety-nine chronic paranoid schizophrenic males.

INTEGRATION BELOW THE FIFTH PERCENTILE. Few or no I scores indicate poor ability to organize and use intellect. Subjects with I scores below the fifth percentile show little interest in seeking relationships between different aspects of experience. Low I scores reveal both the organically limited and the immature individual. In a study of the HIT responses of juvenile delinquents (average age 15.5 years) I scores were low and similar to those of seventh graders. These low scores reflect immaturity—the same immaturity observable in the overt behavior of these individuals which led to their confinement (Megargee, 1965).

INTEGRATION ABOVE THE NINETY-NINTH PERCENTILE. Scores this high may reflect an affective push of ideas if impairment in the overall quality of the percept and vague abstractions are also present. FA may be in the average range and pathology may not be evident in the verbalization.

DEVELOPMENTAL TRENDS. Thorpe and Swartz (1965) found a regular increase in the number of I scores with increasing age from five to twenty years. Holtzman, Thorpe, Swartz, and Herron (1961), in their standardization populations, found that five-year olds, chronic schizophrenics, and mental retardates obtain extremely low I scores, and nearly 50 per cent have no I score at all. Scores comparable to those of the five-year olds were found among emotionally disturbed ten-year olds. College students have significantly higher I scores than has any other group. The college-age group is also the only normal group in which I scores are normally distributed (the mean score is 11.1 compared with 4.8 for other average adults).

Popular (P)

People who are able to give P responses are usually conventional and in good contact with reality. They are aware of the values of society and are able to assume at least a surface propriety. Even persons of superior intelligence obtain high P scores, despite the overall creativeness of their responses. They are persons who recognize conventional requirements of groups and are often the ones who set group standards (Beck, 1952). Bohm (1958) believes that high scores in popular reveal the ability to understand and be understood by the man on the street.

POPULAR BELOW THE FIFTH PERCENTILE. Persons who give no populars (or very few) are frequently detached from the influences of practical societal demands. Schizophrenics, particularly those who are autistic, often give few or no P responses, reflecting their weak ties to reality. The L and FA scores of these schizophrenics are also low. When L and FA scores are at least within the average range, the loss of reality contact indicated by low P scores is contraindicated. Few popular responses are found in the records of some adult neurotics. Such records indicate conscious rebellion. Anxious persons are sometimes overwhelmed by the inkblot task; their total responsiveness including populars is arrested (Beck, 1952).

Children are not expected to share adult attitudes and reactions and are limited participants in the community. However, a low number of popular responses (or none at all) suggests little or no ability to participate in the adult world. The child may not be developing as might be expected. The slow development may be attributable to limited intelligence or to avoidance of adult experiences because of emotional, social, or interpersonal difficulties.

POPULAR ABOVE THE NINETY-NINTH PERCENTILE. A very large number of P responses reflect guardedness and conformity. Other factors in the record indicate the extent of the conformity. Beck (1952) reports that some homosexuals give numerous popular responses. He interprets this behavior as an attempt to cover up their nonconventional sexuality by overconventionality in other areas. Bohm (1958) identifies two personality types who score high in popular responses. If an individual scores high in P and low in A and FD, he is probably a ruminative, uninteresting bore. If, however, he scores high in FD and P and low in A, he may play an important role in public life, displaying political talent or journalistic skill. People in these occupations are required to produce ideas of their own and must also be able to understand and appreciate the interests and points of view of the common man. The ability to identify with people (high P score) and the capacity for ideational creativity (high FD score) are useful in those occupations.

Abnormally high numbers of P responses given by children suggest an approach to the environment which is different from that of most other children. Often, these children with high P scores are able to participate better with adults than with peers. Halpern (1953) suggests that they are insecure and have an exaggerated need to conform to adult authority.

DEVELOPMENTAL TRENDS. Holtzman, Thorpe, Swartz, and Herron (1961) found P responses fairly normally distributed with a standard deviation of about 3 for all groups. Among the normative samples, the highest P scores are obtained by college students and the lowest by five-year olds, first graders, chronic schizophrenics, mental retardates, emotionally disturbed children, and emotionally disturbed adolescents. Neurotic and alcoholic subjects score lower on P than do average adults and depressives. These findings are consistent with those of earlier Rorschach studies.

RESEARCH. Megargee (1969), in a comparison of the HIT scores of Negro and white juvenile delinquents, found that the white subjects scored higher on P.

Barrier (Br)

The barrier concept defines the degree of definiteness of the body-image boundary. It reveals the basic feelings that a person has about himself as an entity separate from his environment. Thus, it indicates how he experiences his body and organizes his perceptions about it as a frame of reference in making judgments. Level of maturity and tolerance of stress are personality variables associated with the body image. In certain respects the body image and such dynamic qualities as the ego, the self, and the self-concept overlap (Fisher and Cleveland, 1958).

The body-image boundary demarcates a space in the perceptual field which is identified with the sense of individuality that a person possesses. The body-image boundary grows out of the organization of his internalized self and is therefore determined by forces from within more than from actual characteristics of his body. It does not always mirror the body surface but represents attitudes and others' expectations which have been projected onto the body periphery.

BARRIER BELOW THE FIFTH PERCENTILE. Research findings show a relationship between very low Br scores and persons who are passive, low in achievement orientation, and low in goal-direction (Cleveland and Morton, 1962; Megargee, 1965; Fisher and Renik, 1966; Fisher, 1968). The absence of well-defined body-image boundaries indicates minimum internal stability to tolerate stress. In new situations these persons are likely to create external conditions which artificially provide substitute barriers. For example, in small groups they attempt to structure the situation so that one individual takes the lead and relieves everyone else of responsibility, or they try to define relationships within a group in order to stabilize the demands that can be made on them. Under stress, they tend to react internally (for instance they may experience increased heart action). If they become physically ill, their symptoms are also likely to be internal, such as duodenal ulcer or colitis.

Individuals with poor body-image boundaries are believed to come from settings which create insecurity and frustration. If parents are threatening, destructive, and disrupting, and serve as poor models, the home setting promotes fear and the expectation of being hurt by the parents. Lack of a positive parental relationship prevents establishment of realistic body boundaries, and individuality is blocked. If these conditions exist during adolescence, the individual suffers confusion and uncertainty regarding sex roles, identity, life goals, proper modes of behavior, and a general philosophy of life. Normative data show that low Br scores are typical of mental retardates, emotionally disturbed children, and five-year olds.

BARRIER ABOVE THE NINETY-NINTH PERCENTILE. High Br scores suggest excessive self-protection from the impact of threatening situations. This guardedness may act against the person's best interests because he sets up controls in relationships with others in order to avoid interference with his person.

Hammerschlag, Fisher, DeCosse, and Kaplan (1965) used the HIT to determine why some women delay seeking confirmation of breast cancer symptoms. They found significantly higher Br scores for women who delayed seeking help than for those who sought help early. The study made use of twenty-five of the forty-five blots, and the mean Br score was 5.3 for a group of fifteen subjects used in a preliminary review. The prorated mean score for the forty-five blots places this group above the ninetieth percentile. The authors suggest that women who delay seeking help are less threatened by their symptoms than are women who seek help early. The women who delay also have difficulty in being submissive and subordinating themselves to physicians. These women may possibly also prefer to protect themselves against the threat of knowing that their symptoms are cancer.

Normative HIT data show that neurotic and alcoholic populations are among the three groups with the highest mean Br scores. Persons in these categories set up controls in order to shut out external threats. These controls act against their best interests. The other group with very high mean Br scores is the elementary-school sample. These children tend to be more inhibited than five-year olds. They have longer RT, higher L scores (use of more small blot areas), and higher Sh and M scores. They try to exclude threatening stimuli at an age when they are trying to incorporate external values. They are among the highest scorers in the normal population on anxiety and hostility.

DEVELOPMENTAL TRENDS. Holtzman, Thorpe, Swartz, and Herron (1961) found the distribution of Br scores only slightly skewed except for five-year olds, chronic schizophrenics, and mental retardates. In these three groups, as well as among emotionally disturbed children, the mean score is considerably lower than it is for all other groups. The variability in Br scores is greatest for elementary-school children and depressed patients. The mean scores for elementary-school students, neurotics, alcoholics, emotionally disturbed adolescents, and college students are significantly higher than they are for any of the other groups. Normal adolescents have a lower mean Br score than that of other normal groups. The adolescent is under the pressure of physiological changes that take place at puberty and is also undergoing a conflict between ego identity and ego diffusion (Erikson, 1950). The individual who has difficulty establishing his ego identity continues to experiment with various roles; the greater the degree of ego diffusion the more he clings to these experimental roles. Ego diffusion is associated with problems of the changing body image. Therefore a low Br score is expected for the adolescent group.

The lower Br scores for five year olds and emotionally disturbed children will be better understood from a viewpoint of the development of the body image. Body image is molded by interactions with others. If these interactions are faulty, the body image will be inadequately developed (Schilder, 1942). Adequate development of the body image must be consistent with reality. The development of the body image (or self-concept) requires viewing the self as an object apart from the world. When the child is very young, he has only a vague perception of himself. As experiences increase, self-perception becomes increasingly clear and strong. The self-concept evolves from experiences with significant persons. These experiences determine his ability to accept or reject himself or to see himself as weak or strong, capable or inadequate.

In crystalizing behavior patterns, the child naturally strives to follow those patterns which he believes will win approval and love. However, his responses are modified and altered by the nature of his feelings for significant persons in his environment and by his own needs and drives. His interactions from earliest childhood produce the ultimate pattern of the self, including the self-concept, the "set" regarding the self and the incorporation of parental values (Halpern, 1953). Early treatment of the infant determines the later self-concept. Emotions surrounding feeding (as reflected in the amount and nature of fondling) contribute to his perception of his effectiveness as a human being. The child thinks of himself as he believes others feel about him. Once he develops a concept of himself, he selects those aspects of his experiences which reenforce that concept. The happy child selects from the reactions of his parents those behaviors which signify cheerfulness, contentment, and goodwill. The child who sees himself as unloved creates situations to prove this and manipulates interpersonal relationships accordingly. The frustrated child selects patterns which reenforce his feelings of anxiety and aggression.

Holtzman, Thorpe, Swartz, and Herron (1961) found that schizophrenics who have a poor sense of body-boundary definiteness or poor ego identity have low Br scores. Cleveland (1960) found that most neurotics and schizophrenics have significantly lower Br scores than do normal subjects. Fisher and Cleveland (1958) also found low Br scores in schizophrenic populations. Fisher (1970) now states, however, that as a result of the study of multiple samples, the Br score does not consistently differentiate normals and schizophrenics, although some schizophrenics occasionally obtain lower Br scores than do normals.

Holtzman, Thorpe, Swartz, and Herron (1961) found lower Br scores in depressed patients than in normal populations. These scores probably do not relate primarily to ego identity, however, because the depressed patient has higher Br scores than do both the adolescent and the schizophrenic populations. Cleveland and Fisher (1960) found that the improvement which patients experience following psychotherapy is concomitant with an increase in the Br score (and a decrease in the penetration score).

RESEARCH. Barrier is useful as a *measure of behavior*. Cleveland and Morton (1962) believe that an individual who is confident of his body boundaries relates to others differently from one who is uncertain of the border separating him from others and from the outside world. In a study using delegates to a human relations training laboratory, Cleveland and Morton compared Br scores with various sociometric nomination data and found that members who score high in Br receive significantly more nominations as being able to function independently of authority figures than do those who score low in Br. They also behave in a more democratic manner in group deliberations and are more accepted than those scoring low on Br. The latter are the least influential group members and are reliant on external authority for guidance and support. The authors repeated this study using a psychiatric population and again found that those who score high on Br have the highest nominations as being the most influential group members. They did more to keep the group active, goal directed, and independent of external leaders than did those who scored low in Br. The authors concluded that persons who score high in Br are less influenced by their peers in decision-making than are those who score low. Such persons are also perceived by their peers as being influential in persuading others to change their opinions. These findings are consistent with those concerning the body-image concept. When an individual has established and defined objectives and goals, he experiences little threat in relating to others. Having his own internal system of guides and values, he relies little on external cues or aids for leadership to attain his goals or make decisons. However, if the internalized image is obscure and uncertain, the individual is likely to look for guidelines and leadership outside himself and to seek cues in his decision-making.

Barrier is useful as a *measure of tolerance of stress*. Fisher and Cleveland (1958) found that college students with the best-developed sense of ego identity have the highest Br scores and are independent enough to be capable of expressing anger openly in a frustrating experimental situation. Asserting one's self appropriately is an adaptive trait, and expressing anger at a frustrating experiment is an appropriate reaction requiring good ego identity. Megargee (1965), in his study of juvenile delinquents (whose behavior generally reflects lack of tolerance for stress), found that their Br scores are significantly lower than the HIT norms for populations of lower ages (seventh graders). Within this sample (mean age 15.5 years), he found that the more seriously delinquent subgroup had significantly lower mean Br scores than did the less seriously delinquent subgroup. The low-scoring group is more aggressive and impulsive and their behavior is more maladaptive than is the behavior of the higher scoring group.

Barrier is a *measure of body focus*. Individuals with a definite sense of body boundaries appear to be more aware of the exterior of the body than of interior body sensations. Fisher and Renik (1966) found that individuals with high Br scores experience more skin and muscle sensations than do those with low Br scores (who experience internal heart-and-stomach sensations). In a study of normal female subjects, using the HIT as one measure, they found that subjects who were directed to focus their attention on external body-boundary areas increased their Br scores significantly compared with subjects who were asked to focus their attention on interior body regions or those who were given no direction of focus. The interior-focus group tended to decrease their Br scores although not significantly.

Body sensation plays an important role in shaping projected imagery. In 1968 Fisher and Renik repeated their experiment using male subjects and found that men whose attention was directed toward the external aspects of their bodies increased their Br scores (compared with subjects directed toward internal aspects of their bodies). Those whose attentions were directed toward the internal aspects of their bodies decreased their Br scores. The researchers found that when focusing on the interior of the body, males showed a greater decrease in Br scores than did females.

Fisher (1965b) suggests that individuals who are more aware of external body areas, such as skin and muscle, behave more autonomously and self-assertively than do those who are more aware of internal body areas. Fisher and Cleveland (1958) found in both males and females that the more predominant the body-boundary concept (identified by a high Br score), the less acquiescent is the subject.

Barrier is a *measure of self-awareness* as judged by the clarity with which a person defines himself. The Br score is believed to reflect the ability to communicate with the self and with others. It is also believed to define the consistency and definiteness of internalized goals and values. Fisher (1964), judging behavioral patterns in an interview situation, found that subjects with high Br scores are better able to communicate with others than are those subjects with low Br scores. Ramer (1963) found that females with definite body boundaries are autonomous, which facilitates their ability to relate closely to others and adapt to stress. Fisher (1963) found that persons with high Br scores are interpersonally active and restless. In a later study (1968) he found that an increase in the Br score was correlated with increased interest in communication and a readiness to invest energy in perceptual receptivity. Perceptual vividness allows the perceiver to experience the world as lively, stimulating, and interesting. Persons scoring high on Br find the world exciting, provocative, and demanding of self-investment.

R. Fisher (1968), in a study of the body-image boundary in relation to the affective behavior of boys in a classroom situation, found that the Br score could predict classroom behavior. Those who score high in Br are more effective, mature, and controlled in the classroom setting than those who score low in Br. These results verify the association of the body-image boundary with achievement drive and goal-determining self-steering behavior. Swartz (1965) found that children with high anxiety have lower Br scores than do those children with low anxiety. R. Fisher (1968), studying body-image boundary and achievement behavior in elementary school, found that students with high Br scores were achievement oriented. Fisher and Cleveland (1958) found that persons with high Br scores are more resistant to suggestion and better able to recall a large number of incompleted tasks than are persons who score low on Br. They also found that boys scoring high in Br have greater achievement motivation than do those scoring low on Br and that academic performance is positively correlated with scores for both sexes.

The high Br scorers are in direct contact with reality, and experience the world in a vivid way. Body boundaries are definite, and clearly set these individuals apart from the environment. High Br scorers value things associated with success. Researchers speculate that the parents of these persons provided good models with definite value standards and ways of doing things. The parents, especially the mother, are expected to have been well adjusted and flexible. The person who scores high on Br carries a protective screen and is moderately impervious to the impact of threatening situations. He does much better than the low Br subject under stress. Physiological responses to stress are likely to be in the periphery of his body (in the skin and muscles). Somatic symptoms, if they do develop, are expected to be neurodermatitis or rheumatoid arthritis (Fisher and Cleveland, 1958). Cleveland and Fisher (1960) found that arthritic patients have higher Br scores than do ulcer patients.

The variables in this chapter reflect how the individual organizes ideas. They reflect both directed and associative thinking and indicate the role of personal drives and desires as compared with the demands of external reality. They show the availability of complex intellectual effort and of creative resources.

Content

VIII

The relative importance of content to inkblot interpretation has been a source of controversy for many years. Some clinicians believe that the formal aspects of the response, the determinants, are of primary importance for interpretation. Others all but ignore these aspects and base their interpretation primarily on the content of the response. Fortunately we do not have to take sides in this controversy since a third group of clinicians assigns importance to both. I feel that the record is inevitably more meaningful using both the formal aspects and the content in interpreting protocols.

From clinical experience with the HIT, I find that the content of the response is as important as the sensory perceptual elements of the blot because the subject does not operate independent of his environment. Content variables reflect how the individual relates to external reality, what kind of social interactions he has, how he perceives his psychological and physiological self, and the nature of his impulse drives. The content also suggests the scope and nature of the subject's interests. Age, sex, cultural background, and the pressure of pathology are known to influence responses. The variety of the content increases with age and with experience. Very young children cannot conceptualize present happenings and have few ways of expressing their experiences except through motor activity. They are concrete in their thinking and their narrow range of interests results in gross discriminations. Halpern (1953) states that for these reasons the response content of very young children (between age two and one-half and age four) is limited (on the average) to one or two categories and that more than three or four categories is unusual. As the child grows older, accumulates experience, and gains an accurate perception of reality, his content categories increase commensurate with his increased power to verbalize and discriminate.

Content is frequently used to measure the subject's degree of involvement with the inkblot task. Involvement can range from a minimal, matter-of-fact interaction (typified by only popular or stereotyped responses) to responses which are highly idiosyncratic and include affective components. The level of involvement reflects the interaction effect between the subject and the examiner. Involvement level is a reliable cue in assessing whether personality facets are being revealed and whether the content is typical of the person's response pattern. Unusual or unique content is specific to the subject and reveals his personal psychological needs better than does the usual stereotyped content. The repetition of content in a number of responses may reveal deep anxiety or conflict concerning the material revealed.

When the response content is very limited, inner resources are also few. The individual may focus on a particular topic, for instance, animal. Occasionally (but rarely) the entire record deals with a single content. When such fixations occur, the subject appears to be shutting out normal diverse interests and perseverating on a single theme. Perseveration may be the result of limited native endowment, brain damage, or emotional disturbance. When the cause is emotional dysfunction, the individual is hampered in the free use of his intellectual faculties because of psychological defenses. These defenses inhibit his ability to act independently and to take initiative in reaching out for what is new or different. If the person is sufficiently disordered, the dominating theme may be the clue to possible delusional ideas or hallucinatory percepts. In the relatively intact individual, neurotic defenses serve as a protection, offering withdrawal into a safe circumscribed area.

At the other extreme, the subject may verbalize so wide a variety of content that the ideas show no connection to one another. Rapid changes in theme reveal emotional pressures. The more unique the themes, the more we can assume that the individual is withdrawing into a private world, making autistic solutions to problems, and expressing bizarre or personal (including paranoid) thinking. Strong feelings which beset the individual appear to be breaking through (Beck, 1952).

The interpretation of content is presented for the variables human, animal, anatomy, sex, and abstract. Other content categories which appear more than occasionally are also considered. In this chapter I also discuss sequence analysis of the content. The stimulus values of selected Form A blots are identified by content.

Human (H)

Studies (both HIT and Rorschach) indicate that persons giving H responses have a capacity for warm, empathic relationships and are interested in and sensitive to the feelings of others (Rapaport, 1946; Phillips and Smith, 1953; Piotrowski, 1957; Holtzman, Thorpe, Swartz, and Herron, 1961; Fernald and

Linden, 1966). Thus, the number and type of human responses indicate the subject's degree of interest in other people and the extent to which the subject is able to relate. Rorschach research indicates that H responses measure social maturation and differentiate between those who maintain reality-oriented social contacts and those who tend to retreat into self-blame, inactivity, and fantasy (Haley, Draguns, and Phillips, 1967). Megargee (1965) found that juvenile delinquents have significantly low mean H scores.

The subject's capability for social contact can be evaluated by the extent of involvement revealed in the human content. The response, for instance, may merely identify people in the percept, or it may contain many adjectives, actions, or events which describe them. The degree to which an individual can perceive relationships with people is also derived from the total number of H responses.

Human responses are of three varieties: H 2, and two kinds of H 1. The H 2 response includes the whole person (masculine, feminine, or not specified). The H 1 response includes less than the whole person. The subject may report the head, the face, or the body (torso) of a human. The third H response (also scored H 1) includes caricatures of humans such as fairies, angels, monsters, witches, giants, and statues.

The type of human response reveals the potential for interpersonal involvement and the availability of intellectual resources. Murstein (1965), using the Rorschach, found that members of professions in which a high degree of social interaction is required give a large number of H 2 responses. H 2 responses in the records of persons with pathology indicate the maintenance of reality orientation in social contacts. A more favorable prognosis can be made for them than for those with psychopathology who are unable to give H 2 responses. The ability to give H 2 responses is considerd typical of persons of high intelligence and with good socioeconomic backgrounds (Beck, 1952; Bohm, 1958). Such persons give significantly more H 2 than H 1 responses. The subject's elaboration and the particular variety of content also reflect the breadth and scope of the individual's intelligence and background. When the number of H 1 responses exceeds the H 2 responses, the subject is operating at a lower level of intelligence than if the ratio were reversed. This constriction may be due to lack of capacity, inhibition of intelligence, depression, or anxiety. The greater the number of H 1 over H 2 responses, the more internal constriction is present.

HUMAN BELOW THE FIFTH PERCENTILE. Few or no H responses indicates a lack of interest in other people. This disinterest is frequently caused by hostility which leads to an intellectual aversion for people. Failure to report H percepts may also indicate lack of conscious control over feelings and impulses in persons who are narcissistic and tend to have little interest in the motivation of others. The lowest mean H scores in the normative samples are found among mental retardates and chronic schizophrenics. One out of every seven of these subjects fails to give even a single H response.

HUMAN ABOVE THE NINETY-NINTH PERCENTILE. When the number of H responses is high, interpersonal relationships may be threatening. An overemphasis on human figures indicates preoccupation with the behavior of humans and may reveal a fear of people and their intentions (depending on the content). If the latter is apparent, caution and wariness in relating to people are expected. This interpretation gains weight if several of the human responses are H 1.

H 1 (HUMAN DETAIL) RESPONSES. A head or a face is the most frequent H 1 response. Persons who are preoccupied with this response tend to deal with external persona qualities in relationships. When the subject defines only the body detail, he may have difficulty in intellectual areas and prefer to relate on a primitive, biological level. Persons who give more H 1 responses than H 2 responses experience more anxiety than do those who give more H 2 responses than H 1 responses (Bohm, 1958).

H 1 (OTHER) RESPONSES. Caricatures of humans reflect a variety of symptoms from hostility to depersonalization, depending upon the total ego structure as derived from the entire record (Zubin, Eron, and Schumer, 1965). Psychologists believe that when the subject reports mythical persons or statues in the percept he is not identifying closely with the actions and behaviors reported. He is pushing the fantasy away from his conscious awareness. Halpern (1963) states that children normally identify with the supernatural. By doing so, the child is exercising infinite power and retaliating for wrongs done to him and others. Through symbolic persons he creates roles which reflect his attitudes and feelings toward the world. The roles also reflect the degree of hostility that his frustrations have produced. Responses such as ghosts, dwarfs, giants, angels, and witches are expected to increase up to age ten, but such content should disappear at least by adolescence. A continuation of such responses after puberty shows a poor grasp on reality, a wishful immaturity, and possibly a continuation of superstitious beliefs. Persistence of this omnipotent type of response reveals maladjustment. The individual is believed to be still preoccupied with childhood imagery and rejects acceptance of an adult nurturant role for himself (Beck, 1952).

HUMAN RESPONSES RELATING TO SPECIFIC MODES OF ADJUSTMENT. Brecker (1956) found that a sample of maternally overprotected male schizophrenics gave more female human responses in their Rorschach records than did those with a history of maternal rejection. Shafer (1954) suggests that both males and females with sexual identity problems who fear or reject the conflict over their tendency to identify with the opposite sex frequently give H responses in which the sexual characteristics are either blurred or reversed. Males with a fearful conception of the male role tend to place phallic-aggressive emphasis in the content of their H responses. The content of their H responses may be symbolic of disparagement and castration feelings. Such feelings are reflected in responses such as dwarfs, gremlins, or little men. Similar responses by adult females with identity problems refer to flat-chested females, women gossiping, and so on. Frequent reference by a male subject to small, incomplete male figures (a castration theme) suggests anxiety and weakness with a regressive self-image and orientation. Such references given by a female suggest a competitive, disparaging attitude toward males. These females may also be viewed as revealing a counterphobic defense—a denial of anxiety coupled with a regressive self-image and orientation. Females who are not counterphobic are usually able to express their anxiety directly in conflict themes including females.

Halpern (1953) found that human responses including twins or Siamese twins are given more often by schizophrenics than by any other groups. The twin response reflects feelings of being more than one person, of being unable to integrate aspects of the self because they are bound together in a handicapping way. Halpern (1953) believes that an emphasis on numbers (for example, *two* people) reflects a need for balance. It reveals a quasi-ritualistic approach to life. When these responses are given frequently by children, they may indicate uncertainty, insecurity, and anxiety, even though children are inclined to be ritualistic.

H responses with no reference to sex (such as people or persons) are frequently found in the records of individuals who perceive social interactions vaguely. These persons deal with the superficial aspects of relationships without becoming physically or socially involved. They tend to be more self-oriented than other-oriented.

DEVELOPMENTAL TRENDS. The number of H responses increases with age and intelligence. Holtzman, Thorpe, Swartz, and Herron (1961) report that the lowest mean H scores among the normal samples are obtained by five year olds. College students give the greatest number of H responses. Their mean score is at least ten points higher than that of average adults or children.

H responses normally begin to appear about age four as the child is increasing his discriminative ability, vocabulary, and experiences (Halpern, 1953). Normal eleventh graders give considerably more H responses than do other normal groups (except the college population), and their H scores are similar to those of emotionally disturbed adolescents. During the adolescent developmental period, the individual reworks his self-image and is concerned with the attitude of others toward him. The adolescent is also becoming socialized and other-oriented. The typical uncertainty and ambivalence in interpersonal relationships accounts for the high H content in the records of both the normal adolescent and the emotionally disturbed adolescent. The emotionally disturbed group, however, has significantly higher scores in anxiety, hostility, penetration, and pathognomic verbalization than does the normal adolescent group. Average adults and depressed patients do not differ in the number of H responses. These findings are substantially in agreement with those reported in Rorschach literature. Neurotics and alcoholics, who have difficulty in their relationships with others, give more H responses than average adults, showing their concern with humans.

The age and population to which the person belongs is relevant in examining human content responses. Shafer (1954) gives as an example the response "a gigantic threatening figure." For an eighteen year old, this response reflects a feeling of smallness, weakness, and vulnerability. He sees others as big, violent, strong, and overwhelming in contrast to himself. In late adolescence the individual is striving for independence from parental bonds but may still be required to submit to authority figures. The same response given by a person of forty who has a background of meeting occupational, community and family demands and who is a driving, successful, and compulsive individual reveals current anxiety and depression. The response indicates that his needs are alien to the way he sees himself or are breaking through a reaction formation and other defenses and stirring up internal distress.

RESEARCH. Fernald and Linden (1966) tested four hypotheses concerning the meaning of H responses in the HIT. They predicted that the number of H responses varies directly with social interest and empathy and varies inversely with social isolation and functional pathology. The subjects used to test pathology were a group of hospitalized patients and a normal control group of firemen. The other hypotheses were tested on an upper socioeconomic level college population. Social interest and functional pathology are related to H responses as predicted. Lack of significance of the other two hypotheses is attributed to the homogeneity of the subject population and needs further sampling. Empathy and social isolation may prove to be related to the H response in later studies.

Megargee (1965) found below average mean H scores (as well as low form appropriateness, form definiteness, integration, movement, and pathognomic verbalization scores) on the HIT protocols of a group of seventy-five male juvenile delinquents (average age 15.5). These scores are comparable to those of the seventh-grade standardization population. The overt immature behavior which led to the confinement of the juvenile delinquents reinforces the hypothesis that low H scores reflect immaturity.

Animal (A)

Animal responses reflect the degree of effectiveness with which a person can utilize intellectual resources spontaneously. The absence of both A and H responses reveals stereotyped thinking, which may also be predicted from records in which the A responses are virtually the only content of the percept. In such instances, H responses are absent, and when color responses are given, they are C 2 rather than C 1. When A responses are absent and H responses predominate, the individual is intellectually introversive but not particularly overcontrolled. In this instance, C 1 responses are expected when color is used. Stereotyped thinking has many different causes. It may be due to lack of intelligence, intellectual inertia, or conventionality. Intellectual inertia may be caused by emotional disturbances such as depression in mood, anxiety, or schizophrenia. It may result from organic deterioration both in young persons and in the very old. It may also reveal a conscious effort at response control. Ames, Learned, Metraux, and

Walker (1952) report that studies of senile subjects from seventy to ninety years show almost one hundred per cent use of A in responses to the Rorschach. Responses are seldom more specific than "animal." Such responses may be attributable to intellectual inertia caused by associative difficulties or to organic deterioration. Herron (1964) administered the HIT to college students both in the standard manner and as a "test of intelligence." The only constriction of response when given as a "test of intelligence," was a decrease in A, Pn, Hs, and V content.

Haley, Draguns, and Phillips (1967) see only indirect relevance between the number of A responses and a determination of pathology or intellectual level. The immediate value of the number of A responses is as an indicator of the subject's outlook toward the world. A responses reflect the way he uses his intelligence and other resources and reveals the defense mechanisms he employs.

Animal responses, like human responses, are of three varieties. The A 2 response includes the whole animal. The A 1 response includes less than the whole animal. The other A 1 response includes the animal as a mythical or anthropomorphic cartoon figure or an insect. When the number of A 1 responses exceeds the number of A 2 responses, the subject is expected to show signs of inhibition either in cognitive functioning or in the expression of affect. This ratio may also indicate a critical attitude revealing inner tensions. Haley, Draguns, and Phillips (1967) report that a great number of A 1 responses are given by maladjusted children and other groups who are either socially handicapped or internally tense, including normal adolescents and deaf mutes. Haley, Draguns, and Phillips also found significantly more A 1 responses among schizophrenic subjects than among normal subjects.

The ability to give A responses without having them dominate the content indicates flexibility in thinking. Before the examiner concludes that a subject possesses cognitive mobility, however, he should assess the record for other forms of stereotyped content which may be replacing a preponderance of A responses. For example, the record may have a preponderance of a particular response, such as, anatomy, flowers, or rocks. The subject may also demonstrate some vocational inflexibility, for example, a high number of anatomy or histology responses given by a medical student. In the absence of other indicators, however, A responses in the average range indicate an ability to synthesize and organize intellectual resources and to give adequate numbers of responses in various categories (Bohm, 1958).

ANIMAL BELOW THE FIFTH PERCENTILE. Few or no A responses implies pathologically lowered ego control or greater than normal preoccupation with original content. Unique thinking of this type tends to be nonadaptive and may indicate inadequacy in knowing environmental stimuli because of undue preoccupation with these original ideas (Beck, 1952). Beck found extremely low Rorschach A scores on the records of schizophrenics who are so original in their thinking that they have no equal. Their originality is an imbalance. When low A responses indicate adaptive regression, the themes of the responses show the regressed preoccupation and reveal the individual's needs (Haley, Draguns, and Phillips, 1967).

ANIMAL ABOVE THE NINETY-NINTH PERCENTILE. Animal responses above the ninety-ninth percentile reveal specific ego weaknesses. Such scores indicate a stereotyped approach to associations and a lack of spontaneity. The individual is not alert to events in the world around him and draws heavily on inner needs. He may be fearful of people and represses this fear by projecting his feelings onto animals. This practice leads to intellectual inertia and may have positive and negative implications. On the positive side, these persons react in a predictable fashion to the routine aspects of the environment because of their constriction and inflexibility. They lack impulsiveness. On the negative side, the high A scorer demonstrates resistance to change and a potential for confusion and disruption in situations that make more than average demands. Mental retardates have the highest mean A score, indicating the use of this variable by persons whose cognitive functioning is impaired.

ANIMAL CONTENT. Halpern (1953) states that children between the ages of five and eight tend to express aggression and identify with aggressive forces. During this period they try to appear strong and independent, and their use of aggressive animal content need not indicate destructive impulses. However, when aggressive animals are overemphasized and accompanied by a marked lack of control and judgment (as indicated by other variables such as hostility) the implications are negative, revealing the desire for destructive aggression or a need for self-assertion and independence.

The adolescent normally moves toward self-assertion and independence. Aggressive A responses given by this age group should therefore be evaluated with due consideration to the appropriate adolescent norms. As in the case of younger children, however, if the aggressive animal content is grossly emphasized (high animal and hostility scores) and if the adolescent gives evidence of marked lack of control and judgment, the implications are negative.

Phillips and Smith (1953) state that the animal percepts given by children under age ten are typically bee, cat, chicken, duck, horse, and rabbit. In adults, these responses are rare and reflect childish immaturity. After age eleven, A content becomes generic—fish, insect, animal—and includes such animals as bat, crab, and snake.

Goldfarb (1945) found that animal responses in children indicate their attitude toward adults, especially family members. Phillips and Smith (1953) support this finding. They state that large-animal content represents a child's attitude toward parents. Small-animal content represents the way in which the child sees himself or his siblings. Phillips and Smith found the same symbolic significance of animal content representing the intrafamilial constellation among adults. However, no significant relationship was found between small-animal content and self-representation in adults. As a result of empirical observation by these authors, a symbolic-content analysis yielded five main personality variables relating to specific animal content: (1) relationship to mother figure, (2) relationship to father figure, (3) immaturity, (4) hostility, (5) passivity.

(1) **Relationship to mother figure.** The A content cow and deer represent a mild, kind, easily led mother figure. Fish, scarab, and spider content reflect maternal overprotection. Spider also symbolizes active but unsuccessful striving for independence from a dominant, possessive mother as does octopus. Bug, crab, and jellyfish represent a rejecting, punitive, destructive mother figure, resulting in failure in social adjustments. When such content is emphasized, the individual has chronic expectations of rejection. He defends himself against such rejection with a cocky attitude which hides his deep-rooted nurture needs.

(2) **Relationship to father figure.** Unresolved relationships with a strong father (which are generalized to other authority figures) are symbolically expressed in such content as ape, bear, bison, buffalo, bull, eagle, gorilla, horse, and tiger. Those who see the father as threatening or potentially destructive symbolize this fear through the A content ape and gorilla. Gorilla content also implies derision and contempt for the father. Tiger content implies fear of being overpowered and destroyed. Eagle content implies suspicion, usually of a male figure. Bear suggests a benign and sympathetic father figure but one who is a benevolent despot.

(3) **Immaturity.** Immaturity without personality distortion (but reflecting inability to resolve current problems) is seen in the adult who gives responses such as cat, dragon, elephant, rabbit, or seahorse. In these responses, the focus is turned toward childhood, which in fantasy is deeply satisfying and nurturing.

Immaturity with inadequate personality development is revealed by A content such as bird, frog, bug, chicken, and crab. Records of psychopaths frequently include birds, frogs, and bugs. Frequent chicken responses suggest the love-starved individual with a history of rejection and affectional deprivation. Crab, fish, frog, and seahorse are commonly found in records of alcoholics and enuretics.

Bacteria, germs, bee, and fly responses are rare among normal subjects and suggest extensive regression implying pathology. Schizophrenics and severe hypochondriacs report bacteria and germs. Children, paranoids, and schizophrenic patients respond with bee and fly.

(4) **Hostility.** Persons with a negative attitude who are active and destructive give animal responses such as alligators, crocodiles, lizards, rats, foxes, and wolves. These persons are likely to have little compunction about using underhand means in achieving their goals. Those who report fox and wolf are also shrewd, hostile, and aggressive. Bug responses are often given by acting-out or assaultive individuals. Crab responses reveal underlying resentment and hostility.

(5) **Passivity.** Animal-response content such as jellyfish, moth, and rabbit implies weakness, feelings of inferiority and inadequacy, and lack of drive. Such responses indicate an extreme passivity which may be a defense against the expression of destructive impulses. Fish responses are given by passively inert,

clingingly dependent persons who relinquish their strivings for independence in the face of an overwhelmingly possessive mother figure. Bat responses (other than to a popular bat area) suggest painful morbid anticipation of unpleasantness. Butterfly responses imply a feminine attitude with feelings of well-being (Phillips and Smith, 1953).

The above five categories of interpretation are the result of studies with the Rorschach. Until comparable evidence is secured with HIT data they should be applied cautiously, especially when a particular animal response occurs infrequently.

ANTHROPOMORPHIC ANIMALS. This category includes the Disney-, cartoon-, and Alice in Wonderland-type animals. These A responses occur most often in the records of children. When they appear in adult records they may indicate infantile character identification or regression. They may also occur in the records of creative, intellectual persons. (The balance of the record should be consulted for the appropriate hypothesis.)

DEVELOPMENTAL TRENDS. Animal responses are numerous at all ages. They first appear in the very young child (about age four) as he becomes differentiated and feels a oneness with animals. Normative data show that A responses increase from age five and reach a peak in the fourth-grade population, which has the highest mean A score. The fourth grade is a stormy period when pent-up aggressive impulses and frustrations in the struggle with authority compete with needs for love and approval from the same source. The A responses of this group usually deal with aggression in animals as reflected in the fact that this group also has the highest hostility score of all normal groups (with the exception of the college students). Emotionally disturbed children (average age 9.8) have significantly lower A scores. These low scores suggest an inability to project aggression to animals. Their human scores are also low and comparable to those of five year olds (suggesting regression to inanimate content). Their hostility scores are low as well—considerably lower than those of their normal counterparts, the fourth graders. Of the adult populations, depressed patients and schizophrenics have the lowest A scores. These score are approximately the same as those of very young children and seventh graders. They reflect regressed preoccupation with personal needs.

A total lack of animal or human responses indicates stereotypy. A subject who gives animal but no human responses demonstrates immaturity, spontaneity, and intellectual stereotypy.

Anatomy (At)

Anatomy responses are of two kinds: At 1 and At 2. At 1 responses include X rays, medical drawings, and bone structures. At 2 responses include visceral, crude anatomy, and all other references to soft internal organs. The response "blood" is only sometimes scored for anatomy in the original HIT work. However, personal clinical evidence and Rorschach usage have proven that the blood response should always be interpreted as an anatomy response, and I do so in this book. Blood is scored At 2 because blood would not be visible without penetration or implied penetration of the body wall. Anatomy responses are rare. Persons who do give them give only a few (Holtzman, Thorpe, Swartz, and Herron, 1961). Excessive At responses reveal body preoccupation, anxiety, and thought disturbances. The number and kind of At responses and the balance of the record indicate the degree of disturbance. Self-absorption may be so extensive as to be a withdrawal into autism, or it may be a self-oriented concern associated with physiological changes which the subject may believe are taking place; for instance, during the onset of climacteric, pregnancy, or some prolonged physical illness. Exaggerated concern over body functions and body integrity is accompanied by a concomitant lessening of interest in the external world (Murstein, 1965; Haley, Draguns, and Phillips, 1967). Rav (1951) found that restriction of and reduction in intellectual drive increase At responses.

Phillips and Smith (1953), from their work with the Rorschach, found that anatomy responses reveal concern with destructive impulses, although the At responses alone are not sufficient evidence for predicting acting-out behavior. Excessive At responses indicate that hostility tends to be turned inward or at most that it would be discharged through verbal expression. These authors suggest that skeletal responses (At 1) are particularly contraindicative of direct acting out of hostile or other impulses and that the individual is unaware of his underlying hostility. These persons tend to be naive regarding their motivation. Wolf (1957) concluded from his work with the Rorschach that anatomy responses plus a knowledge of the strength of the subject's hostility drive are needed before the examiner can diagnose acting out behavior.

AT 1 RESPONSES PREDOMINANT. Rorschach (1942) reported skeletal types of anatomy responses chiefly in the records of neurotics who complain of inner emptiness, loneliness, and emotional coldness.

Psychologists consider X-ray responses as an intellectualization—an attempt to cover up anxiety in the individual who lacks the emotional insight necessary to deal effectively with his problems. He may be attempting to discover more about himself by trying to probe the body. Often this individual may be a compulsive worker, keeping busy to prevent anxiety from breaking through (Klopfer, Ainsworth, Klopfer, and Holt, 1954). Phillips and Smith (1953) state that X-ray responses are given frequently by persons who have a morbid apprehension of being physically harmed.

AT 2 RESPONSES PREDOMINANT. Visceral responses (At 2) suggest a turning inward of the subject's concerns and energies (Kuhn, 1963). These responses occur with more-than-average frequency in the records of neurotics and of other clinical groups who displace anxiety and whose conflicts concerning the body are higher than normal. In the HIT normative groups (with the exception of first graders) the highest mean At scores are found in the records of alcoholic patients, emotionally disturbed children, emotionally disturbed adolescents, and neurotics. The percepts of subjects in these groups are often idiosyncratic. Their elaboration includes diseased processes such as cancerous tissue, which reveals a distortion of the body image. Such responses are also found in the records of some schizophrenics. Feelings of depersonalization are suggested both in concepts of diseased processes and in responses concerning skeletons and dead bodies (human or animal). Malignant thought processes are almost always present in subjects giving many pathological responses dealing with internal body functions (Beck, 1952).

Blood responses reveal deeply negative emotions and reflect the manner in which the subject handles aggressive and sexual impulses. Murstein (1965) states that blood responses appear most often in the Rorschach records of persons whose ego controls are disturbed because of psychosis. These responses are also found in the records of persons who have been apprehended for aggressive acts or sexual offenses. When blood is the exclusive reaction to any card, it implies the presence of sadistic and destructive impulses in the subject (Phillips and Smith, 1953). Three or more blood responses in a record would reveal problems with self-control.

A high number of At responses in the records of persons in the medical profession reveal vocationally influenced stereotypy. It reflects the imposition of intellectual mastery over the ambiguous inkblot configuration. However, even in the medical professions a high number of At responses is a negative indicator and may reveal a tendency toward overpreoccupation with body processes (Bohm, 1958).

RESEARCH. In studies with the Rorschach, At responses given together with H responses are associated with self-report measures of anxiety and with suicidal attempts and ruminations (Haley, Draguns, and Phillips, 1967). Barnes (1963), using the HIT and other selected measures as predictors of brain damage, found high At scores in brain-damaged subjects. Swartz and Swartz (1968) compared test anxiety and performance on the HIT in 120 normal school children (60 girls and 60 boys) in three age groups (6.7 years, 9.7 years, and 12.7 years). The students with high test anxiety have higher scores in anatomy, movement, penetration, and affect arousal, which indicate greater body concern in these children than in their classmates. Megargee (1966), in a comparison of the HIT scores of Negro and white juvenile delinquents, found that Negroes score significantly higher on At than do whites.

Sex (Sx)

Under normal conditions of administration most persons avoid Sx responses and give responses which are more acceptable socially. Researchers have found, however, that when the sex of the subject and that of the clinician are the same, sex responses are facilitated. When the patient and clinician are of the opposite sex, however, the subject may feel inhibited in verbalizing percepts with sexual content. Freedom to produce sexual responses in the presence of a person of the same sex is often found in emancipated individuals. Persons who are either neurotically inhibited or inhibited by the test situation are not likely to give overt sexual responses, although sexual implications may be symbolically represented.

Sometimes sex responses are displaced, and the individual puts a distance between his sexual thoughts and the expression of them. Anatomy responses dealing with the bowel, pelvis, and lower parts of the body reflect this displacement.

Three or more Sx responses indicate a conflict attributable to sexual maladjustment. The conflict may range from sexual repression to the chaotic sexuality of the schizophrenic. Whether the Sx responses reflect deep-seated conflicts or whether they suggest aberrant behavior depends upon how they fit into the total personality structure. Interpretation is based on the adequacy of the defensive mechanisms (Beck and Molish, 1967).

The most blatantly idiosyncratic Sx responses (Sx 2) are frequently found among schizophrenics. Holtzman, Thorpe, Swartz, and Herron (1961) found chronic schizophrenics to be one of the two groups who give repeated Sx responses. The other group is depressed patients. (Emotionally disturbed adolescents, alcoholics, and neurotics also give many Sx responses.) Zolliker (1943) reports a high number of female Sx responses in depressed pregnant females. These responses were accompanied by an absence of male genital responses (either overt or symbolic). Blatant Sx responses may sometimes also be found in the nonschizophrenic who is in a current state of emotional upheaval or perhaps as a result of psychoanalysis. Before making a diagnosis, however, the examiner should investigate other indices of ego dysfunction (Beck and Molish, 1967). Blatant Sx responses suggest interest in sexual activity and preoccupation with heterosexual life. Klopfer, Ainsworth, Klopfer, and Holt (1954) state that subjects who give many Sx responses involving genitalia may be trying to prove that they are sufficiently mature to make such responses. These researchers believe, however, that such individuals are covering up a preoccupation with pregenital sexuality and that they are probably fixated at that stage of development, being unable to carry out either a heterosexual or a homosexual relationship. Studies indicate that when Sx responses and blood responses are higher than average, they provide significant information on how the individual handles sexual and aggressive impulses. Above average numbers of Sx and blood responses in the Rorschach are found both in individuals whose ego controls are disturbed through psychosis and in individuals apprehended for aggressive or sexual acts. The latter group demonstrates a great number of blatant Sx responses. In the former group, blood responses predominate (Haley, Draguns, and Phillips, 1967).

The content "breasts" in a Sx response is associated with an oral-receptive dependency orientation (Zubin, Eron, and Schumer, 1965) and indicates frustration of affectional needs from the mother or a similar significant maternal figure (Klopfer, Ainsworth, Klopfer, and Holt, 1954). Sx responses that reveal concern with reproduction and generative activities include references to the birth process (ovaries, uterus, womb, fetus, and pregnant females). Beck (1952) believes that subjects giving a large number of birth-process responses have a need relating to the rebirth fantasy. Such responses also reflect an effort toward regressed rebirth in the service of rebuilding the ego.

The age of the subject is important in evaluating Sx responses. Shafer (1954) believes that reproductive responses in the young female (age eighteen or nineteen) may indicate curiosity, hope, and perhaps fear of childbirth. In the older female (especially past age fifty), these responses may suggest grief at the loss of vitality, attractivenes, and the nurturent role. Cultural differences are also important in assessing the meaning of Sx responses. An Sx response referring to intercourse given by a member of the lower socioeconomic community, possibly rural, is serious. It indicates failure to establish the defenses appropriate to the subculture and indicates rejection of cultural traditions. This Sx response given by a person in a socioeconomic culture that sanctions free use of sexual terminology, however, is not as significant.

Sex responses may also indicate conflict in accepting an appropriate sex role. Shafer (1954) suggests that persons with inadequate sexual identity or homosexual orientation often show uncertainty and ambiguity in defining the sex of characters seen in the inkblots. They may define sexual characteristics in an arbitrary manner or reject their own sexual identity by showing an exaggerated preference for the opposite sex. They may report bisexual figures, change the sex specified in the original response, or see symmetrical figures as being one male the other female. Shafer reports persons with sexual identity problems also refer to perversions, such as members of their own sex embracing or wearing clothing typical of the opposite sex. The male may reveal a fear of the masculine role through phallic-aggressive emphasis, for example, gigantic penis or double-barreled shotgun. The female may reveal a hostile, fearful rejection of feminine characteristics, for example, shrew or flat-chested woman. The homosexual demonstrates an increase in sexual, anal, and oral imagery (Shafer, 1954). Anderson and Seitz (1969) found Shafer's signs diagnostically useful in detecting sex-role disturbances and overt homosexuality in a hospitalized male population. These Sx responses alone are not sufficient to identify the homosexual. However they do detect the individual who has a conflict and is ambivalent regarding his sexual identity. Many homosexuals who are not disturbed by their homosexuality do not give responses of this kind. Female homosexuality is difficult to identify and that label should not be used without substantial evidence.

Studies with the Rorschach show that when subjects are asked to give sexual responses, they give more female than male responses. This reaction appears to be a function of the structure of the blot—with intercard differences in sexual properties favoring female over male responses (Pascal, Reusch, Devine, and Suttell, 1950; Shaw, 1948). The stimulus value of the HIT in eliciting male or female sex responses needs to be examined.

Holtzman, Thorpe, Swartz, and Herron (1961) found the distribution of Sx responses extremely truncated in all groups. Sex responses are virtually nonexistent in the records of normal children and rarely occur among average adults. Occasional Sx responses are found among college men, depressed patients, chronic schizophrenics, alcoholic patients, neurotic patients, and emotionally disturbed adolescents. Repeated Sx responses are exceedingly rare except among chronic schizophrenics, depressed patients, and emotionally disturbed adolescents.

Abstract (Ab)

Abstract responses express ideas or moods and bear no association to specific objects, concrete realities, or actual occurrences. These responses may be triggered by the color in the blot or by inner feelings which may find expression in inanimate movement.

Abstract responses are usually given by persons with superior intelligence and sensitivity. Codkind (1964) found that persons with a high degree of fantasy acceptance give more Ab responses to the HIT than do those who are not able to use fantasy. Holtzman, Thorpe, Swartz, and Herron (1961) found that only college students give an appreciable number of Ab responses, and even among these subjects most fail to give any. Abstract responses are almost nonexistent among mental retardates and young children. An occasional abstract response is given by the average adult, chronic schizophrenic, depressed patient, neurotic patient, and emotionally disturbed adolescent.

The abstract response often reflects a fantasy which the individual would like to experience but which is not present in his life, for example: "It reminds me of gaiety," "It is light and cheerful," or "It gives me a feeling of power." The Ab response may also reflect some psychological inner feeling which he is experiencing. Abstract responses may be either negative or positive. Negative abstract responses are exemplified by verbalizations such as: "It is very depressing" or "It reminds me of gloom and despair." Rorschach (1942) interpreted the impressionistic abstract responses as indicating an incapacity for maintaining a grip on a central thought, thus revealing a passive orientation.

Abstract responses derived from the color stimulus of the blot may be positive or negative. A positive Ab response suggests elation in mood and reveals the excited, impressionable, expressive individual. Some examples of positive Ab responses derived from the color stimulus of the blot are: "It reminds me of gaiety because it is red," "It reminds me of truth because it is blue," "It reminds me of purity because it is white," or "It reminds me of spring because it is green." Negative Ab responses derived from the color stimulus of the blot suggest depression in mood and reveal the impulsive, restless, belligerent, irreconcilable individual. Some examples are: "It reminds me of death because it is black," "It reminds me of gloom because it is black," or "It reminds me of despair because it is gray." Persons who give many color-dominated abstract responses are dominated by their feelings. They take chances and act impulsively. A strong ego is required to cope with such strong emotions. In schizophrenics, hypomanics, and neurotics, emotions projected in this way are usually dissociated from the direct control of the individual, although dissociation is rare among neurotics. The examiner should be careful in interpreting positive color-instigated Ab responses because they appear in the records of healthy, elated individuals as well as in the records of overexuberant hypomanics. The differentiating factor between normality and abnormality is the number of such responses. Negative color-instigated Ab responses are found in the Rorschach records of psychopaths, organics, and epileptics. Schizophrenics who give this response tend to discharge frustration in overt motor behavior, namely, suicide attempts. Among nonpathological subjects, Piotrowski (1957) reports finding these responses in the records of adolescents and superior individuals who are leaders, reformers, and doers. Few validation studies have been made on the significance of abstract content. Interpretations must be cautious and in conjunction with other variables.

RESEARCH. Jortner (1966) investigated cognitive aspects of schizophrenics, using the HIT as one of the measures. The specific cognitive aspects which he found were preoccupation with abstract ideas, with the supernatural, and with symbols. Schizophrenics are generally more concerned with abstract ideas such as good versus evil than with concrete things such as a wife and a job.

Other Content

The five HIT categories discussed above are generally sufficient for a complete evaluation of content. Sometimes, however, in examining the themes of the forty-five blots, the examiner finds other content used repetitively. The most frequently used categories are discussed in this section. The evaluation of this content is appropriate when the subject overemphasizes one of these categories or when scant use of other categories limits interpretation.

NATURE AND ARCHITECTURE RESPONSES. Nature, plant and simple architecture responses are among the earliest percepts given by children and are therefore grouped together. Nature responses (rocks, snow, rain, sky, and rainbow), plant responses (trees, leaves, and flowers), and simple architecture responses (houses, and bridges) are common in the records of very young children (age four or four and one-half). At this age the child feels a oneness with the simple, primitive forms of life in nature and plants and a security in the familiar simple representations of houses. These responses begin to drop out when the child is about four and one-half and are replaced by animal and then by human responses.

Psychologists who emphasize symbolism in their interpretations believe that the child's concern with these simple forms of life is symbolic of his dependency on the family. Architecture responses (such as bridge and house) and some nature response (rocks and caves) are believed to reflect the child's need for security. The tree response is symbolically interpreted as revealing the child's outlook on the family. The branches and leaves represent his feelings about himself. If the branches and leaves are on the tree, he has a greater degree of security than if the branches and leaves have fallen off. A sad, happy, or dead tree often indicates the way in which a child perceives the family situation (Halpern, 1953). When rock and landscape content is high in the records of children over age five and in adolescents, the subject often has a history of family strife or institutional placement. Rock and landscape responses are also given frequently by schizophrenics and individuals with a schizoid tendency. A schizophrenic record containing many rock responses implies a poor prognosis (Haley, Draguns, and Phillips, 1967).

Persons who give a preponderance of nature responses tend to be superficial and intellectually evasive. Nature responses are usually indistinct and impermanent and represent either a direct evasion (a near rejection) or stereotypy. In the latter case, the individual is either poorly endowed intellectually or cannot use his abilities because of emotional problems or some other interference. Sometimes natural objects are seen in a deteriorated state—torn, or decayed—or misformed (oddly shaped leaves). This kind of response is given almost exclusively by psychotics who project their own weakness and feelings of personal disintegration onto plant life, the vitality of which is even lower than that of a human or animal. Architectural responses given by adults may reveal compensation for an inner insecurity by projecting firm and rigid structure.

CLOTHING. Clothing responses are usually hat, dress, coat, or cape. These responses are rare and are therefore considered significant. Articles of clothing by themselves are scored barrier as are articles of clothing worn by animals and birds. Clothing worn by a person is scored Br only if the clothing is unusual or decorative. In addition to the interpretation of clothing as a Br score, preoccupation with clothing indicates concern with social status and attractiveness. Clothes are a passive method of drawing attention to the self and this response is more typical of females who are generally more passive than males. The clothing response is significant when given by male subjects because it implies feminine interests. Feminine interests, however, should not be equated with overt or covert homosexuality.

EMBLEMS. Emblems and insignia appear frequently in some records. These responses indicate strong prestige drives in persons with inadequate personalities. These persons may be ambitious for achievement and recognition and seek to dominate their environment. But they nevertheless feel inadequate and are usually unable to compete successfully with others (Lindner, 1946; Phillips and Smith, 1953).

MASKS. Mask responses represent a disguise, a hiding of the face. Researchers have suggested that this response may reveal a tendency to misrepresent and to appear as something which one is not. This interpretation is strengthened when human movement occurs together with a mask response. When no human movement is given with this response, the hiding and disguise symbolized by the mask may represent a fear of the hypocrisy in other people rather than a defense. If the mask represents fear of hypocrisy, the subject feels that people in the environment are presenting a facade and are not always what they seem to be. Kuhn (1944) found that a large number of mask responses is associated either with persons who show disturbances in identity formation or with persons who use denial as a defense. This interpretation ties in with the disguise interpretation. Kuhn believes that excessive mask responses indicate a pathological condition which would be evidenced by phobias, hysteria, or even depersonalization. However, a pathological diagnosis should not be made on the basis of mask responses alone.

FOOD. Food responses which occur frequently in a record suggest a dependent orientation—an overconcern with the supply and demand of oral needs. Food responses frequently occur in conjunction with food objects, such as a pan or a decanter.

TEETH. Teeth responses when mentioned with some frequency suggests that the individual is reacting to frustration of dependent needs. Teeth responses are immature and imply feelings of resentment and rejection. Cotte (1964) found that teeth responses are predominant in the Rorschach records of children who come from broken homes or in children with aggressive behavior. This finding is consistent with the interpretation which hypothesized frustration of dependent needs —such frustration is certainly felt by youngsters from broken homes. Aggressive acting-out behavior in a child frequently reflects the need to have someone pay attention to him because he feels rejected. In another Rorschach study, Haley, Draguns, and Phillips (1967) associated the use of many teeth responses with schizophrenia both in children and in adults. Authorities widely believe that many schizophrenic patients have not had their dependent needs met or that those needs have been frustrated. The schizophrenic also feels rejected by the environment and responds to this rejection with hostility. In the normal adult population, the teeth response is given almost exclusively by females. Women giving this response usually lean heavily on others, are chronically dependent and immature, and have feelings of rejection. Teeth responses sometimes also suggest sibling rivalry (a reaction to frustration of dependency needs).

EYES. The eyes seen in an inkblot nearly always belong to humans even though the response is often just eyes with no identification of human or animal. Many responses of this kind indicate a high degree of sensitivity to the opinion of others. Unless the response is elaborated—"eyes looking at me" (which may indicate hallucinations and imply psychosis) eye responses should not be construed as indicative of a paranoid attitude.

POSITIVE AND NEGATIVE CONTENT. Studies have been made of the populations that give negative content responses to inkblot tests. Fisher and Cleveland (1958), in a study of naval air cadets, found that unhealthy content such as smoke, explosions, and blood distinguished significantly between cadets who are prone to air sickness and those who are not.

Haley, Draguns, and Phillips (1967) cite Rorschach studies which demonstrate that the verbal affective property of the content of a response may suggest antilife moods. White and Schreiber (1952), in studying subjects with indications of suicidal ideation, found that those who have the highest suicidal potential verbalize themes of mutilation, death, flight, suspense, darkness, aggression, passivity, and restlessness. They also found that percepts including mutilation, weapons, and fighting are greater in suicidal patients than in homocidal patients. Responses also associated with suicide (but less strongly so than the responses above) include ice, shadows, smoke, and clouds.

SEQUENCE ANALYSIS OF CONTENT THEMES. The content of a protocol reveals both adaptive and defensive mechanisms and expressions of drives and impulses. In general, content reflects adaptive behavior. However, severely disturbed persons and persons who are unable to repress their feelings express their drives and impulses directly in the content. But an individual's mode of adaptation, his basic drives, or the strength of his impulses cannot be derived from a single response. An analysis of major content trends over the forty-five blots is necessary. An examination of content themes on the clinical summary sheet determines content emphasis. Even when the subject has rejected cards, the examiner usually has a sufficient number of responses to identify consistent and recurring themes, the sequence in which themes occur, and the manner in which themes follow one another. The content also indicates the conceptualizing ability of the subject as he interacts with the blots. After the evaluation of the variables, of affect arousal, and of other test behavior, the qualitative assessment of the overall content and its sequence is made. This analysis requires an empathic identification with the subject. The subsequent judgments are frequently subjective, based on how the examiner perceives the subject during the test. Klopfer, Ainsworth, Klopfer, and Holt (1954) believe that most problems in sequence analysis result from lack of criteria and the poor validity of hypotheses that have thus far been established. They believe that the examiner will have difficulty validating any basic interpretative hypothesis which is taken out of context. The examiner must consider the total picture from which that hypothesis has been formed, that is, the relationship of any one response to the ones preceding and following it. The clinician evaluates the content sequence by forming hypotheses. These hypotheses are verified from interpretive theories derived from the scoring variables and from other tests.

The distance the subject places between himself and the described content is a clue for determining the extent to which he is consciously aware of his motivation and inner drives. In human responses distance is achieved by changing the sex or the age from that of the subject, by placing the person in another time period, or by identifying a fantasy figure. Human responses appearing late in the record reveal inhibition. The later they appear, the greater the inhibition.

A sequence analysis is also concerned with sequential relationships or variations—consistencies in reaction time, responses to color stimuli and shading implications, and so on. Some persons habitually use a rigid and orderly approach to situations and handle their responses in the same manner. They deal with the same size area and the same content in each blot. They are more concerned with logical order and reasoning than with flexibility in having the approach suit the stimulus. Such rigid sequence is usually given by pedants or by subjects who are anxious, feel inferior, and hesitate to veer from a given course. A rigid approach is also associated with a self-critical attitude. Flexibility is revealed when the subject can respond to various blots in different ways—to the entire location in some and in others to detail areas—and when he is able to respond to the variants of the stimulus with a variety of determinants and content. At the opposite extreme, the response themes are sometimes so scattered that they can be interpreted only as lability of mood.

The sequence analysis may reveal the degree of intellectual control. The task of responding to forty-five blots in sequence requires sustained effort and focused attention, which demands disciplined thinking. Sometimes the subject verbalizes many good responses early in the protocol but the response content deteriorates later. Such deterioration indicates a lack of staying power or an inability to maintain defenses in the presence of the unstructured blot stimuli. Sometimes a record shows the reverse situation. The subject gives poor responses at the beginning, but as he progresses he mobilizes his resources and the responses become more appropriate. This improvement reveals the need to be familiar with a situation before the individual can relax enough to use his cognitive ability.

STIMULUS PROPERTIES OF SELECTED BLOTS IN FORM A. The stimulus value of particular HIT blots is readily apparent and can be clearly formulated much as Schachtel (1966) formulated the stimulus value of the Rorschach blots. However, with forty-five cards in each form it is not practical to do this for every one. Therefore, cards in Form A with the most predominant themes have been selected for this purpose. The characteristics described below have been found empirically from the records of a group of 115 emotionally disturbed adolescents (69 males and 46 females). These data should be applied cautiously to any other group. Further sampling may require modification. It may be found that different themes emerge for other groups; or these themes may be applicable to all groups.

Card 1A: Depression. The shading and darkness of this blot evoke primarily depressive themes. Forty per cent of the subjects respond with content such as black storm clouds, smoke, or anatomy responses dealing with disease and dissection. Another 20 per cent verbalize animate percepts. These persons typically report either side as heads of animals or creatures often seen in violent interaction with each other or with the center L 2 area labeled d 1 in the Guide. Evasive themes included neutral nature content such as continents, maps, rocks, and mountains.

Fourteen subjects (four male and ten female) gave coping themes. These responses were given by avoiding the largest part of the blot and responding to the center L 2 area, which was seen as two people (often interacting with one another). Those who are able to integrate this area with the balance of the blot report an element of threat to the people.

Card 2A: Aggressive sexuality and castration. The shading and protuberances bring out hostility and covert masculine sexual themes. Fifty-five per cent of the subjects responded to the figures on each side. Typically, they reported persons in aggressive interaction with each other using symbolic phallic attacking objects (knives, spears, and so on). Castration themes are evoked in 13 per cent of the subjects (tree stumps, dead branches, split trees with limbs hanging). Two females directly reported male phalluses. For many, however, the phallic threat provokes regressive ideation and they report aggressive fantasy figures (witches, ghosts, monsters, devils), or the threat was further removed (statues).

Card 3A: Fear of destruction. Both the high-saturated color and the unstructured shaded areas arouse affect revealing inner turmoil connected with fear of destruction. Themes reported by 60 per cent of the subjects deal with nature, volcanic eruption, nuclear explosion, fireworks, storm clouds, and so on. When animals or humans are reported, they are assaultive, threatening, or devouring (gorillas, beasts, monsters, football players, devils, spooks).

Inner fears of destruction are further revealed by an additional 20 per cent of subjects who report blood and germ responses and abstract responses such as death, evil forces, and confusion. Two female sex responses were given by males.

Some deny the threatening stimulus and give evasive themes which are more neutral, for example, sunset. Often, however, the denial is incomplete, and the dark areas are brought in as storm clouds blocking the sun.

Card 4A: Displacement or denial of aggression and paranoid ideation. This card has two dominant areas and themes: the "animal and rider" on each side, which elicits aggressive movement responses, and the partial face on the top which evokes feelings of guilt and threat. The color is too low in saturation to arouse enough affect to interfere with a response. Only one subject in the entire sample rejected this card.

Two themes were reported by 80 per cent of the subjects. Half of the subjects displace their aggression onto a socially accepted percept. The percept is often to the animal (in most cases a horse) and figure in interaction, (usually readying to attack one another or representing abstract forms of war and evil). The others, who deny the threat of aggression, give evasive themes, typically dealing with amorphous or destructive nature content (fog, smoke, fire, explosion). Only 4 per cent give coping themes, distanciating the threat to art forms such as cave paintings or cowboy scenes. Persons with paranoid ideation are attracted to the top area and report such percepts as the face of God, someone watching, or eyes watching.

Card 5A: Anxiety and loneliness. This card is asymmetrical in black and white. It has an overall dotted effect with darker areas. Over 60 per cent of the sample were unable to impose structure on the blot. The textural shading characteristics of the blot evoke themes related to cold and desolate feelings. Such responses reveal anxiety and loneliness. Typical responses were snow, mist, fog, blizzard, snowstorm, and dust storm. Coping themes were seen in the area on the right and were reported as a head, head and shoulder, or full human figure by 13 per cent of this sample.

Card 6A: Sexual pathology, hysteria. The high-saturated color (chromatic and achromatic) arouses enough affect to interfere with the process of inhibition which would result in a "good" response. Seventy-five per cent of the subjects report percepts whose main theme contains disturbed content, more than half of which reveals pathology. This card evokes more At 2 responses than does any other card. Twenty-one subjects report such percepts as blood, lungs, and intestines. Some elaborate on diseased processes. Anatomy responses coupled with sex responses are also high. The dominant content is female genital relating to the birth process and fetuses (in one case the fetus being ripped out of the mother). When animals are reported they are threatening, aggressive [attacking] types, or passive types being attacked.

Evasive themes are color dominant and include nature responses such as flowers, garden, and art. Coping themes, given by only thirteen of the subjects, relate to humans (H 1 and H 2).

Card 8A: Adult male sexuality. The L 1 center projectile form (labeled D 2 in the Guide) on this blot evokes phallic attacking fantasies in both male and female subjects. These fantasies are mostly symbolically represented. Forty per cent of the percepts include either shooting objects in action, such as rockets, jets, missiles, or cannons, or explosions and eruptions. Evasive themes include nature responses, such as sunshine and sky.

Card 10A: Masochism, castration anxiety, or both. The fragmented areas of this blot elicit masochistic fantasies concerning victimized persons. Although the most popular response to this card (over 50 per cent) was the center L 1 figures (labeled D 3 in the Guide) as persons, 20 per cent of subjects report persons as being dismembered and dissected. Castration fear is present, with limbs often the disjointed object. Others place the damage at a distance by reporting cells that are diseased or cancerous. Coping themes include people as dancers or angels.

Card 11A: Unresolved Oedipal anxiety. This dark, threatening card elicits percepts suggesting fear, threat, or oral aggression in 75 per cent of the responses. The content includes such threatening concepts as monsters, spiders, sting rays, and teeth. It also includes the results of aggressive attack, for example, skinned, squashed, smashed, bloody, distorted, and dead animals or faces. Evasive themes include dark clouds and thunder storms. Coping themes are masks.

Card 12A: Interpersonal relationships. This card is well structured and elicits warm, active percepts from 70 per cent of the subjects in the sample. A typical percept is "persons dancing or walking around a campfire or monument." Some persons reveal passive, submissive attitudes in their reports of "persons sacrificing or worshipping in ritual acts." Over 25 per cent of subjects give themes which evade the interpersonal themes and respond with phallic aggressive content (for instance, reporting the center area as rockets blasting off).

Card 14A: Anxiety aroused by mother figures. The black "figures" on the outer edges elicit fear of menacing, aggressive attacks from displaced mother figures. The majority of subjects (80 per cent) associate with these figures (either alone or in interaction with the balance of the blot). Threatening imagery includes such content as monsters, witches, genies, skeletons, evil spirits, and spiders. Action responses report things being torn or ripped apart. Evasive themes are in the center area, which elicits At 1 responses such as ribs, X rays, and backbone.

Card 16A: Fear of pathology. This highly saturated color card arouses threatening affect in 80 per cent of subjects. The whole blot is frequently seen as a face, often reported as blown apart, tortured, mad, or a monster. When the halves are reported separately, they are often seen as aggressive animals physically assaulting each other. Evasive themes include nature responses such as flowers or sun.

Card 19A: Interpersonal relationships. The well delineated figures in this card stimulate human-action responses, which reveal attitudes toward interpersonal relationships. Over 90 per cent of this sample report human figures in various degrees of action reflecting positive aggressive attitudes, such as dancing or picnicking, or negative aggressive impulses such as war and fighting (including hostile implements). Many respond to the center figures as hanging (thus revealing their fear of threatened aggression).

Card 21A: Authority. This card evokes superego conflicts of guilt and innocence concerning authority. Forty per cent of the subjects give responses related to religious themes (manger scene, Mary and Jesus, nuns, angels, chapels, churches, thrones, and crosses). Such responses reflect innocence and denial of guilt. An equal number give passive animal responses (ducks, birds, and sheep). Sixteen of the subjects relate phallic aggressive themes to the center and upper center areas (bats, clubs, poles, dart guns, phallic symbols).

Card 23A: Death and destruction. Card 23A is one of the two most disturbing cards. It evokes threatening fantasies of depression, mutilation, and death. Twenty per cent of the subjects rejected this card. The responses emphasize the darkness of the blot. Very few human responses are given. Only one human response was given by a male and nine were given by females. Those given involved Ku Klux Klan figures, witches, and dark angels. Animal responses are mostly bats and vampire bats. Butterfly responses appeared but were frequently seen as ripped, dead, or cut up. Nature responses also reflect fearfulness and depression and include many dark caves and tunnels. Abstract responses given to this card are Hades, doom, and gloom. Evasive themes deal with clothing (shirt, vest, coat).

Card 24A: Masochism. Card 24A is an unstructured, disturbing card which arouses masochistic feelings of destruction and mutilation. This card was rejected by 20 per cent of the subjects. Nature responses reflect coldness and desolation (ice, snow, smoke, storm). Twenty per cent of the subjects give anatomy responses, most of which are blood even though this is an achromatic card. Lacerated and cut hands are frequently reported as are mutilated bodies, disease, and bacteria.

Card 30A: Feelings of adequacy in coping with pressures. This card generates movement responses of the m variety. Over 50 per cent of the subjects report themes of threatening, noncontrollable action such as storms, hurricanes, monsoons, rain, and winds. Many, in addition, report a building (straw hut, shack, thatched roof, house) in most instances being threatened by a storm. The inner feelings expressed are those of inadequacy to withstand external forces. Evasive themes deal with nature responses such as trees, grass, and sunlight.

Card 31A: Oral aggression. This card evokes themes of oral aggression. Devouring animals such as lions, dragons, alligators, and snakes are reported in 40 per cent of the responses. The animals are often seen as sticking out tongues or fangs or spouting fire, suggesting the projection of fear experienced at verbal attacks from persons. Anatomy responses suggestive of the aftermath of aggression are reported by an additional 10 per cent of the subjects. Evasive themes include nature themes (valley, sunset, mountain).

Card 35A: Ideas of reference. This highly saturated color card arouses affect, which makes it difficult to respond to the card. Twenty per cent of the subjects reject the card. Those who respond give predominantly animal and human-head responses but emphasize the darkness and the eeriness of the setting. Heads are reported as distorted and include staring eys. Nature responses include threatening clouds and oil fires. Evasive themes include sunglasses, bottles, and art.

Card 39A: Dependency and passivity. The characteristics of this card evoke responses revealing oral dependency and aggressive fears. The black figures on either side are the stimuli for dependence, the red center the stimulus for aggression. Forty per cent give passive themes concerned with newborn babies and animals, passive recipients of food, and passive oral aggressors (insects feeding on petals). Twenty per cent express aggressive fears to the red center, which is seen as blood resulting from being hit. Thirty-five per cent respond to the upper half of the outer figures, which are most frequently seen as eyes, sad eyes, or eyes that have been hit or are tearing. Evasive themes include eyeglasses, sunset, and mask.

Card 41A: Guilt and punishment. Feelings of being judged and punished are typically expressed in 35 per cent of the responses to this card. Subjects frequently see humans or mythical figures (Jesus, witches, and so on) being sacrificed, burned, or crucified. Twenty-five per cent are unable to express these feelings directly and give nature responses expressing destructive, punishing forces such as volcanoes. Sexual themes (overt and covert) are given by 7 per cent of the subjects (nudes, fan dancers, totem poles, phallic symbols). The evasive themes given include objects, for example, cocktail glasses (usually overflowing), bridges, buildings, and statues. Coping themes are girls dancing or waterfall.

Card 43A: Depression caused by guilt. This card evokes depressive guilt themes concerned with the aftermath of aggression. Forty per cent of the subjects report the center figure as a person struggling, destroyed, or already dead, or as animals threatened or threatening (swarms of insects, animals running, snakes, or spiders). Nature responses are also threatening (explosions, storms, or lightning). Ten per cent give evasive themes, for example, rocking horse or cave drawing.

Disturbed Thought Processes

IX

Psychopathology of the thought processes and emotional disturbances are revealed in fantasy production. The content of the subject's responses as well as his side remarks and personal references help identify disordered thinking, bizarre perception, or disturbed inner fantasy life.

Thought processes range from healthy, highly developed, logical thinking to highly disturbed, autistic thinking. Autistic thinking is a subjective form of thinking, the content of which is derived largely from the person's fantasy rather than from occurrences in the real world. Autistic thinking is a turning away from reality. The individual's unconscious makes the largest contribution, distorting intellectual processes through emotions which dominate the individual (Arieti, 1955). Goldman (1962) describes this kind of thinking as a regression to a diffuse and global stage. In the interaction with the inkblot, the autistic individual (like the young child) is stimulus bound and therefore passively subjected to sensory stimulation, revealing weak emotional control (Werner, 1949).

Logical thinking is characterized by clarity and ease of thinking. A logical thinker organizes stimulus events well, reasons objectively, and is reality oriented. His associations reflect the demands of the stimulus situation.

The thinking of most individuals falls somewhere along a continuum between logical thinking and autistic thinking. The individual may also shift in his ability to retain certain capacities and capablities in intellectual functioning. When the shift is in the direction of autistic thinking, we term it regressive (because autistic logic represents an elementary form of thinking typical of the young child). Autism reveals lability of thinking and emotional dominance. A partial, temporary shift to autisticlike thinking may occur consciously in the well adusted individual as a creative maneuver. Kris (1952) refers to such a shift as a regression in the service of the ego. The individual is cognizant of the liberties he is taking and dips back into imagery, drawing on fantasy associations. He is frequently aware that he has regressed and is capable of verbalizing the process. The balance of the record reveals whether the individual has an intact ego.

Sometimes, regression is habitual as in severe schizophrenics. In these patients, outer pressures or inner conflicts may stimulate the autistic thinking (Shafer, 1954). In the true regressive situation, the content of the individual responses is similar to subjective symbolic dream (or daydream) representations. Images well up in the individual and he may feel that he is only a passive observer as he reports a stream of ideas. The record reveals lack of control over thought processes and identifies the individual with disordered thinking. This chapter deals with the identification of such disturbed thought processes through test scores on pathognomic verbalization, anxiety, hostility, penetration, and affect arousal.

Pathognomic Verbalization (V)

Pathognomic verbalization (V) is the prime indicator of disordered and disorganized thinking. The V score is a qualitative measure of mental disturbance. It reveals poor reality testing and autistic thinking. V scores result from the failure of repressive defenses and from ego weakness. When the defenses fail, regressive responses result, reflecting the loosened fantasies and bizarre themes of the borderline or full psychotic state (Shafer, 1954).

Repression is an indispensible defense and in some ways is adaptive to the test situation. A test should not break down basic repressive barriers. The inkblot technique, however, tends to circumvent repressive barriers. The individual is usually not aware of this circumvention, although he may fear it. Responses to the ambiguous inkblot require creative imagination, which depends on free access to preconscious and unconscious ideation. The individual who is overrepressed or whose repressive barriers are precarious cannot tolerate resorting to free fantasy and spontaneity in thought. When repressive defenses fail in these persons, perverse, morbid, and fantastic thoughts often flood the stream of consciousness. The more anxious the person is over his bizarre content, the more likely it is that he is compensating into a borderline or full psychotic state. The more bland the individual appears concerning his bizarre content, the more likely it is that he has a stabilized character disorder with borderline or full psychotic trends (Shafer, 1954).

Extremely bizarre content indicates regression in the ego organization of the individual. Energy normally available for advanced, adaptive thought functioning is tied up in aggressive and libidinal urges and conflicts. Concept formation tends to be organized around drives, conflicts, and fears, instead of relationships that exist in reality between objects and their properties.

Autistic thinking is not solely revealed in pathognomic verbalizations. A strong prevalence of M responses, especially human movement with a marked lack of C is further verification of autistic or unrealistic thinking (Rapaport, 1946). V accompanied by a large number of C and Sh responses implies failure of the defenses (Shafer, 1954). Below I discuss the nine subcategories of pathognomic verbalization.

FABULATION (FB). Fabulated responses are frequently given by introspective, sensitive individuals who enjoy a play on language containing high affective components. Normal individuals are aware of the fanciful liberties they take. Swartz (1969) found that normals gave significantly more FB responses than did mental retardates or schizophrenics. Between normals and depressives, the latter group has a greater percentage of FB responses, although the difference does not reach significance.

Codkind (1964) found that persons high in the acceptance and use of imagery score higher on FB than do those who reject imagery. These persons have an ability to enliven and enrich the blot material with affective qualities. Therefore the presence of some FB responses is not proof of psychopathology. A high number of FB responses is sometimes characteristic of clinical groups with quantitatively and qualitatively rich ideation whose thinking is not so unrealistic as to be judged clearly psychotic. Persons with excessive fantasying may reveal a pathological amount of autistic thinking. However, other pathological elements must be present to diagnose pathology (Rapaport, 1946).

FABULIZED COMBINATION (FC). Responses in this category reflect a loss of distance between the subject and the inkblot. The subject accepts the blot as immutable reality with its own real affective and logical properties. He thereby relinquishes critical control over his response. His approach to the blot is unrealistic, often demonstrating a breakdown in the distinction between fantasy and reality. Shafer (1954) believes that such responses occur involuntarily despite defensive efforts. He suggests that the bizarre verbalizations, although not strictly out of control, are not completely in hand. The FC response, he states, is not specifically autistic.

Studying the V scores of normals, depressives, schizophrenics, and mental retardates, Swartz (1969) found FC responses more common among depressives and normal populations than among schizophrenics and mental retardates. Well organized normals and neurotics who give FC responses are aware of the irregularity of their responses. In a nonpsychotic population, FC is often found in the records of obsessive-compulsive individuals. The FC response reveals their passive relativistic feeling that any combination of things is possible. The world around them does not appear meaningfully integrated or amenable to integration. Such ideation suggests a pathological tendency and may reveal a preschizophrenic condition in which thinking is based on fantasy and autism, replacing an adherence to objective reality in everyday situations.

QUEER RESPONSE (QR). QR is the most subjectively determined score in the HIT and depends upon the internalized standards of the scorer. It should therefore be cautiously applied. Such responses imply psychotic reasoning, although the illogical reasoning may not be directly revealed. These responses indicate poor reality testing and a partial breakdown of the reasoning processes. They point to the influence of inner-directed fantasies which are not consistent with the demands of reality.

Jortner (1966) found schizophrenics high in QR responses. Swartz (1969), however, found that the only difference in use of QR among the subject groups in his study was a significantly higher incidence of QR for mental retardates than for normals.

INCOHERENCE (IC). IC responses reveal a complete breakdown of rational control. No attempt is made by the individual to regulate his thinking from without. His verbalizations reflect directly his inner thoughts and demands. Such responses are quite rare. When they occur, they reveal the schizophrenic with disturbed thought processes. Swartz (1969) found no IC responses in the records of normal or depressive subjects. Schizophrencis or mental retardates are likely to give several such responses rather than just one.

AUTISTIC LOGIC (AL). AL responses are scored when the subject gives faulty, fantastic reasoning to justify his response. AL is also scored for responses in which a small portion of the blot triggers off a percept involving a larger area, even though the area bears no resemblance to the percept. Responses in which parts of a percept are determined solely by their position on the card are also scored for AL. The AL response reveals poor reality testing and thought disorders.

Evidence indicates that such responses are almost always conclusive indicators of schizophrenia (Rapaport, 1946; Jortner, 1966; Swartz, 1969). Swartz found that both schizophrenics and mental retardates give significantly more AL responses than do depressives.

CONTAMINATION (CT). CT responses reveal a loss of distance from the blot. The subject blends discrete and separate percepts into one another without any semblance of reality in the relationship. The CT response reflects the schizophrenic's increasing inability to keep percepts and their corresponding concepts distinct. It reveals a variety of autistic, unrealistic thinking which assumes that everything ultimately belongs with or is related to everything else. CT is considered one of the most reliable indicators of schizophrenia (Rapaport, 1946; Jortner, 1966; Swartz, 1969).

Bohm (1958) reports occasionally finding this type of response in the Rorschach records of preschool children, especially females around age five.

SELF-REFERENCE (SR). SR responses, whether in the form of side remarks or as part of the percept, reveal bizarre self-preoccupation and serious loss of distance between the individual and the blot. Ann Q. Hozier (in Jortner, 1966) believes that as long as the body is not sufficiently cathected to become bounded and differentiated from everything that is not body, the individual has no frame of reference from which to judge the reality of events in the external world as compared with the reality of those events that derive from his psychological experiences. This lack of body-image boundary results in inability to distinguish the uniqueness of the individual from the environment and reveals depersonalization and preoccupation with the self. Swartz (1969) found that the highest number of SR responses (20 and 19 per cent, respectively) are given by depressive and schizophrenic subjects. By comparison, only 5 per cent of normals and mental retardates give SR responses.

DETERIORATION COLOR (DC). The diagnostic implication of DC is deterioration of thought processes. The percept is an extremely haphazard association to a specific object which is colored like an area of the blot but bears no resemblance to it. The inquiry usually reveals the presence of deterioration implicit in these responses (Rapaport, 1946). Swartz (1969) found that, although rarely given, the DC response is common among schizophrenics and mental retardates.

ABSURD RESPONSE (AB). AB responses show a complete disregard for the form qualities of blots whose form qualities are not normally ignored. Perseverations often result in AB responses. Swartz (1969) found these responses clearly indicative of mental retardation.

DEVELOPMENTAL TRENDS. The distribution of V is skewed and truncated in all the standardization population groups, especially the normal populations, in which the score is generally low. Among the normal groups, five year olds have the highest mean V scores. The V scores begin to drop (but are still high) for first graders. Swartz (1969) found high V scores in subjects age 6.7 with a decline, although not monotonic, to the lowest mean scores in the twelve- to fourteen-year age range. These findings are consistent with scores of the seventh-grade HIT sample. The mean scores rise for eleventh graders and college students although the scores are not nearly as high as those obtained for the youngest age groups. In the young child, V scores are typical. Autisticlike thinking is expected of the young child. The ability to draw on inner fantasies for percepts is considered healthy. The V scores for children load positively on Factor 1 (which defines, in part, integration of ideational activities).

Swartz (1969) found that with increasing age, significantly more children give FB responses and fewer of them give AL, CT, and AB responses. Over a six-year age span, FC, QR, and DC responses remain steady. Almost none of his sample gave IC or SR responses. Of the abnormal populations, chronic schizophrenics have the highest V scores. Emotionally disturbed children have the lowest mean V scores (somewhat lower than those of their normal counterparts). The scores of depressed patients are next lowest but are higher than are the scores of normal average adults. Mean V scores for mental retardates, emotionally disturbed adolescents, neurotics, and alcoholics fall in between and are higher in all instances than are those of normal subjects.

RESEARCH. Jortner (1966) studied the cognitive aspects of schizophrenics, using the HIT. He specified that, in general, cognitive aspects reflect reality testing and thought disorders. Specifically, he believes that autistic thinking and contamination are revealed by broken boundaries. He found schizophrenics high in QR and AL responses, revealing poor reality testing and thought disorders. They also scored high in CT. Their SR 3 and SR 4 scores reflect bizarre self-preoccupation and a breakdown in the sense of reality involving a breakdown of the body self.

Megargee and Swartz (1968) factor analyzed the extraversion and neuroticism scales of the Maudsley Personality Inventory (MPI) with the HIT scores. They found no significant loading with extraversion. However, the neuroticism scale loads on factors reflecting psychopathology and correlates positively with V, Ax, Hs, and M, and negatively with FA and R.

Megargee (1966), in a comparison of scores of white and Negro male juvenile delinquents, found significant differences on three of the twenty-two HIT scoring variables. White subjects scored significantly higher on V than did Negro subjects. (Negroes scored higher on At, and whites scored higher on P.)

Richter and Winter (1966) found that females high in creativity (as measured by the intuitive-perceptive scales of the Myers-Briggs Type Indicator) score higher in V (as well as FD, M, H, I, C, Ax, Hs, and Ab) than do females low in creativity. Megargee (1965) found a low mean score on V for a group of seventy-five male juvenile delinquents awaiting court hearing. This score, as well as their low scores on FD, FA, I, M, and H, is similar to the scores obtained by the seventh-grade standardization population. Herron (1964) found that when the HIT is administered to a college population and structured as an intelligence test, scores on V, Hs, and Pn are lower than when the test is administered in the standard manner. Moseley, Duffey, and Sherman (1963) found a positive correlation between a guilt scale on the Minnesota Multiphasic Personality Inventory (MMPI) and V, At, and FA scores in a population of depressed patients.

Anxiety (Ax)

The scoring of anxiety in the HIT is patterned after the original work of Elizur (1949) and is based on a direct relationship between the amount of conscious awareness of anxiety and the anxiety content in the percept. Elizur defines anxiety as an inner state of insecurity, which may take the form of fears, phobias, lack of self-confidence, extreme shyness, ideas of reference or marked sensitivity. The anxiety score reflects the level of anxiety and implies a long-term personality characteristic of the individual rather than a transitory reaction to stress. Ax reflects the degree of anxiety, not the way in which the individual expresses or attempts to reduce it. In order to assess how the individual copes with anxiety, his defensive style must be derived from other scoring variables. Anxiety is scored on the basis of symbolic content, which is strictly at the fantasy level. Neither the presence nor absence of anxiety is a sign of ego weakness; how the anxiety is handled indicates whether the personality is healthy or disturbed.

Normal anxiety is based on reality and warns the individual of outside dangers. Expression of normal anxiety indicates ability to deal with threats without becoming overwhelmed. A free expression of anxiety that does not violate the demands of reality may indicate ego strength, awareness of internal experiences, and may be a healthy way of handling problems. Persons capable of creative thinking are free in their use of imagery. They score higher on Ax (and other HIT variables) than do those who are not so endowed, without sacrificing the reality demands of the stimulus situation (Codkind, 1964; Clark, Veldman, and Thorpe, 1965; Richter and Winter, 1966).

Speilberger (1966) discusses two different types of anxiety concepts—anxiety as a transitory state, which he calls state anxiety and anxiety as a personality trait, which he calls trait anxiety. State anxiety, like normal anxiety, is a reaction which takes place "now" in response to a stimulus, external or internal, which is perceived as dangerous. The anxiety reaction leads to behavior designed to avoid or otherwise deal with the danger or to reappraise cognitively the original assessment of danger. Anxiety for some is a relatively stable reaction to certain stressful situations. Such trait anxiety reflects the residual of past experiences that in some way determine the individual's latent disposition to see certain situations as dangerous and thus to evoke an anxiety state. The experiences, Speilberger suggests, probably date back to the parent-child relationship regarding punishment. Anxiety as Elizur (1949) defined it and as it relates to the Ax score, reflects trait anxiety rather than the transitory anxiety state.

Anxiey as a trait is generally considered a negative emotion. It is experienced as a vague, objectless, free-floating, pervasive state of discomfort. The subject may be aware of the situations and conditions under which this feeling of anxiety is experienced, but he may not be aware of the cause. Anxiety is a threat to the core of the personality, the self-image, and threatens the existence.

The essential features of trait anxiety are uncertainty, helplessness, and anticipation of failure. The individual feels physically and mentally powerless to do anything about some personal matter and believes inevitably that he is in some danger. He tends to remain tense and alert as if facing an emergency. The self-absorption which this state creates interferes with the effective solution of real problems. He has doubts concerning the nature of the threat and his ability to cope with it. The focus of attention, however, is his feelings of personal inadequacy. These handicap and disturb relationships between the individual and others. Conscious and active attempts to overcome anxiety often intensify the feeling, resulting in complete lack of activity or in restless, intense activity which, if exacerbated, may eventually become destructive. Physical symptoms of anxiety intensify the individual's concern. These symptoms may involve cardiac spasms or palpitation, breathing distress, blood circulation problems (visceral and muscle tension), intestinal spasms including diarrhea or constipation, nausea, or tremors. Sometimes tension becomes so great that the individual will do anything to get rid of it. He may even attempt suicide. Anxiety states on the other hand may be mild and may be accompanied only by an increase in overt activity. The individual may appear outwardly calm and the inner anxiety state may go unnoticed. Or he may develop pathological fears to relieve the anxiety. These fears usually develop slowly and unconsciously. Therefore they are not likely to be controlled. Phobic and fear reactions may reduce temporarily the anxiety, but they are also a liability because the task of blocking these symptoms causes the anxiety to reappear. Other responses to anxiety may include rigidity in thinking (the individual refuses to accept and learn any new truths and sticks to certain dogma for security), aggression, withdrawal, blocking, and frantic compulsive activity (such as alcoholism or sexual activity).

Different individuals have different thresholds of anxiety. The inability to solve the problems which cause anxiety creates the fundamental roots of the neurosis. Neurotic anxiety is anxiety which is either out of proportion to the danger encountered or which exists without external danger. The danger in neurotic anxiety stems from the individual's own unacceptable impulses. Patterns of neurotic responses to anxiety include repression, inhibition, and sometimes somatic symptoms (if the anxiety cannot otherwise be tolerated).

Anxiety in children is manifested in loss of control and recourse to defenses. The defenses may take many forms. The children may demonstrate severe and exaggerated repression or complete denial of the conflict. They may retreat into fantasy or engage in frequent disrupting outbursts with loss of intellectual and emotional control. These manifestations are believed to be accompanied by unusual feelings of inadequacy (Halpern, 1953).

The anxious individual is tense, timid, apprehensive, and sensitive to the opinions of others. He is easily embarrassed and worries. He has inferiority feelings and has difficulty in making decisions because he is afraid of making mistakes. His posture is generally tense. He is excessively vigilant, has a fidgety manner (especially in the activity of his hands and feet), and his voice may be uneven. In stress situations his pupils may be dilated and his hands and face may perspire. He is frequently scrupulous, overconscientious, ambitious, and feels that he must live up to self-imposed standards.

The development of anxiety starts early. The very young child is considered in harmony with his environment. As he develops self-awareness and begins to move toward individualization, he comes into conflict with the demands of his parents. Increasing growth toward independence may lead to open conflict with parental demands and feelings of guilt ensue. The more creative the child, the more autonomy he seeks. As conflicts increase, so do feelings of guilt and anxiety. Anxiety in the child is generally related to his relationship with his parents. He needs their love and approval, and he has difficulty expressing negative feelings toward them because this behavior increases his anxiety. He therefore displaces his anxiety by developing fears of imaginary objects or animals which could be considered hostile.

Inconsistency in child training is the worst offender in creating anxiety because the child becomes uncertain, isolated, and mistrustful. Any threat to the child's need for self-worth and prestige creates anxiety. Another source of anxiety in children is deprivation. The child who is ignored, treated as if he were insignificant, and deprived of affection anticipates being unloved and unlovable, which makes him anxious. Deprived children lack controls and are afraid they will never gain them. If the child is overcontrolled, he fears failure and frequently responds with rebellious behavior. Overaffection also causes anxiety. The child fears being smothered. The surfeit of affection is more than he can tolerate.

The anxious child becomes restricted in his psychological growth and in his awareness. He has difficulty clarifying his feelings because he believes he has no dependable sources of interpersonal interaction available. In the young child (under age nine) anxiety produces disorganization and irritability. Children rarely react to anxiety in a mature adaptive fashion before this time and in many cases do so only considerably later (Halpern, 1953).

ANXIETY ABOVE THE NINETY-NINTH PERCENTILE. When the Ax score falls above the ninety-ninth percentile, the individual may be experiencing feelings of insecurity and personality conflicts. Excessive Ax responses also indicate that defenses may be beginning to fail, particularly in depressive individuals (Shafer, 1954). The content often helps to identify the type of anxiety which the individual is experiencing. Phobic anxiety is revealed in content involving threats from animals, persons, or mythical creatures. The highest mean Ax scores are obtained by emotionally disturbed adolescents who as a group have personality conflicts. Alcoholics and neurotics also score very high on Ax.

DEVELOPMENTAL TRENDS. The HIT normative sample evidences irregular developmental trends in the anxiety scores of the five normal populations. College students have the highest scores, average adults and five year olds the lowest. The distribution in slightly skewed in most groups but especially among the five year olds and the three abnormal standardization groups. Although chronic schizophrenics and average adults do not differ in their mean scores, the two groups differ strikingly in the range of their scores. The variance of schizophrenics is almost six times the variance of average adults (Holtzman, Thorpe, Swartz, and Herron, 1961). The variance for emotionally disturbed adolescents, neurotics, and alcoholics is also high.

Anxiety loads high on Factor 3, for all groups where it is a marker variable. Anxiety also loads high on Factor 1 for school children, average adults, and mental retardates. When Ax scores are given in these three groups, two other factors should be considered. The first is the controlled, differentiated, but integrated ideational activity characteristic of the variables defined in Factor 1 (M, I, H, FD, and P). The second is the component defined by pathological thought processes and emotionally disturbed fantasies as reflected in Factor 3. The scores for V, Hs, and M should be reviewed together with Ax for implications of this nature.

RESEARCH. The higher the level of anxiety in the schizophrenic, the greater the likelihood that he is still struggling with conflicts (a positive sign). Grauer (1953) reported greater improvement in a group of schizophrenics with a high anxiety level than among those with a low anxiety level. Stotsky (1952) also found that anxiety-level scores were higher for remitting schizophrenics than for nonremitting schizophrenics. Goldfried (1966), in a review of anxiety content, found a high level of anxiety in neurotics, adolescent delinquents, coronary patients, and psychiatric patients who present diagnostic problems. Anxiety is also higher on admission for schizophrenics who have a higher rate of remission than for those who do not.

Megargee (1965), studying a population of male juvenile delinquents, found lower anxiety scores for delinquents than for a normal adolescent group. However, the delinquent population was aware that their responses would affect the results of their impending court hearings. He speculated that they were responding to the blots not at the projective level (which would reveal fantasy behavior), but on the basis of overt controlled behavior.

Megargee and Swartz (1968) compared the HIT scores of college students with the extraversion and neuroticism scales of the MPI. They found a positive correlation between high neuroticism and high Ax scores (which accompanied high scores in V, Hs, and M) and negative correlation with R and FA.

Clark, Veldman, and Thorpe (1965) studied the relationship between junior high students who scored high in convergent thinking and those who scored high in divergent thinking and scores on the HIT. They found that the high-divergent thinkers score higher on anxiety (as well as Hs and M) than does the other group. These results indicate a consistent tendency for the divergent subjects to give free reign to imagination when given the opportunity. They are able to regress in the service of the ego without sacrificing the demands of reality (as evidenced by adequate FA and FD scores and low V scores). Fantasy production for this group is free and active without being pathological.

Codkind (1964) studied the relationship between subjects who readily accept the imaginary and those who do not. She found that the accepting group scores significantly higher on Ax (as well as Hs and M) than does the nonaccepting group. These scores occur together with other indicators of a high level of personality integration for the former group and an ability to respond in a normal manner (no V content). Codkind's findings agree with the findings of Clark, Veldman and Thorpe (1965).

Richter and Winter (1966) studied the correlation between creativity and various HIT scores. They used the intuitive perceptive scales of the Myers-Briggs Type Indicator to define high and low creativity in female subjects and found that those high in creativity have significantly higher scores in Ax (as well as Hs and M) than do those low in creativity. In addition, the creative groups also have high scores in FD, C, H, I, V, and Ab.

Hostility (Hs)

Hostility is expressed in themes of external threat and aggressive acts. The fact that an individual reports percepts that have aggressive elements does not necessarily mean that there will be a one-to-one relationship between aggressive content and any single behavioral or ideational expression of aggression. Many factors must be considered in determining the meaning of the aggressive, hostile content. The aggression may mean that the individual has a deep desire to fight or to be competitive whenever a vital value of his is threatened. Or he may not be aggressive at all but may greatly *fear* the aggression of others. Or he may be aware of his feelings and be capable of cognitively discharging them through aggressive fantasy elements. The content, the level and number of Hs scores, and the relationship of Hs to other variables indicate which hypothesis is most likely to be correct.

A highly aggressive, hostile individual is usually ready to fight beyond the call of social circumstances, which is a maladaptive trait (Beck, 1952). The fighting is frequently a defense against an attack of anxiety. It may also be a counterattack against self-attack. Individuals who fear the aggression of others are generally not aggressive toward others even though their responses include hostile implements of destruction, mutilated organisms, or animals with cut-off parts. Themes that deal primarily with fighting between persons with no threat to the individual imply the potential for making a hostile attack if provocation warrants it. However, such an interpretation needs to be supported by other variables and by a knowledge of the individual's general adaptation level, his control over impulses, and his ability to accept his aggression.

Murstein (1956) measured the projection of Hs on the Rorschach in relation to ego threat. Male college students were divided into four groups on the basis of group and self-judgments of hostility. Four experimental groups (twenty subjects each) were labeled hostile-insightful, hostile-noninsightful, friendly-insightful, and friendly-noninsightful. He found that projection of Hs was dependent both on the possession of the trait and on whether the subject accepts that he possesses it. The hostile-insightful group projected more hostility than did the other three groups. In an ego-threatening situation, however, they reacted differently and projected less Hs than did the hostile-noninsightful group. Therefore, self-insight alone is not an accurate measure of the amount of projection for all situations. Murstein concludes that under non-ego-threatening conditions, persons tend to perceive the world according to personal characteristics, provided the self is not so threatened by the perceptual environment that it causes denial of the percept. In ego-threatening conditions, most persons tend to project the negative traits ascribed to them onto others. This reaction is more marked in those who deny possession of the trait which others ascribe to them. The process is a function of the perceived threat to the self (Murstein, 1956).

The individual, then, who is aware of inner experiences and can deal with feelings at a cognitive level is capable of using aggressive elements in responses to the inkblot unless he perceives the situation as ego-threatening. High-average FD and FA scores combined with low V scores reflect an ability to integrate primary and secondary thought processes. Codkind (1964) found an increase in Hs scores in persons with a high degree of acceptance of the imaginary (accompanied by higher scores in cognitive variables) when compared with persons low in the acceptance and use of the imaginary. Clark, Veldman, and Thorpe (1965) found higher scores on Hs for high divergent-thinking junior high school students compared with high convergent-thinking students. FD and FA scores for the former group were adequate, and V was low, revealing the ability to use imagination and express aggressive elements while keeping them under cognitive control. Richter and Winter (1966) also found that women high in intuitive-perceptive creativity had higher Hs scores than did women not so endowed. Among other significantly higher HIT scores were FD, I, M, and H, revealing cognitive control as well.

HOSTILITY ABOVE THE NINETY-NINTH PERCENTILE. When hostile-content scores are excessively high, two hypotheses should be considered. Acting-out behavior would be expected if the individual were provoked, especially if the content of his responses involves overt hostility between persons or animals. Both Zubin, Eron, and Schumer (1965) and Murstein (1965) report elevated aggressive scores in persons who resort to aggressive acting-out behavior in such populations as children, adolescents, and adults convicted of and imprisoned for assault. Finney (1955), in a series of studies, found a positive relationship between assaultive behavior and destructive, hostile ideas. Sturment and Finney (1953) found aggressive thinking prevalent in assaultive mental-hospital patients. Murstein (1956) found that persons who project the most hostility on the Rorschach are hostile and insightful regarding their hostility. Rader (1957) found that when sociocultural conditions sanction aggressive behavior or when ego controls break down or both, high hostility-response content parallels acting-out behavior. However, Rader does not find sufficient evidence to expect this parallel in all cases. Megargee and Cook (1967) found a significant relationship in a juvenile-delinquent population between Hs scores and behavioral criteria of aggression. Fisher (1951) found that self-destructive and self-depreciative themes occurred frequently in the records of suicidal patients. Ulett, Martin, and McBride (1950) also found frequent aggressive and dysphoric associations among suicidal patients.

When the content of the Hs responses deals primarily with themes relating to threats to the individual, the individual often has an inordinate fear of aggression from others, especially if Ax scores are also high. These persons tend to avoid situations which they perceive as threatening. Megargee and Swartz (1968) found a positive correlation between the neuroticism scale of the MPI and high HIT Hs, Ax, V, and M scores and a negative correlation with R and Fa scores. Holtzman, Thorpe, Swartz, and Herron (1961) found higher Hs scores among depressive populations than they did among schizophrenics. Neurotics, alcoholics, and emotionally disturbed adolescents have the highest Hs scores of all groups. Their Ax and V scores are also excessively high.

DEVELOPMENTAL TRENDS. Holtzman, Thorpe, Swartz, and Herron (1961) found a noticeable drop in mean Hs scores accompanied by a drop in the number of individuals with excessively high Hs scores as the normal individual progresses from elementary school to adulthood. Five year olds have the lowest mean Hs scores and college students the highest. The mean Hs score for normals and schizophrenics is about the same, but the variance is much greater for the schizophrenics. The relatively low Hs (and Ax) scores for both chronic schizophrenics and mental retardates are due in part to the fact that the use of these two variables presupposes the availability of active fantasy involving humans in both hostile and anxious situations. Both groups also have unusually low M and H scores, again reflecting their inability to express their feelings directly through human-movement responses. The distribution for Hs shows a mild skewness upward in all groups, accompanied by a truncation in the records of chronic schizophrenics and mental retardates.

As with Ax, Hs loads both on Factor 3 (of which it is a marker variable) and on Factor 1. It loads higher than Ax on Factor 1 for all samples of school children, average adults, and mental retardates. On Factor 3, the loading is low for mental retardates, elementary school children, and the average adult. When Hs scores are present for these groups they should be considered on the basis of their relationship to both factors. Factor 1 variables (which include M, I, H, FD, and P) relate to controlled, differentiated but integrated ideational activity. Factor 3 variables (which include Ax, Hs, V, and M) define pathological thought processes and emotionally disturbed fantasies.

RESEARCH. Megargee and Swartz (1968), in comparing the extraversion-neuroticism scales of the MPI with HIT scores, found a positive correlation between the neuroticism scale and score on Hs, Ax, V, and M, and a negative correlation with R and FA.

Megargee (1965), comparing a population of juvenile delinquents with normals, found that the delinquent group did not have higher scores on Hs, Ax, or C. He suggested that this lack of difference reflects little relationship between overt behavior and fantasy because juvenile delinquents are expected to be impulsive and hostile. Megargee believes, however, that the test attitude of the juvenile delinquents was subjective. They did what they thought was expected of them and were probably not revealing fantasy because they were told that the testing would determine the outcome of their cases. Megargee and Cook (1967) later studied the relationship between aggressive content on projective techniques and overt aggression, using the same juvenile-delinquent population as Megargee (1965). They found a significant relationship between HIT scores including Hs, and their criterion of overt aggression. They also found the aggressive content in the HIT more related to measures of physical aggression than to verbal aggression. The authors feel, however, that no clear-cut statement can be made concerning the relationship between overt aggression and fantasy aggression because of the different criteria for overt aggression. Correlations could be positive, negative, or chance, depending on how one defines overt aggression. Megargee and Cook therefore suggest caution in predicting behavior. They were also aware of the role of the subjects' defensive test attitude.

Herron (1964) found that when the HIT was administered to a group of college students as an intelligence test rather than in the standard fashion, the scores showed a significant decrease in variables which reveal pathological thought (Hs, V, Pn, and A). He reports these results as a tightening up of the cognitive-perceptual process without an accompanying increase in constriction or stereotypy.

Penetration (Pn)

Penetration scores indicate the vulnerability of the body-image boundary. Cleveland (1960) found that Pn scores are negatively correlated with level of maturity and tolerance for stress. This hypothesis was verified by Swartz and Swartz (1968), who found that Pn scores are significantly higher for boys and girls with high anxiety than they are for those with low anxiety. These results indicate emotional immaturity, body preoccupation, and possible psychopathology. Jortner (1966) relates the Pn score to thought disorders and poor reality testing. Weakness of the body-image boundary makes an individual susceptible to attacks from without. He feels that things happening elsewhere or to others are happening to him. The individual cannot set up a line of demarcation which consistently distinguishes his body from the bodies of others. This inability to define body boundaries has a destructive effect on the body image and is associated with hostility toward the self. The hostility is experienced as sensations of disintegration and body decline. Freud (1925) considered the body image to be the total framework for the development of the ego structure. Persons with high Pn scores who have not defined their body-image boundaries would not have developed good ego structures. Fenichel (1945) suggests that body-image distortions of all varieties are among the earliest forerunners of schizophrenic regression.

The highest mean Pn scores in the normative samples are for emotionally disturbed adolescents, alcoholics, and neurotics. High Pn scores are also found among schizophrenics and depressives. Fisher (1970) reports that multiple samples do not show that Pn scores are consistently differentiating between normal and schizophrenic populations (although they are occasionally).

Holtzman, Thorpe, Swartz, and Herron (1961) found the distribution of Pn scores to be skewed and truncated except for college students, where the range is sufficient for a normal distribution. Five year olds and mental retardates have unusually low scores. (Two-thirds of them have none or only one.)

RESEARCH. Jortner (1966) used the HIT to investigate some cognitive aspects of schizophrenia. He studied the general attributes of poor reality testing and thought disorders, specifically preoccupation with abstract content and broken boundaries. He found that schizophrenics score significantly higher on broken boundaries, having higher Pn scores than do normal subjects. He relates the high Pn score to thought disorders and poor reality testing.

Cleveland and Sikes (1966) in a study of alcoholics versus nonalcoholics found that alcoholics score signficantly higher on Pn and perceive their bodies as dirty, disgusting, and deteriorating. The responses included wasted bodies, degeneration, and decadence, verifying the diffuse body-boundary concept associated with a high Pn score.

Conners (1965) compared the HIT records of disturbed children with the records of normal children and found no difference in the Pn scores. This finding is not surprising because body image in the young child is still in the permeable stage and has not yet crystalized. Barnes (1963) found higher Pn scores in brain-damaged subjects than he did in normal controls. Fisher (1964) found that boys tend to have higher Pn scores than do girls. Cleveland and Fisher (1960) found that Pn scores identify persons with interior body symptoms. In these individuals, the body attitude is fixated at a level predating the period when defensive mastery of the body exterior is normally accomplished. Fixation at this level often prevents free experimentation with the potential of the body exterior as a channel of expression and defense.

Herron (1964) studied the influence of test instructions on HIT variables. For some, he structured the HIT as an intelligence test. For others, he structured the HIT as a test of imagination. The responses were influenced by the individual's perception of what he thought he was being tested for. The differences in the results, however, were not large and affected only some of the HIT variables. The major difference was in the Pn score. Herron noted a highly significant decrease in Pn, a significant decrease in V and Hs, and a minimal tendency to reduce spontaneity of expression in favor of safe factual responses when the test was structured as a measure of intelligence.

Affect Arousal (AA)

Verbal or behavioral expressions of affect while responding to the inkblot imply a loss of distance between the individual and the card. The individual perceives the card as a segment of reality and affective feelings are precipitated. The affect may be pleasurable or painful. In either case, it represents the discharge of uncontrolled inner drives. Schachtel (1945) believes that when the affect is very strong, the individual has no time to be detached or objective in responding to the blot or to do any deliberate thinking. He simply reacts emotionally. Affect arousal in response to ten or more cards, whether positive or negative, indicates lability. The subject is unable to maintain the necessary distance toward the task because of the dominance of inner pressures for outward expression, whether appropriate or not.

Swartz and Swartz (1968) using 120 normal children in a study of the effect of test anxiety on the performance of the HIT found AA significantly higher (along with M, At, and Pn) in the high-anxiety group than in the low-anxiety group. The authors suggest that these results confirm the hypothesis that high-anxiety subjects give more subjectively personalized responses than do low anxiety subjects. When AA responses are given by the low-anxiety group, the responses are either pleasant or ambivalent. The responses of the high-anxiety group are almost exclusively unpleasant or ambivalent. These subjects express their fear of the test situation in the form of exclamations over individual blots. The affect is either without direction or is expressed in overtly unpleasant remarks directed to the cards or the subject's own responses.

The variables in this chapter identify thought processes as logical and clear or as disturbed and disordered. They reflect the level of reality orientation and the ability to use adaptive defensive behavior to protect the ego. The manner of outwardly expressing or suppressing inner pressures dealing with personality variables such as affect, anxiety, and hostility is revealed through these variables.

Factor Groupings

X

The twenty-two scoring variables (plus AA) can be treated as independent and should be used independently in the interpretation and analysis of the record. However, consideration of the relationships among some HIT variables often increases the validity of the interpretation. Although attempts to establish intercorrelations for the Rorschach scoring systems have been unsatisfactory, such relationships have been clearly established for the HIT. Serious psychometric flaws in the traditional Rorschach scores (such as the lack of metric properties, the artificial linkage of variables in most scoring systems, and marked curvilinear relationships between most scores and the number of responses) have been eliminated or greatly reduced in the HIT (Holtzman, Thorpe, Swartz, and Herron, 1961).

The computation of intercorrelation matrices of all scores for the standardization samples and the subsequent factor analysis for reducing the observed correlations to a smaller number of factors yielded valuable data. An objective rotational procedure selected the best-fitting orthogonal factors for the hypothesis that five factors are commonly present in HIT correlation matrices. The sixth factor is free to vary as necessary to accommodate the first five (Holtzman, Thorpe, Swartz, and Herron, 1961).

Evaluation of the interrelationships defined by each factor for variable loadings and reference populations provides insight into the meaning of the scores.

The factor groupings are also useful in developing designs for research studies.

Factor 1

Factor 1 consists of the following variables: integration, movement, human, popular, form definiteness, and barrier, and (except for five year olds) these variables (with the exception of H) are treated as a cluster in Chapter Seven ("Ideational Organization"). H is discussed in Chapter Eight. Factor 1 reveals the level of perceptual maturity of the individual. It defines his manner of organizing and integrating ideational activities. It reflects his ability to employ conventional percepts, reveals his imaginative capacity, and indicates his differentiation of ego boundaries and awareness of reality-based concepts. It also reflects the individual's ability to tolerate stress which is encountered in ambiguous situations. Megargee (1966) found that the length of the response has high loading on Factor 1. He interpreted this factor as verbal loquacity.

Hostility and anxiety load on Factor 1 for school children, average adults, and mental retardates. These two variables (as well as M) also load on Factor 3. They correlate with the characteristics associated with Factor 1 and define the pathological thought processes found in the emotionally disturbed fantasies of Factor 3.

Rejections are negatively correlated with Factor 1. Therefore, a high number of rejections reveal a paucity of constructive inner resources. Few or no rejections reenforces a prediction of ability to integrate ideational activity.

Location responses show a small but consistent tendency to be negatively correlated with Factor 1 for normal populations and positively correlated with Factor 1 for abnormal populations. The tendency for normal populations to give responses to the entire blot (low L scores) reflects reality contact and inner resources. Among deteriorated schizophrenics and mental retardates, even minimum perceptual ability to differentiate parts of the blot (L 1 or L 2) shows some limited resources as compared with the vague or absurd responses that these populations usually give and is therefore a positive sign.

Shading and animal responses have significant components which load on Factor 1 for many populations. This loading, however, does not hold for individuals with high ideational activity (such as college students). For the latter group, Sh and A responses are overshadowed by the high use of movement, form definiteness, and integration. Individuals with fewer resources, however (such as young children, mental retardates, and severely depressed patients), show moderate loading. Use of Sh and A by these persons can be interpreted as a positive sign of perceptual maturity and ego differentiation (Holtzman, Thorpe, Swartz, and Herron, 1961).

Factor 2

Factor 2 is defined by color, shading, and form definiteness which is inversely related. These are the major determinants with direct stimulus correlates within the blot. Color, shading, and balance (which also has high positive loading on Factor 2) are all discussed in Chapter Six ("Determinants"). FD is a positive marker variable for Factor 1. When it loads high on Factor 1 it loads low on Factor 2 and vice versa. This is a bipolar factor. When C and Sh are high, FD is low. This pattern reflects overreactivity to the stimulus correlates of the blot with the response predominantly determined by C and Sh. When C and Sh are low and FD high, it reveals an overconcern for form level and lack of attention to affective qualities (C and Sh).

Movement tends to be positively loaded on Factor 2 for children (except for the University of Texas superior group), for the Montrose Veterans Administration hospital schizophrenic group, and for the Austin State School retarded group. For these populations M may have a component in common with C and Sh (as opposed to responses determined solely by form). Persons with rich fantasy lives who respond affectively appear to do so in response to C, Sh, and the projection of M to the percept.

Balance has significant positive loading on Factor 2 for only some of the sample populations (eleventh graders, University of Texas superior, Waco and Montrose VA hospitals' schizophrenic groups, and the Austin retarded group). B is another measure of sensitivity similar to C and Sh.

Penetration is the most consistent variable (with the exception of the three marker variables), which loads positively on Factor 2. Significant loadings were reported in nine of the sixteen sample groups. Affect aroused by C and Sh usually results in diffuseness of response. Diffuseness reveals lack of body-image boundaries—the primary characteristic of high-Pn scorers.

Location has a high negative loading on Factor 2 for nine of the samples. The loading is especially high for the Austin college sample. These findings are consistent with the findings that high use of C and Sh accompany responses to the whole blot (Holtzman, Thorpe, Swartz, and Herron, 1961).

Factor 3

Factor 3 is best defined by the single variable pathognomic verbalization. Other marker variables are anxiety, hostility, and movement. Ax and Hs together with V have consistently high loadings for all groups. Chapter Nine (on disturbed thought processes) includes a detailed discussion of Factor 3 variables V, Ax and Hs (as well as Pn and AA). Factor 3 identifies the individual with psychopathology of thought processes and emotional disturbances. It reveals active and disturbed fantasy life with disordered thinking and bizarre perceptions.

Movement responses have the highest positive loading in the college sample. They have moderately high loadings on the other normal samples and a near zero loading on the abnormal standardization samples. M derives from the creative experience of the individual. Therefore, it contributes to the V score for the normal population, especially the college group. Creativity expressed in M responses derives for the normal populations, plays an insignificant role in the psychopathology of the abnormal group. M for normal populations, especially college groups, is linked with the fabulation or fabulized combination categories of V, both of which are usually high when M is present and both of which show controlled use of fantasy.

M and Factor 2 correlate higher in the samples of emotionally disturbed adolescents, neurotics, and alcoholics than they do in the samples of chronic schizophrenics, depressives, and mental retardates. When M occurs in the former populations it reveals disturbed thought processes. The accompanying V scores are likely to contain such categories as fabulized combination, autistic logic, self-reference, queer response, and deterioration color.

Form appropriateness in the abnormal groups (with the exception of the Montrose schizophrenic group) and in the samples of young children has the highest negative loading on Factor 3. All adult normals load near zero. Thus, V is likely to be linked with poor FA for the psychotic, the young child, and the mental retardate. The type of V response is likely to be incoherence, deterioration color, or absurd response, all of which accompany poor FA. Affect arousal is positively loaded on Factor 3. This relationship is expected because of the loss of distance frequently implied in AA and in the interpretation of Factor 3. Penetration is positively loaded for school children, especially fourth graders (Holtzman, Thorpe, Swartz, and Herron, 1961).

Factor 4

Factor 4 is defined by location and form appropriateness, which show reasonably positive loadings for most normal samples and for the group of Austin retardates. The loading is near zero for the other abnormal samples. Fragmentation of the blot into small parts is generally associated with good form level. Therefore the combination of L and FA is expected. Both these variables show high negative loading on Factors 1, 2, and 3. Thus, Factor 4 reflects those components of L and FA that remain after accounting for the components common to the three previous factors. Space responses tend to show low positive loading on Factor 4. They often involve blot fragmentation and fairly good form. Chapter Five ("Perceptual Differentiation") deals with the interpretation of variables in this factor (L, FA, and S).

Factor 4 can be interpreted in two ways. On the positive side, the interpretation is differentiated responses with adequate form level. This interpretation reveals a critical sense of good form and perceptual differentiation. On the negative side (when both scores are very low) the interpretation is immaturity, diffuse body preoccupation, with thought disturbances, and possible psychopathology (Holtzman, Thorpe, Swartz, and Herron, 1961).

Factor 5

Factor 5 is defined by the variables reaction time, rejection, and animal (reversed). Research shows that the longer the RT and the greater the R score, the lower the score for A.

Location scores tend to show significant negative loadings on Factor 5, which are expected. Psychologists assume that the longer the RT, the greater the blocking (which frequently results in increased rejections) and the subsequent zero scores for L (as well as for all other variables). Another expectation when RT is high is that L tends to be low. (When the response is finally made, it is often diffuse, involving the whole blot.)

Factor 5 is of minor importance compared with the other factors. Factor 5 depends on the interrelationship between RT and R or the relationship with A when R is high. In any case, this factor reflects the ability to respond to the total testing situation. Chapter Four includes a discussion of RT and R. Animal is discussed in Chapter Eight.

Factor 6

Factor 6 is a residual factor that contains those scores that have not been included in the first five factors (anatomy, sex, abstract, penetration, balance, space, and affect arousal.) All the variables included in this factor are sharply skewed and truncated. Therefore it is difficult to make a general interpretation incorporating all of them. A detailed discussion of At, Sx, and Ab appears in Chapter Eight.

In the Waco schizophrenic sample, the clearest pattern for this factor emerged with high loadings for S, Sx, and AA, and lesser loadings on Pn. This sample contained the greatest number of Sx responses, providing an opportunity to examine the inkblot correlations of sexual responses. Sx and Pn also define Factor 4 for the other schizophrenic groups. Sx is replaced by At in eight of the remaining twelve samples. Pn consistently defines variables in all these groups. At and Pn are also linked to Factor 4, so that Factor 6 is a residual of Pn and At, with Sx replacing At in two of the schizophrenic groups. Although the pattern shifts from one sample to another, the three variables, Pn, At, and Sx, stand out. Interpretation, therefore, should be based on them. Persons scoring high on these three variables are preoccupied with the body in a manner which is different from the body preoccupation found in Factors 3 and 4. Also, subjects high in Pn, At, and Sx are emotionally immature with possible psychopathology.

Research

Conners (1965) carried out a study to determine the effectiveness of brief psychotherapy (compared with initial consultation only) on a population of neurotic children. His study also tried to assess the effects of a stimulant drug on children with conduct disorders. Alternate forms of the HIT were used for pre- and posttreatment testing. In evaluating the results, Conners interpreted the scores according to the first five factors. In the group given psychotherapy, he found changes in Factors 2 and 4. The treated group tended to become more responsive to the blots and more differentiated and realistic in their approach than did the other group. The group treated with drugs also showed a trend toward an increase in Factor 2 and a decrease in Factor 4. The responses of the neurotics appeared to be significantly more differentiated than the responses of the children with character disorders as evidenced by significantly higher scores in Factor 4. The neurotic children were also more inhibited than the children with character disorders (Factor 5 is significantly higher). In addition, Conners noted considerable variability within the conduct-disorder group on Factors 1 and 2. The substantial change in Factor 1 for the drug-treated group suggests the feasibility of detecting changes after a short interval. The results also indicate that a more controlled, mature, and differentiated type of response is possible in hyperkinetic children who are treated with the stimulant (drugs).

INTERPRETATION
BASED ON
PERSONALITY VARIABLES

PART THREE

In the previous part, interpretation of the responses is based on the quantitative scores for the HIT variables and the interrelationship of clusters of variables and on qualitative factors. The process of quantitatively evaluating the responses to the inkblots begins with the coding of each percept by variables. These coded data for the forty-five blots are tallied, and the final scores are compared with a normative reference group (or groups). The protocol is then ready for interpretation, which results in the accumulation of postulates concerning the functioning of the subject. To make final use of these data, the hypotheses are coordinated in a manner which facilitates personality assessment and helps answer questions raised concerning the person tested.

In reviewing hypotheses derived from the separate scoring variables, many clinicians look for specific personality functions (for instance, intelligence or thought disturbance). Multiple references (from the individual HIT variables) to the same or similar personality factors strengthen hypotheses and identify significant modes of personality functioning.

Clinicians are able to provide a variety of information about an individual based on the assessment of his personality through many kinds of psychological testing. The information gleaned from the inkblot test is an essential contribution to any report. Personality variables commonly used in evaluating and predicting are cognitive functioning, affective functioning, and self-identity. This part therefore presents an interpretation of these personality variables and relates them to the HIT scoring variables.

Cognitive Functioning

XI

Cognitive functioning refers to the degree of native intellectual endowment and to the processes operating when an individual (through past experience) relates meaning to a situation which he perceives or recalls. For this process to take place, the individual must be able to use his inherent abilities. Thus, cognitive functioning is a complex of factors operating within and upon the individual. Dysfunction of the cognitive processes results from a malfunctioning of the central nervous system (particularly the brain) or from an emotional disturbance. Emotional disturbances often inhibit cognitive functioning and usually occur when a person has been subjected to unsatisfying conditions or relationships at home, at school, or at work. When this happens he develops defensive mechanisms in order to cope with these threatening situations. Hence cognitive functioning is not solely to be equated with intellectual endowment but also with the level of functioning possible in view of external and internal pressures which affect latent efficiency.

Transient events in or outside the test situation may also modify an individual's cognitive functioning. For example, his current physical state may be affected by illness, lack of sleep, hunger, or even the weather. He may also be in a depressed or elated mood. His affective state, basic attitudes, and motivation determine whether he approaches the test as a challenge and uses the cognitive resources available to him or sets up defenses to guard against exposure of his thoughts, resulting in inhibition.

Intelligence

Intelligence here is defined as the capacity to learn and the ability to adapt this learning to the demands of the environment through solving problems in old and new circumstances. The ability to make planned responses to relevant stimuli is basic to all intellectual activity. The behavioral responses of an individual in certain tasks (for instance, an inkblot test) reflect his capacity for dealing effectively with the environment. At each developmental level, from infancy to adulthood, the individual's perception of relevance changes. The greater the number of things that become relevant to the individual, the more intelligent he is judged to be. Few things are relevant to the retarded individual.

The HIT is not a test of intelligence. However, it requires memory, associations, thinking, and the ability to organize these processes in order to make relevant responses. Therefore, the quality of the response to the inkblot provides information which permits assessment of cognitive functioning. Beck (1952) enumerates three advantages of inkblot tests for assessing cognitive functioning: the responses are not directly dependent on schooling, the test material is objective and simple, and the same material may be used to test all levels of intelligence. Another important advantage of the inkblot technique is that responses require an interaction of the individual's intellectual and affective capacities, just as both these capacities operate when cognitive responses are made in a real life situation. Deficient thought processes may result from limited endowment, lack of development, organic brain damage, or emotional interference.

AVERAGE TO SUPERIOR INTELLIGENCE. Individuals whose cognitive functioning is at or above the mean possess both the native intellectual potential necessary for learning and the ability to use this potential for adaptive living without interference from emotional impulsivity. These persons demonstrate adequate reasoning ability and can see and understand relationships. They can synthesize separate facets of experience into a unit and are capable of taking an integrated approach to life situations by assuming an overall view through systematic thinking. They can concentrate, organize, and carry out plans. Their thinking is flexible but controlled and goal-oriented. These persons are well integrated in ideational activities and aware of conventional percepts.

They give a large variety of percepts, using a good vocabulary. Typically, they have average or above average scores for such variables as form definiteness, form appropriateness, color, movement, integration, human, and animal. The FD scores reveal the clearness of their perceptions and intellectual control. A low L score accompanied by FD, FA, and I in the average range or above indicates ability to abstract, theorize, plan, and engage in the overt motor activity necessary to execute their plans. This combination of scores is also associated with problem-solving activity, good recall, and a drive for achievement. The FA score reveals practical intelligence and the individual's ability to maintain contact with reality without interference from emotional impulsivity. The I score reveals realistic logical thinking and intellectual drive.

SUPERIOR INTELLIGENCE. Persons of superior intelligence are capable of advanced levels of problem-solving and can manipulate abstract associations, synthesize, and integrate at a high level of effectiveness. These abilities are revealed by the richness of their responses and the level of the content. Their FD, FA, and I scores are frequently well above the fiftieth percentile with L at or below the thirtieth percentile. The high FD scores reflect their ability to recall sharp memory images, to make good observations, to concentrate, and to persist. The quality of their I responses reveals integration not only of two or more parts of the blot but of color and shading as well. Such integration suggests the capacity to perform work requiring difficult and complex intellectual efforts. Those who are creative as well can use imagination freely and have high scores in movement, anxiety, and hostility, but low scores in pathognomic verbalization (Clark, Veldman, and Thorpe, 1965; Codkind, 1964; Richter and Winter, 1966).

LOW INTELLIGENCE. Mental retardation is associated with below average cognitive functioning and impairment of adaptive behavior. Persons who operate at this level lack the ability to survey and evaluate events. They have difficulty anticipating future happenings and lack the ability for constructive planning. They deal with those concrete situations which are immediately at hand. Their ability to function in society depends largely on the degree of retardation. At the lowest level, these persons are unable to defend themselves against common dangers and need protection. At the upper level, they can often master simple tasks but still require supervision in managing the complex activities of living. As a group, they are dependent on the guidance of others. They are suggestible in their social attitudes and can be easily led. They tend to be impulsive, inconsistent, and undependable when required to function independently. In a therapeutic relationship they are relatively inaccessible and often find it difficult to tolerate a one-to-one relationship. These persons cannot engage in insightful self-evaluation. They lack the ability to work out their feelings because they are incapable of resorting to fantasy, which accounts for their impulsive actions. They have no way of dealing with their feelings other than through overt behavior and emotional reactions remain dominant.

Mental retardates have high rejection scores. When they do respond to the inkblots, the responses are usually diffuse and amorphous, lack organization, and are similar to those of young children. Their A scores are the highest of those for all normal groups except for fourth graders, and they score very low in M and H. Their H scores are the lowest of all, revealing their intellectual inertness and constricted range of interest. They tend to have low FA scores, which reveals their inability to observe environmental events clearly. They have very low scores in L, FD, and I, demonstrating their inability to organize experiences beyond a diffuse global perception. Their V responses are second only to those of schizo-phrenics, and they give more of the absurd or deterioration-color V responses.

Thought Disturbances

Thought disturbances occur in neurotic and psychotic patients, persons with character disorders, and those with organic impairment. A defect in intellectual functioning usually represents a partial loss of the original capacity. The loss may be slight or severe, temporary or permanent. Maladjustment from any source interferes with intellectual functioning. The responses and behavior patterns of the maladjusted person are determined by his needs and drives, regardless of appropriateness to the stimulus situation.

NEUROSIS. Below average intellectual performance may be the result of neurotic inhibition of thought processes caused by the close tie between affective and intellectual functioning. This inhibition does not necessarily imply below average potential. On the contrary, such inhibition is frequently found in individuals with average or above average intellectual capacity.

Depressive inhibition is found in persons whose intellectual processes are slowed down and whose cognitive activity is impoverished as a result of the inhibiting effects of depression. Their FD scores are the lowest of those of all normative populations. The inhibition is also reflected in higher RT and R scores than those of normal adults. The depression inhibits motor functioning as well as intellectual functioning, but unless the depression is chronic, the inhibition is usually transitory, occurring from time to time.

Color, shading, and popular scores are low because of a reduction of involvement with external events. Depressive persons give more pathognomic verbalization and penetration responses than do normal adults, indicating the depressive's self-preoccupation and disordered thinking. The m response (particularly with destructive content) is often found in the records of very disturbed depressive patients who have morbid masochistic ideation.

Neurotic inhibition of intellectual functioning is more lasting than depressive inhibition and rarely is modified wthout psychotherapeutic intervention. It is often accompanied by mild depressive inhibition because some neurotics assume a chronic depressive mood. Examiners must therefore determine the structure of the neurosis and its impact on intellectual functioning.

The combination of high L and FD scores is found in the records of some neurotics who place a pedantic emphasis on accuracy and exactitude. This combination reveals the compulsive defensiveness found at times in this group. The L scores of the normative neurotic sample are generally comparable to those of normal average adults, although FD scores are higher. Neurotics have the highest mean C score of all groups. Predominant C 2 responses suggest sensitivity to the emotional impact of others in the person who is likely to be receptive to suggestion. Predominant C 3 responses suggest the chronic neurotic with diffuse lability and crochety irritability. Sh scores are higher for such individuals than for normal average adults, and light-film shading responses are frequently predominant. Attention to the diffuseness of the shading appears to be a defensive maneuver against the discharge of affective energy. The neurotic develops anxiety because of the strong possibility of affective impulses breaking through. The fear of retaliation for having expressed these impulses causes them to retreat into inactivity and develop passive adjustment as a defense. High scores in M and low scores in FA are also typical of the neurotic who, because of recourse to inner life, is turned in on himself and draws on his own fantasy.

Constricted neurotics are often unable to acknowledge their imaginal processes (Klopfer, Ainsworth, Klopfer, and Holt, 1954). Morbid masochistic ideation is frequently revealed through m responses with destructive content and by the high use of At content (At 2 predominant). This combination is generally found in the records of persons who displace anxiety and conflicts concerning the body. The V scores for this group are among the highest of all groups as are their Ax and Hs scores.

CHARACTER DISORDERS. The individual with a character disorder acts out his problems at the expense of others (in contrast to the neurotic, who conforms with social expectations by taking out his frustrations and anxieties on himself). The person with a character disorder violates societal codes and conventions, assuming no responsibility for his behavior. Basically, he has failed to become socialized and introject the standards of society. Many persons in this category have average or above average intelligence but have failed to develop realistic life goals.

Among the groups of persons with character disorders are juvenile delinquents. Norms for this group are characterized by low RT and high R scores, indicating their inability to become involved with the stimulus. Their low C and Sh scores also reveal their lack of involvement and insensitivity to the enriching qualities of the blot. L and I scores are also low and reflect their lack of motivation to achieve and to discipline the intellect. Their low H scores indicate lack of interest in the motives of other people, and their low P scores are consistent with their rebellious attitude and indifference to conventionality.

PSYCHOSIS. The individual who has a serious mental disorder pays insufficient attention to his immediate surroundings, both physical and social, and yet is unable to be detached or indifferent to them. He lacks the ability for objective thought. His associations are uncritical, based on his inner needs regardless of the demands of reality. He cannot use his intelligence for critical evaluation and has difficulty concentrating. Reality becomes distorted for him because of his disordered thinking and confusion. Many diagnostic categories of psychosis have been defined in the field of psychodiagnostics. The most common are schizophrenia, manic depressive psychosis, and paranoia.

According to Schachtel (1966), the preschizophrenic can be identified when the capacity for active coping, structuring, integrating, and organizing behavior breaks down. Little or no use of color is considered one indicator of the preschizophrenic's inability to integrate. Color in the blot is acutely disturbing to him. Therefore he consciously avoids it lest he reveal underlying chaotic and panicky thoughts (Schachtel, 1966). Failure to use color reveals intellectual and emotional withdrawal and a narrowing of functioning. It indicates inhibition, guardedness, and defensiveness. Such behavior is found in persons who are deficient in the socialization of their emotional impulses and are therefore unable to establish good relationships. They compensate by withdrawing into autistic living. The chronic-schizophrenic normative samples have lower C scores than do most other groups. These schizophrenics at times see animals in human movement, which reflects their disappointment with the world and is accompanied by prolonged depressive moods (Beck, 1952).

Some schizophrenics use a great deal of color, and their C 3 and C 2 responses exceed their C 1 responses. Norms for the paranoid-schizophrenic sample show C scores which are among the highest for all groups. Although these scores reflect affective expression, they show that the individual is still maintaining some control; he is able to integrate color and some form. The use of color typifies the sporadic outbursts of schizophrenics but it is a positive sign (Beck, 1952).

Excessive At responses are given by the paranoid schizophrenic and reveal his self-absorption and overconcern with his body. The restriction of or reduction in intellectual drive is revealed by the high At scores and by the low FD, FA, and I scores obtained by all schizophrenics. The low FD, FA, and I scores (along with the subject matter of the content), reflect poor planning, lack of persistence and drive, and lack of integration. The largest number of rejections for all samples is given by schizophrenics (and mental retardates) who lack inner fantasy life and are incapable of interacting with the stimulus except in a superficial and limited manner.

When nature content, such as rocks and landscapes, is seen in a deteriorated condition, and the examiner also has other indicators of psychosis, the individual is projecting his own feelings of weakness and personal disintegration onto these objects. Such responses suggest a poor prognosis (Haley, Draguns, and Phillips, 1967).

V is the prime indicator of disordered and disorganized thinking. It is a qualitative sign of mental disturbance, revealing autistic thinking, failure of repressive defenses, and ego weakness. Failure of the defenses leads to regressive responses, often revealing loosened fantasies and bizarre themes such as are found in the borderline or full psychotic state (Shafer, 1954). Schizophrenic samples have the highest V scores, indicating little interest in seeking relationships and poor reality content. Chronic paranoid schizophrenics have significantly higher self-reference, deterioration-color, incoherence, and contamination types of pathognomic verbalization content than do normals. They also produce more SR responses than do mental retardates, and more autistic logic responses than do depressives. Schizophrenics give fewer absurd responses than do mental retardates and fewer fabulation responses than do depressed subjects (Swartz, 1965). High penetration scores are often found in psychotic populations. Fenichel (1945) found body-image disortion to be among the earliest forerunners of schizophrenic regression.

ORGANIC BRAIN DAMAGE. When there is brain damage present the degree of impairment varies with the location and extent of the damage. In some patients, the damage results in minimal disruptions of behavioral functioning, while in others the interference in functioning is great, with loss of ability to abstract, impairment of memory, inability to make associations, and stereotyped thinking.

Some persons with organic brain damage obtain high L scores because they find it easier to produce a good percept to a small part of the blot than to produce an integrated response. Others who use the entire blot (scoring low in L) respond with content that is diffuse, showing little attempt to integrate the blot material. The content is often characterized by perseveration. Barnes (1963) found low L scores among his brain-damaged sample as well as low FA scores, revealing poor reality awareness. This lack of awareness may be the result of faulty recall, even when sharp memory traces are present since the organicity may affect either recent or past memories (Bohm, 1958). Organics typically reject blots because they experience difficulty in sustaining the effort necessary to respond to each blot. Barnes (1963) found high C, At, and Pn scores for brain-damaged subjects, revealing body preoccupation and lack of affective controls.

Affective Functioning

XII

Affect relates to feelings and moods within the individual which are predominantly internalized and not always identifiable in overt behavior. These feelings can be positive(happiness, love, curiosity) or negative (depression, anxiety, anger, fear). Affective moods and drives which result in overt action may originate as a consequence of an idea or mental representation of an event, or as a result of an interaction with the environment. Sometimes the affective tone of the individual is obvious (for example, crying or laughing), but, mostly, feelings are contained within the individual and are not readily discerned (such as anxiety and tension). Whether affect will cause overt behavior depends upon the strength of the stimulus which aroused the feeling. It also depends on the personality of the individual. The greater the strength of stimulus, the more likely is the expression of the affect aroused in overt behavior. The ability to control or express feelings also depends upon the individual's emotional maturity and his faculty for demonstrating feelings in an adaptive manner. In order to understand how an individual copes with affect, the examiner must determine the intensity of the internal idea or external event which aroused the feeling as well as the maturity level at which the individual generally functions.

The expression of affect may be adaptive or nonadaptive. Adaptive behavior includes perception of and concern with interactions in the outer world and is either partially or totally under the conscious intellectual control of the individual. The individual is capable of placing appropriate limits on the expression of his feelings and expresses them in a manner that is socialized and acceptable. These individuals have affective stability and can relate well.

Nonadaptive behavior is of two kinds. Labile affect is typical of the egocentric individual whose inner pressures dominate and direct the outward expression of affect, regardless of the appropriateness of their expression. For these persons, affect is easily aroused. They are sensitive to the impact of the actions of others and receptive to suggestion. Their ability to control their feelings is inadequate. The other nonadaptive affective behavior is typified by excessive inhibition. This manner of handling affect is pathological because it is directed primarily toward the reduction of anxiety. The individual is limited in his ability to experience, think, or act in certain areas because these areas evoke anxiety. The result is a constricted inner state. The individual remains anxious and tense because he is unable to handle his affect. Some insensitive normal persons also function at an affective level which is flat. They either lack the incentive to develop the capacity to enjoy the world around them by openly interacting and expressing feelings or lack the opportunity to do so (Schachtel, 1966).

Emotional Maturity

The development of emotional maturity, which includes control of affect, normally proceeds in an orderly manner from birth. The very young child is egocentric with little, if any, drive toward interacting with the environment. He does not experience himself as separate from the world. His emotional reactions reflect this egocentricity. He is demanding, impulsive, and spontaneous in the expression of feelings. The prepubertal child is still dominated by emotional needs, but during this period he also wants to strengthen and regulate relationships with significant persons. In so doing, he starts to become other-directed and identifies with adult concepts, values, and attitudes. Thus, the control of affect begins. By puberty he should experience an increase in emotional controls.

During the early adolescent period (ages twelve to sixteen), the child again becomes self-directed. He is preoccupied with understanding himself and learning to control affect through self-limits rather than through limits imposed from without. By the late adolescent period (beginning with age sixteen or seventeen), he should be increasing the stability of his inner emotions and using cognitive processes to control their expression. Thereafter, affect for the normal individual should be expressed in an adaptive, appropriate manner independent of the intellectual level at which the individual is capable of functioning. If affect control has not developed by late adolescence, emotional maturity lags. The developmental level at which the individual is functioning can be determined by the manner in which he expresses affect; the more labile the affect, the more infantile the emotional level.

Emotional development sometimes proceeds excessively rapidly signaling developmental problems. Strong affective controls instituted before age nine suggests that affect-depressing forms of training have created insecurity in the child, resulting in exaggerated efforts at self-control and compliance. Emotionally mature persons have affective stability and are capable of using cognitive processes effectively. College students and eleventh graders have the highest mean scores among all the normative groups in popular, form definiteness, form appropriateness, and human, and the college students score highest in integration. These two groups also have the highest color and shading scores among the normal populations. The use of P responses in the average range or above reflects an intellectual adjustment to society. The use of Sh and C responses with C 1 predominant represents the ability for affective control, keeping emotions under the control of the intellect. The presence of H responses (both H 1 and H 2) indicates ability to relate to persons. The combination of many H 1, H 2, and C 1 responses suggests human compatibility and the ability to form relationships.

Emotional Immaturity

Persons with labile emotions typically give excessively high C, Sh, and M responses. They may also give excessively high anxiety, hostility, penetration, and anatomy responses. The three normative groups having the highest mean scores in all these variables are the emotionally disturbed adolescents, neurotics, and alcoholics. Paranoid schizophrenics also have high C scores. Such responses are given by emotionally immature persons who are preoccupied with their bodies. Their behavior is similar to that of a young child. Inner forces dominate ideational processes, and these persons are indifferent to environmental pressures.

Persons whose affect is overcontrolled usually give few C, Sh, or M responses. Low C, Sh, and M scores are found among schizophrenics, retardates, and emotionally disturbed children. Location, human, and anxiety scores for emotionally disturbed children, neurotics, and alcoholics are among the highest in the abnormal groups. These scores identify the rigid, compulsive, tense individual whose major defense is repression. These individuals frequently suffer acute neurotic reactions or have severe compulsive disorders which lead to painful distrust, even of their own actions. Withdrawal is accomplished by insulation from the outer world and assumption of a passive, apprehensive mood. Excessive H, Ax, and Hs responses suggest problems in interpersonal relationships because of fear of people. Emotionally disturbed adolescents have the highest scores in these three variables, reflecting their inability to tolerate interpersonal relationships on a one-to-one basis.

Controls

Perceptual autonomy is the ability to use cognitive processes effectively without interference from emotional impulses—the ability to maintain control so that neither unconscious nor emotional elements distort perception. At the other extreme, complete lack of affect control is seen in lack of restraint, impulsiveness, self-centeredness, and emotional reactivity. Such behavior is also seen in the typical emotional reactivity found sporadically in children under five. At this age they are egocentric, demanding, and impulsive. Prepubertal children are also dominated by emotional needs and tend to lack adequate control of emotions, although by age seven or eight emotional controls should be emerging. During puberty, the capacity for empathizing with others and increasing maturity cause emotional controls to become incorporated. In early adolescents (age twelve to sixteen) and for some children during the entire adolescent period, controls fluctuate or decline. This fluctuation or decline is the result both of internal and external pressures which impinge on the adolescent as he develops and begins to know himself. However, during this period, controls are being internalized and should begin to become effective by age sixteen.

Adaptive controls are reflected in average or above average scores in FD, C, Sh, and Br. College students have the highest mean scores in these variables. They are generally capable of performing well under stress. Anxiety is controlled if Ax and FA are also in the average range.

Some persons maintain an intermediate level of control. They seem to desire and strive for controls but nevertheless demonstrate adolescent irritability regardless of age. They have excessively high C scores, revealing lack of capacity to delay affective responses. Adaptation to reality is not precluded, but the excessively high C scores have psychotic implications. Repression of highly charged impulses with some control present (as in the hysterical individual) may also be implied (Beck, 1952).

Emotionally disturbed behavior reflecting lack of internalized controls is seen in the overt actions of children beyond age seven or eight who are uncertain in emotionally charged situations, and in disturbed adolescents. Uncertainty suggests primary behavior patterns which attempt to protect the individual against anxiety caused by feelings of inadequacy and destructive impulses. For the most part, children and adolescents who lack controls are aggressive and bullying. They are unruly, engage in temper-tantrum behavior and minor delinquencies, and do not face reality.

When controls are absent, RT is low and C, Sh, M, and Hs are generally very high with a tendency for C 3 and dark-film responses to be high. The L and FA scores are typically low. The excessively high C scores (particularly when C 3 is predominant) indicate emotional reactivity in persons who are overwhelmed by their feelings. When, in addition, the individual scores high on HM, he may be potentially dangerous, especially when inhibitions lapse. Excessive Sh scores indicate lack of capacity for control and suppression of emotional impulses. When dark-film Sh is predominant, the individual tends to alleviate his anxiety by increasing activity in areas where fear and anxiety are rife. He may take chances and act hastily, often underestimating the dangers ahead. Such behavior may be due to an inability to tolerate anxiety or to feelings of invincibility or both. However, the need to act is based on a desire to avoid anxiety and depression.

Emotionally disturbed adolescents typically score low in RT, L, and FA. C scores are high, and Sh, M, H, and Hs scores are very high. This group also scores very high in V, At, Ax, and Pn, revealing the disturbed nature of their fantasies and their self-preoccupation. They have low P scores, reflecting their rebellious attitude and lack of participation in the adult world.

Another maladaptive reaction is overcontrol, which indicates emotional withdrawal based on a need to avoid dealing with feelings. Some children as young as seven or eight give up the struggle to establish relationships with the outer world and turn inward, ignoring external stimuli and pressures (Halpern, 1953). For some, emotional energy is absorbed in an active fantasy life filled with self-preoccupation. Some fail to make friends because they are unwilling to participate in group activities. Others, however, do not withdraw socially, even though they are overcontrolled and emotionally withdrawn. Nevertheless, their social behavior is highly individualistic because it is basically inner-directed. These persons are sometimes deviant and not accepted because they are demanding, disorganized, impulsive, and egocentric. Emotionally disturbed children have typically overcontrolled reactions. Their RT, L, FA, and I scores are very low, revealing the inability to become actively involved in the task of responding to the stimulus. Although they are able to give C responses, their Sh scores are the lowest of all groups. They are also very low in M, H, A, and P, revealing their inability to express their feelings through normal channels. They have high At scores, reflecting their body preoccupation. They also have low Br scores, which indicates their passivity and inability to tolerate stress. These children tend to be prudent, hesitant, timid, inadequate, and depressed. Excessive control of overt behavior results in low action tendencies. However, their anxiety remains because they do nothing to alleviate these feelings.

When excessive control appears in a child's record, emotional life is inhibited. Such inhibition provides some stability but does not permit spontaneity or the development of affective potential. In fact, excessive controls repress whatever affective potential has been developed. The children find some release in uncontrollable sporadic outbursts. Studies have shown that psychosomatic disorders such as asthma, eczema, and colitis are found in children who place great emphasis on control, conformity, and compliance. Their need to repress aggression and to accept the dictates of authority is so strong that it causes constriction and inhibition of emotional expression.

Anxiety

The overall indications of anxiety discussed here do not relate specifically to the Ax score. Anxiety as a trait is generally an unpleasant affect aroused by unreal or imagined dangers. Both physical and somatic reactions (cardiac, respiratory, and psychological, including unpleasant feelings, sensations, and apprehensions) are associated with anxiety. As the child develops, he gains an awareness of himself and a need to maintain his self-image. He experiences anxiety whenever he is unable to achieve a sense of equilibrium between the inner and outer pressures which impinge on him or when this balance is threatened.

The child also learns that certain traumatic situations result in feelings of anxiety. In time, he is able to anticipate these uncomfortable feelings before the traumatic situations arise, and this anxiety in anticipation, which precedes or accompanies certain events, signals danger and helps the child avoid stress either through ego defenses which he has developed or through avoidance.

Because all persons experience anxiety, it does not in itself signify lack of maturity or stability. A mild dose of anxiety may be pleasurable, and some persons seek ways of stimulating such anxiety. They equate it with excitement, for instance, in automobile racing. Normal anxiety, which Spielberger (1966) refers to as state anxiety, is produced by actual danger from the external world and serves as a warning. Persons with normal anxiety have the ability to deal with threats without becoming overwhelmed. They are capable of functioning adequately in all situations. Their responses show neither excessively high nor exceedingly low scores especially in L, FD, FA, C, Sh, and Ax.

To understand how anxiety affects a person, the examiner must know the intensity of the anxiety, its cause, and how the individual copes with it. In the very young child (before age eight) anxiety is typically handled by repression (denial of the conflict), retreat into fantasy, or disruptive outbursts with loss of emotional and intellectual control. The child may also handle anxiety by developing exaggerated dependence on the environment at the expense of his inner life, which he represses and denies. The content of responses results in low Ax scores. His repression results in lack of emotional investment in a fantasy life. Instead, energies are used to establish emotional relationships with the outside world which are usually based on infantile needs and demands. The responses of anxious children frequently include a high R score, revealing blocking and refusal to respond and indicating conflicts and anxiety. Their very low C, H, and M scores also reflect conflicts and anxiety. They lack the ability to be emotionally responsive to the environment on which they are so dependent and deny their inner life and fantasy. The normative sample of emotionally disturbed children (average age 9.8) shows this pattern of high R scores and low C, M, H, and Ax scores. Their R and H scores are comparable to those of the five-year olds. Their C and Ax scores are lower than those of that group, and their M scores are comparable to the scores of first graders.

Excessive anxiety is associated with maladaptive behavior and is the central feature of neurosis. Anxiety neurosis results primarily from blocking expression of drives and is associated with general irritability and and free-floating feelings of apprehension.

Conversion hysteria is a channeling of anxiety through repression of its original cause to a dissociated bit of behavior. In this substitution, the fear of external danger is replaced by internal danger. Somatic symptoms replace the feared thought content. Conversion reactions are frequently manifested by disturbances in the cardiac function and respiration. Symptoms also include the presence of diarrhea, vertigo, and paresthesia. The substitute symptom converts the anxiety so that it remains bound to the symptom. Such cases are relatively infrequent. However, excessively high scores in Ax, Pn, and At with some blocked movement responses are suggestive of the conversion hysteric. The blocked movement reveals severe doubts and neurotic reactions, which reflect an inability to make decisions either in thought or action. The very high Ax and Pn combination reveals neurotic conflict with excessive body concerns. This combination together with high At scores is found in the neurotic sample.

Neurotic anxiety may also take the form of a phobia. The original fear of an internal drive is displaced and bound to some other object. The phobic anxiety is fixed on some external danger which is exaggerated in relation to the actual danger. Phobic anxiety is a morbid fear associated with morbid anxiety, for example, fear of death, illness, or insects. Individuals who are phobic or counter-phobic often have excessively high scores in Ax, Hs, M, C, At, and Pn. A 1 responses frequently exceed A 2 responses. These scores are found in the normative sample of neurotic subjects. Blood or mutilation themes often appear in the content. The type of movement reveals how the individual copes with aggression. He may respond with counteraggression, with flight, or by doing nothing (playing dead). If the movement is aggressive and the subject also gives some C 2 responses, aggression may be expected. (Such aggression neutralizes the anxiety somewhat.) Readiness for flight is expected when the subject gives no direct sign of aggression. If the movement is passive, the subject tends to withdraw from the outer world or play dead. Phobic anxiety is also seen in morbid anxious content when the subject expresses fear of hostility from the environment or from people or both. It is also suggested by threatening content involving H 1 responses (faces or mythical figures) or a high number of threatening A responses and masks accompanying achromatic color responses.

Another form of neurotic anxiety is obsessive-compulsive neurosis. Anxiety of this nature is usually associated with fear of punishment for aggressive or sexual impulses. It becomes displaced onto overcontrolling behavior which centers on trifling details. Obsessive-compulsive neurosis is characterized by disturbing, unwanted, anxiety-provoking thoughts and impulses to perform certain acts repetitively (such as compulsive counting) whose only purpose is to allay anxiety. Compulsive actions usually accompany the obsessive ideas. An obsessive-compulsive neurosis often manifests itself in a critical attitude toward the imperfections in the inkblots. Such behavior is an attempt to avoid anxiety by clinging to obvious and safe percepts and expressions. Excessively high scores in L, FD, Ax, and M are expected from these individuals. Very low C and Sh scores also reflect insensitivity to the emotional impact of the outer world, although the subject is aware of inner needs and impulses. Obsessive-compulsive persons tend to worry, which increases their fantasy lives and decreases overt behavior.

A high level of anxiety in schizophrenics is considered a positive sign, suggesting a continued struggle with conflicts (Grauer, 1953). Schizophrenics with high anxiety show greater improvement in treatment and a higher remission rate than do schizophrenics with low anxiety.

Defense Mechanisms

Everyone uses defense mechanisms to protect the ego at one time or another. The appropriateness and effectiveness of the mechanism depends on the amount of emotional freedom and constructive personality development it permits. The more emotional freedom possible, the healthier the use of the defense mechanism. Defensive behavior is aimed at avoiding emotional involvement with inner or outer stress. These mechanisms, however, are unconscious, and the person is not aware of the motivation for these acts although he obviously is aware of the acts themselves.

REPRESSION. Repression is the active but unconscious process of keeping out, ejecting, or banishing from consciousness unacceptable ideas or impulses, thereby reducing their influence. Stressful events or thoughts are handled by an intellectual control which ignores the emotional content. When a high level of energy is used to maintain this intellectual control, little or no energy remains available for emotional experiences. Persons who use repression frequently have excessively high scores in RT, indicating an interim process—probably repression of unacceptable content. Alcoholics and depressives have the highest RT scores.

REACTION FORMATION. Reaction formation is a form of defense against impulses which are unacceptable to the ego. The reaction-formation response is usually the extreme opposite of the unacceptable impulse; for example, oversolicitude and friendliness may cover unconscious feelings of hate, or a passive, conforming attitude may cover aggressive drives. By using this defense, the individual is obliged neither to avoid situations which stimulate aggression nor to deny the aggressive impulses. These persons generally have very high P scores. The highest P scores are found among college students and average adults. Emphasis on passive movement in humans and animals may be present and C responses would be predominantly C 1.

DENIAL. Denial is a defense through which either external reality is rejected and replaced by wish-fulfilling fantasy or behavior, or awareness of internal reality, such as wishes, impulses and affects, is blocked. This defense may be observed as anxiety during the test taking behavior. For example, very young children often give a test response such as "it isn't anything." In older persons, the denial response is usually overt denial of a forbidden impulse. For example: "Two people fighting. No, they are not fighting; they are talking."

FLIGHT. Flight is an escape from danger. The danger may be disturbing emotional demands from the outer world or anxiety-arousing fantasies from within. When emotional involvement with the world is disturbing and the emotions are turned back on the self, excessive M, H (and possibly A) responses are expected. Turning inward is normal for eleventh graders and college students. These groups have the highest M, H, and A responses of all groups. The late adolescent is still unable to cope with the demands of the outer world. He is in the process of establishing a rapport between the demands of his outer and inner worlds. This pattern is also found in emotionally disturbed adolescents. In this group, however, the additional high V, Ax, Hs, At, and Pn scores reveal pathognomic fantasy content. The neurotic and alcoholic populations have excessive M and H responses and high A responses. These groups have not learned to cope with the demands of the outer world. If the emotional content of their fantasies causes the distress, the flight away from revealing inner fantasies is indicated by excessive R scores and low FD, M, H, Ax, and Hs scores. Emotionally disturbed children, schizophrenics, and retardates have scores such as these.

PROJECTION. Projection means ascribing one's own unacceptable drives and impulses to others. If the projection is excessive, it interferes with the acceptance of reality and leads to paranoid feelings. The individual believes the world is an evil, threatening place requiring a cautious and wary approach. Responses indicative of projection contain very high Ax and Hs scores. There may also be such qualitative signs as verbalized feelings of someone watching or threatening, or of humans fighting or engaging in brutal or morbid activities. Also H 1 responses may include faces, eyes, or pointing hands. The highest Ax and Hs scores are found among emotionally disturbed adolescents, neurotics, and alcoholics.

REGRESSION. Regression is an emotional return to an earlier stage of development in which the individual felt more secure and satisfied than he feels in his present stage. The young child frequently regresses, but for him it is usually a temporary device. Radical and prolonged regressive behavior indicates a serious disturbance. Responses typical of regressive behavior include perseveration of percepts from one blot to another and excessively high scores in V and Pn. The highest V and Pn scores are found in neurotics, alcoholics, and emotionally disturbed adolescents.

Kris (1952) refers to a temporary shift in associations to reveal imagery and fantasy as regression in the service of the ego. Such regression is under the conscious control of the individual and is a temporary, creative aid. Typical response scores for such individuals show I, H, A, FA, Br, Pn, B, and At in the average range or above, and Sx and L in the low range. If V responses are given, FB predominates.

DISPLACEMENT. Displacement is the transferring of emotional tones from the ideas to which they were originally attached to different ideas. Displaced affect presupposes the displacement of ideas because affect is associated with thoughts rather than objects. Impulses are displaced from one mode of behavior to another as, for example, feelings of motor aggression may be displaced to verbal aggression. In the inkblot responses, hostile affect toward people is often displaced by hostility toward less threatening objects such as animals, mythical figures, or natural forms. Hs scores are usually excessively high in individuals resorting to this kind of displacement. Sexual ideation is often displaced to At responses dealing with lower parts of the body, resulting in excessive At scores. The highest Hs and At scores are found among emotionally disturbed adolescents, alcoholics, and neurotics.

Depression

Depression is a clinical syndrome which consists of lowering of mood tone, difficulty in thinking, and psychomotor retardation (Hinsie and Campbell, 1960). In certain types of depression (especially involutional melancholia, neurosis, and psychosis) the depression may be masked by anxiety, obsessive thinking, or agitation. This masking of depression is particularly common in persons with phobic and obsessional neurosis and in manic-depressive psychosis. A depressive reaction is a normal state caused by an external problem which, when resolved, relieves the depression. Ordinarily, depression means a dejected, sad, gloomy, desperate, or despondent mood. The depressive reaction is an attempt to repress and control threatening, unconscious hostility and aggressive impulses. When aggression cannot be openly expressed, it is turned against the self. Typically, HIT scores identifying self-punitive attitudes are high RT, R, V, Pn, and Ax because such scores indicate an increase in threatening imagery. In addition, C and Sh are often very low. Depressives have the lowest FD scores of all normative samples, reflecting emotional flatness, apathy, and the rigidity which inhibits creativity but serves as a safety device for self-directed aggression. Additional signs of depression include projection of chromatic color (for example, blood) onto achromatic areas, excessive use of black to the exclusion of other chroma, and excessive use of dark-film Sh responses. Depressives tend to seek in the environment those factors which are consistent with their mood of despair. They are sometimes disappointed when good things happen to them. Such disappointment is particularly common for persons with mild forms of depression where reproach and anger are manifest (although these feelings may not be known to them).

Suicidal ideation often accompanies depression. Persons with high suicidal potential respond to the inkblots with themes of mutilation, death, flight, suspension, darkness, depression, passivity, and restlessness. Percepts of mutilation, weapons, and fighting are more likely to be given by suicidal than by homicidal persons. Responses involving ice, shadows, smoke, and clouds also indicate suicidal ideation (White and Schreiber, 1952). When a response is made to a colored area and both the color and shading in the area are used as determinants, the individual is considered a suicidal risk. An example of such a percept is dried blood in response to a colored area where both the color and the texture of the area are determining factors. Applebaum and Colson (1968) found that psychiatric patients who made suicidal attempts give a significantly higher number of color-shading responses than do other depressed patients. They believe that this scoring combination identifies the individual who is dispassionate in carrying out suicidal action. He is able to adopt affective distance in a situation rife with feelings. He thinks or acts as if he were entirely removed from the situation. This kind of dissociation is necessary to carry out the suicidal act. Excessively high Sh scores in which dark-film responses predominate also suggest an increase of hostility toward the self with a concomitant increase in suicidal tendencies.

Aggression

Aggression is defined as violent, attacking, destructive behavior that results in pain to the victim. It is undertaken with the intention of physically harming another person or verbally belittling or ridiculing him. Some researchers believe that aggression is usually a response to frustration (White, 1956; Dollard, Doob, Miller, Mowrer, and Sears, 1939). These authors believe that the young child manifests aggression in temper tantrums thereby releasing tension and securing attention from those who can alleviate the frustrating situation. As the child grows older, he learns to control these explosive outbursts and replaces them with rational, realistic actions which win him relief from frustration. Aggressive reactions differ. Some persons direct aggressive feelings outwardly with the intention of afflicting injury on or destruction to the persons or objects believed to be the source of their frustration. Other individuals cannot direct their aggression toward the frustrating stimuli and harbor resentments and grudges for many years, displacing them onto persons or objects removed from the original source of the frustration.

Others view aggressive behavior as a disequilibrium between an impulse system and a control system. Childhood experiences contribute to the development of the impulse system. The child learns that he can attain gratification through a sense of having injured another person. Such gratification is the aim of the aggressive motive. But the child is also subject to a control system. He assesses consequences, namely, the possibility of external or internal punishment. Guilt and anxiety (the superego tools) are the inner factors which restrict behavior (Murstein, 1965). The highly aggressive and hostile individual is usually ready to fight in spite of insufficient reason. For these persons, aggressive drives exceed the control system. Typically, the aggressive person with antisocial psychopathic behavior or aggressive acting-out behavior has excessively high scores in Hs, Sh with dark film predominant, M, and H with aggressive content. Emotionally disturbed adolescents have the highest Hs and M scores and are among those scoring highest on Sh and H. Individuals convicted and imprisoned for assaultive behavior often have very high hostility scores (Zubin, Eron, and Schumer, 1965; Murstein, 1965). Aggressive HM and AM responses include grabbing, trying to eat something, and fighting or pulling, and indicate assertive, competitive behavior (Schachtel, 1966). Aggressive behavior within normal limits is typical of the adolescent. However, excessively high C and Hs scores accompanying dominant aggressive H and A responses and very low FA scores are not typical of the normal adolescent. Such responses are found in records of emotionally disturbed adolescents. In the very young child, such scores indicate lack of control and poor judgment. In the adolescent they reveal an excessive need for self-assertion and independence. The excessively high Hs score in the adolescent and in the child indicates acting-out behavior.

When inwardly directed, for some persons aggression may take the form of blame and anger against the self, resulting in depression with self-destructive and masochistic behavior. Persons suffering from these feelings believe that they are at fault when frustrating situations arise. They blame themselves for not acting with sufficient wisdom or for provoking the anger in others. Others turn their aggression inward, appear passive and tend to be easy to get along with, providing excessive demands are not made on them. They seek in others what they lack in themselves, preferring others to take responsibility for them and even to share their feelings of anxiety and guilt. Some indulge their passivity by waiting for assistance, while others are able to reach out for help. They all tend, however, to lean on someone stronger under whose protection they can display their full initiative and activity. Passive individuals have difficulty asserting themselves in the face of obstacles. They avoid frustrating situations which may arouse feelings of aggression.

Excessively high scores in Hs, Pn, At, and V, accompanying low L and FA scores are typical of individuals who direct their hostility inward; such scores reflect a sense of disintegration and depersonalization. Destructive impulses suggested by the very high At scores are not necessarily indicative of acting-out behavior. Acting-out behavior can only be predicted if the strength of the hostile reactions is known. If, in addition, A 1 responses are of the dominant animal-movement type, the individual may be unaware of his underlying hostility and unconscious motivation (Phillips and Smith, 1953). The blood response indicates aggressive feelings based on the fear of contact with people and on a need to dissociate oneself from people. Phillips and Smith (1953) state that this response implies sadistic, destructive impulses. The populations with the highest Hs, Pn, At, and V scores accompanying low L and FA scores are neurotics, alcoholics, and emotionally disturbed adolescents.

Identity

XIII

Identity is the sense of self-awareness that emerges as the child strives to separate himself from his parents and peers. The search for identity (a concern with who and what one is), is accomplished through explorations of different identities beginning in earliest childhood. It becomes crystalized when the child commits himself to a personal identity, usually by late adolescence. Self-identity is the core around which the personality develops and sexual identity is an important aspect of the whole self.

Self-Identity

The self-concept is a complex awareness of the individual's perceptions of his physical self, his behavior (past and present), his interactions with others, and his values and goals. People usually try to preserve and enhance the self-concept, which is thus a basic motivational force in human behavior.

The self-concept starts to develop early in childhood and is subject to changes throughout the lifetime of an individual. In the very young child the self becomes differentiated from objects in the environment for the first time as he learns to differentiate himself from his mother, and begins to define body boundaries. As he grows older, the child becomes aware of body sensations and feelings and of the physical image of his body. He then sees himself not only as an entity with feelings, sensations, forms, and image, but also as a doer—an agent who can initiate activities. With further growth, his awareness and knowledge of himself come under the influence of social interactions, particularly with significant persons in his environment. He begins to perceive himself as he believes others perceive him, based on their treatment of him. He carries over the memories of past events and burdens himself with reevaluation. During adolescence, the self-concept is reworked as family ties are weakened and acceptance by the peer group becomes of increasing interest. Toward late adolescence, the self-concept begins to stabilize and becomes the basis of personality organization and behavior. The self-concept is the individual's conceptual formulation of himself. It is derived from inner sources based on his effectiveness and from outer sources based on his interpretation of the opinion of others toward him. Inner sources of perceptual determination of the self-concept are more dependable than is outside opinion. If the self-concept is good, it counteracts negative opinions. However, if the self-concept is poor, the individual continues to depend on external sources for self-evaluation. Dependence on the opinions of others is detrimental to personality growth and development.

A positive self-concept permits a person to withstand external pressures and to draw on inner resources without loss of emotional control. His ego boundaries are well differentiated. He is aware of conventional percepts, yet can maintain his autonomy without being severely hampered by defensive strategies. He has sufficient energy and optimism to use his thought processes effectively, leaving nothing to chance. His imaginative capacity is good and readily available. He is independent and assertive, can define achievement goals, and can take a forceful approach toward them, valuing things associated with success. He is independent enough to be capable of accepting his impulses and dealing with them effectively. He can express anger openly, is reality-oriented, and experiences the world in a vivid way. The individual with a well developed ego identity sees the world as exciting, provocative, and demanding of self-investment. He demonstrates an affective drive for achievement and a willingness to risk tackling situations without necessarily having all the facts available to him. The flexible, adaptive individual is capable of regressing in the service of the ego without loss of control. His HIT scores are low in L and high (but not excessive) in integration, form appropriateness, color, movement, anxiety, hostility, and penetration (Codkind, 1964; Clark, Veldman, and Thorpe, 1965; Richter and Winter, 1966). Good ego functioning is further revealed in the ability to give human-movement responses. The individual sees the world as peopled and can empathize with them. Maturity, spontaneity, and a good value system are indicated by his use of color, human-movement, animal-movement, popular, anxiety, and hostility responses while still maintaining good form appropriateness and not excessive pathognomic verbalization.

A negative self-concept removes a person from the influence of society, resulting in poor ties with reality and weak ego strength. These persons tend to be passive, need-achievement is low, and there is little goal direction. They have a limited capacity for active coping, structuring, integrating, and organizing behavior. Disturbed thinking is often present, revealed in low location, integration, form-definiteness, and form-appropriateness scores and high pathognomic verbalization scores. Schizophrenics and mental retardates have this scoring pattern.

Neurotic and alcoholic populations have low FD and FA scores and high V scores. Emotionally disturbed children have low FD, FA, and I scores but their V score is also low. Emotionally disturbed adolescents have low L and FA scores and high V scores. A paucity of constructive inner resources is revealed by low scores in HM and high R scores. Schizophrenics, mental retardates, and emotionally disturbed children have the lowest M and H scores and the highest R scores of the normative samples. These cognitive difficulties are often accompanied by feelings of personal inadequacy and a poor sense of body-boundary definiteness reflected in excessively high anatomy, anxiety, and penetration scores. Neurotics, alcoholics, and emotionally disturbed adolescents have high scores in these three variables. Schizophrenics have high At and Pn scores.

Sexual Identity

When a boy or girl becomes identified with the socially prescribed masculine or feminine role, he has achieved sexual identity. Sexual identity is not only determined by the biological characteristics of the child but by the cultural expectations of his life style. Sex is biologically determined, but the sex role is determined by the culture in which the individual lives. Sexual identity begins to develop in earliest childhood when the socially approved cultural stereotype is reinforced by the parents' responses to the child. Preparation for adult sexuality starts very early and continues over a long period. During this time, the child moves from narcissistic autoerotic preoccupation to the desire for and capability of obtaining gratification from the opposite sex. Responsible parents give the child knowledge, satisfying his curiosity and providing training in proper sexual habits.

Sex differences are not just physical but psychological as well. Traits, attitudes, and values appropriate to the sex of the child must be defined and cultivated. The child learns what it means to be a boy or a girl early in childhood by dress, types of toys, behavioral expectations, and body differences. In the process of developing mature sexual identification, a significant adult serves as a model. Freud (1925) considered the resolution of the Oedipal conflict the turning point in the ability of the child to make the appropriate identification with a member of the same sex. Briefly, he theorized that the small boy becomes attracted to and develops a love relationship with his mother. The result of this incestuous desire for his mother creates fears in him because of his father, who has now become his rival. As the child begins to understand that his relationship with his father is not only one of danger but one of affection and his relationship to mother is not only one of love but one of resentment for discipline, he resolves the conflicts by repressing his desires and his fears. He incorporates aspects of the father's image, and the threat of disapproval disappears as he learns to accept the love and dependability of both parents. A similar conflict exists for the female child and resolves itself in a similar manner. The goal, then, is identification with the parent of the same sex. If a satisfactory adjustment takes place, the child identifies with and incorporates the appropriate role. One aspect of this identification is a normal sexual desire for a member of the opposite sex—a channeling of sexual energies into socially approved mature patterns of heterosexual behavior. The child may also sublimate his sexual energy in other socially acceptable ways. By late adolescence, the individual should be capable of playing the appropriate sexual role, accepting this role, and respecting the role which society expects of members of the opposite sex.

Knowledge of the cultural stereotype does not of itself guarantee that the child accepts his role or is sufficiently motivated to pattern his behavior in accordance with society's expectations. Sex-role acceptance depends on the attitudes of the child's significant adults toward sex. Their attitudes may interfere with appropriate sexual identification. The child may learn that sexual behavior is terrible and dangerous and may develop a warped attitude toward heterosexuality. Failure to establish close and affectionate ties with parents and to resolve the Oedipal conflict may also hamper the child's ability to relate to others, resulting in a continuation of self-centered attitudes aimed at personal gain and manipulation of others. Failure to identify with the appropriate sex role results in sexual aberrations and a heightened interest in sexuality. Sexual aberrations or maladjustments express themselves in various ways, such as homosexuality, sexual inversion, frigidity and impotence, and promiscuity.

HOMOSEXUALITY. Homosexuality is the state of being in love with a person of the same sex. Homosexuality does not necessarily involve sexual acting-out behavior. It is a pathologic sexual adaptation caused by pervasive fears of expressing heterosexual impulses. This reaction is created by an incapacitating fear of the opposite sex which is expresed in a fear of disease, a fear of personal injury, or an aversion to feminine genitalia. Heterosexual behavior is avoided because of excessive anxiety. This incapacitating fear of the opposite sex results in retarded maturation, and the self becomes the love object (Freud, 1925). The individual who remains autoerotic remains fixated at a preadolescent or pregenital level of development and seeks love objects which represent himself. These desires are translated into a strong need to possess his own sex. Evidence indicates that homosexual males have strong fixations on their mothers. This exaggerated identification with the mother takes place in early childhood. Later, because of this identification, the male child finds it easier to become stimulated by males rather than females. Investigations also suggest that a psychopathological relationship was present in the early parent-child interaction, and the child was obliged to interact with two emotionally disturbed parents. When the child comes from such a background, psychologists speculate that the mother's frustrated romantic wishes reinforce the child's incestuous desires during the Oedipal stage, intensifying his fear and rivalry with the father. Thus, he is further alienated from a father who has become hostile to both of them. Mothers of homosexual males are extremely close and seductive toward the sons, who in childhood were probably their favorites and the ones in whom they confided. Fathers of homosexuals are hostile and detached toward their sons. Bieber (1962), in an extensive study on homosexuality, indicates that three-fourths of his sample of homosexual males has an incapacitating fear of the opposite sex, compared with one-third of the heterosexual population. He states that half of the homosexuals, as compared with a very small number of the heterosexual males, come from homes where the mother dominates and the father's role is minimized. Because of these parental attitudes and the need to circumvent the fear and anxiety related to heterosexual interactions, Bieber believes that sexual gratification with members of the same sex becomes the pathological alternative.

SEXUAL ROLE INVERSION. When the individual adopts inversion as his mode of sexual functioning, he identifies with and adopts the identify of the opposite sex in thoughts, feelings, attitudes, interests, and preferences. Such behavior affects his total personality. The result is an individual who belongs physically to one sex but has the psychological make-up and personality of the opposite sex. Persons with this inverse identification are often homosexuals, but not always. Homosexuals generally prefer to play their own sex role, although their love object is a person of their own sex. Role inversion is found more often among males than it is among females. The male with this life pattern has overidentified with his mother or some other female. This identification may have resulted from a relationship which was so pleasant and ego satisfying that it fostered a continuance of the feminine identification. Or, it may have resulted from the lack of a male figure with whom to identify in the formative years. The father figure may have been absent or his relationship to the child may have been forbidding. In the latter case, the child may have rejected the father (or male figure) because he was more harsh and punitive and less warm and accepting than the woman. Or the father may have been a weak, ineffectual, psychological nonentity who did not win the respect and admiration of the child. When sexual inversion occurs in a female, she has usually overidentified with the father, and the Oedipal conflict has not been resolved in the appropriate manner.

Persons with sexual inversions tend to give human responses in which they reject their own sex by showing an exaggerated identification with persons of the opposite sex. They may also emphasize clothing of the opposite sex. Homosexuality is considered pathological because a continuing fear of heterosexuality in late adolescence and adulthood is contrary to the expectations of society and therefore of reality. Researchers have carried out very few studies on female homosexuality. Society seems to have less interest in and greater acceptance of homosexual behavior in females than they do of such behavior in males. The incidence and frequency reported in Hinsie and Campbell (1960) are far less for females than for males.

The substance of the H and A responses, particularly those with sexual content, reveals the degree and type of sexual identification. Male homosexuals often include the following content in their responses: sex responses involving the buttocks (male, female, or animal); bisexual figures having both male and female characteristics; exhibitionistic human movement involving exposure of primary or secondary sexual areas (for example, fan dancer, lower part of a male bent over); males wearing female gowns; figures of mixed species (such as mermaids and centaurs); emphasis on feminine objects (for instance, corsets, stockings, jewels, or cosmetics); or reference to perversions (for instance, males or females embracing or males using cosmetics). They may also give hostile, fearful concepts of masculine roles which emphasize aggressive phallic symbols such as club, arrow, ape-man, double-barrel shotgun, in conjunction with hostile, fearful, rejecting descriptions of females, such as Amazon, witch, shrew, as well as castration themes, such as amputated, crippled, withered, or stunted objects, tweezers, nutcrackers, dead branches, missing or blind eyes, or unfinished figures (Piotrowski, 1957; Shafer, 1954). Sometimes human stances suggest homosexuality when the pose is contrary to that expected from the sex of the figure (Beck, 1952). Responses in which the sexual characteristics are blurred are frequently given by both males and females with problems of sexual identity who fear or reject their tendency to identify with the opposite sex.

Sexual responses and the content of these responses identifies conflict in accepting the appropriate sex role. Although the HIT responses are not always sufficient to identify the homosexual, they identify ambivalence in sexual identity. A scoring pattern which suggests homosexual identification does not mean that the individual is engaging in homosexual behavior.

FRIGIDITY AND IMPOTENCE. Frigidity and impotence result in lack of emotional warmth in heterosexual interactions. When these occur, they reflect an unfavorable attitude toward the sexual act. The unfavorable attitudes originate in early childhood and reflect the negative attitude of the parents toward sex. Sexual information when imparted is represented in such a way that sex appears animallike or painful, creating disgust or fear in the child. These early attitudes interfere with the establishment of a satisfactory heterosexual relationship. Sex responses using genitalia usually cover up preoccupation with pregenital sexuality. Klopfer, Ainsworth, and Holt (1954) suggest that these responses show an inability to carry out either a homosexual or a heterosexual relationship.

PROMISCUITY. Promiscuity is another maladaptive response to inappropriate sexual identification, which society terms sexual delinquency. Promiscuity is a constant seeking for a love object and an inability to find satisfaction with any one love object. In the male, extreme promiscuity results in aggressive sexual attacks on females of all ages. In the female, such sexual delinquency takes the form of prostitution or of bearing many illegitimate children.

High Sx scores on the HIT are rare and reveal overpreoccupation with sexuality, thereby identifying the individual who is sexually maladjusted. Not all sexually maladjusted persons, however, have high Sx scores. The greatest number of Sx responses among the standardization populations are given by schizophrenics and depressed persons (Holtzman, Thorpe, Swartz, and Herron, 1961). Additional norms show numerous sex responses among emotionally disturbed adolescents, neurotics, and alcoholics. Excessively high scores in Hs, C, Sh or high scores on At and Pn (or high scores in all five variables) in addition to high Sx scores indicate aggressive acting-out potential. The content of the responses determines whether the individual will act out sexually. Excessively high Sx, At, and Pn scores are associated with individuals who engage in sexually delinquent behavior. Emotionally disturbed adolescents, neurotics, and alcoholics have the highest scores in Hs, C, Sh, At, and Pn as well as high Sx scores. In records of sexual delinquents, the content of At responses usually includes blood. Evidence indicates that individuals apprehended for sexual or aggressive acts give a high number of sex and blood responses. Those apprehended for sexual acts have a predominant number of blatant sex responses. Those apprehended for aggressive acts have a predominant number of blood responses (Haley, Draguns, and Phillips, 1967). A predominance of blatant Sx 2 responses is characteristic of the extreme chaotic sexuality of the schizophrenic and reveals ego dysfunction.

CASE ANALYSES

PART FOUR

The final step in evaluating the HIT is the preparation of the report based on the analysis of scoring and personality variables. Clinicians have different styles of reporting these data. Some prefer a long detailed account of the findings; others prefer a short presentation. The cases which follow illustrate the variability in approach. Cases A and B are reported in a detailed, comprehensive style: one on the basis of scoring variables, the other based on personality variables. Cases C, D, and E are in a short form.

Case A is in two parts. It is a test-retest of the same patient, using first Form A then Form B. All cases with the exception of case C are records of patients referred for psychological evaluation. Case C is the record of a normal college student. In each case, the anonymity of the subject is assured by changes in the identifying data. These changes, however, have not altered the basic personality dynamics.

Adolescent Making
Schizoid Adjustment

XIV

The evaluation of case A, Henry Brown, is detailed, according to the scoring variables. It is a test-retest study of a boy making a schizoid adjustment to his problems. Henry, age thirteen, in the eighth grade, was referred by a psychiatrist for diagnostic evaluation and personality assessment because he was preoccupied with morbid thoughts. He had been withdrawing for more than a year by remaining alone in his room for long periods of time when not in school and avoiding interactions with people. Specific questions were: "Has he the ego strength to undertake psychotherapy?" and "How tenuous are his controls?"

Observations

Henry is a tall, good-looking boy, who appears much older than his thirteen years. He displayed great interest in the testing and responded carefully with complete answers. As the testing shifted from structured to nonstructured tasks, his affect increased markedly. He became increasingly more excited, talked louder, and gestured as he produced stories to the Thematic Apperception Test (TAT) cards. His associations to the inkblots which followed were accompanied by intense affect, manifested both physically and verbally.

Ψ

HOLTZMAN INKBLOT TECHNIQUE
RECORD FORM

Form A

Name_____ Henry Brown _____ Age__ 13 __Sex__ M ____Date 10/4/66 _____

Address_____ Phone_____ Educational Level 8th Grade _____

Examiner_____ E. F. Hill _____ Previous Administration (Form and Date)_____

Symbols: QL —question regarding location;   Qc —question regarding characteristics;   QE —question regarding elaboration;
>V< —change in card position;   R.T. —reaction time in seconds.

X R.T. __3__	A bat; winged animal that flies by night. L 0 c. Shape. e. No.
Y R.T. __6__	A skeleton. L 0 c. Lines and outline. e. Not like a human skeleton, more like an X-ray of a dress model.
1A R.T. __8__ Beings' heads experiment	Something out of a science fiction movie. Two beings looking at an experiment. L 0 c. Could be a ray gun because electricity is running back and forth between them.
2A R.T. _10_ head arm spike cart	A double impression, two people standing together, wild creatures, far out beings, holding a spike with three prongs, medieval variety. They're standing on a cart with a gun spraying out slime, sticky stuff, suspension. L 0 c. Sprayed effect and sticky looking.
3A R.T. __9__ eyes head evil power	Five different creatures, four are of the same nature, head and knobby things which represent arms, could be from another planet, mutations. Red thing is a red mastermind. Could be commanding something, hypnotizing, it's awesome. L 0 c. Just the looks of it.

Printed in U.S.A.   Copyright © 1958. All rights reserved. The Psychological Corporation, New York 17, N.Y.   61-118 AS

4A **R.T.** _12_	Something out of a comic-like fairy tale. One figure imposed on another like 3D. It's an atomic explosion reaction. Here's someone's face, looks like Dr. Strange, awesome. Here's warriors on horses. Gorilla creatures battling with a bunch of arms to defend themselves, like a converging force is bringing them out. All created by the explosion. **L O** c. Color & behind it the stuff, grey dots, l.l.fallout.(Rub)
5A **R.T.** _12_	Mystic thing, man's head, and bats are flying around. Cloudy. Magician, it's confused, a mystic master mind for a criminal organization. Man is sitting. Criminal below. Does not see that one of the criminals is looking on. Like I may be a criminal looking on. L O c. Blurriness.
6A **R.T.** _22_	(Hmm.) Double print of a space creature. Heads of space creatures talking to each other. Line between them could be a docking pen. They're tied up to each other and can't get away. Red part could be other planets or something. L O c. Shape.
7A **R.T.** _9_	Lagoon to a small Pacific Island. Mountains, beaches. Red spots look like where water is hot and bubbling up from a volcano. It's an aerial view. L O c. Shape, looking down at it.
8A **R.T.** _10_	An explosion. A space vehicle, came through force field waves, the vehicle is disintegrating and burning up. L O c. Color and impression of smoky look.
9A **R.T.** _11_	Battle scene in a volcano, crablike creatures. Dinosaur creatures with guns or flame throwers going to attack, poised for battle. Looks like shell plate, aerial view, looking down at it. L O c. Redness.

10A	R.T. 30	Something coming out of a duplicating machine because of the edges, some sort of creatures, hunchbacks, as if being manufactured. L O c. Double and looks like gates are coming on top and out of the bottom. Looks like they're being crushed and mashed into one thing. Not 3D.
11A	R.T. 3	Spiderlike creature. L O c. Face with huge eyeballs, tiny body, very strong pincers, huge head.
12A	R.T. 7	Looks like taking off, like a rocket on a moon. Two suns. L O c. Blackness like from monoxide or ammonia gas. Black smoke, flame and projection type of material.
13A	R.T. 17	Something under a microscope, little beings, on a slide under a microscope. L O c. Blurred and moving back and forth.
14A	R.T. 8	Entrance to mystical places. Jackal type creatures, sneaky, standing. Doorway made out of backbone of human skeleton. Flame shooting out. L O c. Spiders are shooting out flame.
15A	R.T. 8	Space ship. L O c. Outlines; darker parts would be regular parts. Yellow, orange and red are reactions in a bubbledome which shoots out. Passenger compartment. Retrorockets.

16A R.T. __8__ 	A trap. The Vietman walks on top. Rotating jaws and spikes are pushing him down into a cavern with bugs, he can't get out. The cavern that the Viet Cong or subhuman race live in. Once in it's more like a subterranean village. L O
17A R.T. __31__ 	Engine in operation, spewing out smoke and the reaction creates light. c. Color, fuel tanks, and billowy smoke. L O
18A R.T. __6__ 	Animal with horns, it's an Xray. Mouth is up and down instead of sideways. I'm looking straight at it. c. Different shades. L O
19A R.T. __10__ 	Scene, Hallowe'en, horrifying. People hanging, guards with guns, people with hats. Scary spooks with swords in back of the people's heads. c. Red flame bug of death, head with two pincers, mystic sign of the cult. L O
20A R.T. __16__ 	(Wow!) Two people looking at one another. Imprints, messed up picture. c. Billowing out of a bottle like genies. Brown could be the main body, and purple could be like jelly. L O
21A R.T. __25__ 	Two people carrying a pole, like fishing pole, to support a house or something. c. Don't know, looks like sunglasses or big eyes. L 1

22A R.T. __17__ jaw bone 	Skull of animal, separated. Teeth in it. c. Jaw taken off the head and placed under it but separate. L O
23A R.T. __19__ 	Blind, curtain or door. Behind it a scientist is working on experiments. c. Yellow color could be heat radiating from the experiment. L O
24A R.T. __18__ 	Space ship taking off. Cockpit where the man sits. L O.
25A R.T. __13__ serpent 	People, Roman gladiators running along together with swords and separated, with a serpent in one hand and a sword in the other. L O.
26A R.T. __18__ Hydrofoil fronts exhaust reactors	Like a boat. In here turbines turning the propeller in the rear which goes into the gear works. c. Looks like a luxury liner. L O
27A R.T. __23__ geese bulls	People, like praying to these sacred bulls or geese at a lake. Red would be the sacrifices. c. Ground and hazy reflection on lake. L O

28A	R.T. 28	Launching craft, ship being launched.
		c. Red signifies shooting off reaction as ship flies in air.
		L 0

29A	R.T. 24	Fancy vase.
	(base, ornaments, handles)	
		L 0

30A	R.T. 3	Looks like storm.
		c. Lines and looks like clouds, rain, thunder and very slippery.
		L 0

31A	R.T. 9 (volcanic reaction, tongues, dead carcass)	Two creatures, lizards of dinosaur age, rivals glaring at each other and fighting over dead carcass in middle.
		c. Red. There's a volcanic reaction in the background.
		L 0

32A	R.T. 3	Creatures charging, bursting out of a container.
		c. Scales on back, caged in a well.
		L 0

33A	R.T. 2	Snow storm.
		Lines look like Christmas trees on side of hill, there's a forest in background.
		c. Blue has appearance of winter, lines look like trees. Overall blur is the storm.
		L 0

34A R.T. 4 legs	(Mmm) Two people running toward each other. Abstract football. One has the ball, the other is charging him. L 0	
35A R.T. 39	Head without a jaw. c. Like a skeleton of a head, skull. L 1	
36A R.T. 5 back front legs pincers	Froglike creature. L 0	
37A R.T. 3 legs	Birds, vultures standing in the water, strange. Looking at, holding and eating (red thing) that they just killed. L 0.	
38A R.T. 13	Top view of a river delta. Looking down at it. Marshy appearance Mountains River L 0	
39A R.T. 2 Brain eyes	Something with eyes. Cross section, Xray of brain and eyes. c. Shape. Jaws with teeth sticking in them. L 0	

40A R.T. __8__ head legs wings, to fly	Scorpion in 3D. L O
41A R.T. __13__	Volcanoes. Mainly in background, side and in front lava heavy looking. c. Smoking lava, exploding and black billowing clouds. L O
42A R.T. __3__ lungs backbone stomach	Stomach, lungs, backbone. c. Because it's more transparent. Stomach to go along with lungs because stomach is usually below lung. L O

43A R.T. __5__	Relief map, mountain ranges.
	
	c. The darker, the higher the ranges;
	   the lighter, the lower.
	
	   3D effect.
	
	L O

44A R.T. __15__ decanter neck	Wine decanter. Fancy. L O
45A R.T. __8__	People conducting something like an orchestra. Baton. L O

SUMMARY SHEET   HOLTZMAN INKBLOT TECHNIQUE   Form: (circle) (A) B

Name **HENRY BROWN** _____ Age _13_ Sex _M_ Date _10-4-1966_

Examiner _E.F.HILL_ _____ Previous Administration (Form and Date) _____

Card No.	RT	R	L	S	FD	FA	C	Sh	M	V	I	H	A	At	Sx	Ab	Ax	Hs	Br	Pn	B	P	AA
1	8				1	1			3m	AL1	1	1o	1o				1	1					
2	10				2	1		1f	1			1	1o					1	1		1	1	
3	9				1	1	1-		1ma	QR2		1o	1o				1						1-
	RT	R	L	S	FD	FA	C	Sh	M	V	I	H	A	At	Sx	Ab	Ax	Hs	Br	Pn	B	P	
4	12				3	1	1-	1vt	3m	FC3		1H	1o				2	2			1	1-	
5	12				3			1f	2	SR2		2MP	2A				1	1			1		
6	22				1	1			2	FC2		1o	1o				1			1		1±	
7	9		1		2	1		1v	4m								1	1					
8	10				1		3-	2f	4m								1	2	1				
9	11				2	1	1-	1v	3	FC2		1o					1	1	1				
	RT	R	L	S	FD	FA	C	Sh	M	V	I	H	A	At	Sx	Ab	Ax	Hs	Br	Pn	B	P	
10	30				1	1			3ma	QR3	1o						2	3	1	1	1		
11	3				1							1o					2	1					
12	7				2	1	1-	1df	4m	FC2								1					
13	17				1			2f	2m														
14	8				2	1-			3m	FC3		1o	1				2	2					
15	8				2		1N		4m									1					
	RT	R	L	S	FD	FA	C	Sh	M	V	I	H	A	At	Sx	Ab	Ax	Hs	Br	Pn	B	P	
16	8				2			2	3ma	QR3		2MA					2	2	1	1			
17	31					1	3N	1f	4m									1					
18	6				1	1		1f		SR2		1						1	1				
19	10				3	2	1-		1	QR2		2OP					2	2			1	2-	
20	16				1		1-	1f	3ma	FC4		1o	2					1	1		1	2-	
21	25	1			2	2			2		1	2OP									1		
	RT	R	L	S	FD	FA	C	Sh	M	V	I	H	A	At	Sx	Ab	Ax	Hs	Br	Pn	B	P	
22	17				1	1						1					1						
23	19				1	1	2N			AL1								1					
24	18				2				4m									1					
25	13				3	1			3	FC2		2MA	2P				2	1			1		
26	18				2				2m														
27	23				3	1		1f	1	FB1		2OP	2P				2	1			1		
Sub-total: Items 1-27	RT 380	1	1		FD 44	21	C 16	Sh 14	M 62	35	I 3	H 19	A 13	At 5			Ax 24	Hs 23	Br 8	Pn 7	B 3	P 8	6- 1±

Fold the top of this page down to this line, so that sub-totals for Items 1-27 may be seen on this side.

#	RT	R	L	S	FD	FA	C	Sh	M	V	I	H	A	At	Sx	Ab	Ax	Hs	Br	Pn	B	P	
28	28				1	1	2N		4m														
29	24				2	1												1					
30	3					1	2f	4m 2m									1	1					
31	9				2	1	1-	1vt3	FB1			1o					1	2	1				
32	3				1	1		4			1o	1o					1		1	1			
33	2				1	1	2N	1vf4m									2	1					
	RT	R	L	S	FD	FA	C	Sh	M	V	I	H	A	At	Sx	Ab	Ax	Hs	Br	Pn	B	P	
34	4				2	1			3	1	2OP										1	1±	
35	39	1			1									1			2						
36	5				2	1						1o						1					
37	3				3	1			2	FC2		2A					2	2	1				
38	13					1		1vf										1					
39	2				1	1							2					1		1			
	RT	R	L	S	FD	FA	C	Sh	M	V	I	H	A	At	Sx	Ab	Ax	Hs	Br	Pn	B	P	
40	8				4			1v				1o					2	1		1			
41	13				2	1	1-Ac	1vf 4m									2	1		1			
42	3				2			1f	AL2			2								1			
43	5					1		1v															
44	15				2													1					
45	8				3	1			2	1	2OA									1			AA
Uncorr. Total	559	✕	✕	✕	73	35	✕	✕	40	✕	✕	✕	✕	✕	✕	✕	✕	✕	✕	✕	✕	✕	
Score	12.4	0	2	1	73	35	22	23	92	40	5	24	19	10	0	0	37	33	13	12	3	10	6⁻/2±
Percentile*	13	24	4		30	6	72	97	>99	>99	79	92	52	99			>99	>99	95	99	>96	84	

Note. — Except for **RT, FD, FA,** and **V,** the **Score** for each variable is the total of the scores on each of the 45 cards. These totals should be entered in the row labeled **Score.** For **RT,** write the sum in the row labeled **Uncorrected Total,** divide this by 45, and enter the quotient as the **RT Score.** For **FD, FA,** and V, write the sum in the **Uncorrected Total** row, see Table 3 of the Guide, and enter the corrected total as the **Score.**

*Norms Group SEVENTH GRADE

HILL CLINICAL SUMMARY
for the
HOLTZMAN INKBLOT TECHNIQUE

Form (A) or B

Name: HENRY BROWN

Norms: SEVENTH GRADE

Date: 10-4-1966

CATEGORIES

	I					II			III					IV					V				VI
	RT	R	L	FA	S	C	Sh	B	FD	M	I	Br	P	H	A	At	Sx	Ab	Ax	Hs	V	Pn	AA
Final Score	12	0	2	35	1	22	23	3	73	92	5	13	10	24	19	10	0	0	37	33	40	1	6- / 2±
Percentile	13	24	4	6		72	97	>96	30	>99	79	95	84	92	52	99			>99	>99	>99	99	
High (a) Stim. Color	16		1	9		10	5	1	24	28	0	6		2	9	5	7		11	7	18	5	5- / 1±
Low (b) Stim. Color	9	0	13			2	9	1	21	27	1	5		2	5	7	2		10	10	7	3	

Form A (a) 3, 6, 9, 15, 16, 17, 19, 20, 26, 27, 28, 35, 39, 42, 44
      (b) 1, 2, 5, 7, 18, 22, 24, 29, 30, 32, 33, 36, 37, 38, 43
Form B (a) 3, 6, 7, 11, 15, 17, 21, 24, 29, 34, 36, 39, 41, 42, 44
      (b) 2, 5, 8, 9, 10, 16, 18, 19, 23, 25, 26, 30, 32, 33, 45

COLOR

Score	+	-	N	Ac
1		9	1	1
2		3		
3		1	1	

SHADING

Score	Texture	Light Film	Dark Film	Vista
1	2	9	2	9
2			3	

MOVEMENT

	HUMAN									ANIMAL					m	
	1			2						1			2		Inanimate	Animate
Score	H	B	O	P	A	P	A	P	A	H	B	O	P	A		
1	1			3			1	1		2						1
2				1	1	1		1		1			2	3		
3				1		1		1		2			3	3		
4				1						1				10		
NO M				1						3	2					

PATHOGNOMIC VERBALIZATION

FB	FC	QR	IC	AL	CT	SR	DC	AB
2	8	4		3		2		

Notes: THE EXCESSIVELY HIGH SCORES ARE NOT TYPICAL OF ANY OF THE ABNORMAL GROUPS

SEQUENCE ANALYSIS

1. 2 BEINGS LOOK AT EXPER. RAY GUNS
2. CREATURES W. SPIKE SPRAYG SLIME
3. 5 MUTATION CREATURES, MASTERMIND COMMANDG
4. EXPLOSION CREATG GORILLA CREATURES
5. MAGICIAN·MASTERMIND CRIMINAL ORGAN.
6. H.D. SPACE CREATURES TALKING TIED TOGETH.
7. LAGOON - BUBBLG WATER F. VOLCANO
8. EXPLOSION-SPACE VEHICLE DISINTEGRATG
9. CREATURES BATTLE IN VOLCANO
10. HUNCHBACKS MFG'D IN DUPLICATG MACHINE
11. SPIDER-LIKE CREATURE
12. ROCKET TAKG OFF MOON-GAS-FLAME
13. BEINGS UNDER MICROSCOPE
14. SPIDERS SHOOTG FLAMES-H. SKELETON DOORWG
15. SPACE SHIP
16. TRAP JAWS PUSH MAN IN CAVE W. BUGS
17. ENGINE SPEWING SMOKE
18. XRAY A. W HORNS MOUTH UP AND DOWN
19. PEOPLE HANGG - FLAME OF DEATH
20. PEOPLE BILLOWG OUT OF BOTTLE - GENIES
21. PEOPLE CARRYG POLE TO SUPPORT HOUSE
22. A SKULL JAW OFF HD. SEPARATE
23. SCIENTST BEHIND CURTAIN WORKG EXPER.
24. SPACE SHIP TAKING OFF
25. GLADIATORS RUNNG W. SWORD & SERPENT
26. BOAT TURBINES TURNG PROPELLER
27. PEOPLE PRAYG · SACRED BULLS · SACRIFICE
28. SHIP LAUNCHG
29. FANCY VASE
30. STORM · RAIN · THUNDER - SLIPPERY
31. LIZARDS FIGHTG OVER DEAD CARCASS
32. CREATURES BURSTG OUT OF CONTAINER
33. SNOW STORM · CHRISTMAS TREES
34. 2 PEOPLE-ONE W. BALL-OTHER CHARGG
35. SKULL WITHOUT JAW
36. FROG-LIKE CREATURE
37. VULTURES EATG THEIR KILL
38. RIVER DELTA
39. XRAY BRAIN, EYES, JAWS W. TEETH
40. SCORPION IN 3-D
41. VOLCANOES-SMOKG LAVA-EXPLODG
42. STOMACHE LUNGS
43. RELIEF MAP - 3D
44. WINE DECANTER
45. PEOPLE CONDUCTG ORCHESTRA

Findings

Reaction time is low in the average range, showing a seven-second difference between the high and low stimulus-strength color cards. The nine-second
average RT to the low stimulus-strength color cards is fast, reflecting Henry's
ability to associate, respond quickly, and get away from the blot. The average RT
of sixteen seconds to the high stimulus-strength color cards indicates that some
internal process was interfering with the response. Arousal of affect required a
longer time for selection of a response from among the push of affective ideas.

Location scores are low and at the extreme for his normative group, indicating almost exclusive use of the entire blot. A form-appropriateness score as low
as the sixth percentile indicates that the responses are inconsistent with the reality
demands of the stimulus and are under the control of inner fantasies and imagination. The content reflects poor planning, lack of persistence, and confusion. The
pathognomic verbalization score above the ninety-ninth percentile further indicates poor reality contact and a lack of ability to use intelligence for critical evaluation of tasks. The low FA score also reveals immaturity, self-preoccupation, and
disturbed thought processes. The combination of low FA and L scores indicates
that Henry relies on perceptual defenses to modify the stimulus so that he can
deal with it.

Although the color score is at the seventy-second percentile and in the
average range, C-minus responses predominate, indicating avoidance of intimate
relationships. Persons who give C-minus responses tend to be self-centered and
disregard the rights and feelings of others. The C-minus response is frequently
found in the records of schizophrenics. Henry is drawn toward and reacts more
to the color on the high stimulus-strength color cards than to the color on the low
stimulus-strength cards, where he is better able to ignore it.

The shading score at the ninety-seventh percentile indicates an extreme
sensitivity to the variations in the blot, suggesting a similar sensitivity to emotional overtones and undercurrents in the environment. For example, Henry is
aware of the presence or absence of hostility, approval or disapproval, anxiety,
and tension in the environment. The excessive number of Sh responses also reveals anxiety in relationships with other people and in his attitude toward himself.
Anxiety is confirmed in his Ax score, which is above the ninety-ninth percentile.
Vista Sh responses are high, suggesting a gloomy attitude and self-depreciation.
They reveal destructive intrapunitive behavior. The additional large number of
light-film Sh responses suggests conscious feelings of inferiority. Defenses typical
of persons with feelings of inferiority are passivity and submissiveness. These
defenses are accompanied by a low energy level, leading to and aggravating feelings of depression and anxiety. Henry's sensitivity to the diffuse quality of the
shaded areas of the blot suggests feelings of lack of solidity in his life. It indicates
undifferentiated emotional reactions and reveals anxiety and frustration of affectional and security needs.

The form-definiteness score is in the average range, revealing the availability of memory engrams and the ability to fantasize and articulate. Thinking processes, however, must be interpreted as very disturbed because of the pathognomic content. For example, the movement score above the ninty-ninth percentile includes some human and animal content, but m is predominant. Although the HM content is principally aggressive, aggressive behavior is not necessarily a basic personality trait. The overall content indicates unconscious difficulty in self-assertion and deals largely with mythical, magical figures—a paranoid projection of human movement perceived as alien. Magicians, masterminds, and other supernatural beings are the cause of the actions in the percepts, thereby relieving Henry of the responsibility for this projected movement. The predominance of m responses indicates the presence of drives which he feels incapable of fulfilling. He feels as if things outside of him are directing his behavior without his involvement. Here again Henry projects his feelings but this time through inanimate objects, again relieving himself of the responsibility for the actions. The explosive content indicates the wish to release the inhibitions he places on his impulses and the fear of doing so. The m content also reveals the desire for lack of restraints. However, through repression he avoids attaining this goal. His maximum effort remains in the realm of daydreams and self-observation, which considerably reduce overt activity. His ability to attribute varieties of movement to the blot indicates a complex and rich inner life and the capability of introspection.

The high barrier score, which indicates excessive rigidity and control, reveals a tendency toward oversocialization through repression. He places a barrier between himself and the outside world. Popular responses are high in the average range, indicating the ability to partake in general community thinking. He is aware of the values of society. In spite of his disturbed fantasy life, he is still cognizant of conventional requirements.

The human content is childlike and immature, dealing largely with supernatural beings who have infinite power to retaliate for wrongs. He creates roles which reflect his need for omnipotent manipulation of the environment. This continuation of wishful immaturity is nonadaptive. His animal content is also predominantly of the "nonreal" variety, again showing his infantile preoccupation. Anatomy responses at the ninety-ninth percentile reflect self-absorption and withdrawal into autism. At best, he discharges aggression through verbal expression, but his aggression is essentially turned in on himself. He has morbid fears of possible body harm. The numerous nature responses reveal his need for security —a need which is also identified in the Sh responses.

The sequence analysis and review of the blot characteristics show involvement with fantasy and disturbed ideation. Henry's record shows a repetition of unique content, notably masterminds who influence and control the behavior of others by mystical means. These themes indicate that Henry is living in a private world and finding autistic solutions to his problems. His thinking is bizarre, and strong feelings appear to be on the verge of breaking through into conscious awareness. The content of his responses reflects physical and mental destruction, aggressive feelings, and fear of others. Fear of aggressive sexuality is revealed in the responses to cards 2, 8, and 21. Henry also expresses anxiety over the mother figure in cards 11 and 14. He achieves distance from his associations by projecting them onto characters which are nonhuman and nonanimal. The content of his responses is more disturbed at the beginning of the test, but with time he is able to mobilize resources and to repress pathognomic verbalization. He reveals a distinct need to be familiar with ambiguous situations before he can relax enough to effect sufficient controls and use his cognitive ability.

Disturbed thinking and psychopathology are revealed in bizarre and autistic percepts. Aggressivity is expressed in daydreamlike content, most of which reflects a minimum of control over ideas. The excessively high V score reveals the disordered thinking, the failure of repressive defenses, and ego weakness. The bizarre themes reveal a borderline psychotic state. Morbid, fantastic thoughts seem to be flooding his consciousness, disclosing regression. Libidinal urges and conflicts are also present. The high fabulized-combination score shows a loss of distance between himself and the blots, with no critical control over responses. The queer responses identify psychotic reasoning; the autistic-logic responses also show faulty reasoning with poor reality testing; the self-reference responses show bizarre self-preoccupation with serious loss of distance, suggesting feelings of depersonalization. The Ax score is excessive, showing basic insecurity and personality conflict. It reinforces the V-score findings of failure of the defenses to hold up. The hostility score above the ninety-ninth percentile indicates that aggression is largely self-directed. Sufficient fantasy aggression is present to consider potential acting-out if Henry were provoked. The penetration score at the ninety-ninth percentile confirms the feelings of depersonalization, schizophreniclike regression, and poor ego structure.

Validation Evidence from Other Tests

Henry's high intelligence as revealed in the vocabulary and content of the HIT is consistent with the (WISC) results. Henry has a full-scale WISC IQ of 138, a verbal IQ of 138, and a performance IQ of 131, which places him in the top 2 per cent of the population for his age group.

His persistent anxiety and need for security are confirmed in the TAT responses. For example, for TAT card 3B he relates the story of a child who burns himself while playing with a soldering gun. The rug catches fire, but his mother comes in to take care of him just at the right moment and saves him from harm. The mother figure confirms Henry's need for mothering and attention. The mother's concern in the story, however, is contrary to his report in the interview that his own father and mother are cold and indifferent. Henry reported that his mother is also punitive and rejecting. Henry's aggression fantasy is revealed in TAT content where members of cults are involved in death rituals.

Summary

Henry is an intellectually superior boy who is functioning at a reduced level because of severe mental disturbances. He is making a schizoid adjustment. He lives in a world of disturbed fantasy in which he imagines himself as all-powerful in a destructive, aggressive role against the world. Along with his feeling of aggression are equally strong fears of people, which oblige him to institute powerful inhibitory controls over his behavior. An acutely stressful event, however, may break through his controls and release his acting-out potential against himself or others. Henry has many assets that can work for him. In addition to his superior intelligence, he has adequate controls in neutral situations in which no undue demands are made on him. Furthermore, in ambiguous stressful situations, given enough time, he can inhibit the expression of his inner needs. He has the potential for interpersonal involvement and is aware of the conventional demands of society. He has an active inner life and is capable of introspection.

Henry needs psychotherapy, but it will be a long, slow process because of the severity of his pathology and his difficulty in making a one-to-one relationship. Although his ego strength is low, his controls under most circumstances are adequate, and he can be treated in an open setting.

Part Two of case A is a re-test of the patient, using HIT Form B. The evaluation is short, including both the new data and a comparison with the scores and content of the initial testing. Henry, now age fourteen, was reevaluated after eighteen months of individual psychotherapy because he was still experiencing difficulty opening up his feelings in therapy, although he had been attending regularly. His psychiatrist wished to determine what, if any, basic changes had taken place and if continuation of therapy was indicated.

Observation

Henry was more poised during the second testing session than he was at the initial testing, and his feelings were considerably more under his control. He appeared comfortable and interested throughout and suppressed overt verbal and behavioral manifestations of affect.

Form B

HOLTZMAN INKBLOT TECHNIQUE
RECORD FORM

Name_____Henry Brown_____ Age __14__ Sex __M__ Date_ 6/23/68 _____

Address_____Phone_____Educational Level___9th Grade_____

Examiner_____E. F. Hill_____Previous Administration (Form and Date)_____

Symbols: QL —question regarding location;   Qc —question regarding characteristics;   QE —question regarding elaboration;
 >ᵛ< —change in card position;   R.T. —reaction time in seconds.

X R.T. 6	Xray.
	c. Looks like backbone is prominent.
	(e. Could be of bird a/c wings.)
	L O

Y R.T. 26	(Mmm)
	Xray a/c bones, looks like they're trying to find something wrong because of the red thing in the middle.
	L O

1B R.T. 8	Looks like a rocket or bullet has split through. Dogs watching were thrown away, catapulted back.
smoke streaming out like retro rocket	c. Smoke type stuff like powdered pieces flying and smoke going straight up middle of cloud.
	L O

2B R.T. 4	Teapot like an urn.
urn	c. Center shape.
handles	e. Egyptian art ornamental decorations; looks like two snakes and two centaurs coming up to behead them.
	L O

3B R.T. 8	Sunset through clouds.
sun clouds	c. Color radiating from middle, also on the water, on eye level reflection at lower half on water.
	L O

4B apes	**R.T.** __6__	From the movie "Planet of Apes." Apes like men, they keep people trapped in cages. Lines look like cages, random people inside, don't see them. The apes are running on outside. L O
5B 	**R.T.** __2__	Snow storm. c. Everything blurred a/c small dots. e. Very thick storm, seems to be confusion in traffic after awhile. L O
6B smoke reaction	**R.T.** __12__	(Hmm) Bottom cone of rocket. L O c. Yellow. e. Cone looks like overheating on edges, blurred and bulged out, cannot take the blast very well. It got too hot.
7B eyes smoke feet	**R.T.** __10__	(Hmm) Oriental, mouth with goatee, breathing smoke. c. Appearance of face, smoke billows out. e. No expression, bland-like, doesn't need emotions because he has smoke coming out of him. L O
8B Mountain in background woods	**R.T.** __17__	(Mmm) Meteor coming down through air. c. A red thing coming down, blue is the water, coming down and through the air with smoke trailing. Colors red and blue, one crashed into a desert and made such a huge hole it was a lake when filled. L O
9B Incense burning Fumes	**R.T.** __16__	(Hmm) Entrance into mosque, religious place. Hollow, with decoration, looks like a mosque, top of minaret bulging on two sides. c. Fumes and orange incense burning. L O

10B R.T. __12__	Something under a microscope. Blurred, and the balance is filmy water that you are looking through. c. The darker part seems out of focus. L O
11B R.T. __20__	(Mmm, nice color green; I like it.) Looking down on a 3D jungle. Green and yellow part of the middle could be a darker jungle because of the light and dark green color. L O
12B R.T. __6__	Looks like the heart has been taken in two. Red with veins in it, looks like a heart, looks like it's split in two. c. A/c not together. I don't know why they split them apart. Could be two different ones because of different colors. Could be comparing two cross sections; it don't have to be two hearts. L O
13B R.T. __11__	Stick drawings on a cave wall. Could be a moose leaning forward, stick figure. Smaller is like people who are hunting it, that's what's drawn on the walls. c. Forms, not fully rounded. L O
14B R.T. __17__	Two people having a race and a camera is in the middle. Two cars are coming. c. You are standing in the middle and both are racing by. Dark looks like people racing on the edge. e. Both running very hard trying to win; very close because they're right beside each other. L O
15B R.T. __7__	Palace in the sky, like a cartoon on TV where Thor races up the rainbow to his palace. c. Shape, clouds look billowy and the palace rests on top of it. L O

16B R.T. __14__		A Sugar Daddy, candy on a stick. c. Edge where stick comes out. e. It's a big sucker. L 1
17B R.T. __13__		Tunnel going down, outside looking in. Edges come out and looks like it's getting smaller, curving over and appear like a roof. e. Idea of two things like two halves standing next to each other. L 0
18B R.T. __14__		(Mmm) Picture of night because lines through it, like aurora borealis. Tiny specks of what could be stars. e. Very cloudless night because see stars, nothing in the way and moonless. L 1
19B R.T. __8__		A catapult on an airplane. This opening could be a guide holding back the plane and it will throw it forward into the track. Balance could be the mechanism to pull forward, when you let go it will fire forward. L 1
20B R.T. __20__		Looking down on city. Brown could be looking down through clouds. Purple parts are city lit up, with more or less lights in the business section because everyone has gone home, closed up. e. Contrast between color and river filled in and brown could be clouds you are looking down through. L 0
21B R.T. __18__		(Hmm) Very large nutcracker, pull up the lever, crack the nut and it falls down, ready to eat. L 0

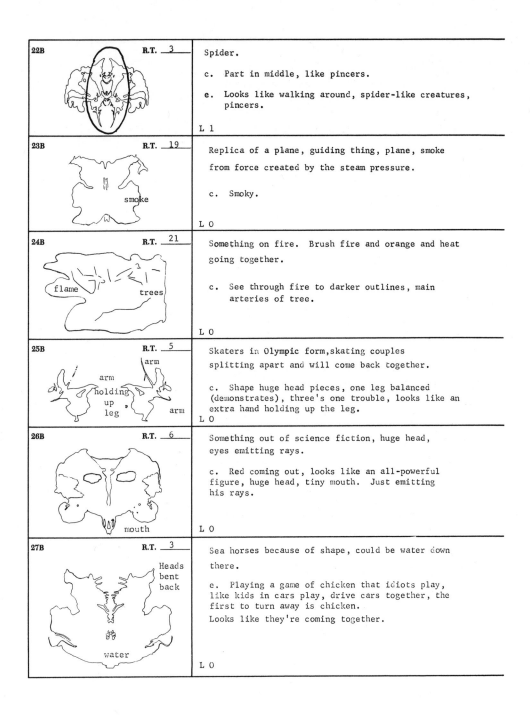

22B	R.T. 3	Spider. c. Part in middle, like pincers. e. Looks like walking around, spider-like creatures, pincers. L 1
23B	R.T. 19	Replica of a plane, guiding thing, plane, smoke from force created by the steam pressure. c. Smoky. L 0
24B	R.T. 21	Something on fire. Brush fire and orange and heat going together. c. See through fire to darker outlines, main arteries of tree. L 0
25B	R.T. 5	Skaters in Olympic form, skating couples splitting apart and will come back together. c. Shape huge head pieces, one leg balanced (demonstrates), three's one trouble, looks like an extra hand holding up the leg. L 0
26B	R.T. 6	Something out of science fiction, huge head, eyes emitting rays. c. Red coming out, looks like an all-powerful figure, huge head, tiny mouth. Just emitting his rays. L 0
27B	R.T. 3	Sea horses because of shape, could be water down there. e. Playing a game of chicken that idiots play, like kids in cars play, drive cars together, the first to turn away is chicken. Looks like they're coming together. L 0

28B head R.T. _8_	King Henry. c. Coat and costume in a scene of play. Huge coat billowing, looking down, and he's coming at you, huge overstuffed legs strutting down. e. Color and legs. L O	

28B   head   R.T. _8_

King Henry.

c. Coat and costume in a scene of play. Huge coat billowing, looking down, and he's coming at you, huge overstuffed legs strutting down.

e. Color and legs.

L O

29B   R.T. _3_

nose
eyes
upper jaw

Skull of some sort of dog or something.

L O

30B   R.T. _10_

Birds, long tails and standing up. Looks like out in the woods, bushes and shrubs around.

c. Long tails and the balance fits in well.

e. Looks like talking to each other, like house-wives talking across a fence.

L O

31B   R.T. _6_

Gears, jagged pieces, mesh in neutral also curved, like one part of two huge gears.

L 2

32B   R.T. _7_

bridge

pedestals

Bridge but very fancy, comes down, winding bridge.

c. Flat line like roadway along edge.

e. Pedestals to stand on, two look cut off.

L O

33B   R.T. _8_

masts

Two ships having a battle, old sailing ships, both sinking because of masts. Balance are lines for ships, both on an angle, sinking, rammed each other and both sank. A draw.

L O

34B **R.T.** ___2___ 	Two people talking, mouth, nose, sitting in an enclosed area, looking through window, bargaining because both looking at each other. They're behind the window and you are looking from the outside in. L 2
35B **R.T.** ___11___ 	Ships amidst battle. Red looks like rockets going off, balance is smoke and flames and smoke is hiding everything and we cannot see it. L 0
36B **R.T.** ___9___ 	Monsters, eyes looking down, going to pick up something, he's hunched over, darker and fuller and a big thing looking down. Could be a wooly bear type. c. Eyes, hands. L 0
37B **R.T.** ___12___ 	Lobster, just the hand which looks like a tuning fork. c. Color and prickly things on and joined together. L 2
38B **R.T.** ___3___ 	Two giraffes talking in the jungle, light color and tallness and looking at each other. Swamp shrubbery because milkiness like water with plants sticking up. L 0
39B **R.T.** ___18___ 	Cross section of a bowl or some sort of thing that holds stuff because empty here. Could be a plant vase split in half lengthwise. c. Edges L 0

40B R.T. <u>22</u> eyes / nose / L 0	Skull on display. Skull set into an ornamental base of some kind. Balance is the ornamentation, like a trophy.
41B R.T. <u>9</u> Birds / L 0	Fire, volcanoes because mountains sticking up. Red lava flowing down, red being thrown up in no special form, heaved at random, shades look like mountains. Two birds watching it, flying and looking back at it.
42B R.T. <u>2</u> huge flower / base / legs of bowl / L 0	Big flower on a base. c. Account of yellow and everything.
43B R.T. <u>2</u> lighter / legs around bottom / L 0	Big tent. c. Fullness effect, top, skylight a/c lighter shading. e. Could be looking at a fair because it's open all around where people would be. Legs around bottom, people come in and see the displays.
44B R.T. <u>18</u> L 0	Wrapper, like a candy wrapper that has been pulled down, that looks like litmus paper and gets lighter. Darker where the light hasn't gotten to it. c. Peeled back and progressively lighter as it goes up and the color.
45B R.T. <u>15</u>	Inside of cave, mystical one, cave stalactite. Cauldron. Hands making brew, withered hands, fist inside looks like they're growing out of rock, mystical thing.

SUMMARY SHEET   HOLTZMAN INKBLOT TECHNIQUE   Form: (circle) A Ⓑ

Name __HENRY BROWN_____ Age __14__ Sex __M__ Date __6-23-1968__

Examiner __E.F.HILL_____ Previous Administration (Form and Date) __FORM A 10-4-1966__

Card No.	RT	R	L	S	FD	FA	C	Sh	M	V	I	H	A	At	Sx	Ab	Ax	Hs	Br	Pn	B	P	AA
1	8		1w	2	1			1f	4ma		1		2P				2	2		1		1	
2	4			3	1				1		1	1o	1o				1	1	1				
3	8				1	3+	1f															1	
	RT	R	L	S	FD	FA	C	Sh	M	V	I	H	A	At	Sx	Ab	Ax	Hs	Br	Pn	B	P	
4	6			3	1				3		1	2oP	2A				1		1				
5	2				1			2f	4m								2	1					
6	12			1	1		2-	1f	4m									1	1	1		1±	
7	10		1w	3	1			1f	2ma	AL2		1o							1		1	1±	
8	17				1		3-	2f	4m								1	1	1			1±	
9	16				1	1	1N	1f	2m								1		1	1			
	RT	R	L	S	FD	FA	C	Sh	M	V	I	H	A	At	Sx	Ab	Ax	Hs	Br	Pn	B	P	
10	12				1			2f															
11	20				1	3-	1v															2+	
12	6			1		2-			AL1				2				1		1				
13	11			2	1					1	1o	1o					1	1					
14	17			3	1			3	FC2	2oA										1			
15	7			2	1	1f										1	1						
	RT	R	L	S	FD	FA	C	Sh	M	V	I	H	A	At	Sx	Ab	Ax	Hs	Br	Pn	B	P	
16	14	1		2	1																		
17	13				1												1	1	1				
18	14	1			1		2t														1±		
19	8	1	1w	2				4m									1						
20	20				1	3N	2vf										1						
21	18			2	1													1			1±		
	RT	R	L	S	FD	FA	C	Sh	M	V	I	H	A	At	Sx	Ab	Ax	Hs	Br	Pn	B	P	
22	3	1		2	1			2				1o					2	1			1		
23	19			2	1	1f												1					
24	21				1	2-		4m									1	1					
25	5			3	2			3	CT2	2oA										1			
26	6			1	1	2-		2ma				1H	1H				1	1	1				
27	3			4	1			3	FC2	2A							2	2		1			
Sub-total: Items 1-27	RT 300	R	L 4	S 32	FD 39	FA 27	C 21	Sh 19	M 42	V 9	I 4	H 10	A 10	At 2	Sx	Ab	Ax 13	Hs 14	Br 10	Pn 9	B 1	P 7	5± 2+

Fold the top of this page down to this line, so that sub-totals for Items 1-27 may be seen on this side.

#	RT	R	L	S	FD	FA	C	Sh	M	V	I	H	A	At	Sx	Ab	Ax	Hs	Br	Pn	B	P	AA
28	8				4	1	1N		2				20A					1	1			1	
29	3				1	1								1			1						
30	10				2	1			2	FB1	1		2A									1	
31	6	2				1																	
32	7				1	1																	
33	8				3	1			3m									2	1				
	RT	R	L	S	FD	FA	C	Sh	M	V	I	H	A	At	Sx	Ab	Ax	Hs	Br	Pn	B	P	
34	2	2			2	2			2	ALI	1		20A						1			1	
35	11				1	1	2-	1f	4m									2	1	1			
36	9				1	1		1t	1			1o						1	1			1	
37	12	2			3	1	1-					1B						1					
38	3				3	1	1N	1f	2	FB1	1		2A						1	1			
39	18				1	1												1	1				
	RT	R	L	S	FD	FA	C	Sh	M	V	I	H	A	At	Sx	Ab	Ax	Hs	Br	Pn	B	P	
40	22				1	1											1						
41	9				2	1	1-		2 4m		1		2A				2	1		1		1	
42	2				1	1	2+																
43	2				2	1		1f											1				
44	18					1	1N	1t															
45	15				1	1			2mma FC2								1		1				
	RT	R	L	S	FD	FA	C	Sh	M	V	I	H	A	At	Sx	Ab	Ax	Hs	Br	Pn	B	P	AA
Uncorr. Total	465	✕	✕	✕	68	46	✕	✕	14														
Score	10.3	0	10	3A	68	46	30	23	64	14	9	14	18	3			19	22	17	14	1	12	5±/2+
Percentile°	9	24	20		22	57	93	97	98	>99	92	58	52	67			94	98	>99	>99		96	

Note. — Except for **RT, FD, FA,** and **V,** the **Score** for each variable is the total of the scores on each of the 45 cards. These totals should be entered in the row labeled **Score.** For **RT,** write the sum in the row labeled **Uncorrected Total,** divide this by 45, and enter the quotient as the **RT Score.** For **FD, FA,** and **V,** write the sum in the **Uncorrected Total** row, see Table 3 of the Guide, and enter the corrected total as the **Score.**

°Norms Group _SEVENTH GRADE_____

Summary Sheet for
Holtzman Inkblot Technique
Copyright © 1958 by The Psychological Corporation, New York, N. Y. 10017
All rights reserved as stated in the Guide and Catalog.

Printed in U.S.A.   65-368S

HILL CLINICAL SUMMARY
for the
HOLTZMAN INKBLOT TECHNIQUE

Form A or Ⓑ

Name: **HENRY BROWN**

Date: **6-23-1968**

Norms: **SEVENTH GRADE**

CATEGORIES

	I			II		III			IV					V					VI				
	RT	R	L	FA	S	C	Sh	B	FD	M	I	Br	P	H	A	At	Sx	Ab	Ax	Hs	V	Pn	AA
Final Score	10	0	10	46	3⅍	30	23	1	68	64	9	17	12	14	18	3			19	22	14	14	5± 2+
Per- centile		9	24	20	57		93	97		22	98	92	99	99	96	58	52	67		94	98	99	99	
High (a) Stim. Color	11	0	2	11	1⍵	15	7	1	16	21	2	4	5	3	3	1			5	5	3	7	3± 2+
Low (b) Stim. Color	10	0	3	15	1⍵	6	10	0	21	23	3	6	2	4	4	0			7	6	5	3	2±

Form A (a) 3, 6, 9, 15, 16, 17, 19, 20, 26, 27, 28, 35, 39, 42, 44
      (b) 1, 2, 5, 7, 18, 22, 24, 29, 30, 32, 33, 36, 37, 38, 43

Form B (a) 3, 6, 7, 11, 15, 17, 21, 24, 29, 34, 36, 39, 41, 42, 44
      (b) 2, 5, 8, 9, 10, 16, 18, 19, 23, 25, 26, 30, 32, 33, 45

COLOR

Score	+	–	N	Ac
1		2	4	1
2	1	5		
3	1	2	1	

SHADING

Score	Texture	Light Film	Dark Film	Vista
1	2	9		1
2	1		5	

MOVEMENT

Score	HUMAN								ANIMAL						m	
	1				2				1				2		Inanimate	Animate
	H	B	O	P	A	P	A	P	A	H	B	O	P	A		
1			1											2		
2						2					1	1	3		1	3
3						3							2	1		
4													7	1		
NO M	1		1							1	1	2				

PATHOGNOMIC VERBALIZATION

FB	FC	QR	IC	AL	CT	SR	DC	AB
2	3			3	1			

Notes:

SEQUENCE ANALYSIS

1. ROCKET CATAPULT'G DOGS
2. CENTAUR BEHEAD'G SNAKES - ON URN
3. SUNSET THRU CLOUDS REFLECT ON WATER
4. APEMEN RUNN'G CAG'G PEOPLE. LK MOVIE
5. SNOWSTORM - BLUR - CONFUSION
6. ROCKET CONE TOO HOT CAN'T TAKE BLAST
7. BLAND ORIENTAL GOD BREATH'G SMOKE
8. METEOR CRASH DESERT LV. LG. HOLE
9. ENTRANCE TO MOSQUE INCENSE BURN'G
10. SOMETHING UNDER MICROSCOPE - BLURRED
11. LOOK'G DOWN AT JUNGLE 3-D
12. HEART SPLIT IN TWO
13. PEOPLE HUNT'G MOOSE CAVE DRAW'G
14. 2 PEOPLE EA. RAC'G TO WIN
15. PALACE IN SKY REST'G ON CLOUDS
16. CANDY ON STICK - SUGAR DADDY - TO SUCK
17. OUTSIDE TUNNEL LOOK'G IN
18. CLOUDLESS MOONLESS NIGHT W. STARS
19. PLANE HELD BACK TO BE CATAPULTED
20. LOOK'G THRU CLOUDS AT CITY LIGHTS
21. V. LG. NUTCRACKER PULL LEVER CRACK NUT
22. SPIDER CREATURE PINCERS WALK'G
23. PLANE SMOKE FR. STEAM PRESSURE
24. BRUSH FIRE
25. SKATERS BALANC'G EXTRA HAND EACH
26. HUGE HEAD EYES EMITT'G RAYS
27. SEA HORSES COM'G HD ON PLAY'G CHICKEN
28. KING HENRY OVERSTUFFED COAT- COM'G AT YOU
29. SKULL OF DOG
30. BIRDS TALK'G LK HOUSEWIVES ACROSS FENCE
31. GEARS - JAGGED
32. FANCY BRIDGE
33. SHIPS BATTL'G - BOTH SINK'G
34. 2 PEOPLE TALK'G SEEN THRU WINDOW
35. SHIPS BATTL'G SMOKE HID'G EVERYTHING
36. MONSTER PICK'G UP WOOLY BEAR THING
37. LOBSTER CLAW - PRICKLY
38. 2 GIRAFFES TALK'G IN SWAMP
39. CROSS-SECTION OF BOWL
40. SKULL ON ORNAMENTAL BASE TROPHY
41. VOLCANO FIRE LAVA - BIRDS LK'G BACK FLY'G
42. HUGE FLOWER ON A BASE
43. TENT AT A FAIR
44. CANDY WRAPPER PULLED BACK
45. CAVE - CAULDRON - HANDS GROW'G OUT OF ROCK

Findings

The improvement in Henry's manner of coping with external reality, both in controls and ideation, is revealed in his HIT scores in form appropriateness and in the content of his responses. Psychopathology is still present, and autistic thinking is revealed in the content of his fantasy. However, his autistic thinking is less severe than it was eighteen months before. The improvement is evidenced in the following scores: Form appropriateness went from the sixth to the fifty-seventh percentile, pathognomic verbalization from a score of 40 to 14, movement from a score of 93 to 64, and anatomy from a score of 10 to 3. The bizarre content in the original record with its projected magical grandiosity is replaced by more relevant associations. He is now concerned with explosive violent acts. With further therapy and increased understanding and acceptance of his inner conflicts, this explosive violence should be replaced by percepts depicting violence between people.

Although Henry is somewhat more accessible than he was previously, he is also more reserved and remains detached, lonely, and socially wary. (Light-film shading responses are still predominant, barrier scores are higher than before, and human scores are reduced.) He continues to be hypersensitive to environmental pressures and therefore is anxious about people and himself (reflected in his Sh and Ax scores). He overemphasizes conventionality and conforms without giving sufficient consideration to his own likes and dislikes (reflected in the P and Br scores). His behavior is rigid, and he presents a facade of appropriateness which conceals evasion and lack of commitment. He is like a nonparticipating observer in interpersonal interactions (reflected in the Br score). He still uses withdrawal as a defense in order to decrease fear and anxiety when under stress (reflected in RT, light-film Sh, and At). The conscious maintenance of controls tends to depress his cognitive functioning (FD and RT are both lower than they are in the previous testing). Ideational activity in dealing with unstructured situations is not as good as it was at the previous testing.

Henry is more mature and less self-preoccupied than in the initial testing, but he is still self-centered (reflected in FA, At, C-minus, Ax, Hs, and Pn scores). Sexual identity problems are indicated by castration fears (blots 2, 4, 16, 21, 32, 45). He is still experiencing difficulties originating from his poor self-concept. He sees himself as inferior and judges his worth by the way people act toward him. He is, however, experiencing some pressure toward striving for independence and autonomy. This pressure for independence will increase his already high level of anxiety but is nonetheless movement in the right direction (reflected in S, HM, and AM scores).

Summary

Positive changes are taking place in Henry's internal frame of reference. Conflicting inner pressures, formerly repressed and released through magical, mystical fantasies, are more keenly experienced as free-floating anxieties and are released through illusions of explosive acts of violence. His internal orientation is shifting. He is currently experiencing conflicts which need resolution, namely, dependency versus independence, castration fear versus acceptance of a masculine role, and withdrawal versus coping with anxiety and tension. Evidence indicates that Henry is profiting from the therapeutic relationship in spite of his apparent detachment. His regular attendance shows that he is able to tolerate a one-to-one relationship, even though it may be stressful. Henry needs more time to work through his problems. Individual therapy should be continued. Group therapy as an adjunct to individual therapy would also be helpful. He can learn through his peers that other have problems, and he can discover how they work to resolve them. Group therapy may help him loosen up and express his feelings openly.

Adult Neurotic

XV

Case B is evaluated in detail based on personality variables. Jon Waters is a neurotic adult with hysterical conversion symptoms. He is forty-two years old, a social worker, and was an inpatient in a private psychiatric hospital. He was referred for psychological testing to determine whether his problems were attributable to organicity or emotional pathology. He developed cardiac symptoms after both his parents died from heart attacks. Doctors found no physiological basis for these symptoms. He was also experiencing sexual fantasies involving women whom he had been counseling. These feelings were followed by such severe feelings of guilt that he was unable to articulate appropriately. Before being admitted to the hospital, he experienced recurring thoughts of raping his daughter and killing his wife.

Observations

The patient is a tall, nice-looking man, neatly dressed and very quiet. He appeared concerned about the impression he was making and seemed eager to please. He was compulsive in his need for instructions, both in the copying of the Bender-Gestalt figures and in the drawings. He revealed rigidity in the block design of the Wechsler Adult Intelligence Scale (WAIS). If one block in the design was incorrect, he started over, even though the design was otherwise correct and almost complete. He manifested nervousness by a tremor in his left hand. When he was performing the digit symbol of the WAIS, his hand shook so badly that he had to press it tightly against the desk. He was cooperative but not spontaneous in his conversation, except in his need for elucidation of the instructions.

HOLTZMAN INKBLOT TECHNIQUE
RECORD FORM

Form A

Name_____Jon Waters_____Age__42__ Sex__M__ Date__4/3/69_____

Address_____Phone_____Educational Level_Graduate School_

Examiner_____E. F. Hill_____Previous Administration (Form and Date)_____

Symbols: Qʟ —question regarding location;   Qᴄ —question regarding characteristics;   Qᴇ —question regarding elaboration;
>ᵛ< —change in card position;   R.T. —reaction time in seconds.

X R.T. __3__	A bat.
	c. Formation of wing and body structure.
	e. Just an animal that you have to be aware of.
	L 0
Y R.T. __2__	A body.
	c. Formation, shape of woman's body.
	e. Just the outline.
	L 0
1A R.T. __10__ rocks	Two people talking and a background formation of rocks.
	c. Size.
	e. They just seem to be out in the open spaces with the rocks behind them.
	L 0
2A R.T. __11__	Nothing.
	Rejected.
3A R.T. __15__ eyebrows	Face in background.
	c. Color and it's in back of the black part.
	e. Looks like it's in agony and suffering badly.
	L 1

4A R.T. _10_	A cave as you are looking out through the opening. c. Structure around it and the walls. e. It has an opening and you look out through it. L 0
5A R.T. _11_	Dots. c. The appearance. e. No. L 0
6A R.T. _3_	A butterfly. c. Body, wings. e. Looks like it hasn't decided what color to be. L 0
7A R.T. _11_	Bone. c. Looks like a pelvic bone. e. It's an Xray. L 0
8A R.T. _13_	Cloud formation over water with sun reflecting. c. The wavering effect of the color. L 0
9A R.T. _15_	Nothing, except someone made a mess of things. They made a mistake. c. Color. L 0

10A R.T. 11	Little animals under a microscope, taking a look at their cells. c. All through a microscope. e. They're being moved around. L O
11A R.T. 11	A butterfly or animal again. c. Wings and the tail section, butterfly. e. Just resembles it to me. L O
12A R.T. 10 smoke	A campfire. Looks like the smoke is rising and people are standing around. Flame in it. c. Smoke and flame. e. Seems to be in a twilight time of evening. L O
13A R.T. 9	Green markings, that's all it is. L O
14A R.T. 45	Two dogs may be fighting. c. Down here. e. They're not fighting, seem to be barking and making noises, like they're frightened. L 1
15A R.T. 38 door	A building with the door open, it l. l. a church. c. You can see into it. e. Just inside looking out. L 1

16A R.T. __18__	Formation of an ape. c. Arms. e. Just seems to be standing. L 0
17A R.T. __22__	I just see color, that's all. L 0
18A R.T. __32__	(What in the world!) Rejected.
19A R.T. __7__	People. I don't know what they have around their necks. May be hanging by something. e. The others don't seem to be interested in the two that seem to be hanging or caught. L 0
20A R.T. __45__	May be a bird over here. c. Here. e. Seems to be flying, but seems to be after something. It's a vulture. L 1
21A R.T. __13__	A couple of angels standing by an open tomb. c. The shape of it. e. Just standing there. L 1

22A R.T. _25_	Nothing, just some kind of marks. Rejected.
23A R.T. _32_	I'm getting worse instead better. I don't see anything. Rejected.
24A R.T. _30_	Rejected.
25A R.T. _5_	Two people dancing. c. Looks like it. e. Just reaching out for each other. Think they're possibly swinging each other, making steps together. L 0
26A R.T. _11_	May be some kind of butterfly but I don't know what kind. c. The way it looks. e. Seems to be resting. L 0
27A R.T. _21_	Reflection in a pool. c. Looks like reflection, blurry at the bottom. e. Don't know what it is, trees and rocks and shrubs. L 0

28A R.T. __27__ L 0	Just color. e. No.
29A R.T. __28__	Rejected.
30A R.T. __15__ L 2	May be a figure in there; hazy, not very clear. c. Looks like he's standing in the doorway. e. Standing, waiting, alert, as if he's afraid something's going to happen.
31A R.T. __10__ L 0	A giant crab. c. Structure. e. I'd love to have some, I'm hungry.
32A R.T. __10__ L 0	Two birds on a perch. c. Here and here. e. Seem to be waiting for something to happen, they're in danger.
33A R.T. __8__ L 0	Blue blotting. c. Dots. e. That's all.

34A R.T. 6	Two men pointing at each other. c. Looks like it. e. Seem to be getting ready to run together. L O
35A R.T. 16	Looks like some kind of flying animal. It's a bird. c. Has two wings. e. Just seems to be flying. L O
36A R.T. 11	Nothing. Rejected.
37A R.T. 34	I'm trying to see something but I'm having an awful time, except black spots with a little red. e. Just black and red. L O
38A R.T. 23	A big butterfly. c. Shape. e. Just seems to be flaked out, resting. It looks translucent, it's drying its wings, just escaped from something. L O
39A R.T. 22 hands	A man holding something in his hands. c. Hands, holding something. e. No. L O

40A **R.T.** _5_	Looks like a vampire bat. c. Wings, body. e. Looks like he might be reaching to grab for something or about to land on something he's going to attack. L O
41A **R.T.** _13_	Four types of structures holding up something. c. Four supports. e. Just holding up some kind of ceiling. L O
42A **R.T.** _2_	A pretty butterfly. c. Color. e. Just seems to look like one. L O
43A **R.T.** _5_	Looks like a desert. c. Nothing there, it's empty (touching). e. I just used to fly and see these things, they look so barren and desolate. L O
44A **R.T.** _13_	Nothing, except a mistake, that's all. Rejected.
45A **R.T.** _8_	Cactus trees in a desert. c. The form, looks like sand, barren, empty (touch). e. Wasted, deserted. L O

SUMMARY SHEET   **HOLTZMAN INKBLOT TECHNIQUE**   Form: (circle) Ⓐ B

Name __JON WATERS__   Age __42__   Sex __M__   Date __4-3-1969__

Examiner __E. F. HILL__   Previous Administration (Form and Date) _____

Card No.	RT	R	L	S	FD	FA	C	Sh	M	V	I	H	A	At	Sx	Ab	Ax	Hs	Br	Pn	B	P	AA
1	10				3	2		1✓	2		1	20A								1			
2	11	1																					2-
3	15		1		1	1		1✓	FB1		1H	1H				2	1						
RT	R	L	S	FD	FA	C	Sh	M	V	I	H	A	At	Sx	Ab	Ax	Hs	Br	Pn	B	P		
4	10					1		1✓										1	1				
5	11					1		1t															
6	3					2		1-	AL2			1o											
7	11					2	1	1✓						1					1				
8	13						1	3N 2✓															
9	15						1	3-															2-
RT	R	L	S	FD	FA	C	Sh	M	V	I	H	A	At	Sx	Ab	Ax	Hs	Br	Pn	B	P		
10	11				1	1			1ma										1				
11	11				2	1						1o								1			
12	10				3	2	1+	1✓	1mv		1	20P								1			
13	9					1	3N																
14	45	1				2			2			2A				1							
15	38	1	1N		2	1		1✓											1	1			
RT	R	L	S	FD	FA	C	Sh	M	V	I	H	A	At	Sx	Ab	Ax	Hs	Br	Pn	B	P		
16	18				3				1			2P						1					
17	22					1	3N																
18	32	1																					2-
19	7				3	2			1ma		1	20					2	2		1			
20	45	1			2	1			2			2A					2						
21	13	1	1N		2	1		1	FC2			1o					2	1	1	1			
RT	R	L	S	FD	FA	C	Sh	M	V	I	H	A	At	Sx	Ab	Ax	Hs	Br	Pn	B	P		
22	25	1																					
23	32	1																					2-
24	30	1																					
25	5				3	1			3		1	20A								1			
26	11				1				1			1o											
27	21				1	1		1✓															
Sub-total: Items 1-27	RT 484	R 5	L 5	S 2N	FD 33	FA 21	C 14	Sh 10	M 15	V 5	I 4	H 10	A 10	At 1	Sx	Ab	Ax 9	Hs 4	Br 3	Pn 5	B	P 6	8-

Fold the top of this page down to this line, so that sub-totals for Items 1-27 may be seen on this side.

Item	RT	R	L	S	FD	FA	C	Sh	M	V	I	H	A	At	Sx	Ab	Ax	Hs	Br	Pn	B	P	AA
28	27					1	3N																
29	28	1																					
30	15		2		1	1		1f	1				1o				2	1					
31	10				2	1				SR2			2				2						
32	10				2	1			1				2P				2						
33	8					1	2N	1t															
	RT	R	L	S	FD	FA	C	Sh	M	V	I	H	A	At	Sx	Ab	Ax	Hs	Br	Pn	B	P	
34	6				3	1			3	1		2MA						1				1	
35	16				2	1			2				2A										
36	11	1																					
37	34					1	3N^Ac																2-
38	23				2	1		1f	1				1o					1		1			
39	22				2				1	FC2		2MP											
	RT	R	L	S	FD	FA	C	Sh	M	V	I	H	A	At	Sx	Ab	Ax	Hs	Br	Pn	B	P	
40	5				3				2				2A				2	1					
41	13				1	1												1					
42	2				2	1	2+						1o									1	1+
43	5				1			1t		SR2							1						1-
44	13	1																					2-
45	8				1	1		1t			1						1						
	RT	R	L	S	FD	FA	C	Sh	M	V	I	H	A	At	Sx	Ab	Ax	Hs	Br	Pn	B	P	AA
Uncorr. Total	740	✕	✕	✕	54	34	✕	✕	11	✕	✕	✕	✕	✕	✕	✕	✕	✕	✕	✕	✕	✕	
Score	16.4	8	7	2▲	64	40	24	15	26	13	6	15	20	1			18	6	4	7		8	13- / 1+
Percentile*	42	82	2		31	19	80	83	59	95	80	55	46	45			98	56	37	97		49	

Note. — Except for **RT**, **FD**, **FA**, and **V**, the **Score** for each variable is the total of the scores on each of the 45 cards. These totals should be entered in the row labeled **Score**. For **RT**, write the sum in the row labeled **Uncorrected Total**, divide this by 45, and enter the quotient as the RT Score. For **FD**, **FA**, and **V**, write the sum in the **Uncorrected Total** row, see Table 3 of the Guide, and enter the corrected total as the **Score**.

*Norms Group AVERAGE ADULTS

Summary Sheet for
Holtzman Inkblot Technique
Copyright © 1958 by The Psychological Corporation, New York, N. Y. 10017
All rights reserved as stated in the Guide and Catalog.

Printed in U.S.A.   65-368S

HILL CLINICAL SUMMARY
for the
HOLTZMAN INKBLOT TECHNIQUE

Form (A) or B

Name: JON WATERS   Date: 4-3-1969

Norms: AVERAGE ADULT

CATEGORIES

	I			II		III			IV					V					VI				
	RT	R	L	FA	S	C	Sh	B	FD	M	I	Br	P	H	A	At	Sx	Ab	Ax	Hs	V	Pn	AA
Final Score	16	8	7	40	2	24	15	0	64	26	6	4	8	15	20	1			18	6	13	7	13-/1+
Percentile	42	82	2	19		80	83		31	59	80	37	49	55	46	45			98	56	95	49	
High (a) Stim. Color	18	1	3	11	1	12	3		21	8	1	1	2	5	10	0			4	4	5	1	7-/1+
Low (b) Stim. Color	18	6	2	10	0	5	7		10	5	1	0	2	3	3	1			6	0	2	3	3-

Form A (a) 3, 6, 9, 15, 16, 17, 19, 20, 26, 27, 28, 35, 39, 42, 44
       (b) 1, 2, 5, 7, 18, 22, 24, 29, 30, 32, 33, 36, 37, 38, 43
Form B (a) 3, 6, 7, 11, 15, 17, 21, 24, 29, 34, 36, 39, 41, 42, 44
       (b) 2, 5, 8, 9, 10, 16, 18, 19, 23, 25, 26, 30, 32, 33, 45

COLOR

Score	+	-	N	Ac
1	/	/		
2	/		/	
3		/	5	/

SHADING

Score	Texture	Light Film	Dark Film	Vista
1	4	5		4
2			1	

MOVEMENT

	HUMAN										ANIMAL					m	
	1				2						1				2		
					M		F		O								
Score	H	B	O	P	A	P	A	P	A	P	H	B	O	P	A	Inanimate	Animate
1			2	1				1				2	2			1	2
2							1								4		
3						1											
4																	
NO M	1							1			1		3		1		

PATHOGNOMIC VERBALIZATION

FB	FC	QR	IC	AL	CT	SR	DC	AB
1	2			1		2		

Notes:

SEQUENCE ANALYSIS

1. 2 PEOPLE TALK'G - ROCK BACKGROUND
2. R.
3. FACE IN AGONY SUFFER'G
4. CAVE LOOK'G OUT THRU OPENING
5. DOTS
6. BUTTERFLY - HASN'T DECIDED RE COLOR
7. XRAY PELVIC BONE
8. CLOUD OVER WATER
9. SOMEONE MADE A MESS
10. LOOK'G AT ANIMAL CELLS - MICROSCOPE
11. BUTTERFLY
12. CAMPFIRE PEOPLE STAND'G SMOKE RISING
13. GREEN MARKINGS
14. 2 DOGS FIGHT'G NO - FRIGHTENED
15. CHURCH - DOOR OPEN - INSIDE LOOK'G OUT
16. FORMATION OF APE - STAND'G
17. COLOR
18. R.
19. PEOPLE - 2 HANGED - OTHERS NOT INTERESTED
20. VULTURE FLY'G
21. CPL. ANGELS STAND'G BY OPEN TOMB
22. R.
23. R.
24. R.
25. 2 PEOPLE DANC'G
26. BUTTERFLY REST'G
27. REFLECTION IN POOL
28. COLOR
29. R
30. FIGURE STAND'G IN DOORWAY AFRAID
31. GIANT CRAB - (I'M HUNGRY)
32. 2 BIRDS ON PERCH - IN DANGER
33. BLUE DOTTING
34. 2 MEN POINT'G - READY TO RUN TOGETHER
35. BIRD - FLY'G
36. R
37. BLACK AND RED
38. BUTTERFLY FLAKED OUT DRY'G - ESCAPED
39. MAN HOLD'G SOMETHING
40. VAMPIRE BAT GRAB SOMETHING TO ATTACK
41. 4 SUPPORTS HOLDING SOMETHING
42. PRETTY BUTTERFLY
43. DESERT, BARREN DESOLATE
44. R
45. CACTUS IN DESERT BARREN WASTED

Findings

Cognitive functioning is adequate, evidenced in the FD, RT, and P scores, all in the average range, and in the excess of H 2 over H 1 responses. The I score in the high-average range indicates a capability for integrating and grasping relationships. The P and Br scores reveal awareness of conventional demands. Mr. Waters can control his thoughts in situations where the demands on him are not intense. He accomplishes this control by repressing and inhibiting affect. He rejected eight blots by controlling his associations. The cards he rejected are predominantly low in stimulus strength of color. The average RT for the eight blots rejected is twenty-three seconds, compared with the average RT of sixteen seconds for the blots to which he responded. In addition, there are nine near rejections, again showing the ability to inhibit affect by keeping the responses neutral. He can defensively block free-floating associations when the stimulus pressure is weak.

Under stress, however, he cannot sustain the inhibitory effort and gives amorphous responses which, together with the high V scores, reveal pathology. Mr. Waters gave only one I response to a high stimulus-strength color card. The pressure of emotional impulses interferes with his cognitive functioning, and he is unable to concentrate, integrate, or deal effectively with the stimuli. This inability is reflected in the low FA score and in the color-naming responses. He has difficulty sustaining enough effort to organize percepts when affect is present. The blot content early in the test is varied. About half way through, however, after associating "angels standing at an open tomb," reflecting superego conflicts of guilt, he rejected three blots. He was then able to mobilize enough resources to give a good response, "two people dancing." The balance of the responses are spotty and irregular and he ended with a rejection and two safe nature responses. Under stress, inner conflicts interfere with the use of his intellectual capacity. These conflicts are revealed in the low HM and excessive Ax scores. Depression appears to be cutting him off temporarily from his creative capacity.

Mr. Waters' thought processes are disturbed. The combination of R scores in the very high average range and near rejections reveals repression and control of associations. Poor reality contact is revealed in the low L and FA scores and the high V score. The high V score also reveals disturbed inner fantasy in which emotional dominance distorts intellectual efforts. The patient loses the distance between himself and the blot (reflected in the high use of AA and the SR responses).

Affective functioning is disturbed as evidenced by a predominance of C 3 responses, low L and FA scores, high numbers of AA, and high V. These scores identify the patient's immaturity, diffuse body preoccupation, and the self-orientation which leads at times to insufficient differentiation from the environment. Anxiety and tension are high, especially in relationships with people. This behavior is reflected in the Ax score at the ninety-eighth percentile, the Sh score at the eighty-third percentile, and few HM responses. Mr. Waters' H responses deal primarily with people rather than male or female persons. These responses are associated with distanciation. He is dependent but pessimistic about fulfillment of his dependent needs. His pessimism is revealed in percepts such as barren desert and people not interested in other people who are hanging. His need for security is reflected in nature responses, percepts involving caves and houses, and passive H content. The high Ax content reflects long-term feelings of anxiety, fears, and phobias.

Inner conflicts, internal stresses, and external pressures overwhelm his emotions, as evidenced by R, C 3 responses, and near rejections. Although inner pressures to express affect outwardly are strong, his responsiveness to the environment makes him capable of temporarily blocking his affect to protect the ego. The rejections and near rejections show that he inhibits affect by evasion—doing nothing—thus avoiding confrontations. This constriction creates affective discomfort, preventing spontaneity. He is cautious, restrained, and inhibited, and avoids handling interpersonal relationships directly or openly. Human and animal stances show that he has little, if any, desire to act. Despite avoidance and excessive controls, he is susceptible to attack from without. He tries to mask his feelings with neutral content, but his excessive Pn score shows that he cannot be detached. The V scores suggest weak ego control and distortion of reality, with responses determined by inner needs and drives. Inner unrest and instability are also suggested in the high-average C responses (eightieth percentile) with a predominance of C 3 and excessive Ax responses. Mr. Waters' efforts to control affect may be reflected in the neutral content and R scores, but the strong need to release his feelings is expressed through side comments, elaboration, and many AA scores. Disturbed thoughts protrude into his consciousness, and his repressive defenses are precarious.

The low L and FA scores indicate Mr. Waters' reliance on perceptual defenses to modify or delimit external stimuli so that he can deal with them. He uses inhibition to repress the inner unrest (revealed in m, Ax, and V scores). Passive content, denial of aggression (card 14), and vista and light-film Sh responses indicate a passive-submissive adjustment which conceals aggressive elements. Mr. Waters is depressed and may be entertaining suicidal thoughts. Suicidal ideation is indicated by his color and shading responses to the same chromatic area in blots 8 and 33, the high Ax score, and his smoke and cloud responses.

Mr. Waters' self-concept is poor. He sees himself as inadequate, as is evident in the high Ax score and the vista and light-film Sh responses. The patient is self-depreciating, unhappy, and lacking in self-confidence (which was evident in his test behavior). His body-image boundaries are not well integrated. The Pn score is excessive. In two of the three percepts in which Br is scored, Pn is also scored, so that although he verbalizes the desire for the protection of a cave and shelter (Br), openings which are scored Pn make the protection ineffectual.

Mr. Waters has conflicts concerning his sexual identity. Although the HIT record is devoid of sex responses, one At percept, pelvis, and the response to card

34, two men getting ready to run together, have possible sexual implications. Sexual responses are apparent in the symbolic content of other tests.

Validation Evidence from Other Tests

Other tests verify Mr. Waters' capacity for good mental functioning. Although the results of the WAIS place him in the average range of intelligence, these results are not a true measure of his potential. In that test, he experienced difficulty in concentrating and applying himself. He showed some rigidity in speed tasks, particularly the digit symbol. Part of his low score was attributable to his hand tremor. Although there was a speed loss on the block design and the digit symbol, his perceptual processes do not seem to be disturbed, as he was able to complete all the block designs accurately when given enough time. Speed loss is found in persons with organicity but it is also common in people with emotional problems. Many signs were counter-indicative of organicity. Mr. Waters' memory and capacity for new learning on the Wechsler Memory Scale were very good, and he had no difficulty perceiving depth.

He evidenced passivity and withdrawal in the sentence completion test and in the TAT, as well as in the HIT. In response to TAT card 1, he indicated his typical sit-and-do-nothing behavior: "The boy does not want to play the violin which is forced on him and just sits and watches it." In TAT card 3 "the boy cannot get a toy he wants so he sits and cries." Mr. Waters' depression is also indicated in TAT card 12M: "The father sees if his son is dead; he is not sure; but he finds that his son is really dead."

He was able to verbalize his fear of losing control of himself more openly in the sentence-completion test than in the HIT and indicated that he could lose his temper if he were to let himself go. In the sentence-completion test, he also revealed his feelings of inferiority concerning his inability to be verbally fluent and less selfish. He expressed feelings of guilt that people may think him better than he is.

The drawings reveal castration difficulties. The top of the head is cut off, there are no legs, and there are other accepted castration symbols on the drawings. In the sentence-completion test, he reported that his relationship with his father was very poor and that he had problems relating to him. In response to TAT card 2, "the school girl is attracted to the male who is married; in the end he stays with his wife." The response to TAT card 13MF concerns guilt over adultery. He does not see himself as virile and has difficulty contending with masculine sex symbolism. Perhaps his strong need for contact affection and approval gets mixed up with his sexual drive and contributes to his fantasies concerning women. Is he using sex fantasies to work out his aggression toward females because of deprivation of affection from his mother, wife, or both? The

castration fears and strong feelings of guilt seem to suggest unfulfilled and repressed sexual needs and undue tensions.

Summary

Mr. Waters is a rigid, defensive individual who deals with superficial
aspects of relationships without becoming either physically or socially involved
with people. He tries to avoid revealing himself and exercises strong inhibitory
forces to maintain an appropriate external facade. Conflicting inner needs of
aggression and affection strive for outward expression. But an equally strong need
to maintain control over his behavior prevails. The result is long periods of anxiety
and depression with possible suicidal ideation.

Mr. Waters evidences psychological disturbances in intellectual and emotional functioning. Under stress, he becomes stimulus bound and is able to perceive only the threatening situation. He is unable to integrate or deal with stress
effectively. He reveals neurotic constriction with obsessive-compulsive behavior,
ritualistic thinking, and hysterical conversion symptoms. He cannot acknowledge
his impulses through overt action or through imaginal processes. The test gives
evidence of self-preoccupation. The high Ax scores suggests physical symptoms
such as cardiac spasms or palpitations which are verified by Mr. Waters' presenting symptoms. His ego structure is threatened and pathology is indicated.

Mr. Waters has many assets which can be used to help him. He has the
ability to objectify his problems and is capable of introspection. He generally tries
to adapt to anxiety when it is elicited, although he may not always be able to
handle the stress encountered. He can see his world peopled and has a capacity
for empathy with people, which is an affective resource considering his depression.
He is also aware of social values and recognizes conventional requirements.

Mr. Waters needs to learn to assert himself, however difficult it may be.
He needs to understand and accept himself—his strong needs for affection and
security—and not be so concerned with the opinions of others. In addition to
the individual therapy he is receiving, I would suggest group therapy. The ability
to be open with other people in a group setting will be useful to future interactions when he leaves the hospital. Art therapy might also be a useful adjunct to
psychotherapy because he needs help in loosening up and expressing himself. His
phobic sexual fears need to be worked through in terms of his sexual immaturity,
his fear of castration, and his desire for contact affection. He needs support in
attaining a masculine identity.

Normal College Coed

XVI

Case C, Sarah Fuller, is illustrative of the record obtained from the normal college student of superior intelligence. The HIT scores are evaluated on the basis of personality variables. Sarah, age nineteen, is a sophomore of superior intelligence (full scale WAIS IQ 145, verbal IQ 143, performance IQ 141) who is successful in her academic pursuits. She is not fully sure of herself in group social interactions with strangers, although she has established close relationships with individuals in her peer group, both male and female.

Observations

Sarah is an attractive, slim girl, who was relaxed and interested in the test.

Normal College Coed

HOLTZMAN INKBLOT TECHNIQUE
RECORD FORM

Form A

Name _____ Sarah Fuller _____ Age __19__ Sex __F__ Date _4/20/67_

Address _____ Phone _____ Educational Level _College_
Sophomore

Examiner _____ E. F. Hill _____ Previous Administration (Form and Date) _____

Symbols: Q$_L$ —question regarding location; Q$_C$ —question regarding characteristics; Q$_E$ —question regarding elaboration;
      ⊁⊀ —change in card position; R.T. —reaction time in seconds.

X head **R.T.** __2__ tail	A bat. c. Black and wings, head and tail L 0
Y **R.T.** __9__	Shape of body. c. Lines look like rib cage, top part, torso. L 0
1A **R.T.** __22__ apple trees shadows	People facing and talking to each other in an orchard with trees around them. c. Spread out appearance, looks like apple trees. These are shadows cast by the people, logically they would be in the same direction. L 0
2A **R.T.** __4__ forks tables	Two people sitting back to back, looks like they're sitting at tables. They have forks in their hands. c. Shape. L 0
3A **R.T.** __4__	Sun setting behind trees, over water because of reflection. c. Colors and unclear effect of reflection. L 0

4A R.T. <u>9</u>	Desert, looks like sand (touch), horses or could be camels with people on top of them. c. Color and hilly aspects. e. Looks like a battle, they're riding toward each other. Horses look like bucking with one foot up in the air. L O	
5A R.T. <u>12</u>	A painting by Duchaps. He uses geometric forms. Looks like two guys fencing. c. The straight lines look like legs and swords here, and motion. e. It's vague. L O	
6A R.T. <u>23</u>	A guy reading, he has a long nose, here's the book. c. Shape. e. No. L 2	
7A R.T. <u>22</u>	Two butterfly-like forms facing each other. Looks like dancers with arms up, on toes like a ballet. c. Shape. L O	
8A R.T. <u>16</u>	Reflection on the water. c. Because of division, looks like a repeat in the water, repeating because of color and variations. L O	
9A R.T. <u>15</u>	Horseshoe crabs in the sand. c. Texture, dots look like sand and color shape of crabs. e. No. L O	

10A R.T. __6__	Two people. c. Shape. e. They're meeting and greeting each other. L 1	
11A R.T. __21__	A butterfly. c. Shape wings. e. No. L 0	
12A R.T. __7__	Bonfire in the middle. Some kind of birds, like swans, around fire. People standing, women with wide skirts. Clouds overhead in horizon. c. Color, shapes, and cloudy effect. L 0	
13A R.T. __12__	Motion, like something went by very fast, leaving an after-image. c. The repeated lines and forms in one direction. L 0	
14A R.T. __16__	Skeletons, skull looks like head shape and has a bony look. L 1	
15A R.T. __27__ Temple Elephants Robed figure	Has Oriental appearance, looks like a collage or composite, colorful. There's a Siamese Temple, and here are elephants with their trunks rolled up, and here there's a robed figure, like a monk. L 0	

16A R.T. _30_ eyes beak	A birdlike head, two eyes and a beak. c. Shape. e. No. L 0
17A R.T. _13_	Faces, nose, open mouth, chin, looks like masks. c. Like a clown mask because of exaggerated nose. Both are the same. e. No. L 2
18A R.T. _17_	Landscape, trees, lake, mountain areas, looking down at it. c. Feeling of depth and texture. L 0
19A R.T. _8_	Bunch of people, two kneeling, two sitting and two dancing. c. Looks like these two are hung because of the lines and heads bent down. These two have hats on. L 0
20A R.T. _32_	A series of animals jumping over something, like you would see on a wood block. c. Brown looks like a wood block of a print, the extra dots look like a place where all the wood is not taken out. L 0
21A R.T. _12_	Angels with wings and long robes. They have halos but they have no heads. c. The way it looks. e. No. L 1

22A R.T. __12__	Two caterpillars because of all the legs, looks like they're rearing up. c. Shape. L 2

23A R.T. __13__	Bat hung upside down. c. Wing shape, black color. e. No. L 1

24A R.T. __18__	Water color. Paint allowed to spread on wet paper, fuzzed up. Looks like a ski scene, pine trees. c. Black against the white. L 0

25A R.T. __9__	Two forms reaching out to each other. Looks like a Michelangelo fresco, the one of God reaching out to man. c. Shape. L 0

26A R.T. __3__	Primitive mask with mouth and eyes. c. Oval shape. L 0

27A R.T. __10__	Ducks, buffalo with horns, horses, shape of head. All around the water. c. Shape and blurred effect of the water. e. Friendly, the ducks are standing on top of a couple of the others. They're communicating with each other. L 0

28A	**R.T.** _8_	Two women bowing down, looks like they're bowing to each other. One hand is back and one down. L 1
29A	**R.T.** _9_	Stonehinge type of place. Top looks like stones and leaned on each other. c. Shapes, geometric. L 0
30A	**R.T.** _4_	Japanese strokes or lettering like a painting. c. The lines. L 0
31A	**R.T.** _17_	Dragons with long tongues that look like snakes. Looks like they may have wings. c. Shape. e. Looking across at each other from over rock or something. L 0
32A	**R.T.** _22_	Horse's head and bent front leg. c. Shape. e. No. L 1
33A	**R.T.** _4_	Fossils of fish. c. Grainy texture. L 0

34A R.T. 6	Two fat angels, cherubs, holding a wishbone, with a bumblebee in the middle. Pink part looks like a cutaway to view the insides and makes them look like mechanical figures, showing how they operate. c. Color and shape. L 0
35A R.T. 25	Little fat birds sitting on logs. c. Shape. e. No. L 2
36A R.T. 10	A sheep's head. c. Shape. L 0
37A R.T. 12	Swordfish jumping in the waves. c. Shape. L 1
38A R.T. 26	Landscape, mountains in background, trees in front. Vague shapes looking down at them. L 0
39A R.T. 22	Insects with big buggy eyes and little legs, sitting down. c. Shape. e. Looking at each other. L 0

40A R.T. __19__	Landscape containing a pyramind form and trees. c. Shape. L 0
41A R.T. __9__	Cocktail glasses. c. Triangular shape with stems, looks like have something in them that's greenish. L 1
42A R.T. __7__	Butterfly c. Color and shape. e. It's also fuzzy, not very well defined but suggests a butterfly. L 0
43A R.T. __14__	Person laying on the ground, looks like a stick figure. c. Lines, look very skinny. e. No. L 0
44A R.T. __7__	Face, nose, mouth, eyes, in color; looks like it has sunglasses on. e. The even shapes around the eyes. L 0
45A R.T. __6__	Cactus in desert, looks like distance, in background maybe a tree. c. Tree looks smaller, therefore more distant. Color looks like sand. L 0

SUMMARY SHEET   **HOLTZMAN INKBLOT TECHNIQUE**   Form: (circle) (A) B

Name **SARAH FULLER**   Age **19**   Sex **F**   Date **4-20-1967**

Examiner _____ Previous Administration (Form and Date) _____

Card No.	RT	R	L	S	FD	FA	C	Sh	M	V	I	H	A	At	Sx	Ab	Ax	Hs	Br	Pn	B	P
1	22				2	2			2		1	20A							1			1
2	4				3	1			1		1	20A					1					1
3	4				1	1	2+	1f														
4	9				4	1	1-	1vt	4		1	20P	2A				2					1
5	12				2	1			2			1o					1					
6	23	2			3	1			1		1	2MP							1			
7	22				3	2			1		1	20P										
8	16					1	3N 2f															
9	15				4	1	1N 1t						2P						1			
10	6	1			2	1			2		1	20A										1
11	21				2	1						1o										1
12	7				3	2	1N	1f	2m		1	2FP	2P						1			1
13	12					1			3m								2					
14	16	1			1	1					1					1						
15	27				4	1	1+				1	1o	1o						1			
16	30				2							1H										
17	13	2			1	1														1	1	
18	17				1	1			1vt													
19	8				3	2			3m		1	20A					2	1	1			1
20	32				1	1		1t	3		1	1o							1			
21	12	1			2	2				QR2		1o					1	1	1			1
22	12	2			2	1			2			1o										
23	13	1			3	2	1Ac		1			2P					1					
24	18				1	1	2Ac N	1t			1											1
25	9				4				1			1o					1					1
26	3				1	1																
27	10				4	2			2	FB1	1		2A									1
Sub-total: Items 1-27	393		10		59	32	12	9	30	3	12	20	15	1		2	6	6	6	2	1	12

Fold the top of this page down to this line, so that sub-totals for Items 1-27 may be seen on this side.

#	RT	R	L	S	FD	FA	C	Sh	M	V	I	H	A	At	Sx	Ab	Ax	Hs	Br	Pn	B	P
28	8	1			3	1			2		1	2FA								1		
29	9				1												1					
30	4				1																	
31	17				2	1			1		1	1o					1	1				
32	22	1			4	1						1H										
33	4					1	2t															
	RT	R	L	S	FD	FA	C	Sh	M	V	I	H	A	At	Sx	Ab	Ax	Hs	Br	Pn	B	P
34	6				3	2	1N		1	FC2	1o	1o	1						1			1
35	25	2			2	1			1		1	2P										
36	10				3	1						1H										
37	12	1			3	1			2			2A										
38	26				1	1		1v														
39	22				1	1			1		1	1o										
	RT	R	L	S	FD	FA	C	Sh	M	V	I	H	A	At	Sx	Ab	Ax	Hs	Br	Pn	B	P
40	19				3	1																
41	9				3	2	1N											1				
42	7				2	1	1N	1t				1o										1
43	14				1	1			1			1o										
44	7				3	1	1N					1H						1				1
45	6				1	1	2N	1v	1													
	RT	R	L	S	FD	FA	C	Sh	M	V	I	H	A	At	Sx	Ab	Ax	Hs	Br	Pn	B	P
Uncorr. Total	620				94	52			5													
Score	13.7	15			94	52	18	14	39	5	17	25	25	2		2	8	7	8	3	1	16
Percentile°	17	33			79	97	33	41	45	63	85	53	66	51			34	24	52	25		97

Note. — Except for **RT, FD, FA,** and **V,** the **Score** for each variable is the total of the scores on each of the 45 cards. These totals should be entered in the row labeled **Score.** For **RT,** write the sum in the row labeled **Uncorrected Total,** divide this by 45, and enter the quotient as the RT Score. For **FD, FA,** and **V,** write the sum in the **Uncorrected Total** row, see Table 3 of the Guide, and enter the corrected total as the **Score.**

°Norms Group __COLLEGE STUDENTS__

Summary Sheet for
Holtzman Inkblot Technique
Copyright © 1958 by The Psychological Corporation, New York, N. Y. 10017
All rights reserved as stated in the Guide and Catalog.

Printed in U.S.A.   65-368S

HILL CLINICAL SUMMARY
for the
HOLTZMAN INKBLOT TECHNIQUE

Form (A) or B

Name: SARAH FULLER

Date: 4-20-1967

Norms: COLLEGE STUDENTS

CATEGORIES

	I		II			III			IV					V				VI				
	RT	R	L	FA	S	C	Sh	B	FD	M	I	Br	P	H	A	At	Sx	Ab	Ax	Hs	V	Pn	AA
Final Score	14		15	52	0	18	14	1	94	39	17	8	16	25	25	2	0	2	8	7	5	3	
Per-centile	17		33	97		33	41		79	45	85	52	97	53	66	51		68	34	24	63	25	
High (a) Stim. Color	16		7	16		6	4	1	36	13	7	4	6	8	11	0		0	2	1	1	1	
Low (b) Stim. Color	14		3	17		2	6	0	26	11	4	1	4	8	5	0		0	1	2	0	0	

Form A (a) 3, 6, 9, 15, 16, 17, 19, 20, 26, 27, 28, 35, 39, 42, 44
(b) 1, 2, 5, 7, 18, 22, 24, 29, 30, 32, 33, 36, 37, 38, 43
Form B (a) 3, 6, 7, 11, 15, 17, 21, 24, 34, 36, 39, 41, 42, 44
(b) 2, 5, 8, 9, 10, 16, 18, 19, 23, 25, 26, 30, 32, 33, 45

COLOR

Score	+	–	N	Ac
1		2	7	1
2	1		2	1
3			1	

SHADING

Score	Texture	Light Film	Dark Film	Vista
1	6	3		4
2		1	1	

MOVEMENT

	HUMAN								ANIMAL						m	
	1				2				1				2		Inanimate	Animate
Score				M	F	O										
	H	B	O	P	A	P	A	P	A	H	B	O	P	A		
1			2	1		1		2					4	3	2	
2			1				1		2			1		2	1	
3							1						1		2	
4							1						1			
NO M			1							4		1	1			

PATHOGNOMIC VERBALIZATION

FB	FC	QR	IC	AL	CT	SR	DC	AB
1	1	1						

Notes:

SEQUENCE ANALYSIS

1. PEOPLE TALK'G IN APPLE ORCHARD
2. 2 PEOPLE SITT'G BACK TO BACK FORKS IN HAND
3. SUN SETT'G BEHIND TREES
4. HORSES W. PEOPLE ON THEM BATTLE
5. PAINT'G GEOMETRIC FORM 2 GUYS FENC'G
6. GUY READ'G LONG NOSE BOOK
7. DANCERS BALLET BFY-LIKE
8. REFLECTION ON WATER
9. HORSESHOE CRABS IN SAND
10. 2 PEOPLE MEET'G GREET'G
11. BUTTERFLY
12. BONFIRE PEOPLE STAND'G BIRDS AROUND FIRE
13. MOTION FAST LEFT AFTERIMAGE
14. SKELETONS
15. ORIENTAL COLLAGE, TEMPLE, ELEPH'T, MONK
16. BIRD-LIKE HEAD
17. CLOWN MASK-EXAGGERATED NOSES
18. LANDSCAPE-LOOK'G DOWN AT
19. FIGURES 2 HUNG 2 SITT'G 2 DANC'G
20. WOOD BLOCK ANIM. JUMP'G OVER SOM'G
21. ANGELS, ROBES, WINGS, HALO NO HEADS
22. 2 CATERPILLARS REAR'G UP
23. BAT HUNG UPSIDE DOWN
24. WATER COLOR OF SKI SCENE
25. MICHELANGELO FRESCO-GOD REACH'G TO MAN
26. PRIMITIVE MASK
27. ANIMALS AROUND WATER-FRIENDLY
28. 2 WOMEN BOW'G TO EACH OTHER
29. STONEHENGE PLACE
30. JAPANESE STROKE OR LETTER'G
31. DRAGONS W. LONG TONGUES LOOK'G AT EA. OTH.
32. HORSES HEAD AND BENT FRONT LEG
33. FOSSILS OF FISH
34. 2 FAT ANGELS, MECHANICAL HOLD'G WISHBONE
35. LITTLE FAT BIRDS SITT'G ON LOGS
36. SHEEPS HEAD
37. SWORDFISH JUMP'G IN WAVES
38. LANDSCAPE -MOUNTAIN -TREES
39. INSECTS W. BUGGY EYES LOOK'G AT EA. OTHER
40. LANDSCAPE PYRAMID TREES
41. COCKTAIL GLASSES SOMETHING IN IT
42. BUTTERFLY
43. SKINNY PERSON LAY'G ON GROUND
44. FACE W. SUNGLASSES
45. CACTUS IN DESERT

Findings

Cognitive functioning evident of superior intelligence is revealed throughout the test. RT low in the average range shows the availability of inner resources without undue interference of affect. The combination of L scores low in the average range and high scores in FD, FA, and I reflects high mental functioning. She can integrate ideas, organize them, and verbalize her perceptions. In addition to the scoring pattern indicated, the use of color in the average range with C 1 predominant reveals creativity and the ability to regress in the service of the ego. This creativity is also seen in the many human-movement responses. M, Ax, Hs, and A in the average range reflect free and active fantasy with good imaginative production and flexibility in thinking. The high popular score shows that although Sarah is capable of creativity, she can recognize conventional requirements.

Sarah's affective functioning is typical of that of the mature person who is aware of inner feelings and can express them appropriately. This maturity is revealed in the FA, FD, Ax, Hs, and V scores. Aggressive feelings typical of the adolescent who is moving toward self-assertion and independence are also indicated. These feelings are not predominant, however, and are under control, as evidenced by the Hs scores in the average range. Sarah is experiencing normal anxiety based on reality and can deal with threats without becoming overwhelmed, as revealed in the scores on Ax, Br, L, FD, FA, and I. Her self-control is at the conscious level, without any unconscious or emotionally disturbed perceptions. Her behavior and rational functioning are therefore consistent and predictable. She is capable of functioning well under stress.

Sarah is also capable of smooth interpersonal relationships because she is considerate of others and sensitive to their needs. This behavior is revealed in her C, Sh, and H responses. She has some needs for closeness and dependency, but she would seek gratification from appropriate sources, as indicated in her use of texture in Sh and passive H and A movement responses.

Sarah's self-concept is favorable, and she has appropriate ego control. Her strong sense of self-identity is revealed in the FD, FA, and Br scores. She is independent and assertive. Her use of aggressive H and A movement responses shows that she has a good sense of responsibility toward herself and others. She shows confidence and self-reliance and should be able to pursue her goals without much reliance on others.

Summary

Sarah is typical of the college student of superior intelligence who has no marked inner conflicts. She is self-accepting, original, and creative. She is capable of acting on her own ideas. She is sensitive and introspective, yet fully oriented to reality and aware of societal demands.

Adolescent with Brain Damage

XVII

Case D, Carl Miner, considers the record of a young man with brain damage. His case is evaluated in summary form with only those scoring variables pertinent to the findings indicated. Carl, age fourteen, was referred for psychological evaluation to determine the cause of his lack of impulse control in school and at home.

Observations

Carl is a tall, thin, attractive boy with a severe case of acne. He bites his fingernails. At times he behaved in a childish, teasing manner. At other times, when he was unable to cope with a task, he had a perplexed look as if puzzled by his inability to deal with the stimulus, even after regarding it from many angles. He was able to verbalize his frustration at not being able to perform test tasks as he would have liked. He talked freely about himself and was preoccupied with events relating to aggressive activities.

HOLTZMAN INKBLOT TECHNIQUE   Form A
RECORD FORM

Name_____Carl Miner_____Age__14__ Sex__M__ Date__7/10/67__

Address_____E. F. Hill_____Phone_____ Educational Level__7th Grade__

Examiner_____Previous Administration (Form and Date)_____

Symbols: QL —question regarding location;   Qc —question regarding characteristics;   QE —question regarding elaboration;
⧸⧹⧸⧹< —change in card position;   R.T. —reaction time in seconds.

X	R.T. 2	A bat.
	head	
	wings	
		L 0

Y	R.T. 2	Insides of a human.
	8	c. Shape and blood, red looks like blood.
		L 0

1A	R.T. 2	South America and North America but they're not hooked together.
	So. America No. America	c. The thing on the end, except it's together.
		L 0

| 2A | R.T. 2 | Two letters, not sure, could be E but it's the wrong way. |
| | | L 1 |

3A	R.T. 5	Clouds, sun coming up out of the clouds.
	color	c. Clouds all full and black and the color of the sun.
	black	L 0

4A R.T. __2__	Bat in a small cave coming at you. c. Here. e. He's under water, but bats can't see under water. I'm sure he cannot. He moves his wings up and down just enough. L 1
5A R.T. __5__	Rejected.
6A R.T. __10__	(Holds card at arm's length.) Looks like a butterfly. c. Color. L 0
7A R.T. __8__	Rejected.
8A R.T. __2__ V	A jet going sideward. c. The rocket's going up sidewards, that's strange. . L 0
9A R.T. __13__	(Card held at arm's length.) Rejected.

10A R.T. __4__	Rejected.
11A R.T. __5__ mouth	A face with a mouth. c. Face with mouth. L 0
12A R.T. __2__	Rocket ship going off from the clouds. (Touch) c. Clouds, air all around it, rocket. L 0
13A R.T. __8__	Looks like something I did at home, spilling a paint can, going everywhere; green paint. c. Looks exactly like it. L 0
14A R.T. __4__	Fish, sting ray. Shape. L 0
15A R.T. __4__ V feet head	Someone standing in front of a tree, in the weeds. c. Feet and head. e. No. L 0

16A R.T. __10__	(Held card at arm's length.) Looks like an owl. c. Eyes, teeth-like. L 0
17A R.T. __5__	(Held card at arm's length.) Rejected.
18A R.T. __8__	Rejected.
19A R.T. __7__	(Held card at arm's length.) Two people getting hanged. c. Head, rope. L 1
20A R.T. __11__	(Held card up over his head.) Rejected.
21A R.T. __13__	(Held card at arm's length.) Rejected.

22A R.T. _11_	Looks like someone's insides. L 0	
23A R.T. _13_	Rejected.	
24A R.T. _4_	Gas tank, also like gas can. Shape. c. The pipe that sticks out. L 0	
25A R.T. _10_	(Held card at a distance.) Looks like someone dancing, stupid. I tell you it is. I don't dance like that. Maybe someone else, not me. L 1	
26A R.T. _6_	Rejected.	
27A R.T. _5_	Rejected.	

28A R.T. 8	Big rock with drawing on it. c. Shape. L 0
29A R.T. 6	Rejected.
30A R.T. 6	A box that someone stepped on, but it is not in the right shape. L 0
31A R.T. 2	Two eyes looking at me. L 2
32A R.T. 2	Eyes. Skeleton eyes, hollow. c. No eyeball or anything. L 2
33A R.T. 5	A mummy. c. The body, the way it is. L 0

| 34A | R.T. __8__ | Rejected. |

| 35A | R.T. __3__ | (Held card away from him.)

 Big face, a donkey face, the shape (I hope).

 L 1 |

| 36A | R.T. __6__ | Looks like nothing except an idiot.

 c. A deformed animal in bad shape.

 L 0 |

| 37A | R.T. __9__ | Rejected. |

| 38A | R.T. __5__ | A horseshoe.

 c. Here.

 I had a horse and used to love him.

 L 2 |

| 39A | R.T. __5__ | Two big eyes.

 c. Color.

 L 2 |

40A R.T. 7	Rejected.	
41A R.T. 11 trees butter- flies	Two hills with two butterflies. c. Smoke going up in the middle of two hills with clouds above. L 0	
42A R.T. 8	Rejected.	
43A R.T. 5	Snake hole under ground or mole hole. c. Tunnels. L 1	
44A R.T. 3 nose eyes teeth	Clown's face, got makeup on. c. Nose, eyes, teeth. L 0	
45A R.T. 10	Two clouds going to have a fight. They're dumb to say they make rain which will go to the ground and then come back up and down. L 2	

SUMMARY SHEET **HOLTZMAN INKBLOT TECHNIQUE** Form: (circle) (A) B

Name _CARL MINER_ _____ Age _14_ Sex _M_ _____ Date _7-10-1967_

Examiner _E·F·HILL_ _____ Previous Administration (Form and Date) _____

Card No.	RT	R	L	S	FD	FA	C	Sh	M	V	I	H	A	At	Sx	Ab	Ax	Hs	Br	Pn	B	P
1	2		1		4																	
2	2		1		2	1																
3	5					1	3^{Ac}_{N}	1 4														
4	2		1		3				2	QR2		2A					1					
5	5	1																				
6	10				2	1	1_N						1o									
7	8	1																				
8	2				2	1			4m													
9	13	1																	1			
10	4	1																				
11	5					1	1					1_H	1_H									
12	2			1_a	2	1		1f	4m									1	1			
13	8					1	2-															
14	4				3								2				1		1			
15	4				2	1			1			2OP										
16	10				3								2									
17	5	1																				
18	8	1																				
19	7		1		3	2			1			2OP					2	2				1
20	11	1																				
21	13	1																				
22	11													1				1				
23	13	1																				
24	4				2	1												1				
25	10		1		2	1			3	SR2		2OA										1
26	6	1																				
27	5	1																				
Sub-total: Items 1-27	179	11	4	1_a	31	12	6	2	15	4		7	8	1			4	5	3			2

Fold the top of this page down to this line, so that sub-totals for Items 1-27 may be seen on this side.

Item	RT	R	L	S	FD	FA	C	Sh	M	V	I	H	A	At	Sx	Ab	Ax	Hs	Br	Pn	B	P
28	8					1																
29	6	1																				
30	6				1	1													1	⌐		
31	2	2	1		1	1			1	SR2		1o	1o					1				
32	2	2	1											1					1			
33	5				2	1												1				
	RT	R	L	S	FD	FA	C	Sh	M	V	I	H	A	At	Sx	Ab	Ax	Hs	Br	Pn	B	P
34	8	1																				
35	3		1		3	1						1H										
36	6				1	1				QR1		1o						1				
37	9	1																				
38	5		2		3	1												1				
39	5		2		1	1	2N					1o	1o									
	RT	R	L	S	FD	FA	C	Sh	M	V	I	H	A	At	Sx	Ab	Ax	Hs	Br	Pn	B	P
40	7	1																				
41	11				2	1			1f	2m		1o							1			
42	8	1																				
43	5		1			1												1				
44	3				2	1	1N					1H										1
45	10		2			1			4m	FC3								1	1			
	RT	R	L	S	FD	FA	C	Sh	M	V	I	H	A	At	Sx	Ab	Ax	Hs	Br	Pn	B	P
Uncorr. Total	288	✕	✕	✕	47	24	✕	✕	10	✕	✕	✕	✕	✕	✕	✕	✕	✕	✕	✕	✕	
Score	6.4	16	16	2	73	37	9	3	22	16	0	10	13	2			4	8	7	4		3
Percentile	2	81	32	76	30	9	39	32	54	>99	18	37	24	67			27	55	68	68		8

Note. — Except for **RT, FD, FA,** and **V,** the **Score** for each variable is the total of the scores on each of the 45 cards. These totals should be entered in the row labeled **Score.** For **RT,** write the sum in the row labeled **Uncorrected Total,** divide this by 45, and enter the quotient as the **RT** Score. For **FD, FA,** and **V,** write the sum in the **Uncorrected Total** row, see Table 3 of the Guide, and enter the corrected total as the **Score.**

°Norms Group **SEVENTH GRADE**

Summary Sheet for
Holtzman Inkblot Technique
Copyright © 1958 by The Psychological Corporation, New York, N.Y. 10017
All rights reserved as stated in the Guide and Catalog.

Printed in U.S.A.

65-3688

HILL CLINICAL SUMMARY
for the
HOLTZMAN INKBLOT TECHNIQUE

Form (A) or B

Name: CARL MINER Date: 7-10-1967

Norms: SEVENTH GRADE

CATEGORIES

	I		II			III			IV					V					VI				
	RT	R	L	FA	S	C	Sh	B	FD	M	I	Br	P	H	A	At	Sx	Ab	Ax	Hs	V	Pn	AA
Final Score	6	16	16	37	12 2	9	3	0	73	22	0	7	4	10	13	2			4	8	16	4	
Percentile	2	81	32	9	>76	39	32		30	54		68	68	37	24	67			27	55	>99	68	
High (a) Stim. Color	7	6	4	9	0	7	1		16	2		0	0	6	5	0			2	2	0	0	
Low (b) Stim. Color	6	5	5	7	1	0	0		15	0		5	2	0	1	2			0	2	1	2	

Form A (a) 3, 6, 9, 15, 16, 17, 19, 20, 26, 27, 28, 35, 39, 42, 44
(b) 1, 2, 5, 7, 18, 22, 24, 29, 30, 32, 33, 36, 37, 38, 43

Form B (a) 3, 6, 7. 11, 15, 17, 21, 24, 29, 34, 36, 39, 41, 42, 44
(b) 2, 5, 8, 9, 10, 16, 18, 19, 23, 25, 26, 30, 32, 33, 45

COLOR

Score	+	-	N	Ac
1			2	
2		1	1	
3			1	1

SHADING

Score	Texture	Light Film	Dark Film	Vista
1		2	1	
2				

MOVEMENT

Score	HUMAN									ANIMAL					m	
	1			2						1			2		Inanimate	Animate
				M		F		O								
	H	B	O	P	A	P	A	P	A	H	B	O	P	A		
1								2				1				
2														1	1	
3									1							
4															3	
NO M	2		2							2		4	2			

PATHOGNOMIC VERBALIZATION

FB	FC	QR	IC	AL	CT	SR	DC	AB
	1	2				2		

Notes: SCORES TYPICAL OF MENTAL RETARDATES

SEQUENCE ANALYSIS

1. SO. AND NO. AMERICA
2. 2 LETTER E
3. SUN COM'G THRU BLACK CLOUDS
4. BAT IN CAVE COMING AT YOU
5. R
6. BUTTERFLY
7. R
8. JET GOING UP SIDEWAYS
9. R
10. R
11. FACE WITH MOUTH
12. ROCKET GOING OFF FROM CLOUDS
13. SPILLED PAINT JUST LIKE I DID
14. STING RAY
15. SOMEONE STAND'G IN FRONT OF TREE
16. OWL
17. R
18. R
19. 2 PEOPLE GETT'G HANGED
20. R
21. R
22. SOMEONES INSIDES
23. R
24. GAS CAN PIPE STICK'G OUT
25. SOMEONE DANC'G STUPID NOT LIKE ME
26. R
27. R
28. BIG ROCK DRAW'G ON IT
29. R
30. BOX STEPPED ON WRONG SHAPE
31. 2 EYES LOOK'G AT ME
32. EYE'S SKELETON'S NO EYE BALLS
33. A MUMMY
34. R
35. BIG FACE - DONKEY'S
36. IDIOT - A DEFORMED ANIMAL
37. R
38. HORSESHOE - I HAD A HORSE I LOVED
39. 2 BIG EYES
40. R
41. 2 HILLS - BUTTERFLIES SMOKE IN MIDDLE
42. R
43. SNAKE HOLE UNDERGROUND
44. CLOWNS FACE W. MAKE UP
45. 2 CLOUDS GOING TO FIGHT

Findings

The test gave evidence of brain damage involving central nervous-system impairment. Carl's thinking is concrete. He uses basic (lower level) skills (FD, RT, and content) but is not able to use complex skills involving higher levels of learning, such as abstracting, synthesizing, generalizing, and problem solving. Problem solving for Carl is accomplished on the basis of trial and error. He is not mentally alert, has a paucity of inner resources, has difficulty concentrating, and lacks control over his thoughts (evidenced in RT, R, FA, and content). He has a poor memory (he could not remember his birth date) and is not alert to events in the world around him (evidenced in his FA, P, and V scores).

Carl's behavior problem is typical of persons with organic brain damage. He is stimulus bound and dominated by inner feelings. He has no frame of reference except himself. His reality contact is limited. He is primarily self-preoccupied and experiences a loss of distance between himself and the outer world (evidenced in V, FA and P responses). He has a restricted fantasy life which limits his ability to act out aggressive impulses. He also lacks the cognitive faculties for suppression and later evaluation of affect necessary to develop mature behavioral controls. Thus, he cannot always deal effectively with environmental demands because he cannot set his own limits. Under stress, he discharges aggressive impulses on the spot because he has no other way of coping with strong feelings (evidenced in R, RT, I, and content responses). He therefore looks for structure and guidelines from without, which makes him feel inadequate and helpless. He is seeking a dependent relationship and wants someone to take care of him. He is basically passive and fears both oral and physical aggression from others. Because he feels unable to defend himself, he avoids threatening situations whenever possible (evidenced in light-film Sh, R, RT, and the content of cards 4, 11, 19, 30, 31, 43).

Validation Evidence from Other Tests

Carl's full-scale WISC IQ is 77, his verbal IQ is 77, and his performance IQ is 80. Subscales measuring higher levels of functioning (for example, arithmetic and similarities) are extremely low. He has a speed disturbance, evident in his excessively low scores on coding and arithmetic. He can verbalize the shape of forms, verifying the availability of sensory input, but he is unable to control his responses. He recognizes this inability to reproduce forms accurately. These results suggest a psychomotor deficit rather than sensory impairment (Bender-Gestalt, WAIS).

Recommendations

Carl will be best served in a school for brain-damaged children, where his needs can be understood and met. He requires training to develop those skills that are within the limits of his intellectual capacity. Motor tasks that are not complex and which involve simple discriminations can be learned through step-by-step learning. He has enough intelligence to do certain manual tasks which require some decision or choice. Therefore, he can be trained in a useful occupation, but he needs a stable, structured, nonstressful environment. When he is able to achieve some successes within the framework of what can reasonably be expected of him and when his needs can be understood and met, his frustrations and the subsequent emotional outbursts should begin to subside.

Adolescent Schizophrenic

XVIII

Case E, Barry Levering, is briefly summarized and is illustrative of the record of a process schizophrenic. Barry, age seventeen, was referred for a diagnostic evaluation because he was having difficulty following instructions and comprehending. He does not relate well with people and prefers to be alone or with his mother. His mother is overprotective. His father is aloof.

Observations

Barry is short and heavy and looks much younger than his seventeen years. He showed annoyance and hostility during the testing. His responses, although adequate, were either snapped out or grunted in a hostile tone.

HOLTZMAN INKBLOT TECHNIQUE
RECORD FORM

Form A

Name____Barry Levering_____ Age__17____ Sex__M____ Date__9/8/66_____

Address_____Phone_____Educational Level__11th Grade__

Examiner_____E. F. Hill_____Previous Administration (Form and Date)_____

Symbols: QL —question regarding location;   QC —question regarding characteristics;   QE —question regarding elaboration;
              >∨< —change in card position;   R.T. —reaction time in seconds.

X R.T. __3__ eye	**A moth.** c. Shape. L 0
Y R.T. __3__ heart blood bones	Part of a body. L 0
1A R.T. __10"__ 22" left side right side feet	Nothing. **A buffalo.** c. The hugeness. e. No. L 0
2A R.T. __15__	(Hmm) Rejected.
3A R.T. __20__	Heart of some animal. c. Because of the color. e. No. L 1

4A R.T. __10__	Cow. c. Eyes and horns, head. e. No. L 1
5A R.T. __6__	(Hmm) Someone looking through a stained glass window. c. The color, it's like winter at Christmas time. L 1
6A R.T. __3__	Lungs. c. The appearance and the way they are taking in air and taking out air. L 0
7A R.T. __18__	Antlers of a deer. c. Because of the shape. e. No. L 0
8A R.T. __12__	A mouth. c. Inside of the mouth, looks like palate because of the color. L 1
9A R.T. __18__	The underside of a cow, where you pump milk. c. The shape of the points made me think of a cow. L 1

10A R.T. __20__	Rejected.
11A R.T. __2__ Shape / Feelers	A moth. c. Shape and feelers. e. No. L 0.
12A R.T. __28__	(Mmm). A mouth. c. Like the mouth is open because of the color. L 0
13A R.T. __5__	Grass. c. Grass is green. L 0
14A R.T. __3__ Lungs / Bones	Part of an animal's body, a cow. c. The color. This part has to do with the excretory system. L 0
15A R.T. __20__	Part of a body of some animal. c. Looks like Eustachian tube. L 2

16A R.T. __5__ *Bones*	Skeletal system of some animal. c. Bones. L 0
17A R.T. __8__	Lungs. c. Color. L 2
18A R.T. __7__	Has something to do with the body, the inside of the body, animal body. c. Color. (What are these doing here?) L 0
19A R.T. __6__	Inside of body of animal. c. Color of the circulatory system and bones and lungs. L 0
20A R.T. __8__	The brown are lungs. c. Because of the color. L 0
21A R.T. __8__	Lungs. c. Because of the color. L 2

22A R.T. __6__	Jaws, one up, one down. c. Color. L O
23A R.T. __12__	Two horses' heads. c. Heads close together, touching. L O
24A R.T. __8__	Pig. c. Ears, snout. e. No. L O
25A R.T. __5__	Parts of inside of body. c. The black is the lungs because of the color. L O
26A R.T. __3__	Black area = lungs. It's the circulatory system of the body. c. Because of the color. L O
27A R.T. __8__	Lungs. And the yellow and pink have to do with the excretory system in the body. c. Color. L O

28A R.T. __3__	Excretory system. c. Color. L O	
29A R.T. __2__	Skeletal system, shape of the bones. c. Color. L O	
30A R.T. __5__	Inside of a thatched hut. c. Color. L O	
31A R.T. __4__	Skeletal system, because of the shape of the bones. c. Color of it. L O	
32A R.T. __3__	Skeletal system. Bones and color. L O	
33A R.T. __7__	Somebody in the snow. c. Two feet, two arms, looks like a man, arm appears to be dislocated, it's separate. The color of snow. L 1	

34A R.T. __8__	Two angels each pulling ends of a wishbone. c. Wings, shape. (Don't know what these are.) L O
35A R.T. __11__	(Hmm). Digestive system. c. Because of the color. L O
36A R.T. __11__	Skeletal system. c. Looks like it; bones. L O
37A R.T. __4__	Skeletal system because of the color of bones and shape. L O
38A R.T. __4__	Skeletal system. c. Shape and color. L O
39A R.T. __3__	Heart and this must be the lungs. c. Color. L O

40A R.T. 8	Excretory system. c. Because of the color. L 0
41A R.T. 10	Feet of a goose. c. Shape. L 2
42A R.T. 15	Yellow excretory system. c. Pink, heart. L 0
43A R.T. 5	(Hmm) Branch of a tree. c. Shape and the way it looks. L 1
44A R.T. 7	Excretory system. c. Color and shape. L 0
45A R.T. 8 Bones	(Oh boy!) Bones. Excretory system. c. Color. L 0

SUMMARY SHEET   HOLTZMAN INKBLOT TECHNIQUE   Form: (circle) (A) B

Name **BARRY LEVERING**   Age **17**   Sex **M**   Date **9-8-1966**

Examiner **E.F. HILL**   Previous Administration (Form and Date)

Card No.	RT	R	L	S	FD	FA	C	Sh	M	V	I	H	A	At	Sx	Ab	Ax	Hs	Br	Pn	B	P	AA
1	22				3					AB3			2					1					
2	15	1																					1±
3	20	1			1	1	2-			AL1			2										
4	10	1			3							1H											
5	6	1			2	2	1+	1f	1			1o							1	1			1±
6	3				2				2ma	QR2			2							1			
7	18				1	1											1						
8	12	1			2		2-			AL1			2							1			
9	18	1			3					AL2			1B	1									
10	20	1																					
11	2				2	1						1o									1		
12	28				1		1-			AL2										1			1±
13	5				.	1	3H													1			
14	3				1		2-						2	1						1			
15	20	2			1	1							2										1±
16	5					1							1			1							
17	8	2			1		2-						2							1			
18	7					1	2-						2							1		2-	
19	6				1		2-						2							1			
20	8				1		2-			AL2			2							1			
21	8	2			1		2-			AL2			2							1			
22	6				1	1	1N						1					1					
23	12				3							1H											
24	8				3	1						1H											
25	5				1		2^{Ao}_-			AL2			2						1				
26	3				1		2^{Ao}			AL2			2										
27	8				1		2-			DC2			2	1									
Subtotal: Items 1-27	286	2	11		36	11	28	1	3	21		1	7	28	3		1	2	2	11		2	4± 2-

Fold the top of this page down to this line, so that sub-totals for Items 1-27 may be seen on this side.

#	RT	R	L	S	FD	FA	C	Sh	M	V	I	H	A	At	Sx	Ab	Ax	Hs	Br	Pn	B	P
28	3					1	2-							2	1			1				
29	2				1	1	1-							1								
30	5				1	1	2N											1	1	1		
31	4					1	2-							1								
32	3					1	2-							1								
33	7	1			2	1	1Ac-		AL1	2M								1				
	RT	R	L	S	FD	FA	C	Sh	M	V	I	H	A	At	Sx	Ab	Ax	Hs	Br	Pn	B	P
34	8				3	1			2	Fc2		1o					1				i	3-
35	11					1	2-		AL2				2									
36	11					1							1									
37	4					1	1-		AL1				1									
38	4					1	1-						1									
39	3				1	1	1-			FC2			2									
	RT	R	L	S	FD	FA	C	Sh	M	V	I	H	A	At	Sx	Ab	Ax	Hs	Br	Pn	B	P
40	8					1	2-		AL1					2	1							
41	10	2	3		1						1o											
42	15					1	2-		DC3					2	1							
43	5	1				1																1±
44	7					1	2-							2	1							
45	8					1	2-							2	1							2±
	RT	R	L	S	FD	FA	C	Sh	M	V	I	H	A	At	Sx	Ab	Ax	Hs	Br	Pn	B	P / AA
Uncorr. Total	404	✕	✕	✕	47	29	✕	✕	✕	33	✕	✕	✕	✕	✕							
Score	8.9	2	15		49	30	51	1	5	35	0	4	8	48	8		2	3	3	13		4 / 7±5-
Percentile 1	12	85	11		8	2	>99	3	4	>99	7	5	5	>99	>99		20	22	27	>99		10 / 5-
Percentile 2	14	41	46		24	32	94	26	45	76		40	31	>99	>99		44	55	55	94		51

Note. — Except for **RT**, **FD**, **FA**, and **V**, the **Score** for each variable is the total of the scores on each of the 45 cards. These totals should be entered in the row labeled **Score**. For **RT**, write the sum in the row labeled **Uncorrected Total**, divide this by 45, and enter the quotient as the **RT** Score. For **FD**, **FA**, and **V**, write the sum in the **Uncorrected Total** row, see Table 3 of the Guide, and enter the corrected total as the **Score**.

°Norms Group 1—(ELEVENTH GRADE) AVERAGE ADULT
2—CHRONIC SCHIZOPHRENIC

Summary Sheet for
Holtzman Inkblot Technique
Copyright © 1958 by The Psychological Corporation, New York, N. Y. 10017

HILL CLINICAL SUMMARY
for the
HOLTZMAN INKBLOT TECHNIQUE

Form (A) or B

Name: BARRY LEVERING

Date: 9-8-1966

Norms: AVERAGE ADULT [1] AND CHRONIC SCHIZOPHRENIC [2]

CATEGORIES

		I			II		III			IV					V				VI				
		RT	R	L	FA	S	C	Sh	B	FD	M	I	Br	P	H	A	At	Sx	Ab	Ax	Hs	V	Pn	AA
Final Score		9	2	15	30	0	51	1	0	49	5	0	3	4	4	8	48	8		2	3	35	13	7± 5-
Per- centile	(1)	12	55	11	2		>99	3		8	4	7	29	10	5	5	>99	>99		26	22	>99	>99	
	(2)	14	41	46	32		94	26		24	45		55	51	40	31	>99	>99		44	55	76	94	
High (a) Stim. Color		9	0	6	8		21	0		13	2		0	0	0	1	27	5		1	0	18	5	1±
Low (b) Stim. Color		8	1	2	14		12	1		14	1		3	1	3	3	8	0		0	2	4	2	3± 2-

Form A (a) 3, 6, 9, 15, 16, 17, 19, 20, 26, 27, 28, 35, 39, 42, 44
     (b) 1, 2, 5, 7, 18, 22, 24, 29, 30, 32, 33, 36, 37, 38, 43
Form B (a) 3, 6, 7, 11, 15, 17, 21, 24, 29, 34, 36, 39, 41, 42, 44
     (b) 2, 5, 8, 9, 10, 16, 18, 19, 23, 25, 26, 30, 32, 33, 45

COLOR

Score	+	–	N	Ac
1	1	6	1	1
2		19	1	2
3			1	

SHADING

Score	Texture	Light Film	Dark Film	Vista
1		1		
2				

MOVEMENT

	HUMAN								ANIMAL						m	
	1			2						1			2		Inanimate	Animate
Score	H	B	O	P	A	P	A	P	A	H	B	O	P	A		
1			1													
2			1													
3																
4																
NO M			1							3	2	1		1		

PATHOGNOMIC VERBALIZATION

FB	FC	QR	IC	AL	CT	SR	DC	AB
	2	1		12			2	1

Notes: PERSEVERATION

SEQUENCE ANALYSIS

1. A BUFFALO
2. R
3. HEART OF ANIMAL
4. HEAD OF COW
5. SOMEONE LOOK'G THRU STAINED GLASS WINDOW
6. LUNGS TAK'G AIR IN AND OUT
7. DEER ANTLERS
8. INSIDE MOUTH
9. UNDERSIDE-COW WHERE PUMP MILK
10. R
11. MOTH
12. MOUTH OPEN
13. GRASS
14. EXCRETORY SYSTEM OF COW
15. EUSTACHIAN TUBE OF ANIMAL
16. SKELETAL SYSTEM OF ANIMAL
17. LUNGS
18. INSIDE ANIMAL'S BODY
19. CIRCULATORY SYSTEM-BONES-LUNGS
20. LUNGS
21. LUNGS
22. JAWS
23. HORSES HEADS TOUCHING
24. PIG
25. INSIDE BODY LUNGS
26. LUNGS CIRCULATORY SYSTEM
27. LUNGS YELLOW AND PINK EXCRETORY SYST.
28. EXCRETORY SYSTEM
29. SKELETAL SYSTEM
30. INSIDE THATCHED HUT
31. SKELETAL SYSTEM
32. SKELETAL SYSTEM
33. MAN IN SNOW ARM DISLOCATED
34. 2 ANGELS PULL'G WISHBONE
35. DIGESTIVE SYSTEM
36. SKELETAL SYSTEM
37. SKELETAL SYSTEM
38. SKELETAL SYSTEM
39. HEART LUNGS
40. EXCRETORY SYSTEM
41. FEET OF GOOSE
42. YELLOW EXCRETORY SYSTEM PINK HEART
43. BRANCH OF TREE
44. EXCRETORY SYSTEM
45. BONES · EXCRETORY SYSTEM

Findings

Barry has all the symptoms of a process schizophrenic whose affective life is deteriorating (evidenced in the V, At, Pn, FA, and C responses). Test results suggest that he was an autistic child who never made the separation from his mother. His father apparently has little to do with him. Barry is still orally dependent with basic needs for food, shelter, and security (seen in his responses to cards 8, 9, 12, and his Pn and M responses). He has a weak ego and is an emotionally flat, passive person who is preoccupied with sensations and perceptions of his own body because of his restricted contact with the world of people (evidenced in his At, Pn, C-minus, Sh, H, and A responses). He is subject to a serious loosening of contact with reality and an inability to relate to people (evidenced in his V, FA, P, H, and A responses). He expresses no aggression because he lacks an imaginative inner life in which he can discharge feelings by fantasizing humans or animals in interaction (evidenced in A, H, and Hs responses). His behavior reflects only impatience and undirected tension. He does not experience anxiety but through his bland affect tries to dispel depressive feelings (seen in Ax, Sh, and C responses to achromatic cards). He is preoccupied with sexuality, which he displaces to excretory-system responses (seen in Sx responses and content).

He can function moderately well when dealing with things rather than people. He has some resources (seen in L and I responses). Under the emotional stress of dealing with people, however, their usefulness is questionable (evidenced in M, H, A, and Sh scores). This inability to relate to people accounts for his difficulty in comprehending and following instructions.

Validation Evidence from Other Tests

Validating evidence of cognitive resources is found in Barry's WAIS scores. His full-scale IQ was 96, his verbal IQ was 100, and his performance IQ was 90. These all put him in the average range of intelligence. He is attending school and obtaining passing grades.

Summary

Barry is a process schizophrenic with evidence of a long-term inability to relate to people. Psychotherapy is recommended with a therapist who can relate well to his type of pathology. The therapy will be a long-term process with a guarded prognosis. Through the therapeutic relationship, Barry may be able to make at least a marginal adjustment to community living.

Appendix: Normative Samples

The normative samples contained in this section are for use in evaluating HIT hand-scored records which have been administered either individually or in a group. To determine the significance of the scores obtained by the subject, the examiner should compare the subject's score with the scores for an appropriate reference group. The relevant group is the one to which the subject currently belongs (either one of the normal groups or the appropriate pathological group). For normal persons, the reference group should be determined on the basis of age and level of schooling. If the subject is no longer in school, reference is based on the average adult norms. Norms for eleventh graders are included in average adult norms. The subject may also be compared with various pathological groups to determine which one the record best matches.

Table 2 contains information concerning the samples which constitute the normal normative groups. They are identified by group, age when available, number in the sample, and source of the sample. Table 3 contains information concerning the abnormal normative samples. Tables 4 through 18 contain the normative samples.

Table 2

Normative Samples of Normal Groups

Reference Group	Number in Sample	Age	Source of Sample	HIT Form
Five year olds	122	5	61 boys and 61 girls from nursery schools in Austin, Tex.[a]	A&B
First Graders	133	6.7	Participants in a 6-year longitudinal study in Austin, Tex.[b]	A
Elementary School	60	7-11	30 girls and 30 boys from a parochial Catholic school in a middle-class neighborhood in Austin, Tex. (12 children from each grade, 2 through 6.)	A&B
	72	9	Fourth graders from a public school in Hamden, Conn.[c]	B
Fourth Graders	142	9.7	Participants in a 6-year longitudinal study in Austin, Tex.[d]	B
Seventh Graders	197	12	From four communities in Texas.[e]	B
Average Adults	72	16.5-17.5	Eleventh graders from Chicago	A&B
	100	19-65 (mean 38)	Middle-class housewives from a random house-to-house canvass of two Texas communities: a lower middle-class community in Austin, and a small town east of Austin.	A&B
	80	21-63	Firemen from Austin, Tex.[f]	A&B
College Students	140	17-19	Students seeking routine educational and personal counseling at the Univ. of Texas Testing & Counseling Center plus volunteers from freshman and sophomore classes.	A&B
	66	17-19	Freshmen from Austin College: approx. equal numbers of males and females.[g]	A

[a] Holtzman, Thorpe, Swartz, and Herron (1961) through the courtesy of the authors. Reproduced by permission. Copyright © 1958 by the Psychological Corporation, New York, N.Y. All rights reserved.

[b] Holtzman (1965) through the courtesy of the author.

[c] *Ibid.* a.

[d] *Ibid.* b.

[e] *Ibid.* a.

[f] *Ibid.* a.

[g] *Ibid.* a.

Table 3

Normative Samples for Abnormal Groups

Reference Group	No. in Sample	Age	Source of Sample	HIT Form
Emotionally Disturbed Children	99	6 to 12 (mean 9.8)	Patients in a psychiatric outpatient clinic for emotionally disturbed children in Baltimore, Md., being studied for effectiveness of treatment procedures.[a]	A
Emotionally Disturbed Adolescents	114	12 to 21 (mean 16.6)	Patients seen by the author both in Johns Hopkins Hospital and in private practice.	A
Juvenile Delinquents	75	11.1 to 17.9 M 15.5	Awaiting court hearing at Alameda County Juvenile Hall, Calif.[b]	A
Mental Retardates	50	15 to 50 (mean 25.1)	24 males and 26 females at Woodward State Hospital & School, Woodward, Iowa.	B
	50 (100 Total)	16 to 39 (mean 21.1)	25 male and 25 female retardates from Austin State School.[c]	B
Depressed Patients	90		75 males and 15 females in a cooperative study in which 11 V.A. hospitals participated.[d]	A&B
Chronic Schizophrenics	140 (99)	23 to 63 (mean 42.2)	Chronic paranoid schizophrenic males at Waco V.A. Hospital, Tex. Hospitalization from 20 mos. to 22 yrs. (average 10.5 years).	B
	(41)		Schizophrenic males in Montrose V.A. Hospital, N.Y. Hospitalization 1 yr. to 29 yrs. (median 11 yrs).[e]	A&B
Neurotics	99	18 to 53 (mean 31.4)	Pretherapy records of adult male and female patients in a Maryland State Hospital. Part of a controlled study of LSD therapy with neurotics (MH-10001).[f]	A&B
Alcoholics	106	22 to 59 (mean 41.4)	Pretherapy records of adult male and female patients in a Maryland State Hospital. Part of a controlled study of LSD therapy with alcoholics (MH-08474).[g]	A&B

[a] Conners (1965), courtesy of the author.

[b] Megargee (1965), courtesy of the author.

[c] Holtzman, Thorpe, Swartz, and Herron (1961), courtesy of the authors. Reproduced by permission. Copyright © 1958, 1961 by The Psychological Corporation, New York, N.Y. All rights reserved.

[d] *Ibid.* c.

[e] *Ibid.* c.

[f] Grant administered by Friends of Psychiatric Research, begun at Spring Grove Hospital and completed at Maryland Psychiatric Research Center under the direction of Albert A. Kurland, M.D., and Charles Savage, M.D.

[g] *Ibid.* f.

VARIABLES

Table 4
Percentile Norms
for
Five Year Olds

(122 Cases)

Raw Score	RT	R	L	S	FD	FA	C	Sh	M	V	I	H	A	At	Sx	Ab	Ax	Hs	Br	Pn	B	P	Raw Score
80					84																		80
79					84																		79
78					84																		78
77					79																		77
76					79																		76
75					75																		75
74					75																		74
73					75																		73
72					75																		72
71					69																		71
70					69																		70
69					69																		69
68					61		99																68
67					61		98																67
66					61		98																66
65					50		98																65
64			99		50		98																64
63			98		50		97																63
62			98		46		97																62
61			98		46		97																61
60			98		46		97																60
59			97		40		96																59
58			97		40		96																58
57			97		40		96																57
56			97		35		96																56
55			96		35	99	96																55
54			96		35	98	95																54
53			95		28	97	95																53
52			95		28	97	95																52
51			94		28	95	95																51
50			94		24	93	94																50
49			93		24	92	94																49
48			93		24	91	94																48
47			93		19	89	94																47
46			93		19	88	94																46
45			92		19	85	93						99										45
44			92		15	80	93						98										44
43			91		15	77	93						98										43
42			91		15	70	93						97										42
41			90		12	66	91																41

(continuation of table)

Raw Score	FD
96+	99
93-95	98
90-92	97
87-89	94
84-86	93
81-83	88

262

Raw Score	P	B	Pn	Br	Hs	Ax	Ab	Sx	At	A	H	I	V	M	Sh	C	FA	FD	S	L	R	RT
40										97			99	99		91	61	12		90		
39										96			96	98		90	56	12		89		
38										96			96	98		90	51	10		89	99	
37						99				95			96	97		89	47	10		86	98	
36						98				95			96	97		89	43	10		86		
35		98 per cent give zero or one response				98				93	99		96	96		87	35	8		83	98	
34						98				93	98		93	96		86	31	8		83	98	
33						98				92	98		93	94		85	28	8		78	98	
32						98				92	98		93	94		84	26	7		78	95	
31						98				91	98		93	93		83	21	7		73	94	
30			68 per cent give zero or one response			98	98 per cent give zero or one response			91	98		93	93		82	16	7		73	93	
29						97		99 per cent give zero or one response		89	97		90	90		79	15	6		69	93	
28						97				89	97		89	90		78	10	6		69	92	
27						97			60 per cent give zero or one response	84	97		89	89		77	8	6		66	92	
26					99	97				84	97		88	89		76	7	4		66	91	
25					98	97				75	96	65 per cent give zero or one response	88	84		75	7	4		59	90	
24					98	96				75	96		87	84		74	4	4		59	88	
23					98	96				71	95		87	80		72	3	3		55	84	
22					98	95				71	94		85	80		70	3	3		55	82	
21					98	95				65	93		84	76		68	2	3		50	81	
20					98	94				65	91		82	76		67	2	3		50	80	99
19					98	94				60	89		81	71		61	2	3		44	77	98
18					98	94				60	86		80	71		58	2	3		44	75	
17					98	93				51	84		79	68		56	1	2		39	72	
16					97	93				51	79		76	68		52		2		39	70	
15	99			99	97	93				43	78		75	63	99	49		2		28	68	98
14	98			98	96	89				43	74		74	63	98	47		2		28	65	97
13				98	95	87				38	67		70	58	96	45		2	84 per cent give zero or one response	22	63	96
12					92	86				38	63		66	58	95	43		2		22	60	95
11					90	84				31	58		64	54		39		2		15	58	93
10	98			98	89	80				31	53		62	54	93	34		2		15	56	89
9	97			98	84	73				23	48		57	48	89	28		2		10	55	86
8	93			94	82	70				23	44		55	48	84	25		1		10	54	83
7	87			92	75	63				18	38		50	38	78	23		1		8	52	71
6	76			86	69	61				18	34		44	38	70	19		1		8	50	58
5	68			80	60	53				9	29		39	29	64	16		1		6	47	48
4	54			69	48	44				9	20		34	29	60	16		1		6	44	37
3	44			61	39	34				4	12		27	22	52	12		1		6	42	20
2	31			48	30	25				4	10		22	15	40	7		1		3	38	6
1	16			30	19	17				2	6		20	15	29	5		1		3	35	
0	5			14	7	12				2	2		16		13	3		1		1	26	
Raw Score	P	B	Pn	Br	Hs	Ax	Ab	Sx	At	A	H	I	V	M	Sh	C	FA	FD	S	L	R	RT

VARIABLES

Table 5

Percentile Norms

for

First Graders

(133 Cases)

Raw Score	RT	R	L	S	FD	FA	C	Sh	M	V	I	H	A	At	Sx	Ab	Ax	Hs	Br	Pn	B	P
80			99		78		98															
79			99		76		98															
78			98		75		98															
77			98		72		98															
76			97		70		97															
75			97		68		97															
74			97		65		97															
73			96		62		97															
72			96		60		97															
71			95		59		97															
70			95		57		97		99													
69			94		56		96		99													
68			94		54		96		98													
67			93		53		96		98													
66			92		51		96		98													
65			91		50		96		97													
64			91		48		96		97													
63			90		46		96		97													
62			89		44		96		96													
61			88		42		95		96	99												
60			86		40		95		96	99												
59			85		38		95		95	99												
58			84		37		95		95	99												
57			82		35		95		95	99												
56			81		33		94		94	98												
55			80		32		94		94	98												
54	99		80		30		94		93	98												
53	99		79		28		93		93	98												
52			79		27		93		92	98												
51			78		25		93		92	98												
50	99		78		23		92		91	98												
49	98		77		22		92		91	98												
48	98		77		20	99	92		90	98			99									
47	98		77		19	97	92		90	97			99									
46	98		76		18		91		89	97			98									
45	98		76		18	95	91			97			98									
44	97		75		17	92	91			97			98				99					
43	97		75		16	90	90			97			98				99					
42	97		74		15	85	90			97			97				99					
41	97		72		14	80	89			97			97									

(continuation of table)

Raw Score	FD	C
105		
104		
103		
102		
101	99	
100	98	
99	98	
98	97	
97	97	
96	96	
95	96	
94	95	
93	94	
92	94	
91	93	
90	92	
89	92	
88	91	99
87	91	99
86	90	99
85	88	99
84	85	98
83	82	98
82	80	98
81	79	98

Raw Score	P	B	Pn	Br	Hs	Ax	Ab	Sx	At	A	H	I	V	M	Sh	C	FA	FD	S	L	R	RT	Raw Score
40					98					97			97	88		88	75	13		71		97	40
39					98					96	99		96	87		87	70	12		70		97	39
38					98					96	98		96	86		86	65	12		68		96	38
37					98					96	98		96	85		85	60	11		65		96	37
36					97	99				96	98		96	85		85	55	10		62		96	36
35					97	99				95	98		96	84		84	50	10		60		96	35
34					97	98				95	97		96	83		83	45	9		57		96	34
33					97	98				93	96		96	82		82	40	9		53		95	33
32					97	98				92	96		96	81		81	37	8		50		95	32
31					96	98				90	96		96	80		80	33	8		49		95	31
30					96	97			99	88	95		95	78		79	30	8		47		94	30
29					96	97			98	85	92		95	77		78	25	7		46		92	29
28					96	97			98	82	90		95	75		77	24	7		44		91	28
27					95	97			97	80	89		95	70		76	22	6		43		90	27
26					95	96			97	78	87		95	68		75	21	6		41	99	88	26
25					95	96			96	75	85	99	94	66		74	20	5		40	99	86	25
24					94	96			95	72	83	97	94	65		73	18	5		38	98	84	24
23					94	96			94	70	81	95	93	64		72	16	5		36	98	82	23
22					93	95			94	67	80		92	62		71	14	4		34	98	80	22
21					92	95			94	63	78		92	60		70	12	4		32	98	78	21
20					91	94			93	60	75		91	59		68	10	4		30	97	77	20
19					91	92			92	55	73		91	57		66	8	4		28	97	75	19
18					90	91			92	50	72		90	56		64	5	4		27	97	70	18
17					88	90			91	45	70		89	54		62	4	3		25	96	65	17
16					86	88			91	40	65		88	53		60	3	3		22	96	60	16
15			99	99	84	86			90	35	60	99	86	51	99	55	3	3	99	20	96	57	15
14			98	98	82	84			89	30	55	97	85	50	97	50	2	2	97	18	96	53	14
13			97	96	82	82			87	25	50	95	84	47	95	47	1	2	95	16	95	50	13
12			97	95	80	80			86	22	45		82	43	92	43		2	90	14	95	40	12
11			96	90	75	76			84	20	40		81	40	90	40		2	80	12	93	36	11
10	99		95	84	70	72	99	99	83	18	35	92	80	38	85	37		2	65	10	92	32	10
9	97	99	93	78	65	68	95	95	81	15	30	90	75	33	80	33		1		8	90	28	9
8	95	97	92	70	60	64			80	12	25	78	70	30	76	30		1		5	88	20	8
7	92	95	90	65	55	60			75	10	20	65	60	28	72	25				4	86	10	7
6	90	90	84	60	50	50			70	9	15	45	55	27	66	22				2	84	5	6
5	78		78	45	40	42			65	8	10		50	25	60	20				1	82	3	5
4	70		70	30	34	35			60	6	8		35	20	50	15					80	1	4
3	55		60	22	28	22			50	5	5		22	17	40	10					76		3
2	40		45	10	20	16			40		3		14	13	25	5					72		2
1	25		25		10	10			28		1		5	10							60		1
0	10																						0

VARIABLES

(continuation of table)

Raw Score	RT	R	L	S	FD	FA	C	Sh	M	V	I	H	A	At	Sx	Ab	Ax	Hs	Br	Pn	B	P
80			95		58				99													
79			95		58																	
78			95		58																	
77			94		51																	
76			94		51																	
75			93		51				98													
74			93		43				98													
73			91		43				97													
72			91		43				97													
71			88		37				96													
70			88		37				96													
69			86		37				96													
68			86		32				96													
67			85		32				95													
66			85		32				95													
65			84		26				95													
64			84		26				95													
63			83		26				94													
62			83		25				94													
61			82		25				93													
60			82		25				93													
59			81		22				92													
58			81		22				92													
57			79		22				91													
56			79		17	99	99		91													
55			77		17	98	98		89													
54			77		17	97	98		89													
53			74		15	96	98		87													
52			74		15	95	98		87													
51			71		15	93	98		85													
50			71		12	92	97		85													
49			66		12	88	97		84													
48	99		66		12	84	97		84													
47	98		63		10	80	97		80													
46			63		10	73	95		80													
45	98		62		10	69	95		79	99												
44	98		62		8	60	94		79	98												
43	98		61		8	57	92		77	98												
42	98		61		8	46	90		77	98												
41	97		60		6	31	87		74	98												

Table 6
Percentile Norms
for
Elementary School
Children
(132 Cases)

Raw Score	L
90	98
86-89	97
82-85	96
81	95

Raw Score	FD
114+	99
111-113	98
108-110	96
105-107	95
102-104	94
99-101	91
96-98	90
93-95	89
90-92	83
87-89	77
84-86	69
81-83	65

266

Raw Score	P	B	Pn	Br	Hs	Ax	Ab	Sx	At	A	H	I	V	M	Sh	C	FA	FD	S	L	R	RT	Raw Score
40										99	99		98	74		86	29	6		60		97	40
39										98	99		98	73		86	24	6		57		97	39
38										98	98		98	73		84	21	4		57		96	38
37										92	98		98	69		83	18	4		56		96	37
36										92	98		98	69		81	14	4		56		95	36
35										88	98		98	66		80	11	3		54		94	35
34										88	98		98	66		79	10	3		54		93	34
33										85	97		98	63		78	7	3		53		92	33
32					99					85	97		98	63		77	6	2		53		91	32
31					98					81	97		98	61		74	6	2		50		88	31
30					98					81	96		98	61		73	5	2		50		87	30
29					98					75	95		98	58		72	5	2		47		86	29
28					97					75	94		97	58		68	4	2		47		84	28
27					97					66	91		97	57	99	65	2	2		42		83	27
26					97					66	88		97	57	98	64	2	2		42		80	26
25					96	99				55	86		97	53	98	60	2	2		39		78	25
24					96	98				55	83		96	53	98	59	2	2		39		76	24
23					95	95				48	80		96	47	97	58	1	2		37		75	23
22					94	95				48	78		95	47	97	54	1	2		37		72	22
21				99	92	93				36	74		95	42	95	51	1	2		33		71	21
20			99	98	91	92	99 per cent give no response	99 per cent give zero or one response		36	73	99	94	42	94	45		1	66 per cent give zero or one response	33		70	20
19			98	97	90	91				29	68	98	93	35	94	45		1		30		67	19
18			98	97	88	90			56 per cent give zero or one response	29	65	98	92	35	93	42		1		30	79 per cent have no more than one rejection	64	18
17			98	96	86	89				22	61	98	91	32	92	40				26		61	17
16			98	93	84	86				22	53	98	90	32	89	39				26		58	16
15	99		95	91	81	83				17	47	95	89	26	86	35				24		55	15
14	98		91	88	78	82				17	43	95	89	26	82	33				24		52	14
13	96		88	86	73	77				12	38	92	88	22	80	29				18		47	13
12	95		81	83	69	72				12	31	87	87	22	74	26				18		41	12
11	89	95 per cent give zero or one response	77	74	67	67				6	25	80	86	17	71	23				13		39	11
10	73		72	64	58	60				6	20	73	86	17	65	18				13		35	10
9	65		67	58	52	54				3	14	68	85	13	60	14				10		23	9
8	55		58	48	46	47				3	11	58	82	13	51	13				10		20	8
7	45		42	39	41	42				2	9	45	80	10	40	12				7		11	7
6	34		26	28	33	38				2	8	34	78	10	36	10				7		7	6
5	25		11	20	26	31				2	7	17	73	8	33	8				5		5	5
4	14			14	21	26				2	6		66	8	20	5				5		2	4
3	9			11	11	20				1	5		59	6	13	2				2			3
2	4			6	6	16				1	3		55	6	8	1				2			2
1	1			5	5	11					2		42	3	6					1			1
0				2	3	5					2		30	3	2					1			0

267

VARIABLES

Table 7
Percentile Norms
for
Fourth Graders
(142 Cases)

Raw Score	RT	R	L	S	FD	FA	C	Sh	M	V	I	H	A	At	Sx	Ab	Ax	Hs	Br	Pn	B	P	Raw Score
80					50																		80
79			99		45																		79
78			98		40																		78
77			98		37																		77
76			97		33																		76
75			96		30																		75
74			96		25																		74
73			95		23																		73
72			94		22																		72
71			94		20																		71
70			93		19																		70
69	99		93		18																		69
68	99		92		17																		68
67	99		92		16																		67
66			91		15																		66
65	98		91		15				99														65
64	98		90		14				98														64
63	98		89		13				98														63
62	98		88		12				98														62
61	98		87		11				97														61
60	97		86		10				97														60
59	97		85		9				96														59
58	97		84		8				96														58
57	97		83		7				95														57
56	97		82		6				94														56
55	96		81		5	99			93				99										55
54	96		80		5	99			92				99										54
53	96		79		4	98			92				98										53
52	96		78		4	98			91														52
51	96		77		4	97			90														51
50	95		76		3	96			89				98										50
49	95		75		3	96			87				97										49
48	95		72		3	95			86				97										48
47	95		70		3	94			85				97										47
46	94		69		2	92			84				96										46
45	94		68		2	91			83				96										45
44	93		68		2	90			81				95										44
43	93		67		1	85			80				95										43
42	93		66		1	80			79				92										42
41	92		65			75			78				90										41

(continuation of table)

Raw Score	FD
110	99
109	98
108	98
107	
106	
105	98
104	97
103	96
102	96
101	96
100	95
99	94
98	92
97	91
96	90
95	88
94	85
93	82
92	80
91	78
90	77
89	75
88	72
87	70
86	67
85	63
84	60
83	58
82	55
81	52

268

Raw Score	P	B	Pn	Br	Hs	Ax	Ab	Sx	At	A	H	I	V	M	Sh	C	FA	FD	S	L	R	RT	Raw Score
40										88				77			70			64		92	40
39										87	99			76		99	65			63		92	39
38										85	98			75		98	60			62		91	38
37										83	98			74		98	55			62		91	37
36										82	97			72		97	50			61		90	36
35										80	96			71		97	48			60		90	35
34										75	96			70		96	45			59	99	89	34
33										70	95			67		96	42			58	99	87	33
32										65	94			63		95	40			57	99	86	32
31										60	92			60		94	38			56		84	31
30					99					57	91			59		94	35			55	98	83	30
29					98					53	90			57		93	32			55	98	81	29
28					98					50	88			56		92	30			54	98	80	28
27					97					47	85			54		91	28			53	97	78	27
26						99				43	82			53		91	25			52		77	26
25					96	97			99	40	80			51		90	20			51	97	75	25
24					96	95				35	75		99	50		88	17			50	97	72	24
23					95	93				30	72		98	48		85	13			48	97	70	23
22					93	92				28	70		97	45		82	10			47	96	65	22
21					92	90				25	67		97	42		80	8			45		60	21
20	99		99	99	90	88			99	20	63	99	96	40	99	78	5			43	96	57	20
19	95		99		88	86			98	17	60	98	95	38	98	75	4			42	96	53	19
18			98		85	84			98	13	58	98	94	35	95	70	3			40	96	50	18
17			98		82	82			97	10	55		93	32	92	68	2			38	95	45	17
16					80	80			97	8	52		92	30		65	1			37	95	40	16
15	90	99	97	97	75	75			97	5	50	97	92	28	90	62				35	95	38	15
14	82	98	97	95	72	70			96	4	40	96	91	25	80	60				33	94	35	14
13	75		97	92	70	67			96	2	35	96	90	22	75	57				32	92	32	13
12	60		96	90	60	63			95	1	30	95	87	20	70	53				30	91	30	12
11	45			86	55	60			95		25	94	83	19	60	50				25	90	25	11
10	35	96	95	82	50	55	99		94		20	92	80	18	50	40			99	20	87	20	10
9	20	95	95	78	45	50	97	99	92		17	91	78	15	40	35			95	18	84	10	9
8	10	92	96	70	40	45	95		91		13	90	75	13	25	30			90	15	81	8	8
7	5	90	85	60	35	40			90		10	87	70	12	10	25			78	12	78	5	7
6		75	80	50	30	28			86		5	75	65	10	5	22			55	10	70	3	6
5			75	35	22	20			82		4	70	60	8		20				8		1	5
4			65	25	16	15			78		2	62	50	7		15				5			4
3			50	20	10	10			70		1	55	35	5		10				4			3
2			30	10	5	5			55			40	22			8				2			2
1			20	3					35			25	5			5				1			1
0																5							0

269

VARIABLES

Table 8
Percentile Norms
for
Seventh Graders
(197 Cases)

Raw Score	RT	R	L	S	FD	FA	C	Sh	M	V	I	H	A	At	Sx	Ab	Ax	Hs	Br	Pn	B	P	Raw Score
80					42																		80
79					42																		79
78					42																		78
77					35																		77
76					35																		76
75			99		35				99														75
74			98		30				98														74
73			98		30				98														73
72			98		30																		72
71			97		25																		71
70			98		25				98														70
69			98		25				98														69
68			98		22				97														68
67			97		22				97														67
66			97		22				97														66
65			97		19				98														65
64			97		19				98														64
63			97		19				97														63
62			97		16				97														62
61			96		16				97														61
60			96		16	99			97														60
59			94		12	97			96														59
58			94		12	97			96														58
57			93		12	97			95														57
56			93		10	96			95														56
55			92		10	96			95														55
54			92		10	94			95														54
53			90		7	92			94														53
52			90		7	92			94														52
51	99		88		7	90			93														51
50	98		88		4	85			93														50
49	98		86		4	79			91														49
48	98		86		4	72			91														48
47	97		84		3	65			91														47
46	97		84		3	57			91														46
45	96		82		3	46			89														45
44	96		82		2	37			89														44
43	96		80		2	36			86														43
42	95		80		2	31			86														42
41	95		76		1	24			82														41

(continuation of table)

Raw Score	FD
123+	99
120-122	98
117-119	97
114-116	95
111-113	93
108-110	91
105-107	87
102-104	83
99-101	79
96-98	73
93-95	68
90-92	63
87-89	57
84-86	52
81-83	48

270

Raw Score	P	B	Pn	Br	Hs	Ax	Ab	Sx	At	A	H	I	V	M	Sh	C	FA	FD	S	L	R	RT	Raw Score
40										99				82		99	19	1		76		94	40
39										98				79		98	15	1		73		93	39
38										98				79		98	13	1		73		92	38
37										97				76		97	9	1		70		91	37
36										97				76		96	7	1		70		89	36
35										94				74		96	6			67	99	87	35
34										94				74		95	4			67	98	86	34
33										91				71		94	3			64	98	85	33
32										91	99			71		94	2			64	98	84	32
31										88	97			69		93	1			61	97	83	31
30										88	97			69		93	1			61	97	82	30
29										81	96			66		91				56	96	79	29
28										81	96			66		88				56	96	76	28
27						99				78	95			62		85				51	95	75	27
26						98				78	94			62	99	82				51	94	72	26
25					99	97				72	93			57	98	81				47	92	70	25
24					98	97				72	92			57	97	78				47	92	67	24
23					98	96				66	88			54	97	75				43	91	65	23
22					98	96				66	87			54	96	72				43	89	62	22
21					98	95				59	83			50	95	70				39	89	58	21
20					98	95				59	82			50	94	69				39	87	54	20
19					97	94				52	81			45	94	64				36	86	50	19
18					94	92				52	78			45	93	62				36	85	45	18
17					92	91				44	75			41	93	59				32	83	38	17
16					91	88				44	70			41	90	56				32	81	34	16
15	99		99	99	85	86			99	34	65	99		34	89	55				28	81	26	15
14	98		98	96	81	82			97	34	58	98		34	87	54				28	75	20	14
13	97		97	95	78	78			96	24	53	98		28	86	50				25	74	15	13
12	96		96	94	75	76			95	24	48	97		28	83	47				25	71	13	12
11	90		94	91	73	70			92	19	40	96		24	76	46				20	69	11	11
10	84		89	89	69	65			87	19	37	95		24	71	42				20	67	9	10
9	75		83	83	62	60			82	14	32	92		19	68	39				14	64	5	9
8	61		77	78	55	51			74	14	30	88		19	61	35				14	60	3	8
7	46		68	68	47	47			67	9	25	86		13	55	30				11	56	2	7
6	30		56	55	40	40			48	9	19	85		13	50	28				11	50	2	6
5	17		41	46	31	35			30	6	15	79		10	40	24				8	45	1	5
4	13		25	38	23	27				6	11	72		10	32	19				8	41	1	4
3	8		13	27	16	16				4	7	62		7	26	16				4	35	1	3
2	5			16	13	9				4	6	53		7	15	9				4	31		2
1	1			8	9	5				3	5	34		4	7	7				2	29		1
0				4	4	4				3	4	18		4		3				2	24		0

B: 96 per cent give zero or one response

Ab: 97 per cent give zero or one response

Sx: 99 per cent give no response

V: 62 per cent give zero or one response

S: 76 per cent give zero or one response

VARIABLES

Table 9

Percentile Norms
for
Average Adults
(252 Cases)

(continuation of table)

Raw Score	FD
120+	99
114-119	98
108-113	97
105-107	96
102-104	95
99-101	94
96-98	92
93-95	89
90-92	85
87-89	82
84-86	77
81-83	70

Raw Score	P	B	Pn	Br	Hs	Ax	Ab	Sx	At	A	H	I	V	M	Sh	C	FA	FD	S	L	R	RT	Raw Score
80																		63					80
79																		63					79
78																		63					78
77																		54					77
76																		54					76
75																		54		99			75
74																		46		98			74
73																		46		98			73
72																		46		98			72
71																		41		98			71
70																		41		97			70
69																		41		97			69
68																		38		96			68
67																		38		96			67
66																		38		95			66
65																		31		95			65
64																		31		94			64
63																		31		94			63
62																		25		93			62
61																		25		93			61
60														99				25		92			60
59														98				19		92			59
58														98				19		90			58
57														98				19		90			57
56																		14		86			56
55														97				14		86			55
54														97			99	14		85		99	54
53														96			98	10		85		98	53
52														96			96	10		81		98	52
51														95			95	10		81		98	51
50														95			90	8		78		98	50
49														94			90	8		78		98	49
48														94			86	8		72		98	48
47														93			80	7		72		97	47
46										99				93			68	7		69		97	46
45										98	99			92			59	7				97	45
44										98	98			92		99	47	6				97	44
43										98	98			90		98	43	6				96	43
42										98				90			35	6				96	42
41										97				88			25	4				95	41

272

Raw Score	P	B	Pn	Br	Hs	Ax	Ab	Sx	At	A	H	I	V	M	Sh	C	FA	FD	S	L	R	RT	Raw Score
40										97	98			88		98	19	4		69		94	40
39										97	98			85		97	13	4		64		94	39
38										97	97			85		97	10	3		64		93	38
37										96	97			81		96	8	3		61		93	37
36										96	97			81		96	6	3		61		92	36
35										95	96			76		96	5	2		57		92	35
34										95	96			76		95	4	2		57		91	34
33										92	95			74		95	2	2		51		91	33
32										92	95			74		94	2	2		51		90	32
31										85	93			70		92	2	2		46	99	88	31
30										85	92		99	70	99	90	2	2		46	98	86	30
29										79	91		98	66	98	88	1	1		42	98	84	29
28		88 per cent give zero or one response								79	90		98	66	97	87	1	1		42	98	83	28
27										72	88		98	59	97	85	1	1		39	98	81	27
26										72	86		98	59	97	83	1	1		39	97	80	26
25				99	99					63	83	99	98	54	97	83	1	1		33	96	77	25
24				98	98					63	79	98	98	54	96	80	1	1		33	95	74	24
23				98	98		93 per cent give zero or one response			54	77	97	98	50	96	78	1			30	95	72	23
22				98	98			98 per cent give zero or one response		54	76	97	98	50	94	73	1			30	94	68	22
21				97	97					46	74	96	97	47	92	70				24	93	62	21
20				96	97	99				46	71	93	97	47	90	67				24	93	59	20
19				94	96	98				37	68	91	97	40	88	63				19	92	52	19
18				91	94	98				37	65	90	97	40	88	58				19	91	47	18
17				86	93	98				26	60	86	96	33	86	52				15	91	44	17
16				80	90	98				26	58	82	96	33	83	48			85 per cent give zero or one response	15	90	42	16
15	99			71	88	96			99	19	55	75	96	25	79	44				11	88	35	15
14	98			63	86	94			98	19	50	65	95	25	73	40				11	86	30	14
13	95			49	82	92			98	14	44	58	95	25	67	35				7	82	26	13
12	90			37	78	89			98	14	39	46	95	20	60	31				7	79	23	12
11	84			27	72	85			97	9	35	30	92	15	52	28				5	77	19	11
10	77		99	17	65	82			96	9	30	15	90	15	46	24				5	71	15	10
9	66		97	6	56	78			93	5	26	7	90	12	41	20				3	68	12	9
8	49		94	2	45	71			88	5	23		87	12	31	15				3	62	6	8
7	36		88		36	66			86	3	16		86	7	23	11				2	55	4	7
6	23		81		27	57			81	3	12		80	7	19	9				2	46	2	6
5	15		67		19	42			66	2	6		77	4	14	8				1	36	2	5
4	10		50		12	35			45	1	5		70	4	9	5				1		1	4
3	5		29		4	26			27	1	2		64	3	6	4							3
2	2		14			20					1		54	3	3	3							2
1	1					10					1		38	2	1	1							1
0						5							27	2		1							0

VARIABLES

(continuation of table)

Table 10

Percentile Norms

for

College Students

(206 Cases)

Raw Score	FD
114+	99
111-113	98
108-110	97
105-107	96
102-104	93
99-101	89
96-98	83
93-95	79
90-92	75
87-89	70
84-86	65
81-83	59

Raw Score	RT	R	L	S	FD	FA	C	Sh	M	V	H	A	At	Sx	Ab	Ax	Hs	Br	Pn	B	P	Raw Score
80					50				99													80
79					50				98													79
78					50				98													78
77					43				97													77
76					43				97													76
75					43				96													75
74					34				96													74
73					34				96													73
72					34				96													72
71					25				95													71
70					25				95													70
69					25				94													69
68					17				94													68
67					17				93													67
66					17				93													66
65			99		12				92													65
64			98		12				92													64
63			98		12				91													63
62			98		10				91													62
61			98		10				89		99											61
60			98		10				89	99												60
59			98		8				86	98												59
58			98		8				86	98												58
57			97		8				83	98												57
56			97		6				83	98												56
55			97		6	99			80	98												55
54			97		6	98			80	98												54
53			96		4	97			77	98												53
52			96		4	96		99	77	98												52
51	99		95		4		99	97	73	98												51
50	98		95		3	95	98		73		98											50
49	97		95		3	92	98		68		98											49
48	97		95		3	86	97		68		97											48
47	97		94		2	81			63		97											47
46	96		94		2	73			63		96											46
45	96		91		2	66	97		59		96											45
44	96		91		2	52	96		59		95											44
43	95		88		2	47	95		55		94											43
42	95		88		2	37	94		55		92											42
41	95		86		1	28	93		50		92											41

274

Raw Score	P	B	Pn	Br	Hs	Ax	Ab	Sx	At	A	H	I	V	M	Sh	C	FA	FD	S	L	R	RT	Raw Score
40										99	91		98	50	97	92	24	1		86		94	40
39										97	90		98	45	97	92	17	1		85		93	39
38										97	89		98	45	97	91	11	1		85		93	38
37										96	88		98	40	96	91	7	1		83		91	37
36										96	85		98	40	96	87	3	1		83		90	36
35										94	83		98	35	95	86	2			79		90	35
34						99				94	80		98	35	95	84	1			79		88	34
33						98				91	77		98	30	94	83	1			76		88	33
32					99	98				91	74		98	30	93	81				76		86	32
31					98	98				84	72		98	25	93	79				73		83	31
30					97	97				84	71		98	25	91	78				73		82	30
29					97	97				80	67		97	20	89	77				70		79	29
28					96	97				80	64		97	20	89	71				70		76	28
27					96	96				75	61		97	15	88	68				65		73	27
26					95	96				75	58		96	15	86	66				65		68	26
25					95	96				66	53	99	96	13	83	61				59		64	25
24					94	95				66	49	98	95	13	82	57				59		62	24
23					91	94				53	44	97	95	11	80	54				53		57	23
22					89	93				53	41	96	95	9	76	52				53		52	22
21					87	91				41	38	93	94	8	74	45				48		46	21
20					85	88				41	35	91	94	8	70	39				48		42	20
19				99	83	86			99	30	28	88	94	6	66	36				43		40	19
18				98	82	83			98	30	25	86	94	6	62	33				43		33	18
17	99			97	81	80			98	19	20	85	93	5	54	30				38		28	17
16	97		99	95	76	78			97	19	18	82	93	5	50	26				38		24	16
15	94		98	93	72	74			97	12	14	80	93	4	45	20				33		21	15
14	90		97	89	67	70			95	12	11	78	91	4	41	17				33		17	14
13	82		96	85	59	65			94	6	8	72	89	3	35	15				28		14	13
12	69		94	79	52	58			93	6	6	67	88	3	31	13				28		12	12
11	55		92	73	46	52			90	3	5	57	87	2	27	9				21		8	11
10	43		88	66	39	48			83	3	3	52	83	2	22	7				21		6	10
9	31		84	61	33	41			76		2	43	77	1	16	6				15		4	9
8	18		77	52	28	34			64		1	35	74	1	11	4				15		3	8
7	12		69	41	24	29			51			27	71		9	3				9		2	7
6	7		58	33	20	23			28			24	68		6	2				9		2	6
5	1		47	21	11	14			15			17	63		4	1				6		1	5
4			35	16	5	10						12	55		2					6			4
3			25	6	3	7						6	47		1					3			3
2			16	3	2	4						3	39							3			2
1			7	2	1	1						1	28							1			1
0			2										20							1			0

Ab: 68 per cent give zero or one response

Sx: 90 per cent give zero or one response

S: 88 per cent give zero or one response

275

VARIABLES

Table 11
Percentile Norms
for
Emotionally Disturbed
Children
(99 Cases)

Raw Score	RT	R	L	S	FD	FA	C	Sh	M	V	I	H	A	At	Sx	Ab	Ax	Hs	Br	Pn	B	P	Raw Score
80					84																		80
79			99		82																		79
78			99		81																		78
77			98		80																		77
76			98		79																		76
75			98		78																		75
74			97		76																		74
73			97		75																		73
72			97		73																		72
71			97		72																		71
70			96		70																		70
69			96		69		99		99														69
68			96		68		99		99														68
67			95		66		99		99														67
66			95		65		99		98														66
65			94		64		99		98														65
64			94		62		98		98														64
63			94		61		98		98														63
62			93		60		98		98														62
61			92		58		98		97														61
60			92		55		98		97														60
59			92		52		98		97														59
58			91		50		97		97														58
57			90		48		97		97														57
56			90		46		97		96														56
55			89		44		97		96														55
54			89		42		97		96														54
53			88		40		97		96														53
52			87		38		97		96														52
51			87		37		96		95														51
50			86		35		96		95														50
49			85		33		96		95														49
48			85		32	99	96		95				99	99									48
47	99		84		30	98	96		94					99									47
46	99		83		29		96		94				99										46
45	98		83		29	97	95		93				98	99									45
44	98		82		28	96	95		93				98	99									44
43	98		81		27	94	95		92				97	98									43
42	97		81		26	93	95		92				96	98									42
41	97		80		26	92	95		91				96	98									41

(continuation of table)

Raw Score	FD
120	99
119	99
118	99
117	99
116	99
115	98
114	98
113	98
112	98
111	98
110	98
109	98
108	97
107	97
106	97

(continuation of table)

Raw Score	FD
105	97
104	97
103	97
102	97
101	96
100	96
99	96
98	96
97	96
96	96
95	96
94	95
93	95
92	95
91	95
90	94
89	93
88	92
87	92
86	91
85	90
84	89
83	88
82	86
81	85

Raw Score	P	B	Pn	Br	Hs	Ax	Ab	Sx	At	A	H	I	V	M	Sh	C	FA	FD	S	L	R	RT
40									98	95				91		94	90	25		79		97
39									98	94				90		94	87	23		78		97
38									98	94				90		93	85	22		77		96
37									98	93				89		92	82	20		76		96
36									98	92				88		92	80	19		75		96
35									97	92	99			87		92	75	18		72		96
34									97	91	98			86		91	72	17		70		95
33					99	99			97	91	98		99	84		90	70	16		68		95
32					98	99			97	90	98		99	83		90	67	14		66	99	94
31					97	98			97	87	98		98	82		89	63	13		64	97	94
30					96	98			97	83	97		98	81		87	60	12		62	95	94
29					95	98			97	80	96		98	80		86	50	11		60	92	93
28					94	97			96	75	96		98	78		84	47	10		58	92	92
27					93	97			96	70	96		98	75		83	43	9		56	89	92
26					92	96			96	68	95		97	74		81	40	8		54	87	92
25					92	96			96	65	94		97	72		80	35	7		52	85	91
24					91	96			96	62	93		97	71		79	30	6		50	83	90
23					90	95			96	60	93		96	70	99	78	28	5		45	81	90
22					88	95			96	58	92		96	67	97	76	25	5		40	80	88
21					85	92			96	56	91	99	96	63	95	75	20	4		38	78	86
20					82	90			95	54	90	98	96	60	93	70	17	4		35	75	84
19					80	88			95	52	88	98	96	58	92	68	13	3		32	72	82
18					76	85			95	50	85	97	95	57	90	65	10	3		30	70	80
17					72	82			95	45	82	96	95	55	85	62	9	3		28	65	78
16			99		68	80			94	40	80	96	94	53	80	60	8	2		25	60	75
15			98	99	64	75		99	93	38	75	95	93	52	76	57	7	2	99	23	58	72
14			98	98	60	72		98	92	35	70	92	92	50	72	53	6	1	95	22	55	70
13	99		97	97	55	70		97	92	32	60	90	91	45	60	50	5	1	90	20	52	65
12	98		96	96	50	60		96	91	30	57	75	90	40	45	47	1		78	18	50	60
11	96		95	95	45	55		95	90	25	53	50	88	37	28	43				16	47	55
10	95		92	90	40	50			88	22	50		86	33		40				14	43	48
9	93		90	84	30	40			85	20	40		84	30		38				12	40	40
8	92		85	78	22	30			82	15	35		82	25		35				10	37	28
7	90		80	70	15	22			80	10	30		80	24		32				9	33	20
6	75		75	55	8				75	8	25		72	22		30				8	30	10
5	60	99	70	40					70	5	20		66	21		25				6		5
4	45		55	30					60		15		60	20		20				5		5
3	30		40	22					50		10		50	15		15						1
2	22		25						40		5		40	10		10						
1	10								30		1		25			5						
0																						

VARIABLES

(continuation of table)

Table 12

Percentile Norms

for

Emotionally Disturbed

Adolescents

(114 Cases)

Continuation of table

Raw Score	FD	M	V
119			
118	99		
117	98		
116	98		
115	98		
114	97		
113	96	99	
112	96	99	
111	96	98	
110	95		
109	94		
108	94		
107	94		
106	93		99
105	92		99
104	92		99
103	92		99
102	91		99
101	90		99
100	90		98
99	88		98
98	86		98
97	84		98
96	82		98
95	80		98
94	78		98
93	75		98
92	72		98
91	70		97
90	68		97
89	66		97
88	64		97
87	62		
86	60		

Main table

Raw Score	RT	R	L	S	FD	FA	C	Sh	M	V	I	H	A	At	Sx	Ab	Ax	Hs	Br	Pn	B	P
80					43				96	97												
79					40				96	97												
78			99		38				96	97												
77			99		36				95	97												
76					34				95	96												99
75			99		32				94	96												
74			98		30				94	96												
73			98		28				93	96												
72			98		27				92	96												
71			98		25				92	96												
70			97		23				91	96												
69			97		22				91	96												
68			97		20				90	96												
67			97		19				89	96												
66			97		18				88	96							99					
65			96		16				87	96							99					
64			96		15				86	95							98					
63			96		14				85	95							98					
62			96		12				85	95							98					
61			95		11				84	95							98					
60			95		10				83	95							98					99
59			95		9				82	95							97					99
58			95		9				81	95							97					99
57			94		8				80	95							97					99
56			94		7				78	94							96					99
55			94		6				77	94		99					96	99				98
54			93		6		99		75	94		98					96	99				98
53			93		5		99		74	94							96					98
52			93		5	99	98		72	94							96					98
51			92		5				71	93							95					98
50			92		4	98	98		70	93		98					95	99				98
49			92		4	96	98		68	93		98					95	98				98
48			91		4	95	97		66	93		97					94	98				98
47			91		4	92	97		64	93		96	99				94	98				98
46			91		3	90	96		62	92		96	98				94	98				98
45	99		90		3	85	96		60	92		96	98				93	97				98
44	99		90		3	80	96		59	92		95	97				93	97			99	98
43	99		89		3	76	95		58	92		94	96				92	97			99	97
42	98		88		3	72	95		57	92		94	96				92	97			98	97
41	98		88		2	60	94		56	92		94	95				92	96				97

278

Continuation of table — additional raw scores for scales P (V), B (M), Pn (FD):

Raw Score (Br)	FD (Pn)	M (B)	V (P)
85	58	98	97
84	55	98	97
83	52	97	97
82	50	97	97
81	47	97	97

Main conversion table:

Raw Score	P	B	Pn	Br	Hs	Ax	Ab	Sx	At	A	H	I	V	M	Sh	C	FA	FD	S	L	R	RT
40					96	91				94	93		91	55		94	55	2		87		98
39					96	91				94	92		91	55		93	50	2		86		98
38					96	91			99	93	92		91	54		92	47	2		85		98
37					95	90			99	92	92		91	53		91	43	2		85		97
36					95	90			99	91	91		91	52		91	40	1		84		97
35					95	88			99	91	90		90	51		90	30	1		83		97
34					94	85			98	90	90		90	50	99	89	28	1		82		97
33					94	82			98	88	88		90	48	98	88	25			82	99	96
32					93	80			98	86	87		89	46	98	86	22			81		96
31					92	79			98	84	85		88	44	97	85	20			80		96
30			99		91	78		99	98	82	83		88	42	97	84	17			79	99	96
29			99		91	76		99	98	80	82		87	40	96	82	13			78	98	96
28			98	99	90	75		99	98	75	80		86	38	95	81	10			77	98	95
27			98	98	88	72		98	97	70	78		85	35	94	80	9			76	98	95
26			97	97	86	70		98	97	67	77		84	32	93	78	9			75	97	95
25			97	96	84	67	99	98	97	63	75	99	83	30	92	75	8			70	97	94
24			96	95	82	63	98	98	97	60	70	97	82	28	91	72	8			68	97	93
23			96	90	80	60	98	98	97	57	67	95	82	27	90	70	7			66	96	92
22			95	80	78	57	97	98	97	53	63	94	81	25	88	65	6			64	96	91
21			95	75	74	53	96	97	96	50	60	92	80	22	85	60	6			62	96	90
20			94	70	70	50	96	97	96	47	57	91	79	20	83	58	5			60	95	86
19			93	65	65	47	95	97	96	43	53	90	78	19	80	55	4			58	95	82
18			92	60	60	43	94	97	96	40	50	80	77	17	78	52	3			56	94	78
17			91	50	57	40	94	97	96	34	45	76	70	16	74	50	3			54	93	70
16			90	40	53	38	93	97	96	28	40	72	68	14	70	45	2			52	92	65
15			87	34	50	35	92	96	96	24	35	60	65	13	65	40	1			50	92	60
14			84	28	45	32	91	96	95	20	30	50	62	11	60	37				47	91	57
13	99		81	20	40	30	91	96	95	15	25	35	60	10	50	33				43	90	53
12	97		78	10	30	28	90	96	95	10	20	25	57	9	47	30				40	88	50
11	95		70	5	28	25	80	96	95	8	18	20	53	8	43	28				35	86	40
10	92	97	60	1	27	22	72	96	90	5	15	10	50	8	40	27			99	30	84	30
9	90	85	55		25	20		95	87	5	12		40	7	30	25			98	25	82	25
8	78		50		20	18		95	83	4	10		37	6	25	22			96	20	80	20
7	65		40		17	15		95	80	4	8		33	5	20	20			95	18	78	10
6	50		30		13	12		92	72	3	5		30	4	17	17			90	15	75	8
5	40		25		10	10		90	60	3	4		28	4	13	13			78	12	70	5
4	30		20		8	5		87	55	2	3		25	3	10	10				10	65	1
3	22		15		5	3		83	50	2	2		22	2	8	5				8	60	
2	15		10		1	1		80	40	1	1		20	2	5					7	52	
1	8								25	1			15	1						5	45	
0													10									

VARIABLES

Table 13

Percentile Norms

for

Male Juvenile Delinquents

(75 Cases)

(continuation of table)

Raw Score	FD
105	
104	99
103	98
102	98
101	94
100	94
99	92
98	92
97	89
96	89
95	89
94	88
93	88
92	85
91	85
90	85
89	81
88	81
87	77
86	75
85	73
84	71
83	68
82	67
81	63

Raw Score	RT	R	L	S	FD	FA	C	Sh	M	V	I	H	A	At	Sx	Ab	Ax	Hs	Br	Pn	B	P	Raw Score
80					60																		80
79					59																		79
78					59																		78
77					56																		77
76					56																		76
75					53																		75
74					53																		74
73					47																		73
72					47																		72
71					44																		71
70					43																		70
69					41																		69
68					37																		68
67					37																		67
66					37																		66
65					33																		65
64					31																		64
63					29																		63
62					27																		62
61					24																		61
60					24																		60
59					24																		59
58					21																		58
57					20																		57
56					20																		56
55					15			99															55
54					15	99		97															54
53			99		13	98		96															53
52			98		9	98		96															52
51					7																		51
50			96		7	98		95															50
49			96		7	96		95															49
48			96		5	96		93															48
47			96		5	88		92															47
46			96		5	85		89															46
45			96		5	81		89															45
44			96		4	72		89															44
43			96		4	65		88															43
42			96		4	60		87															42
41	99		94		3	53		87				99											41

280

Raw Score	P	B	Pn	Br	Hs	Ax	Ab	Sx	At	A	H	I	V	M	Sh	C	FA	FD	S	L	R	RT	Raw Score
40										98				87			44	3		94		98	40
39										98				87			35	3		92		98	39
38										98				85			27	3		92		95	38
37										96				85			25	3		92		94	37
36										96				83			24	3		92		94	36
35										95				81			19	3		92	99	94	35
34										94				80			16	1		91	98	94	34
33										94				80			9	0		89	96	94	33
32										94				77			9			88	96	94	32
31										91				77			9			87	94	94	31
30										91	99			75		99	7			84	94	94	30
29										87	98			75		98	3			83	91	94	29
28										85	96			75		98	3			80	88	91	28
27										77	96			73		98	3			80	88	84	27
26										77	96			72		95	3			80	87	81	26
25					99	99				73	94			71		94	3			77	87	80	25
24					98	98				69	92			67		91	1			75	85	80	24
23					98	96				65	91			63		89	1			71	84	80	23
22					92	96				63	91			57		88	1			69	80	77	22
21					91	95				57	91			56		87	1			65	80	73	21
20					88	92				56	88			53		81	1			57	77	72	20
19					85	89				56	85			43		80	1			51	77	68	19
18					80	85				55	81			41	99	77	1			48	77	64	18
17					77	84				53	77			40	96	76	1			43	77	60	17
16					77	81				47	76			36	95	72	0			40	77	57	16
15					69	77				35	72			35	92	72				35	75	53	15
14					61	71			99	29	65			33	91	67				29	72	44	14
13					55	64			98	25	61			29	88	64				27	69	41	13
12	99		99		45	55			98	25	53			28	77	57				21	69	39	12
11	98		98	99	41	49			98	23	51	99		25	77	53				19	65	36	11
10	95		98	95	35	39			96	23	47	98		23	77	47				13	64	31	10
9	87		98	91	31	36			96	21	44	98	99	21	72	40				11	63	24	9
8	81	99	95	87	28	25	99		95	15	36	98	95	20	64	35				5	61	19	8
7	65	98	94	81	16	19	98	99	92	9	29	96	92	19	57	32				5	56	5	7
6	57	85	92	77	9	13	96	96	87	8	19	92	88	13	45	25				4	55	5	6
5	44		83	71	5	7		91	83	8	15	84	77	12	37	24			99	4	53	1	5
4	36		73	60					73	5	11	76	72	11	29	21			95	3	43	0	4
3	28		69	44					64	4	7	60	68	5	20	19			77	0	39		3
2	17		56	39					49	4	4	43	60	3	15	15					39		2
1	9		35	23					36	1	4	31	47	3	11	12					36		1
0	0		17	13					21	0	4	12	45	1	9	9					28		0

281

VARIABLES

Table 14
Percentile Norms
for
Mentally Retarded
(100 Cases)

(continuation of table)

Raw Score	RT	R	L	S	FD	FA	C	Sh	M	V	I	H	A	At	Sx	Ab	Ax	Hs	Br	Pn	B	P	Raw Score
80					54																		80
79					54																		79
78					54																		78
77					46																		77
76					46																		76
75					46																		75
74					43																		74
73					43																		73
72					43																		72
71					38																		71
70					38																		70
69					38																		69
68					33																		68
67					33																		67
66					33																		66
65					29								99										65
64					29				99				98										64
63					29				98				98										63
62					25								97										62
61					25																		61
60					25				98				97										60
59					23				98				96										59
58					23				98				96										58
57					23				98				94										57
56					22				98				94										56
55					22				98				92										55
54					22	99	99		98				92										54
53					20	98	98		98				90										53
52					20		98		98				90										52
51					20		98		97				88										51
50			99		17	98	98		97	99			88										50
49			98		17	97	97		97	98			86										49
48	99		98		17	97	97		97	98			86										48
47	98		97		13	94	97		97	98			84										47
46			97		13	91	97		97	98			84										46
45	98		97		13	90	96		96	98			83										45
44	97		97		11	86	96		96	96			83										44
43	96		95		11	85	96		96	96			82										43
42	95		95		11	83	96		96	96			82										42
41	94		93		9	78	95		96	96			81										41

Raw Score	FD
126+	99
120-125	98
117-119	97
114-116	95
111-113	94
108-110	93
105-107	92
102-104	90
99-101	87
96-98	85
93-95	80
90-92	73
87-89	70
84-86	66
81-83	61

Conversion table. Columns: Raw Score, P, B, Pn, Br, Hs, Ax, Ab, Sx, At, A, H, I, V, M, Sh, C, FA, FD, S, L, R, RT, Raw Score.

Raw Score	P	B	Pn	Br	Hs	Ax	Ab	Sx	At	A	H	I	V	M	Sh	C	FA	FD	S	L	R	RT	Raw Score
40										81			96	96		94	74	9		93	99	93	40
39										80			94	95		93	71	9		92	98	93	39
38										80			94	95		93	68	8		92	96	92	38
37										79			94	95		89	63	8		90	95	91	37
36										79			94	95		89	57	8		90	94	90	36
35										75			94	94		89	51	6		89	94	89	35
34										75			89	94		89	49	6		89	93	88	34
33										72			89	91		88	46	6		88	92	86	33
32										72			89	91		88	42	5		88	90	85	32
31										69			89	89		88	37	5		84	89	83	31
30										69			89	89		88	35	5		84	87	82	30
29										65	99		86	88		88	31	4		80	86	79	29
28										65	98		85	88		87	29	4		80	84	78	28
27										63	98		84	86		87	27	4		75	82	76	27
26										63	98		83	86		87	25	4		75	81	73	26
25						99				59	98		82	83	99	86	24	4		71	80	72	25
24						98				59	98		81	83	98	85	22	3		71	78	70	24
23						98				54	98		80	79	98	84	19	3		67	76	68	23
22					99	97				54	98		79	79	98	83	17	3		67	75	67	22
21					98	97				47	98		78	76	98	82	14	3		63	73	65	21
20					98	97				47	97		76	76	98	78	13	3		63	68	63	20
19					96	96				40	97		75	73	98	77	12	3		58	65	59	19
18					95	94				40	96		74	73	98	72	8	3		58	64	54	18
17					95	93				32	95		73	68	98	71	7	2		54	63	50	17
16					93	92				32	94		70	68	98	70	6	2		54	60	48	16
15					92	91				26	93		69	65	97	67	5	2		50	58	45	15
14					92	90				26	92		68	65	96	66	5	2		50	55	42	14
13					91	88				23	88		67	59	96	62	4	2		45	53	36	13
12	99			99	90	85				23	86		63	59	95	59	4	2		45	51	30	12
11	97			98	88	81				19	80		62	53	94	54	3	2		39	50	25	11
10	95			97	85	77				19	74		54	53	92	52	3	2		39	50	20	10
9	90			97	80	75				15	70		53	48	89	48	2	2		34	49	13	9
8	85			93	75	71				15	66		51	48	82	44	2	1		34	47	10	8
7	79			91	72	65				12	58		47	42	77	40	2	1		27	44	6	7
6	65			86	65	60				12	49		41	42	66	36	2	1		27	39	5	6
5	56			79	61	54				8	41		38	37	58	35	1	1		20	38	2	5
4	47			75	51	47				8	36		34	37	51	28	1	1		20	34	1	4
3	39			63	43	36				5	31		29	26	49	22	1	1		14	29		3
2	23			53	32	31				5	27		19	26	41	19		1		14	27		2
1	12			47	22	18				2	20		14	18	28	12		1		6	21		1
0	4			30	15	11				2	17			18	13	11		1		6	15		0

Notes for columns with a single statement:

- **B:** 87 per cent give zero or one response
- **Pn:** 65 per cent give zero or one response
- **Ab:** 99 per cent give no response
- **Sx:** 98 per cent give zero or one response
- **At:** 65 per cent give zero or one response
- **I:** 71 per cent give zero or one response
- **S:** 92 per cent give zero or one response

VARIABLES

Raw Score	RT	R	L	S	FD	FA	C	Sh	M	V	H	A	At	Sx	Ab	Ax	Hs	Br	Pn	B	P	Raw Score
80					46																	80
79					46																	79
78					46																	78
77					41																	77
76					41																	76
75					41																	75
74					37																	74
73					37																	73
72					37																	72
71					32																	71
70					32																	70
69					32																	69
68					28																	68
67					28																	67
66	99				28																	66
65	98		99		23																	65
64	98		98		23			99														64
63	98		98		23			98														63
62	98		98		20			98														62
61	98		97		20			98														61
60	98		97		20			98														60
59	97		97		18			98														59
58	97		97		18			98														58
57	97		96		18	99		97														57
56	97		96		15			97														56
55	96		96		15	98		97														55
54	96		96		15	96		97														54
53	95		94		12	95		96														53
52	95		94		12	93		96														52
51	94		90		12	92		95														51
50	94		90		10	89		95	99													50
49	94		88		10	88		94	98													49
48	93		88		10	86		94	98													48
47	93		87		8	79		93	98													47
46	92		87		8	73		93	98													46
45	92		83		8	69	99	92	98		99											45
44	91		83		7	56	98	92	98	99	98											44
43	90		81		7	54	97	90	98	98	98											43
42	89		81		7	47	97	90	98	98	98											42
41	86		81		6	40	96	88	98	98												41

Table 15

Percentile Norms
for
Depressed Patients

(90 Cases)

(continuation of table)

Raw Score	FD
108+	99
105-107	98
102-104	97
99-101	94
96-98	89
93-95	81
90-92	75
87-89	70
84-86	63
81-83	55

Raw Score	P	B	Pn	Br	Hs	Ax	Ab	Sx	At	A	H	I	V	M	Sh	C	FA	FD	S	L	R	RT
40										98	98		98	88		96	38	6		81	99	83
39										97	98		97	87		95	29	6		80	98	81
38										97	98		97	87		94	24	6		80	98	79
37										96	98		97	86		93	22	6		75	98	76
36										96	97		97	86		93	20	6		75	98	74
35										93	97		97	82		92	17	5		72	98	73
34										93	96		97	82		92	12	5		72	97	72
33										91	94		97	79		91	10	5		67	97	71
32										91	93		97	79		91	8	4		67	96	70
31										88	92		97	77		90	7	4		63	95	70
30										88	89		97	77		89	6	4		63	94	69
29										81	89		96	71	99	88	2	3		58	94	67
28										81	88		95	71	98	87	2	3		58	93	63
27										74	86		95	70	98	87	2	3		54	92	56
26										74	83		94	70	98	86	2	1		54	89	51
25					99	99				69	80		94	62	97	85	1	1		50	88	49
24					98	98				69	79		93	62	97	83	1	1		50	88	46
23					98	96				60	77	99	93	55	96	80	1			43	88	39
22					97	95				60	76	98	92	55	96	79	1			43	84	38
21					97	94				56	76	98	92	50	96	78	1			40	83	36
20				99	93	94			99	56	73	97	92	50	96	77	1			40	82	34
19				97	91	93			98	48	69	97	91	48	94	76	1			36	82	33
18				97	90	91			98	48	61	96	91	48	93	75	1			36	81	32
17				96	89	90			97	41	58	94	91	43	89	73	1			28	80	31
16				94	88	89			97	41	53	91	90	43	86	68				28	79	27
15	99		99	91	87	87			92	35	44	88	90	40	85	61	1			21	76	23
14	98		98	89	83	84			90	35	41	84	88	40	84	58				21	72	19
13	94		98	87	79	83			89	27	39	81	87	37	82	53				16	71	17
12	89		96	82	76	80			81	27	37	72	84	37	80	52				16	66	12
11	84		94	73	73	74			79	21	33	68	80	31	77	51				12	63	10
10	80		93	66	70	73			70	21	32	66	77	31	73	47				12	62	8
9	72		89	64	66	70			57	17	29	53	76	27	68	42				8	60	3
8	62		83	57	57	63			39	17	26	46	76	27	63	40				8	54	
7	50		76	46	50	59			26	13	22	34	72	24	52	37				7	52	
6	41		68	36	44	52				13	14	30	68	24	48	30				7	51	
5	37		59	33	36	42				9	12	19	66	20	46	23				6	50	
4	27		49	24	29	34				9	11		59	20	43	19				6	49	
3	21		41	12	21	29				6	8		49	14	34	17				3	48	
2	14		29	8	14	22				6	6		42	14	27	12				3	42	
1	7		12		9	18					3		36	9	17	10				2	34	
0	4					10					1		27	9	4	6				2	21	

Column notes:
- B: *72 per cent give zero or one response*
- Ab: *89 per cent give zero or one response*
- Sx: *78 per cent give zero or one response*
- S: *77 per cent give zero or one response*

VARIABLES

(continuation of table)

Table 16
Percentile Norms
for
Chronic
Schizophrenics
(140 Cases)

Raw Score	FD
117+	99
111-116	98
105-110	97
102-104	96
99-101	94
96-98	90
93-95	88
90-92	86
87-89	83
84-86	80
81-83	76

Raw Score	V
185+	99
165-184	98
150-164	97
130-149	96
120-129	95
105-119	94
100-104	93
95-99	92
90-94	90
85-89	89
81-84	88

Raw Score	RT	R	L	S	FD	FA	C	Sh	M	V	I	H	A	At	Sx	Ab	Ax	Hs	Br	Pn	B	P	Raw Score
80					74					88													80
79					74					86													79
78					74					86													78
77					69					86													77
76					69					86													76
75					69					86													75
74					62					85													74
73					62					85													73
72					62					85													72
71					59					85													71
70					59					85													70
69					59					84													69
68					51					84													68
67					51					84													67
66					51					84													66
65					41					84													65
64					41					83													64
63					41					83													63
62					36					83													62
61					36					83													61
60					36	99				83													60
59					31	98				82													59
58					31	98	99			82			99										58
57					31	97	98			82			98										57
56					29	96	98			82			98										56
55	99		99		29	96	97		99	82			98										55
54	98		98		29	95	97		98	81			98										54
53	98		98		26	93	97		98	81			97										53
52	97		98		26	92	96		97	81			97										52
51	96		97		26	90	96		97	81			97										51
50	95		97		24	89	96		96	81			97										50
49	95		96		24	88	95		96	80			96										49
48	94		96		24	86	95		95	80			96										48
47	94		95		21	86	95		95	80			95										47
46	93		95		21	83	94		95	80			95										46
45	90		93		21	81	94		95	80			94										45
44	89		93		16	74	94		94	78			94										44
43	88		92		16	72	93			78			93										43
42	86		92		16	69	92			78			93										42
41	84		91		16	64	92			78			93										41

286

Raw Score	P	B	Pn	Br	Hs	Ax	Ab	Sx	At	A	H	I	V	M	Sh	C	FA	FD	S	L	R	RT	Raw Score
40										93			78	94		90	61	16		91		83	40
39						99				91			76	94		90	56	16		90	99	81	39
38						98				91			76	94		89	54	15		90	98	79	38
37						98				89			76	94		89	49	15		89	97	77	37
36						98				89			76	94		89	43	15		89	96	76	36
35						98				87			76	92		86	39	15		88	95	75	35
34						98				87			73	92		86	38	15		88	91	73	34
33						98				85	99		73	90		84	36	15		85	91	71	33
32						98				85	98		73	90		84	34	14		85	89	69	32
31						97				81	98		73	88	99	83	34	14		83	87	68	31
30					99	97				81	96		73	88	98	83	32	14		83	86	67	30
29					98	97				76	96		72	87	97	80	31	12		82	84	66	29
28					98	97				76	95		71	87	97	78	28	12		82	83	64	28
27					98	97				74	95		70	87	97	77	28	12		77	81	61	27
26					98	96				74	95		69	87	97	76	27	10		77	80	60	26
25					98	96				70	95		69	86	96	75	26	10		75	79	58	25
24					97	96				70	94		68	86	96	74	25	10		75	79	57	24
23					97	96				65	94		67	86	96	71	19	9		70	77	56	23
22					97	96				65	93		66	86	94	70	18	9		70	76	54	22
21					96	95				61	92		65	85	94	69	16	9		65	74	51	21
20			99		96	95				61	90		65	85	92	65	15	8		65	71	49	20
19			98		96	95				58	89		64	82	91	62	12	8		58	69	46	19
18			98		95	94				58	89		63	82	91	59	10	8		58	69	39	18
17			98		95	94				56	88		62	79	89	56	9	6		52	68	38	17
16			97	99	94	94				56	86		61	79	89	52	8	6		52	67	36	16
15			96	98	94	93				54	85		58	73	88	49	8	6		46	65	33	15
14			96	98	93	92				54	80		56	73	85	46	6	5		46	64	28	14
13			94	97	91	89				48	79		56	68	80	45	6	5		42	62	26	13
12	99		94	94	90	89				48	74		54	68	76	43	5	5		42	60	23	12
11	97		92	91	89	87				38	73		53	64	74	41	4	3		37	59	19	11
10	94		90	89	86	86				38	68		50	64	68	38	4	3		37	56	16	10
9	92		89	87	83	84				31	64		48	57	64	34	4	3		30	54	14	9
8	88		85	85	80	82				31	61		45	57	62	30	3	2		30	51	11	8
7	81		79	78	79	75				25	54		43	53	59	26	2	2		26	51	7	7
6	74		78	74	76	72				25	51		40	53	55	24	2	2		26	50	5	6
5	59		74	69	71	68				17	47		39	45	51	18	2	1		20	47	3	5
4	51		67	65	66	65				17	41		36	45	44	16	2	1		20	46	2	4
3	39		62	55	55	52				11	31		34	40	38	12	1	1		11	43	1	3
2	29		51	41	46	44				11	27		29	40	32	10	1	1		11	41		2
1	19		42	29	33	29				6	23		27	29	26	6	1	1		6	37		1
0	9		25	16	19	22				6	14		22	29	15	6	1	1		6	28		0

Notes for columns with no graduated values:
- B: 83 per cent give zero or one response
- Ab: 90 per cent give zero or one response
- Sx: 90 per cent give zero or one response
- At: 62 per cent give zero or one response
- I: 59 per cent give zero or one response
- S: 84 per cent give zero or one response

VARIABLES

Table 17
Percentile Norms
for
Neurotic Adults
(99 Cases)

Raw Score	RT	R	L	S	FD	FA	C	Sh	M	V	I	H	A	At	Sx	Ab	Ax	Hs
80					54		98			97								
79					52		98			97								
78					50	99	98		99	97							99	
77					48	98	98			97							99	
76					46	97	98			96							99	
75					44		98		99	96							99	
74					42		97		99	96							99	
73					40		97		98	96							99	
72					38		97		98	96							98	
71					36		97		98	96							98	
70			99		34		97		98	96							98	
69			98		32		97		98	96							98	
68			98		30		97		97	96							98	
67			97		28		97		97	96							98	
66			97		27		97		97	96							98	
65			96		25		97		97	96							98	
64			96		22		97		96	96							98	
63			95		20		96		96	96							98	
62			94		19		96		96	96							97	
61			94		18		96		96	96							97	
60	99		93		16		96		96	95							97	
59	99		92		15		96		95	95							97	
58	98		92		14		96		95	95							97	
57	98		91		12		96		95	95							97	
56	98		91		11		96		94	95							97	
55	97		90		10		96		93	95							97	
54	97		89		10		96		92	95							97	
53	97		87		9		96		92	95							97	
52	97		86		9		95		91	95							97	
51	96		85		8		95		90	95							96	
50	96		90		8		95		88	94			99			99	96	
49	96		89		8		95		86	94			98			99	96	
48	95		87		7		95		84	94			98			99	96	
47	95		86		7		95		82	93						99	96	
46	94		85		6		93		80	93						99	96	
45	94		94		6	96	92		79	93		99	97			99	96	
44	93	99	83		5	95	90		78	92		98	96			98	96	
43	93	99	81		5	92	89		77	92		98	96			98	96	
42	92	99	80		5	90	88		76	92		98	95			98	96	
41	92	99	79		5	86	87		75	91		97	92			98	95	

(continuation of table)

Raw Score	Br	Pn / FD	B / C	P / V
120				
119				
118				99
117				99
116				99
115				99
114				99
113		99		99
112		99		99
111				99
110		98		99
109		98		98
108		97		98
107		97		98
106		97		98
105		96		98
104		96		98
103		95		98
102		95		98
101		93		98
100		92		98
99		90		98
98		89		98
97		88		98
96		86		98
95		85		98
94		84		98
93		82		97
92		81	99	97
91		80		97
90		78	99	97
89		77	99	97
88		75	99	97
87		70	99	97
86		68	99	97

288

(continuation of table)

Continuation box (high raw scores)

Br / Raw Score	Pn / FD	B / C	P / V
85	65	98	97
84	62	98	97
83	60	98	96
82	58	98	97
81	56	98	97

Main table

Raw Score	Br	Pn	B	P	Hs	Ax	Ab	Sx	At	A	H	I	V	M	Sh	C	FA	FD	S	L	R	RT
40					99	95	98			90	96		91	74		86	82	4		78	98	91
39					98	95	98			88	96		91	73		84	78	4		76	98	91
38					98	95	98			87	96		91	72		83	70	4		75	98	90
37					98	95	98			85	95		90	71		82	65	4		70	98	88
36					98	95	98			83	94		89	70		81	60	4		69	98	87
35					97	94	98			82	94		88	68	99	80	55	4		67	98	85
34					96	93	98			80	93		88	66	99	78	50	3		66	97	83
33					96	92	97			79	92		87	64	98	77	47	3		64	97	82
32					96	92	97			78	91		86	62	98	75	43	3		63	97	80
31					95	91	97			76	91		85	60	97	73	40	3		61	97	78
30					94	90	97			75	90		85	58	97	72	30	3		60	97	75
29					94	88	97			72	88		84	57	96	70	28	3		58	96	73
28					93	85	97			70	87		83	55	96	68	25	2		55	96	72
27					93	82	97			65	85		82	53	96	67	20	2		52	96	70
26					92	80	97			60	83		82	52	95	65	18	2		50	96	65
25					92	78	97			57	82		81	50	95	63	16	2		47	96	60
24					91	75	97		99	53	80		80	48	90	62	14	2		43	95	57
23					91	73	96		99	50	78		78	46	88	60	12	2		40	95	53
22					90	72	96		98	45	75		77	44	88	57	10	1		37	95	50
21					88	70	96		98	40	72	99	75	42	86	53	5	1		33	95	48
20	99	99		99	87	68	96	99	98	30	70	98	73	40	84	50	5	1		30	94	45
19	98	98		98	85	67	96	98	97	25	65	96	72	38	82	47	4			27	94	42
18	98	98			83	65	96	98	97	22	60	95	70	35	80	43	4			25	93	40
17	97	97			82	63	96	97	97	20	57	93	68	32	78	40	4			22	92	35
16	96				80	62	96		96	18	53	92	66	30	75	37	3			20	92	30
15	96	96		97	75	60	96	96	96	17	50	90	64	28	70	33	3			18	91	25
14	95	96		97	70	50	96	96	96	15	40	87	62	25	67	30	2			16	91	20
13	90	95		96	65	45	96	96	95	13	35	83	60	20	63	28	2			14	90	15
12	88	92		95	60	40	95	95	95	12	30	80	57	18	60	25	2			12	88	10
11	85	90		90	50	35	95	93	92	10	28	75	53	17	55	20	1			10	87	8
10	82	80	99	82	40	30	95	92	90	8	25	65	50	15	50	18	1			9	85	7
9	80	75		75	35	25	95	90	88	7	20	50	45	13	45	15				8	83	5
8	72	70		65	30	20	95	78	85	5	17	35	40	12	40	12				7	82	4
7	60	60		55	28	17	95	77	82		13	22	37	10	28	10				6	80	2
6	55	45		40	25	13	93	75	80		10		33	8	20	8				5	78	1
5	50	30	98	28	20	10	92		72		5		30	5	17	7			99		75	
4	40	22	96	20	15	8	90		60				28		13	5			96		70	
3	35	17	95	10	10	7	78		50				25		10				92		65	
2	30	13	90	5	8	5	75		40				20		8						60	
1	25	8			5		60		28				10		5						50	
0																						

VARIABLES

Table 18
Percentile Norms
for
Alcoholic Adults
(106 Cases)

Raw Score	RT	R	L	S	FD	FA	C	Sh	M	V	H	A	At	Sx	Ab	Ax	Hs	Br	Pn	B	P
80	97				52																
79	97				50																
78	97				48																
77	97				45																
76	97				42																
75	97				40																
74	97				37																
73	96		99		35				99												
72	96				33				99												
71	96				30				98												
70	96		98		28				98												
69	96		98		20				98												
68	96		97		19				97												
67	96		97		18				97												
66	96		96		17				97												
65	96		96		16				97												
64	96		95		15				96												
63	96		94		15				96												
62	96		92		14				96												
61	96		91		13				95												
60	96		90		12				95												
59	95		89		11	99			94												
58	95		88		10	99			94												
57	95		88		9	98	99		94												
56	95		87		9	96	99		93												
55	95		86		8	95	98		92												
54	95		85		7	92	98		92												
53	95		84		6	90	98		92			99									
52	94		83		6	86	97		91			99									
51	93		82		5	82	97		90			98									
50	92		82		5		97		90			98									
49	92		81		5		96		89	99		98									
48	91		80		4		96		88	99		97									
47	90		78		4		96		87	98		97									
46	88		75		4		95		86	98		97				99					
45	85		74		4		95		85	98	99	97				99					
44	82		72		4		94		84	98	99	96				98					
43	80		71		4		94		83	98	98	96				98					
42	78		70		4		93		82		98	96				98					
41	75		69		3		92		81		97	95				98	99				

(continuation of table)

Raw Score	RT	FD
110		
109		
108		
107	99	
106	99	
105	99	
104	99	99
103	99	98
102	99	97
101	99	96
100	98	95
99	98	92
98	98	90
97	98	89
96	98	87
95	98	86
94	98	84
93	98	83
92	98	81
91	98	80
90	98	78
89	98	77
88	98	75
87	97	72
86	97	70
85	97	67
84	97	63
83	97	60
82	97	58
81	97	55

Conversion table of raw scores to percentiles.

Raw Score	P	B	Pn	Br	Hs	Ax	Ab	Sx	At	A	H	I	V	M	Sh	C	FA	FD	S	L	R	RT
40					99	97				94	97		97	80		91	79	3		68		72
39					98	97				93	97		97	78		91	75	3		66		70
38					98	97				92	96		97	75		90	68	3		65		68
37					98	96				91	96		96	72		88	60	3		64		65
36					98	96				90	95		96	70		86	50	2		62		62
35					97	96				88	95		96	68		84	45	2		61		60
34					97	96				86	94		96	67		82	40	2		60		58
33					97	95				84	93		96	65		80	37	2		58		55
32					97	95				82	92		95	63		79	33	2		56		52
31					96	94				80	92		95	62		78	30	2		54		50
30					96	93			99	78	91		94	60	99	76	28	2		52		48
29					96	92			99	75	90		93	57	98	75	25	1		50		45
28					96	91			98	70	88		92	53	97	70	22	1		48		42
27				99	95	90			98	67	87		91	50	96	68	20	1		46		40
26				98	95	87			97	63	85		90	48	95	66	18			44		38
25				96	94	83		99	97	60	83		89	45	93	64	16			42	99	35
24				95	92	80		98	96	57	82		87	42	92	62	14			40	98	32
23				93	91	78		97	96	53	80		86	40	90	60	12			38	97	30
22				92	90	77		97	95	50	75		84	38	87	57	10			35	97	25
21				90	87	75		96	95	45	70		83	35	83	53	8			32	96	20
20				87	85	72		97	92	40	65		81	32	80	50	7			30	95	18
19				83	83	70		96	90	35	60		80	30	75	47	5			28	94	15
18			99	80	80	65		95	88	30	57		78	29	73	43	5			25	92	12
17			98	72	78	60		94	85	28	53	99	75	28	72	40	4			20	91	10
16			96	66	74	58		92	82	25	50	98	72	26	70	37	4			18	90	8
15			95	60	70	55	99	91	80	20	45	96	70	25	65	33	3			17	85	7
14	99	99	90	50	65	52	97	90	75	17	40	95	67	20	60	30	3			15	80	5
13	97	97	86	40	60	50	95	85	70	13	35	90	63	18	55	25	2			13	78	4
12	95	95	82	30	55	40	90	80	65	10	30	84	60	15	50	22	2			12	75	2
11	90	80	78	25	50	37	80	70	60	9	25	78	57	12	45	20	1			10	70	1
10	80		70	20	45	33			50	8	20	65	53	10	40	18	1			9	67	
9	72		65	10	40	30			35	6	18	45	50	8	35	15				8	63	
8	60		60	5	35	28			22	5	16	30	47	7	30	12				7	60	
7	50		50	3	30	25				4	14	22	43	5	25	10				6	50	
6	40		40	1	22	20				3	12	8	40	4	20	8				5	40	
5	30		30		16	17				3	10		30	3	17	5			99	4		
4	22		22		10	13				2	5		25	2	13	4			95	3		
3	15		16		5	10				1			20	1	10	3			85	3		
2	8		10		1	5							10		5	2				2		
1			5			1									3	1				1		
0															1							

References

ADLER, A. *Practice and Theory of Individual Psychology.* New York: Harcourt Brace Jovanovich, 1927.

ALTUS, W. D., AND THOMPSON, G. M. "The Rorschach as a Measure of Intelligence." *Journal of Consulting Psychology,* 1949, *13,* 341–347.

AMES, L. B., LEARNED, J., METRAUX, R. W., AND WALKER, R. N. *Child Rorschach Responses.* New York: Hocher, 1952.

ANDERSON, D. O., AND SEITZ, F. C. "Rorschach Diagnosis of Homosexuality: Shafer's Content." *Journal of Projective Techniques and Personality Assessment,* 1969, *33,* 406–408.

APPLEBAUM, S. A., AND COLSON, D. B. "A Reexamination of the Color-Shading Rorschach Test Response and Suicide Attempts." *Journal of Projective Techniques and Personality Assessment,* 1968, *32,* 160–164.

ARIETI, S. *Interpretation of Schizophrenia.* New York: Brunner/Mazel, 1955.

ARMSTRONG, H. E., JR. "Relationship Between a Dimension of Body Image and Two Measures of Conditioning." *Journal of Consulting and Clinical Psychology,* 1968, *32*(b), 696–700.

BANDURA, A. "The Rorschach White Space Response and Oppositional Behavior." *Journal of Consulting Psychology,* 1954, *18,* 17–21.

BARNES, C. "Prediction of Brain Damage Using the Holtzman Inkblot Technique and Other Selected Variables." Unpublished doctoral dissertation, University of Iowa, 1963.

BAUGHMAN, E. E. In R. I. Murstein, *Handbook of Projective Techniques.* New York: Basic Books, 1965.

BECK, S. J. *Rorchach's Test.* Vol. 3: *Advances in Interpretation.* New York: Grune and Stratton, 1952.

BECK, S J., AND MOLISH, H. B. *Rorschach's Test*. Vol. 2: *A Variety of Personality Pictures*. New York: Grune and Stratton, 1967.

BELLAK, L. "On the Problems of the Concept of Perception." In L. E. Abt and L. Bellak (Eds.), *Projective Psychology*. New York: Knopf, 1950.

BIEBER, I. *Homosexuality: A Psychoanalytic Study*. New York: Basic Books, 1962.

BINDER, H. "Die Helldunkeldeutungen im Psychodiagnostischen Experiment von Rorschach." *Schweizer Archiv fur Neurologie und Psychiatrie*, 1933, 1–67 and 233–286.

BLATT, S. J., AND ALLISON, J. "Methodological Considerations in Rorschach Research: The W Response as an Expression of Abstractive and Integrative Striving." *Journal of Projective Techniques and Personality Assessment*, 1963, *27*, 269–278.

BLOCK, W. E., AND GREENFIELD, L. "Adaptation to Inkblot Stimuli: Effects of Order of Presentation, Context, and Stimuli Characteristics." *Journal of Clinical Psychology*, 1965, *21*, 301–304.

BOHM, E. *Rorschach Test Diagnosis*. New York: Grune and Stratton, 1958.

BOOTH, G. C. "Organ Function and Form Perception. Use of the Rorschach Method with Cases of Chronic Arthritis, Parkinsonism, and Arterial Hypertension." *Psychosomatic Medicine*, 1946, *8*, 367–385.

BRECKER, S. "The Rorschach Reaction Patterns of Maternally Over-Protected and Maternally Rejected Schizophrenic Patients." *Journal of Nervous and Mental Disorders*, 1956, *123*, 41–52.

BRUNER, J. S., AND POSTMAN, L. "Perception, Cognition, and Behavior." *Journal of Personality*, 1949, *18*, 14–31.

BRUNER, J. S. "On Perceptual Readiness." *Psychological Review*, 1957, *64*, 123–152.

CASSELL, W. A. "A Tachistoscopic Index of Body Perception, I Body Boundary and Body Interior Awareness." *Journal of Projective Techniques and Personality Assessment*, 1966, *30*, 31–36.

CLARK, C. M., VELDMAN, D. J., AND THORPE, J. S. "Convergent and Divergent Thinking of Talented Adolescents." *Journal of Educational Psychology*, 1965, *56*, 157–163.

CLEVELAND, S. E. "Body Image Changes Associated with Personality Reorganization." *Journal of Consulting Psychology*, 1960, *24*, 256–261.

CLEVELAND, S. E., AND FISHER, S. "A Comparison of Psychological Characteristics and Physiological Reactivity in Ulcer and Rheumatoid Arthritis Group." *Psychosomatic Medicine*, 1960, *22*, 283–289.

CLEVELAND, S. E., AND MORTON, R. B. "Group Behavior and Body Image." *Human Relations*, 1962, *15*(1), 77–85.

CLEVELAND, S. E., AND SIKES, M. P. "Body Image in Chronic Alcoholics and Non-Alcoholic Psychiatric Patients." *Journal of Projective Techniques and Personality Assessment*, 1966, *30*, 265–269.

CODKIND, D. "Attitudes Toward the Imaginary: Their Relationship to Level of Personality Integration." Unpublished doctoral dissertation, University of Kansas, 1964.

COMMITTEE ON COLORIMETRY. *The Science of Color*. New York: Crowell, Collier and Macmillan, 1953.

CONNERS, C. K. "Effects of Brief Psychotherapy, Drugs, and Type of Disturbance on Holtzman Inkblot Scores in Children." *Proceedings of the 73rd Annual Convention of the American Psychological Association,* 1965, 201–202.

COTTE, S. "A Propos d'une Interprétation Rare, à Thématique Aggressive dans le test de Rorschach." *Cahiers de Psychologie,* 1964, *7,* 71–76.

DANA, R. H. "Six Constructs to Define Rorschach M." *Journal of Projective Techniqnes and Personality Assessment,* 1968, *32,* 138–145.

DOLLARD, J., DOOB, L. W., MILLER, N. E., MOWRER, O. H., AND SEARS, R. R. *Frustration and Aggression.* New Haven, Conn.: Yale University Press, 1939.

DOLLARD, J., AND MILLER, N. E. *Personality and Psychotherapy.* New York: McGraw-Hill, 1950.

DRAGUNS, J. G., HALEY, E. M., AND PHILLIPS, L. "Studies of Rorschach Content: A Review of the Research Literature. Part I: Traditional Content Categories." *Journal of Projective Techniques and Personality Assessment,* 1967, *31*(1), 3–32.

DRAGUNS, J. G., HALEY, E. M., AND PHILLIPS, L. "Studies of Rorschach Content: A Review of the Research Literature. Part II: Theoretical Formulations." *Journal of Projective Techniques and Personality Assessment,* 1968, *32,* 16–32.

DRESCHLER, R. J. "Affect Stimulating Effects of Colors." *Journal of Abnormal Psychology,* 1960, *61,* 323–328.

DUDEK, S. Z. "M an Active Energy System Correlating Rorschach M with Ease of Creative Expression." *Journal of Projective Techniques and Personality Assessment,* 1968, *32,* 453–461.

ELIZUR, A. "Content Analysis of the Rorschach with Regard to Anxiety and Hostility." *Rorschach Research Exchange and Journal of Projective Techniques,* 1949, *13,* 247–287.

ELSTEIN, A. S. "Behavioral Correlates of the Rorschach Shading Determinants." *Journal of Consulting Psychology,* 1965, *29,* 231–236.

ERIKSON, E. H. *Childhood and Society.* New York: Norton, 1950.

FENICHEL, O. *The Psychoanalytic Theory of Neurosis.* New York: Norton, 1945.

FERNALD, P. S., AND LINDEN, J. D. "The Human Content Response in the Holtzman Inkblot Technique." *Journal of Projective Techniques and Personality Assessment,* 1966, *30,* 441–446.

FINNEY, B. C. "Rorschach Test Correlates of Assaultive Behavior." *Journal of Projective Techniques,* 1955, *19,* 6–16.

FISHER, R. L. "Body Boundary and Achievement Behavior." *Journal of Projective Techniques and Personality Assessment,* 1966, *30,* 435–438.

FISHER, R. L. "Classroom Behavior and the Body Image Boundary." *Journal of Projective Techniques and Personality Assessment,* 1968, *32,* 450–452.

FISHER, S. "The Value of the Rorschach for Detecting Suicidal Trends." *Journal of Projective Techniques,* 1951, *15,* 250–254.

FISHER, S. "A Further Appraisal of the Body Boundary Concept." *Journal of Consulting Psychology,* 1963, *27,* 62–74.

FISHER, S. "The Body Boundary and Judged Behavioral Patterns in an Interview Situation." *Journal of Projective Techniques and Personality Assessment,* 1964, *28,* 181–184.

FISHER, S. "Body Boundary Sensations and Acquiescence." *Journal of Personality and Social Psychology,* 1965a, *1,* 381–383.

FISHER, S. "Body Sensation and Perception of Projective Stimuli." *Journal of Consulting Psychology,* 1965b, *29,* 135–138.

FISHER, S. "Body Boundary and Perceptual Vividness." *Journal of Abnormal Psychology,* 1968, *73,* 392–396.

FISHER, S. Personal communication to E. Hill, May 5, 1970.

FISHER, S., AND CLEVELAND, S. E. *Body Image and Personality.* New York: Van Nostrand Reinhold, 1958.

FISHER, S., AND RENIK, O. D. "Induction of Body Image Boundary Changes." *Journal of Projective Techniques and Personality Assessment,* 1966, *30,* 429–434.

FONDA, C. P. "The White-Space Response." In M. A. Rickers-Ovsiankina (Ed.), *Rorschach Psychology.* New York: Wiley, 1960.

FRANK, L. K. "Projective Methods for the Study of Personality." *Journal of Psychology,* 1939, *8,* 389–413.

FREUD, S. "Uber die Berechtigung von der Neurasthenie einen Bestimmten Symptomen-complex auf Angstneurose Abzutrinnen." *Gesammelte Werke.* Vol. I. Leipzig: Internationaler Psychoanalytischer Verlag, 1925, pp. 306–333.

FREUD, S. "Totem and Taboo." In A. A. Brill (Ed.), *Basic Writings of Sigmund Freud,* New York: Modern Library, 1938.

FREUD, S. *The Standard Edition of the Complete Psychological Works.* London: Hogarth, 1953.

GIBBY, R. G., MILLER, D. R., AND WALKER, E. L. "The Examiner's Influence in the Rorschach Protocol." *Journal of Consulting Psychology,* 1953, *17,* 425–428.

GOLDFARB, W. "Psychological Privation in Infancy and Subsequent Adjustment." *American Journal of Orthopsychiatry,* 1945, *15,* 247–255.

GOLDFRIED, M. R. "The Assessment of Anxiety by Means of the Rorschach." *Journal of Projective Techniques and Personality Assessment,* 1966, *30,* 364–380.

GOLDMAN, A. E. "A Comparative Development Approach to Schizophrenia." *Psychological Bulletin,* 1962, *59,* 57–69.

GOLDSTEIN, K. "Some Experimental Observations Concerning the Influence of Color on the Functions of the Organism." *Occupational Therapy Rehabilitation,* 1942, *21,* 147–151.

GRAUER, D. "Prognosis in Paranoid Schizophrenia on the Basis of the Rorschach." *Journal of Consulting Psychology,* 1953, *17,* 199–205.

HALEY, E. M., DRAGUNS, J. G., AND PHILLIPS, L. "Studies of Rorschach Content: A Review of Research Literature. Part II: Non-Traditional Uses of Content Indicators." *Journal of Projective Techniques and Personality Assessment,* 1967, *31*(2), 3–38.

HALL, C. S., AND LINDZEY, G. *Theories of Personality.* New York: Wiley, 1957.

HALPERN, F. *A Clinical Approach to Children's Rorschachs.* New York: Grune and Stratton, 1953.

HALPERN, F. "Children's Rorschach." Paper read at Springfield State Hospital, Baltimore, Apr. 1961.

HAMILTON, R. G., AND ROBERTSON, M. H. "Examiner Influence on the Holtzman Inkblot Technique." *Journal of Projective Techniques and Personality Assessment,* 1966, *30*(6), 553–558.

HAMMERSCHLAG, C. A., FISHER, S., DE COSSE, J., AND KAPLAN, E. "Breast Symptoms and Patient Delay: Psychological Variables Involved." *Cancer,* 1964, *17*(11), 1480–1484.

HELSON, H. *Adaptation-Level Theory: An Experimental and Systematic Approach to Behavior.* New York: Harper and Row, 1964.

HERRON, E. W. "Psychometric Characteristics of a Thirty-Item Version of the Group Method of the Holtzman Inkblot Technique." *Journal of Clinical Psychology,* 1963, *19,* 450–453.

HERRON, E. W. "Changes in Inkblot Perception with Presentation of the Holtzman Inkblot Technique as an Intelligence Test." *Journal of Projective Techniques and Personality Assessment,* 1964, *28*(4), 442–447.

HILGARD, E. P. *Introduction to Psychology.* New York: Harcourt Brace Jovanovich, 1963.

HILL, E. F. "Affect Aroused by Color, a Function of Stimulus Strength." *Journal of Projective Techniques and Personality Assessment,* 1966, *30*(1), 23–30.

HINSIE, L. E., AND CAMPBELL, R. J. *Psychiatric Dictionary.* New York: Oxford University Press, 1960.

HOLTZMAN, W. H. Objective Scoring of Projective Tests. In B. M. Bass and I. A. Berg (Eds.), *Objective Approaches to Personality Assessment.* New York: Van Nostrand Reinhold, 1959.

HOLTZMAN, W. H. *Guide to Administration and Scoring: Holtzman Inkblot Technique.* New York: Psychological Corp., 1961.

HOLTZMAN, W. H. "Cross-Cultural Research on Personality Development." *Human Development,* 1965, *8,* 65–86.

HOLTZMAN, W. H., DIAZ-GUERRERO, R., SWARTZ, J. D., AND LARA TAPIA, L. "Cross Cultural Longitudinal Research on Child Development: Studies of American and Mexican School Children." In J. Hill (Ed.), *Minnesota Symposium on Child Psychology.* Vol. 2. Minneapolis: University of Minnesota Press, 1968.

HOLTZMAN, W. H., GORHAM, D. R., AND MORAN, L. J. "A Factor-Analytic Study of Schizophrenic Thought Processes." *Journal of Abnormal and Social Psychology,* 1964, *69*(4), 355–364.

HOLTZMAN, W. H., THORPE, J. S., SWARTZ, J. D., AND HERRON, E. W. *Inkblot Perception and Personality.* Austin: University of Texas Press, 1961.

JORTNER, S. "An Investigation of Certain Cognitive Aspects of Schizophrenia." *Journal of Projective Techniques and Personality Assessment,* 1966, *30*(6), 559–568.

KLOPFER, B., AINSWORTH, M. D., KLOPFER, W. G., AND HOLT, R. R. *Developments in the Rorschach Technique.* Vol. 1. New York: Harcourt Brace Jovanovich, 1954.

KRIS, E. *Psychoanalytic Explorations in Art.* New York: International Universities, 1952.

KUHN, R. *Über Maskendeutungen im Rorschachschen Versuch.* Basel: Karger, 1944.

KUHN, R. "Über die Kritische Rorschach-Forschung und Einige Ihrer Ergebnisse." *Rorschachiana,* 1963, *8,* 105–114.

LEVI, J., AND KRAEMER, D. "Significance of a Preponderance of Human Movement Responses in Children Below Age Ten." *Journal of Projective Techniques,* 1952, *16,* 361–365.

LEVY, D. M. "Oppositional Syndromes and Oppositional Behavior." In P. H. Hoch and J. Zubin (Ed.), *Psychology of Childhood*. New York: Grune and Stratton, 1955.

LINDNER, R. L. "Content Analysis in Rorschach Work." *Rorschach Research Exchange*, 1946, *10*, 121–129.

LORD, E. "Experimentally Induced Variations in Rorschach Performance." *Psychological Monograph*, 1950, *64*, 10.

MEGARGEE, E. I. "The Performance of Juvenile Delinquents on the Holtzman Inkblot Technique: A Normative Study." *Journal of Projective Techniques and Personality Assessment*, 1965, *29*(4), 504–512.

MEGARGEE, E. I. "The Relation of Response Length to the Holtzman Inkblot Technique." *Journal of Consulting Psychology*, 1966, *30*, 415–419.

MEGARGEE, E. I. "A Comparison on the Scores of White and Negro Male Juvenile Delinquents on Three Projective Tests." *Journal of Projective Techniques and Personality Assessment*, 1969, *30*(6), 530–534.

MEGARGEE, E. I., AND COOK, P. E. "The Relation of T.A.T. and Inkblot Aggressive Content Scales with Each Other and with Criteria of Overt Aggression in Juvenile Delinquents." *Journal of Projective Techniques and Personality Assessment*, 1967, *31*(1), 48–60.

MEGARGEE, E. I., LOCKWOOD, V., CATO, J. L., AND JONES, J. K. "Effects of Differences in Examiner Tone of Administration and Sex of Subject on Scores of the Holtzman Inkblot Technique." *Proceedings of 74th Annual Convention of the American Psychological Association*, 1966, 235–236.

MEGARGEE, E. I., AND SWARTZ, J. D. "Extraversion, Neuroticism, and Scores on the Holtzman Inkblot Technique." *Journal of Projective Techniques and Personality Assessment*, 1968, *32*(3), 262–265.

MOSELEY, E. C., DUFFEY, R. F., AND SHERMAN, L. J. "An Extension of the Construct Validity of the Holtzman Inkblot Technique." *Journal of Clinical Psychology*, 1963, *19*, 186–192.

MUELLER, W. J., AND ABELES, N. "The Components of Empathy and Their Relationtionship to the Projection of Human Movement Responses." *Journal of Projective Techniques*, 1964, *28*, 322–330.

MURPHY, G. *Personality*. New York: Harper and Row, 1947.

MURSTEIN, B. I. "The Projection of Hostility on the Rorschach and as a Result of Ego-Threat." *Journal of Projective Techniques*, 1956, *20*, 418–428.

MURSTEIN, B. I. (Ed.), *Handbook of Projective Techniques*. New York: Basic Books, 1965.

NORMAN, R. D., AND SCOTT, W. A. "Color and Affect: A Review and Sematic Evaluation." *Journal of General Psychology*, 1952, *46*, 185–223.

OSGOOD, C. B. *Method and Theory in Experimental Psychology*. New York: Oxford University Press, 1953.

PASCAL, G. R., REUSCH, H. A., DEVINE, A. A., AND SUTTELL, B. J. "A Study of Genital Symbols on the Rorschach Test: Presentation of a Method and Results." *Journal of Abnormal and Social Psychology*, 1950, *45*, 286–295.

PHILLIPS, L., AND SMITH, J. G. *Rorschach Interpretation: Advanced Technique*. New York: Grune and Stratton, 1953.

PIOTROWSKI, Z. A. *Perceptanalysis*. New York: Macmillan, 1957.

PIOTROWSKI, Z. A. "The Movement Score." In M. A. Rickers-Ovsiankina (Ed.), *Rorschach Psychology*. New York: Wiley, 1960.

RADER, G. E. "The Prediction of Overt Aggressive Verbal Behavior from Rorschach Content." *Journal of Projective Techniques*, 1957, *21*, 294–306.

RAMER, J. "The Rorschach Barrier Score and Social Behavior." *Journal of Consulting Psychology*, 1963, *27*, 525.

RAPAPORT, D. *Diagnostic Psychological Testing*. Vol. 2. Chicago: Year Book Medical Publishers, 1946.

RAV, J. "Anatomy Responses in the Rorschach." *Journal of Projective Techniques*, 1951, *15*, 433–443.

RENIK, O. D., AND FISHER, S. "Induction of Body Image Boundary Changes in Male Subjects." *Journal of Projective Techniques and Personality Assessment*, 1968, *32*(1), 45–48.

RICHTER, R. H., AND WINTER, W. D. "Holtzman Inkblot Correlates of Creative Potential." *Journal of Projective Techniques and Personality Assessment*, 1966, *30*(1), 62–67.

RICKERS-OVSIANKINA, M. A. (Ed.) *Rorschach Psychology*. New York: Wiley, 1960.

RIETI, H. Lecture to the Society for Projective Techniques. New York, 1945. Cited by Z. A. Piotrowski, *Perceptanalysis*. New York: Macmillan, 1957.

RORSCHACH, H. *Psychodiagnostics*. Berne: Huber, 1942.

SANDERS, J. L., HOLTZMAN, W. H., AND SWARTZ, J. D. "Structural Changes of the Color Variable in the Holtzman Inkblot Technique." *Journal of Projective Techniques and Personality Assessment*, 1968, *32*(6), 556–561.

SANDERS, R., AND CLEVELAND, S. E. "The Relationship Between Certain Examiner Personality Variables and Subjects' Rorschach Scores." *Journal of Projective Techniques*, 1953, *17*, 34–50.

SCHACHTEL, E. G. "On Color and Affect." *Psychiatry*, 1943, *6*, 393–409.

SCHACHTEL, E. G. "Subjective Definitions of the Rorschach Test Situation and Their Effect on Test Performance." *Psychiatry*, 1945, *8*, 419–448.

SCHACHTEL, E. G. *Experimental Foundations of Rorschach's Test*. New York: Basic Books, 1966.

SCHAIE, K. W. "On the Relation of Color and Personality." *Journal of Projective Techniques and Personality Assessment*, 1966, *30*(6), 512–524.

SCHILDER, P. E. *Mind, Perception and Thought in Their Constructive Aspects*. New York: Columbia University Press, 1942.

SCHMIDT, H. Q., AND FONDA, C. P. "Rorschach Scores in the Manic States." *Journal of Projective Techniques*, 1953, *17*, 151–161.

SHAFER, R. *Psychoanalytic Interpretation in Rorschach Testing*. New York: Grune and Stratton, 1954.

SHAPIRO, D. "A Perceptual Understanding of Color Responses." In M. A. Rickers-Ovsiankina (Ed.), *Rorschach Psychology*. New York: Wiley, 1960.

SHAW, B. "Sex Populars in the Rorschach Test." *Journal of Abnormal and Social Psychology*, 1948, *43*, 466–470.

SIIPOLA, E., AND TAYLOR, V. "Reactions to Inkblots Under Free and Pressure Conditions." *Journal of Personality*, 1952, *21*, 22–47.

SIMKINS, L. "Examiner Reinforcement and Situational Variables in a Projective

Testing Situation." *Journal of Consulting Psychology,* 1960, *24,* 541–547.

SMITH, J. R., AND COLEMAN, J. C. "The Relationship Between Manifestation of Hostility in Projective Techniques and Overt Behavior." *Journal of Projective Techniques,* 1956, *20,* 326–334.

SPIELBERGER, C. D. "Theory and Research in Anxiety." In C. D. Spielberger (Ed.), *Anxiety and Behavior.* New York: Academic, 1966.

STOTSKY, B. A. "A Comparison of Remitting and Non-Remitting Schizophrenics on Psychological Tests." *Journal of Abnormal and Social Psychology,* 1952, *47,* 489–496.

STURMENT, C. T., AND FINNEY, B. C. "Projection and Behavior: A Rorschach Study of Assaultive Mental Hospital Patients." *Journal of Projective Techniques,* 1953, *17,* 349–360.

SULLIVAN, H. S. *The Interpersonal Theory of Psychiatry.* New York: Norton, 1953.

SWARTZ, J. D. "Performance of High-and-Low Anxious Children on the Holtzman Inkblot Technique." *Child Development,* 1965, *36,* 569–575.

SWARTZ, J. D. "Pathognomic Verbalizations in Normals, Psychotics and Mental Retardates." Unpublished doctoral dissertation, University of Texas at Austin, 1969.

SWARTZ, J. D., AND HOLTZMAN, W. H. "Group Method of Administration for the Holtzman Inkblot Technique." *Journal of Clinical Psychology,* 1963, *19,* 433–441.

SWARTZ, J. D., AND SWARTZ, C. J. "Test Anxiety and Performance on the Holtzman Inkblot Technique." *Journal of Clinical Psychology,* 1968, *14*(4), 463–467.

THORPE, J. S. "Level of Perceptual Development as Reflected in Responses to the Holtzman Inkblot Technique." Unpublished doctoral dissertation, University of Texas, 1960.

THORPE, J. S., AND SWARTZ, J. D. "The Role of Intelligence and Social Status in Rejections on the Holtzman Inkblot Technique." *Journal of Projective Techniques,* 1963, *27,* 248–251.

THORPE, J. S., AND SWARTZ, J. D. "Level of Perceptual Development as Reflected in Response to the Holtzman Inkblot Technique." *Journal of Projective Techniques and Personality Assessment,* 1965, *29*(3), 380–386.

TOWNSEND, J. K. "The Relation Between Rorschach Signs of Aggression and Behavioral Aggression in Emotionally Disturbed Boys." *Journal of Projective Techniques and Personality Assessment,* 1967, *31*(6), 13–21.

ULETT, G. A., MARTIN, D. W., AND MC BRIDE, J. R. "Rorschach Findings in a Case of Suicide." *American Journal of Orthopsychiatry,* 1950, *20,* 817–827.

VAN DE CASTLE, R. L., AND SPICHER, R. S. "A Semantic Differential Investigation of Color on the Holtzman." *Journal of Projective Techniques and Personality Assessment,* 1964, *28,* 491–498.

WERNER, H., AND WAPNER, S. "Sensory-Tonic Field Theory of Perception." *Journal of Personality,* 1949, *18,* 88–107.

WERNER, S. J. "The Color Preferences of Psychiatric Groups." *Psychological Monograph,* 1949, *63*(6), 969.

WERTHEIMER, M. "Perception and the Rorschach." *Journal of Projective Techniques,* 1957, *21,* 209–216.

WHITE, M. A., AND SCHREIBER, H. "Diagnosing Suicidal Risks on the Rorschach." *Psychiatry Quarterly Supplement,* 1952, *26,* 161–189.

WHITE, R. W. *The Abnormal Personality.* New York: Ronald, 1956.

WITKIN, H. A., LEWIS, H. B., HERTZMAN, M., MACHOVER, K., MEISSNER, P. B., AND WAPNER, S. *Personality Through Perception.* New York: Harper and Row, 1954.

WOLF, I. "Hostile Acting Out and Rorschach Test Content." *Journal of Projective Techniques,* 1957, *21,* 414–419.

WOODS, W. A. "Personality Through Color." *Mental Health in Virginia.* Richmond, Va.: Dept. of Mental Hygiene and Hospitals, 1954.

WOODWORTH, R. S., AND SCHLOSSBERG, H. *Experimental Psychology.* New York: Holt, Rinehart, and Winston, 1958.

ZAX, M., STRICKER, G., AND WEISS, J. H. "Effects of Non-Personality Factors on Rorschach Performance." *Journal of Projective Techniques,* 1960, *24,* 33–93.

ZOLLIKER, A. "Schwangerschaftsdepression und Rorschach'scher Formdeutversuch." *Schweizer Archiv fur Neurologie und Psychiatrie,* 1943, *53,* 62–78.

ZUBIN, J., ERON, L. D., SCHUMER, F. *An Experimental Approach to Projective Techniques.* New York: Wiley, 1965.

ZULLIGER, H. *Der Talfeln-Z-Test.* Berne: Huber, 1954.

Author Index

Subject Index